Teaching Geography for a Better World

edited by
John Fien and Rod Gerber

Brisbane College of Advanced Education

D1681093

Oliver & Boyd

Acknowledgements

The publishers thank all those who gave permission to reproduce photographs or other copyright material in this book. Information regarding sources is given in the captions. Although every effort has been made to trace copyright owners, the publishers apologise for any omissions.
The photographs on pages 52–3 were supplied by John Fien and the Wilderness Society, Australia.

Illustrated by Denby Designs, Valerie Lewis and Tim Smith

Oliver & Boyd
Robert Stevenson House
1–3 Baxter's Place
Leith Walk
Edinburgh EH1 3BB

A division of Longman Group UK Ltd

ISBN 0 05 004259 9

First published 1986 by the Australian Geography Teachers' Association with the sponsorship of Jacaranda-Wiley and the Australian Department of Arts, Heritage and Environment
This edition first published 1988

Distributed in the United States by Longman Inc., 1560 Broadway, New York, NY 10036

Set in 9/11 pt Helvetica Light and Medium
Printed in Great Britain by
Bell & Bain Ltd. Glasgow

Contents

Contributors

Mr John Bale,
Education Department,
University of Keele,
Keele, Staffordshire,
United Kingdom.

Ms Jenny Burnley,
Australian International
   Independent School,
Sydney, Australia.

Dr Bernard Cox,
Education Department,
University of Queensland,
Brisbane, Australia.

Ms Leonie Daws,
Department of Educational Studies,
Brisbane College of Advanced
   Education (Kelvin Grove),
Brisbane, Australia.

Mr Noel Gough,
Department of Curriculum
   and Teaching,
Victoria College (Rusden),
Melbourne, Australia.

Mr David Hicks,
Centre for Peace Studies,
St Martin's College,
Lancaster, United Kingdom.

Mr John Huckle,
Geography Department,
Bedford College of Higher
   Education,
Bedford, United Kingdom.

Mr Barrie McElroy,
Geography Department,
South Australian College of
   Advanced Education (Salisbury),
Adelaide, Australia.

Professor Janice Monk,
Executive Director,
Southwest Institute for
   Research on Women,
Tucson, Arizona,
United States of America.

Mr Michael Naish,
Department of Economics, Geography
   and Business Studies,
University of London Institute of Education,
London, United Kingdom.

Dr Toh Swee-Hin,
Education Department,
University of New England,
Armidale, Australia.

Ms Jane Williamson-Fien,
Department of Social Studies,
Brisbane College of Advanced
   Education (Kelvin Grove),
Brisbane, Australia.

Introduction

JOHN FIEN AND ROD GERBER

Significant change occurs when people stop believing in what may once have been true, but has now become false; when they withdraw support from institutions which may once have served them but no longer do; when they refuse to submit to what may once have been fair terms but which are no longer. Such changes, when they occur, are the product of true education. (Reimer, 1971)

The students we teach certainly are a varied lot, displaying all the hopes and uncertainties, and fears and optimism of adolescence and young adulthood. They range from the ambitiously conscientious whom we wish would relent and take their schoolwork a little less seriously to those whom we wish would slow down, co-operate and study a little more. They include those for whom school is an outright bore and a waste of time through to those for whom education and the hope of a 'good job' are the passport to a better life. In between, are the friendly, the impish, the tryers, the trying and the outright rebellious. It is for all of these young people that we are teachers. It is for them and their counterparts all over the world that we seek to create a vision of a better world through our teaching in order to bring about those changes in outlook and action that Reimer (1971) described as 'true education'.

A world of contradictions

Actually describing what that 'better world' will, might or should be like is a difficult task. It always seems far easier to catalogue the ills of the modern world. In Chapter 1, Dave Hicks uses the parable of an inter-galactic report on the state of the Planet Earth to list some of the problems that need to be addressed in order to create a better world. We live in a world of enormous contradictions, in a world where, as Jon-athon Porritt (1984) says:

... it's apparently possible to keep the peace only by threatening the total annihilation of the planet; ... [where] it's possible to achieve 'progress' and further growth only by the wilful destruction of our life-support systems; ... [where] we ravage our best farming land to grow food surpluses that are then thrown away or sold off cheap to the 'enemy'; ... [where] in one part of the world millions die of starvation, while people here die of over-indulgence; ... [where] we spend more on useless weapons than we do on either education or health; ... [and where] we pollute the planet in the very process of trying to get rich enough to do something about pollution.

These contradictions are also apparent in the nature of work and the spectre of unemployment where we find millions of people carrying out soul-destroying work and millions of others unemployed at a time when people should be working to improve the social well-being and the life chances of people everywhere.

These contradictions are also evident in the attitudes to life of many of our students. Mark, a 15 year old from Melbourne (but could he be from your town?) no doubt speaks for many young people all over the world when he says:

You look out into the world, you see headlines like 'Unemployment Rates Go Up', 'Such-and-Such A Strike', and you sort of wonder whether you want to go out into the workforce. You think about it. You've been brought up since primary school with 'What do you want to be when you grow up?' and then when you find you've got to grown-up age, you're not sure if it's all it's been made out to be all those years. You just have to reconsider everything. (Guilliatt, 1985)

A difficult challenge

In teaching for a better world, we have to work with this pessimism and confusion along with the mixture of idealism, lack of interest, and dedication that characterises our young people. Some issues, given the right classroom or media conditions, will inspire most students. Despite some concerns about their ideological soundness, the recordings of *Do they know it's Christmas?* and *We are the World* together with the Live Aid concerts proved that this is possible. Other issues, among different students, will cause cynicism, despair or fear. For example, here is how four more students have described their responses to some local, national and global issues:

> Barbara *(17 years old): I started doing apartheid . . . I'd go home every night and my eyes would fill up. You see it on TV . . . I get so upset when I see these policemen with these huge batons belting people. I just can't believe that it happens and people allow it to happen . . .*

> Ricky *(17 years old): Young people don't wanna know what's happening in the world any more. There's no life beyond the western suburbs, there's no life beyond the football club. I'm jealous of them because I want my place to go to, I want to feel secure like they do, but I can't . . .*

> Catie *(16 years old): The first time I ever found out about the Bomb was when I was in grade five and I had nightmares for about a week, which doesn't sound like a long time, but it was horrifying. When the rain came, I'd get really scared because I'd heard about acid rain. Then about three or four years ago I found out they really did blow a bomb . . . I can remember being really scared when the Falklands War was on. I was really scared that America would start getting in there and Russia would and it would blow sky-high . . .*

> Joel *(13 years old): It's like a vicious circle in that there is always going to be violence and there are always going to be people who oppose it, there is always going to be wanton killing but there should be less . . . As far as nuclear weapons go – and not just nuclear weapons, but politics generally – boys and girls just wanna have fun . . .*
> (Guilliatt, 1985)

Such moral paralysis coupled with the 'new traditionalism' bred by fears of unemployment pose enormous challenges for the teachers who seek to activate student concern for a better world. Hayden Raysmith summarises some of the characteristics of today's young people this way:

> *I think this generation is more likely to be . . . conservative isn't the word I'd use. They are more likely to be politically of the right, in that they will tend to place less importance on social justice, equality, sharing, cooperation, those sorts of values which emerged during . . . the social and economic programs of the mid-seventies . . . This generation will be more*

competitive, more individualistic . . . a response to the more competitive environment they've been brought up in, where there are not enough jobs to go around . . . You've got to compete to win, or you lose.
(Guilliatt, 1985)

A better world

Such views provide a sobering challenge to those of us who believe that school geography can and should play 'a significant role in creating more fulfilled and happy individuals in a fairer and less troubled world' (Huckle, 1983). Yet, the fact that our young people are affected by the conditions they see in the world ought to encourage us to renew our commitment to helping them look forward to and start working for a better world for all. Our youths' feelings of frustration and concern ought to challenge us, as geography teachers, to reflect on the purpose and long-term value of some of the things we teach, and make curriculum decisions to promote the well-being of both our students and the society in which we all live.

What then is a 'better world'? All people have their own individual conceptions of what such a world would be like. To do justice to them all, we can do little more than follow Jonathon Porritt's lead in suggesting a range of necessary pre-conditions for a better world (Porritt, 1984). These include the following.

- A reverence for the Earth and all its creatures.

- Protection for the environment as a pre-condition of a healthy society.

- A willingness to share the world's wealth among all its people.

- A recognition of the rights of future generations in our consumption of resources.

- Harmony between people of every race, colour and creed and positive discrimination to redress present inequalities.

- 'Progress' to be measured by the development of alternatives to the 'rat race' of economic growth.

- A rejection of socially unjust and environmentally wasteful practices involved in areas of mining, manufacturing and consumerism.

- Development of socially useful, personally rewarding and environmentally sound products, jobs and work practices.

- A scaling-down of armaments manufacture, reduced arms spending and the eventual destruction of all nuclear arsenals.

- Development of non-nuclear energy policies based on conservation, greater efficiency and renewable sources of energy.

- Open participating democracy at all levels of society.

No doubt, few people will agree with all of the items in our list. Nevertheless, we offer them as tenets which geography students have a right to explore for themselves, in conjunction with the knowledge, concepts and skills of the geographer, and in caring supportive classroom environments.

Bias in geography teaching

Any geography teaching which explores some of the above issues would differ markedly from that prominent in many current syllabus guidelines and geography textbooks. The following teaching practices suggest some of the many ways by which current geography teaching is biased away from teaching geography for a better world.

- Lessons on world trade that ignore the arms trade.

- Lessons on world landscapes that still focus on the Kalahari bushmen and the Boro of the Amazon but do not question the impact of European pastoralism on the bushmen or consider that the Boro are victims of massive deforestation and road projects.

- Lessons on the local environment that ignore student experiences, feelings and land uses in that environment or the maxim of local planning that 'whosoever has the power, makes the rules'.

- Lessons on nuclear power that ignore the place of nuclear weapons in the nuclear fuel chain.

- Lessons on mining in South Africa that ignore apartheid.

- Lessons on manufacturing that do not explore the ownership of the firms, the use made of the products, alternative products that could be made or the environmental effects of manufacturing.

- Lessons on agriculture that ignore the role of governments in the production of food surpluses, the causes of soil erosion and salinity and the 'circle of poison' in pesticide use.

- Lessons on development that ignore the causes of historical and contemporary underdevelopment, or the role of women.

- Lessons on physical geography that ignore the human role in changing the face of the Earth.

- Lessons on climate that ignore the concepts of acid rain and nuclear winter.

- Lessons on natural hazards that do not question the causes or effects of unnatural disasters.

- Lessons on urban models that ignore the social processes involved.

- Lessons on gentrification and slum clearance that do not ask where the former slum dwellers now live.

Such lessons are all too commonplace as investigations by Gill (1982), Hicks (1982) and Wright (1985) have revealed. They stem from the conservative ideology that has been predominant in geographical education, at least until very recently. All geography teachers have a profound responsibility to familiarise themselves with Gilbert's analysis of the conservative bias in their subject (Gilbert 1984, 1986). After studying all geography syllabus documents and textbooks in England and then interviewing students about the messages they take from their geography lessons, Gilbert concluded that much geography is dominated by economic and environmental determinism, the spatial organisation of capitalist societies and a preoccupation with technology and economic development. Gilbert concluded that, as a result, students are failing to learn anything of the nature of social power or the social processes that create spatial patterns and maintain them in the interests of the wealthy and the powerful. In place of these vital social learnings, the dominant conservative ideology is providing a diet of geographic learnings that clutter the mind with facts, concepts, models and theories which serve to disguise the nature and impact of social processes. And in failing to provide learning experiences that give students active knowledge of 'how decisions are made, with what goals in mind, in the face of what problems and conflicts and with what resources and options' (Gilbert, 1986), geography syllabus writers, textbook authors and teachers have become party to the hegemonic role of conservative education in reproducing present patterns of social structure and control.

Geographical education for a better world

Teaching geography for a better world involves making conscious decisions to challenge the ideology of conservative approaches to education, in general, and to rethink our goals, content, resources and methods in geography teaching, in particular. It also challenges many aspects of the liberal–progressive ideology of education that sees schools as a way of improving society through the education of well-meaning individuals who will be tomorrow's skilled and active citizens. Liberal ideologies overemphasise the role of individuals in causing social, environmental and economic problems, and the ability of individuals to solve them. This does not mean that particular individuals cannot be instrumental in, for example, destroying or saving environments. We only need to look at the work of Daniel Ludwig in Brazil and Bob Brown in Tasmania to see effects that individuals can have on the environment. However, liberal approaches to teaching about such people and issues tend to ignore the broader social, economic and political structures within which transnational companies (Ludwig) or environmental activists (Brown) operate and which are responsible for the success or otherwise of their work.

Teaching geography for a better world necessitates the adoption of educational approaches based upon: an understanding of local, national and global power structures, experience and skill in democratic participation and action, and the goal of liberation from disinterest and non-involvement. Connell *et al.* (1982) argue the case this way:

> In a society disfigured by class exploitation, sexual and racial oppression, and in chronic danger of war and environmental destruction, the only education worth the name is one that forms people capable of taking part in their own liberation.

In teaching geography for a better world, it is important that we are not blind to our own ideology and that we explicate and hold up our own assumptions for critical reflection. The value principles underlying this reconstructionist or socially critical approach to geography teaching include:

- the promotion of social justice, participatory democracy, respect for human rights and ecological sustainability as the values base for society;

- the development of an analysis that identifies the inequities and problems resulting from the often taken-for-granted social structures and processes that contradict these values;

- the development of the insights and skills necessary to question such structures and processes, evaluate them according to principles of social justice, democracy, human rights and ecological sustainability and, in particular, to ask questions about the power relationships involved and about who gains and who loses from any decision or change in the social system;

- the development of a willingness and the skills to propose alternative patterns, solutions and futures, and to work with others to help bring about a more just, democratic and ecologically sustainable world at local, national and global levels.

This is an approach to education with a long tradition in western thought. It was central to the work of John Dewey in the 1930s with his ideas on education for democracy and social reconstruction. More recently, it has been revitalised and explored by curriculum writers such as Geoff Whitty (1980), Michael Apple (1979, 1982), and Kemmis, Cole and Suggett (1984). It is evident in British geographical education in the work of the Association for Curriculum Development in Geography (1983) with its anti-racist policies and Geographical Association policy statements on development education (Bale, 1983) and multicultural education (Geographical Association, 1984). In Australia, calls for the adoption of such approaches to geography teaching have been the hallmark of several national conferences. As far back as 1982, John Sibley (1982) called for geography teaching to be:

> very outgoing and outward looking: Geography out there mixing it in society – in the real world – in real issues . . . concerned with social, economic and environmental justice.

At the same conference, Pat Donnelly (1982) demanded a 'geography for **action in** society not **on** it', while Eleanor Rawling, in her conference keynote address, described 'geography capable of **educating** young people', as a geography that:

> will not accept the status quo in society [but] will question accepted values and situations, demand justifications for actions, request genuine participation in decision-making and hope to change society to improve the quality of life and environments (Rawling, 1982).

The purposes of this book

The 1986 conference of the Australian Geography Teachers' Association adopted the theme of 'Teaching Geography for a Better World' to provide a co-ordinated professional experience for teachers who wanted to explore a socially critical approach to teaching and to develop their insights and skills in this area. This book is one result of the thinking and preparation that went into that conference. It is organised into three sections. The first (Section A) contains three chapters which provide the framework for considering the practical implications of teaching in a number of different areas of geography. These implications are expanded in the nine chapters of Section B which offer ideas, strategies and some resources for classroom teaching. In Section C, Bernard Cox summarises and integrates the themes and issues introduced in teaching geography for a better world, and Michael Naish provides a concluding statement specifically written for this revised 1988 edition.

For this new edition, all chapters have been adapted or rewritten to reflect developments and ideas since the conference in 1986 and to suit an international readership in an endeavour to increase the number of people who want to participate in teaching geography for a better world. In this sense, this book has a clear evangelical function. It is intended as a source of motivation, ideas and skills for teachers to start working now with their students to make the possibility of a better world real in their classrooms and lives. As Martin Luther King said:

We are faced with the fact that tomorrow is today. There is such a thing as being too late. Over the bleached bones of numerous civilizations are written the pathetic words: 'Too late'. If we do not act, we shall surely be dragged down the dark corridors of time reserved for those who possess power without passion, might without morality and strength without sight.

We hope that this book, with its clear messages and treasury of practical classroom advice, will encourage and empower many to start teaching geography for a better world.

Section A

1 Teaching geography for a better world

Better worlds

State of the planet

The children that we are teaching in school now will spend most of their lives in the twenty-first century. We need therefore to be concerned with the future as much, if not more than, the present and the past. Thus, while old maps may be interesting, and indeed informative, drawing new maps – of the future – may be our greatest challenge. But to do this we have to stand back. We must understand how things are, and how they came to be as they are, before we can see how they should change; before we can plan for a better world.

Perhaps we should start with a galactic viewpoint like the following (Adams, 1979):

Far out in the uncharted backwaters of the unfashionable end of the Western Spiral arm of the Galaxy lies a small unregarded yellow sun.

Orbiting this at a distance of roughly ninety-eight million miles is an utterly insignificant little blue green planet whose ape-descended life forms are so amazingly primitive that they still think digital watches are a pretty neat idea.

This planet had a problem, which was this: most of the people living on it were unhappy for pretty much of the time. Many solutions were suggested for this problem, but most of these were largely concerned with the movement of small green pieces of paper, which is odd because on the whole it wasn't the small green pieces of paper that were unhappy.

And so the problem remained; lots of the people were mean, and most of them were miserable, even the ones with digital watches.

Many were increasingly of the opinion that they'd all made a big mistake in coming down
from the trees in the first place. And some said that even the trees had been a bad move, and that no one should ever have left the oceans.

More seriously, perhaps, any galactic visitor could not help but observe that conditions for most of the 5000 million inhabitants on Planet Earth are far from good.

- Tension and violence are on the increase in a world already dangerously overarmed and undernourished.
- 30 children are dying each minute for want of food and inexpensive vaccines.
- At the same time $US1.5 million per minute are being spent on armaments.
- 150 major wars have been fought in the last 40 years.
- Torture of people, animals and the environment has reached epidemic proportions.
- The male of the species, only half of the population, does barely a third of the planet's work yet takes 90% of its income; direct and indirect violence against the female of the species is generally the norm.
- In 40 years the stockpile of nuclear weapons has grown from 3 to 50 000.

World goals

There are many ways of analysing the social, political and economic issues that we see around us and thus also many images of what a 'better world' might look like. Some of the clearest insights have come from those involved in peace research (Galtung, 1980). Thus one can argue, broadly, that there are two basic perspectives for looking at such issues: the *actor-oriented* and the *structure-oriented*.

In essence, the first perspective looks for explanations by focussing on individual people at the social

13

level and individual countries at the global level. Each is seen as fairly autonomous but with the consequent competition between both individuals and countries clearly requiring some sort of regulation. Thus, societies are seen as the sum total of the individuals within them; and evil in the world is seen as arising from the evil intentions of particular people or countries.

The second perspective looks for explanations by focussing instead on the social, political and economic structures of interaction between actors. Relations and patterns between and within structures are thus studied in order to understand more clearly how unequal accumulation of resources may come about. Evil in the world is seen as arising from bad structures which deny many disadvantaged groups and nations access to a 'better world'.

Clearly neither of these two broad perspectives should be used in isolation for they complement each other and it is vital that we do in fact explore issues both in terms of actors and structures. This applies not only to the global village, but to our own societies and the institutions we work in.

At the same time we also need to recall that people's perspectives on the world may vary enormously depending, among other things, on their gender, race and class. Take this comment by James in the *Daily Mail* (James, 1985) about several television series which have dealt with the British Empire:

The sun, they used to tell us, never set on the British Empire. Are we now to believe that the Empire was really a string of lands where the sun never shone?

Open an atlas on any page, and all the bits coloured red were our Empire. Are we supposed to now accept that the colour came from the blood of natives we slaughtered to preserve that dominion?

I ask the question having just been watching a television series about, above all supposedly civilised things, cricket.

Bodyline, over ten long-dragging hours, told the story of a famous Test series in which England's bowlers hurled lethally-fast deliveries at the heads of their Australian hosts . . .

Bodyline, by itself, is a tepid delivery we could easily hook for a contemptuous polemical boundary: but it comes as part of an absolute barrage of programmes and films that have one common theme – the claim that the British Empire was carved out by vicious exploiters, preserved only at gunpoint, and relinquished everywhere only by force.

Think back. Apart from the individual plots, what has been the background against which the stories of Gandhi, Jewel in the Crown, Passage to India *were each told? . . .*

Whether it was to India or Iran, Pacific Islands or Polar wastes, the Britons who went emerge now in this re-cast history as either wicked or weak. Some, maybe much, of this is true. But it cannot be the whole story. The Empire could not have survived a decade had it been such a sunless place of oppressed minorities.

What such actor-oriented statements totally ignore are the structures found in most social systems which ensure that 'the power-ful receive more benefits, gains, advantages and satisfaction than the power-less. Correspondingly the power-less receive more losses, disadvantages and diseconomies than the power-ful. The terms "oppressors" and "oppressed" are frequently therefore preferable to the terms "power-ful" and "power-less"' (Richardson, 1986).

If we really are interested in creating 'better worlds' then we must listen carefully to the voices of the powerless: globally, nationally, locally, and in our own workplaces and relationships. We must also be clear about what criteria we are using to define 'a better world'. Clearly these criteria or goals must be applicable on a variety of scales from the personal to the global. They must also be ones that meet the needs of the dispossessed and powerless.

I would thus like to propose the following five broad goals for a 'better world' (Galtung, 1976). They are:

- economic welfare
- social justice
- participation
- non-violence
- ecological balance

Each can be applied at a variety of scales and in a variety of contexts. For example:

Economic welfare involves appropriate access to food, clothes, shelter, health care, schools, transport and communication. There needs to be a minimum level below which people should not have to go, but also a maximum level since there are outer limits to growth, given that nature is a finite closed system.

Social justice requires that what one 'has' should not be dependent on who one 'is'. Thus neither gender, skin pigmentation, class or culture should act as filters to the distribution of resources.

Participation is the opposite of alienation. It involves opportunities for personal growth and enrichment, for being in control of one's own life choices. It means being free to choose.

Non-violence requires freedom from both direct personal violence and also from indirect structural violence. Thus unjust social, political and economic systems may cause as such suffering to some people as more direct forms of violence.

Ecological balance reminds us that 'a better world' must pay heed to the needs of non-human species, that other living forms including air, water and soil have a right to expect our concerned stewardship.

State of the world

In particular we need to ask ourselves about the state of our planet, our own society and the state of education. Thus it has become increasingly apparent over the last two decades that we are facing a major series of interrelated global crises (Johnston and Taylor, 1986). These range from increasing differences in wealth between and within countries, increases in militarism and authoritarian governments, denial of human rights and civil liberties, to breakdown of law and order, the rapidly escalating arms race and irreversible damage to the biosphere. It is worth noting that the extent of these problems is seldom noticed by those people described by one commentator (Richardson, 1986) as 'the archetypal oppressors' i.e. white middle-class males from the northern hemisphere who hold senior positions in hierarchical institutions. It is possible to deny that the state of the planet gives any cause for concern at all. However, many teachers, including geographers, have noted the seriousness of such issues and are increasingly asking how they can respond to young people's concerns on these matters.

The conflict and violence that are so characteristic of the global stage also affect individual societies, both directly and indirectly. Acts of terrorism, high unemployment, racist attacks, sexual harassment, issues of law and order, alienation and the arms race are all inescapable features of life in the western world. In Britain, for example, government unemployment figures confirm that the country has its own North–South divide (*Observer*, 1987). '96% of the total jobs lost since the Tories took office have been in Scotland, the North, Midlands, Wales and Northern Ireland – where the majority of the population live. The southern triangle – populated by the remaining 42% – has suffered only 6% of job losses.' That British students are also worried about such matters was shown by a national survey of young people aged 10 to 17 (*Guardian*, 1987). Of national problems, unemployment provided the biggest cause for concern, followed by nuclear weapons and nuclear war. In terms of worrying about global problems, famine and poverty came first, followed again by nuclear weapons and nuclear war. Confronted daily by these issues directly, or indirectly via the media, teachers are increasingly wondering about how best to empower young people in the face of such dilemmas.

A growing number of teachers are also concerned about the unpeaceful nature of many schools and classrooms, about why so many young people feel insulted, bored or humiliated by their teachers. Many students are highly critical of their school experiences and only a small proportion express unreserved enthusiasm for their school. R. D. Laing (1978) put it another way when he wrote:

A child born today in the United Kingdom stands a ten times greater chance of being admitted to a mental hospital than to a university . . . This can be taken as an indication that we are driving our children mad more effectively than we are genuinely educating them. Perhaps it is our way of educating them that is driving them mad.

With both primary and secondary teachers reporting growing numbers of aggressive or difficult children a drastic reassessment is needed not only of *what* we teach but *how* we teach as Figure 1.1 shows (Brandes and Ginnis, 1986).

Figure 1.1 How we teach is as important as what we teach (Source: *Inspection and Advice*, Councils and Education Press Ltd)

WAR, FAMINE, PESTILENCE, POVERTY, SEXISM, RACISM — THEY'RE ALL YOUR FAULT PARKIN, BECAUSE YOU **DON'T LISTEN**!

Teaching geography

Recent trends

But, one might ask, is this really anything to do with teaching geography? The central nature of these concerns to our subject is borne witness to by the growth of what has been called a 'geography of concern' over the last decade or so. Thus Smith (1977) has argued that:

> the well-being of a society as a spatially variable condition should be the focal point of geographical enquiry . . . It simply requires recognition of what is surely the self-evident truth that if human beings are the object of our curiosity . . . then the quality of their lives is of paramount importance.

In particular we can look to developments in welfare geography, humanistic geography and radical geography to support us here. These have been usefully reviewed by Bale, Fien and Cook, respectively, in Huckle (1983) and also in Johnston (1983). Welfare geography is concerned with describing, interpreting and predicting patterns of human welfare on a variety of scales. Humanistic geography focuses on our feelings, fears, perceptions and experiences, on our personal and private geographies. Radical geography asks critical questions about the unjust status quo and offers insights from Marxist and anarchist perspectives.

And, always, we need to recall and make explicit the implicit values and assumptions in our geographies (Bailey, 1983):

> There is no escape from value-judgements in teaching or authorship, no matter how hard we try to be neutral. Because we are to some extent products of place and time, we are naturally inclined to think that what we know is normal and that what is unfamiliar is abnormal. It is easy to imply, quite unconsciously, that the values and attitudes of agnostic suburban Britain – about birth control for instance – are a useful basis from which to discuss what happens in rural India or urban Latin America; or that the kinds of economic reasoning with which we are familiar can be applied to a mainly subsistence society in which money is little used by most people. We cannot escape our cultural dependence; our thinking and our customs have been shaped by centuries of history, education and socio-economic control: but by recognising its nature and making its implications explicit we may avoid being unduly prejudiced by it in our own judgements

of different societies. It is important that we do so because only then can we teach our pupils, by example and precept, to do the same. In a world in which inter-regional disparities and tensions are growing increasingly acute, it will be important for all of us that some of our pupils do learn this lesson. Unless the causes of the world's and our own society's inequalities are diminished soon, none of us may survive. The pupils we teach will have to take the necessary political action. Will they understand enough to be effective?

It is also important to recall that we can draw on, and learn much from, developments in other fields that impinge on the concerns of geographers, i.e. development education, multicultural education, education for peace and world studies (Hicks, 1984).

World studies

The overall aim of world studies teaching is to help children develop the knowledge, attitudes and skills which are relevant to living in a multicultural society and an interdependent world. World studies is thus not a new subject but rather a dimension in the curriculum (Hicks and Townley, 1982). All subjects, and perhaps geography in particular, can contribute to a global perspective, and a global perspective can enhance all subjects.

One curriculum project, World Studies 8–13, has been published as a very practical teacher's handbook full of down-to-earth and classroom-tested ideas (Fisher and Hicks, 1985). The project puts a particular stress on active learning to help teachers and younger pupils explore a wide range of issues, for example to do with world development, human rights, peace and conflict, the environment. Thus quite young children are, at their own level, keenly interested in, and knowledgeable about, a wide variety of issues.

All the project's themes relate directly or indirectly to teaching for a 'better world'. Three will be referred to here, and these are to do with understanding conflicts, clarifying personal–global links, and looking at images of the world.

Education for democracy, education for equality, education for a multicultural society and education for justice all require that we help pupils understand conflicts both in their own worlds and in the wider world. Many of the practical activities in the project handbook thus stress and illustrate ways in which skills of co-operation may be developed: the need first to have respect for oneself; the ablity to communicate clearly with others; and the ability to empathise with others.

They also focus on ways of analysing conflicts, both near at hand and more distant, and of examining a range of solutions to ask 'which is best and for whom?' A world perspective should also make us reassess situations we take as 'normal': for example, the relative positions of men and women in our own society, where roles and opportunities are still sharply differentiated on the basis of gender, and women are frequently at a disadvantage. The following UN statistics have produced many a lively and intelligent classroom debate.

- Women make up half the world's population.
- Women do nearly two-thirds of the world's work.
- Women receive one-tenth of the world's income.
- Women own less than one-hundredth of the world's property.

This has to be a totally unacceptable situation and one which *men* must begin to rectify. It also has to begin in our own immediate relationships, homes and classrooms. World studies is particularly concerned with understanding the global webs of interdependence of which we are all inescapably part, the fact that personal worlds, local worlds and more distant worlds are all interconnected. We can no longer afford to ignore the links. In the global system action in one country to resolve a particular problem may not only be ineffective, it may make matters worse elsewhere, as some necessarily simplified examples can illustrate.

> As a result of a labour shortage in Britain during the 1950s many firms encouraged people from the Caribbean to leave their homes and settle in this country. They came expecting to be welcomed but were given a reception that was often less than friendly. For many, good jobs and houses proved difficult to come by. The children of these people were born here and grew up in British society. They, however, were less willing than their parents to put up with the prejudice and discrimination that they often met. One result of this frustration was that many of them felt impelled to join in disturbances in inner cities as the only way left to vent their feelings . . .
>
> The current drive towards rapid economic development by governments of many 'third world' countries seems likely to result in the destruction of half of the world's tropical forests by the turn of the century, with the rest to follow in a few decades. The aim of these governments, who are themselves often at the mercy of multinational corporations, is to acquire more land for the cultivation of cash crops, although after a few years such cleared areas are likely to become desert. The global cost of this process includes the progressive elimination of the earth's main and still largely unclassified store of medical and drug-yielding plants, the destruction of a vast source of new food and energy supplies, and potentially serious world-wide climatic changes, all aspects of life crucial to the future of humankind. (Fisher and Hicks, 1985)

How global interrelationships such as these can be explored with younger children can partly be illustrated by three classroom glimpses.

> In one classroom, a class of thirty pupils are playing a game called The Global Cake. They are sitting in groups representing continents, with the size of each group corresponding to the appropriate percentage of world population. The groups are trading scissors, rulers, pencils and other items which they need to make their prescribed symbols for the 'ingredients': for example, sheaves of corn (for flour), chickens (for eggs), cows (for milk) and so on. At the end of an hour or so, when the symbols have all been fixed to a class mural representing the global cake, the teacher gives every group one or more real pieces of cake according to the actual level of consumption of food in the world. Not surprisingly, Asia's nine players are less than happy with their one and a half pieces, especially when they see North America's two players getting fat on eight and a half pieces.
>
> [The second] classroom is empty. Having spent some time considering the needs of the area, the class is on one of its regular visits to the local city farm, planting and tending a variety of vegetables and assisting with the overall development of the farm. In parallel the pupils are studying the life and work of people in an Indian village. What are the common basic needs and aspirations? How are these met? What are the differences?
>
> In yet another classroom the pupils are studying and discussing work. Specifically, what will it be like in twenty years' time? They are doing this as part of a course on the future which includes a general review of some major global issues, more detailed consideration of housing, nuclear energy and appropriate technology, equal opportunities for women, and an exploration of the pupils' hopes for their personal futures in a multicultural society. (Fisher and Hicks, 1985)

As Patrick Bailey said in the Editorial quoted previously, we all tend to take our cultural viewpoints as normal. But if these may, unwittingly, be damaging, they need gently disinterring and examining. Issues of racism – white feelings of superiority on this planet – and sexism – male presumptions of superiority – and the consequent discrimination in both cases need to be challenged at an early age. For example, in teaching about 'developing countries' we might ask ourselves the following questions (Clarke 1979).

- *The tourist's eye view.* Is everything portrayed as quaint and curious? Is there an emphasis on elephants and snakecharmers and the exotic? Are the local community or members of the class used merely as audio-visual aids for a project on the country they originated from?

- *The packet-of-tea approach.* Are people overseas shown as existing to grow our tea/cotton/sugar, or to provide us with exciting holidays? Is it implied that this is a very convenient arrangement: they are happy natives singing in the sunshine and we are happy tea-drinkers snug around the fire at home?

- *The pathological view.* Is everything shown as absolutely desperate: people everywhere are dying of starvation, floods, hurricanes, earthquakes? Are we shown as the only ones able to rescue them from such disaster?

- *The pat on the head.* Is it implied that 'they' have been a bit behind with their mud huts and things but if they follow our example they'll come out all right in the end? Is it implied that high technology, fast cars, automated industry, are the things that make a country 'developed'?

- *Poverty as an act of God.* Is poverty treated as something that is simply there although, of course, we deplore it? Are some of the fundamental causes of poverty given or only descriptions of its symptoms?

What we must aim for is to accept and appreciate other cultures in the context of their own aspirations and maybe learn from the forms, patterns, insights and attitudes of other cultures.

Education for change

Teaching for a better world, it should be clear by now, requires that we help young people to see how to make their own considered moral and political decisions. Thus we need to cultivate an awareness of the values that young people and others hold in order to understand how value commitments affect people's decisions and actions. What values can we choose from? What are the consequences of different choices? How do we behave if we are to affirm our chosen values? These are the sorts of questions we need to explore. Thus, Huckle (1982) describes a classroom activity in which:

Students are asked to consider 'money and happiness' and the 'good and bad' of life in Britain, as introductions to a study section in which they devise composite quality of life indices for twelve South American countries, and examine their relationship to GNP. This exercise clearly leads to a questioning of conventional definitions of development related to economic values, but also suggests other possibilities for values education. The first item in the Study Section in the book asks students to list 'things that make life enjoyable for you and give you satisfaction'. Such 'things' could well be related to the values they reflect, and the students are then asked 'Well, what sort of life are you hoping for anyway?' By substituting values for 'things' and asking students to list their priorities in life, the teacher could assemble on the blackboard a list which would probably include comfort, excitement, beauty, peace, equality, security, and others. Having discussed their meanings of these values, students would then be asked to rank their top five, and these could then form the basis of their assessment of the quality of life in different countries; the criteria by which they would select and compile statistical and other evidence. The student who considers peace a priority might assemble information on armed forces, weapons, and military alliances in the differing countries, while one who values freedom might explore issues of political repression and human rights. Such an exercise would begin to suggest whether Cuba or Brazil, Argentina or Peru, could best accommodate their chosen values.

At the same time, exercises in values education need to be grounded in the real world. Thus young people need to understand the main political division in the world, the major ideologies, and how governments, political parties and pressure groups work for different sorts of change. To be politically literate requires, among other things, the understanding of basic concepts such as power, authority, justice and dissent. Such exercises, however, only make sense if they are made as real as possible. Our teaching and learning must be both experiential and participatory because the *process* of education is paramount. Young people need to learn how to reflect and act both via simulation and in school, the local community and wider world. Only thus can we prepare them for effective participation in a democratic society.

Rights and responsibilities

The three Ps

One way of looking at the tasks for our pupils and for ourselves is in terms of the three Ps: the personal, the political, and the planetary. While these three interlock and overlap, each emphasises particular concerns, tasks, skills, rights and responsibilities.

Thus, in teaching geography for a better world we must be concerned about the intensely *personal*, about interpreting and understanding personal worlds. An essential part of this has to be valuing each individual's personal worth and trusting in their potential for positive change. Developing our own and others' interpersonal skills is vital if we are to become more fully human. Only as we become more fully human does our need to manipulate and control others diminish: hence our stress on active learning, which is experiential, participatory and essentially person-centred. It is vital that we focus on individuals, on actors, but this is of no value unless we also engage with the political.

By *political*, I mean the politics of everyday life: the need to understand and work to change the social, cultural, economic, patriarchal structures which diminish our human being. They affect not only the society we live in, but the institutions we work in and our own relationships. Essentially politics is about the use and abuse of power and if we are working for a better world then we must be concerned about the redistribution of power. But it is worth remembering that there are many sorts of power (Ferguson, 1982), for example: the power of the person, the power of the network, the power of flexibility, the power of decentralisation, the power of process, the power of the whole, the power of the alternative. The political issues and tasks are contextualised for us by the case studies in this book.

What most of these case studies remind us is that all these issues have a global or *planetary* dimension. Certainly world studies, and I hope also geography, would argue that such issues cannot be fully understood at this point in the late twentieth century unless they are set in their global context. Essentially we must be concerned with justice and, I would argue, not only justice for the human inhabitants of this planet but for all other living species on it. We have our own rights but also responsibilities to our sisters and brothers, whatever created form they may take. Indeed a better world must also involve compassionate stewardship for the planet itself. Nothing less will do.

2 Geography and world citizenship

JOHN HUCKLE

Before we can claim to be teaching geography for a better world, we clearly need an understanding of how the world works, what the causes of its major problems are, and which of the proposed solutions seems most realistic and desirable. This chapter seeks to provide the basis of that understanding by setting out a framework of ideas for promoting political literacy and citizenship through studies in geography. This is done largely in the context of environmental issues. Our first task is to consider some ideas about our troubled world.

The world economy

Over the last 400 years, the world's people and resources have been progressively integrated into a single network of economic production and exchange with a related division of labour (Harris, 1983; Wallerstein, 1979). Today, commodity chains criss-cross the globe linking producers of raw materials with processors, manufacturers, and consumers. The total production from this global economy is sufficient to meet the basic needs of all the world's people, yet millions starve while others live lives of luxury involving considerable waste. The world's people have the knowledge to maintain levels of production while sustaining the health of the natural systems on which they depend. Yet, the earth's ecology faces a growing crisis. The reason for this inequality and environmental destruction is that the world economy is a capitalist economy where the bulk of producers do not consume what they produce but exchange it in a competitive market for the best price. Such production is controlled by a rich minority who produce only what it is profitable for them to produce. Their motivation is the accumulation of capital, a process which can only take place through the exploitation of others.

The dominant agent of such exploitation is now the transnational company, often assisted by financial institutions and nation states. The transnational company sustains and develops ways of expropriating surpluses from other parts of the world which have their origins in colonialism and later forms of imperialism. Expropriation results from processes of unequal exchange which are built into world markets and sustained by political and military power. The location of production processes, in response to market forces, structures the world's spatial and environmental relations. The resulting spatial hierarchy of nation states, based on their dominant production processes, shows a threefold division, into core, periphery, and semi-periphery, which mirrors the global division of labour. Four recent atlases provide overviews of the world system (Kidron and Segal, 1984; Crow and Thomas, 1983; Myers, 1985; Chaliand and Rageau, 1985). These atlases are illustrated in Figure 2.1.

The ability to operate within boundaries wider than any political entity, and continually to transfer capital from political to economic units, largely explains the success of transnationals and the persistence of global capitalism. That there is no political unit with ultimate authority in all the areas embraced by the world economy is an important root of many global problems including those relating to the global environment.

Within the world economy it is possible to recognise four groups of states. The core states, centred on the USA, Western Europe and Japan, are the recipients of capital expropriated from elsewhere in the world. Consisting of the ex-colonial and newer neocolonial powers, these states are the centres of industrial and financial capital. Here are the headquarters of trans-national companies and the homes of the world's ruling class. The economies of core states are broadly based on highly mechanised and profitable processes and it is here that most of the world's research and development, which leads to new product cycles, is concentrated. The majority of people in core states enjoy high wages and standards of living sustained by energy and materials imported from elsewhere, particularly from peripheral states.

Figure 2.1 Four atlases which overview the world system

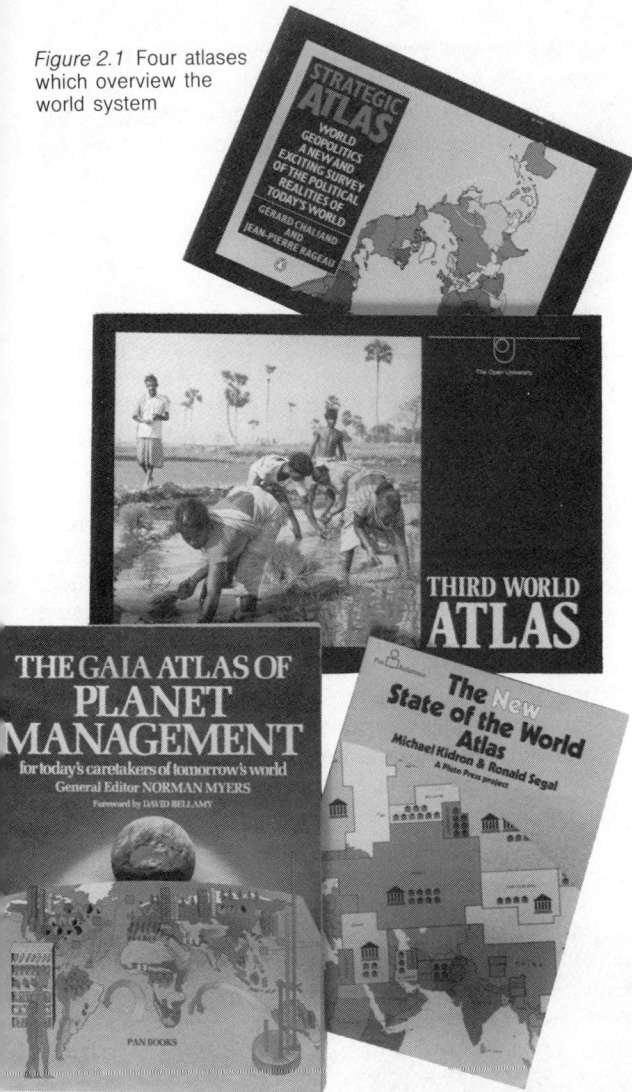

destined to enter the core while others, who remain heavily dependent on outside capital, may return to the periphery. Despite their high level of economic development, there are good reasons for regarding countries such as the UK, Canada and Australia as semi-peripheral states (Crough and Wheelwright, 1981).

The fourth and final group of states consists of the socialist states or centrally planned economies of the Eastern bloc. While socialist economies tend to be more isolated and self-sufficient than those of capitalist states, it is possible to recognise core and periphery within the realm of 'social imperialism' (Galtung, 1975), and to document the increasing dependence of the socialist states on the rest of the world where they have peripheral or semi-peripheral status. Current policy changes in China are the latest indication of their declared need for western capital, technology, strategic raw materials, and management style.

Cyclical and secular trends

As no single agency is in overall control of the world economy, it shows periodic phases of capital over-accumulation when the capacity for economic production exceeds that for consumption. As such periods approach, the rate of profit falls, factories close, and workers are laid off (Sutcliffe, 1983). Major economic recessions, such as the one through which we are currently living, seem to occur every 40 to 55 years and are related to the growth and decline of major product cycles. The upturn which is slowly emerging will be based on the new computer technologies and is likely to see the core of the world economy shift to South East Asia (Smith *et al.*, 1985). In restoring profitability, capital restructures the global network of production processes together with the social and spatial relations associated with them. It does this with the help of nation states which move up or down the spatial hierarchy depending on the nature and profitability of the processes within their borders.

A recurring result of such restructuring has been the extension of the periphery to bring new workers, resources, and markets into the world economy. There are real physical limits to such growth and these are an important cause of the long-term and persistent trend towards crisis within which shorter-term economic cycles are embedded. A further cause is the expansion of oppositional or anti-systemic movements as more and more poor people in the periphery find their lives constrained by new economic and political structures, and more and more people in the core demand a high social wage as their price for co-

It is the peripheral states of the world economy, those countries which Brandt referred to as the South, which are being actively underdeveloped by the process of capital expropriation mentioned above. Predominantly small and powerless, these states have economies heavily dependent on manual labour and the export of raw materials and cash crops. Unable to break free from structures of economic and political dependency, their development is constrained and their futures largely determined outside their borders. While local elites act as the agents of transnational capital and foreign governments, the vast majority of the people find themselves condemned to a life of increasing poverty and powerlessness.

Between core and periphery is found a third group of states, many of them large and resource-rich. Having production processes typical of both core and periphery, these semi-peripheral states have been able to accumulate some capital locally and attain a degree of dependent development. Some may be

operating with the system. Long-term crisis will eventually see the replacement of world capitalism by world socialism.

Ecological crisis

The ecological crisis, documented in such reports as the World Conservation Strategy (IUCN, UNEP, WWF, 1980), results from the workings of the world economy. Competition between capital formations, which must expand their capital in order to preserve it, and between nation states seeking an increased economic power, fuels economic growth. More and more of the earth's living and non-living resources become mere commodities to feed commodity chains and provide goods and services for the global market. Continual pressure to expand and cheapen production inevitably results in such social costs as pollution,

resource depletion, habitat destruction and species extinction (Croall and Rankin, 1981; Peet, 1985).

While the general causes of environmental problems are to be found in capitalist social relations, it is important to recognise that their specific origins and form vary across the four groups of states described above. The continued and accelerating expropriation of surplus from the periphery to the core leads to increased exploitation of people and nature in the countries of the South. Locked into this system people in these countries are forced to over-exploit their natural resources in order to survive. Minerals and timber are sold off to transnational companies to increase cash income and repay national debts. Pastures are overgrazed, soil eroded, and wildlife hunted to extinction, to maintain the power and wealth of ruling elites and to meet the immediate needs of the desperately poor. This leads to the type of disaster currently affecting much of Africa (Timberlake, 1985) and well illustrated by the fuelwood crisis (see Figure 2.2). Dependency means that the majority of people have no alternative but to work their land to exhaustion and to maximise labour availability by having more children. Conventional development often serves merely to increase this dependency.

Those states which have moved to the semi-

Figure 2.2 Young women carrying twigs, Bouza, South Nigeria. Trees supply well over 90% of the energy used in poor, peripheral states. Desertification is a product of 'the other energy crisis' as trees are denuded to provide fuelwood (Photograph: Panos Pictures/Mark Edwards)

periphery have often done so by exploiting their considerable resource base. This is what happened in Australia and Canada, and what is currently happening in countries such as Brazil. Some have been prepared to accept levels of pollution generation no longer tolerated in core regions, but the break-through to mass consumption in these states brings with it a range of new environmental problems. While socialist states have experimented with the public ownership of resources and the central planning of the economy, they have not avoided these problems. Their reforms have unlocked productive capacity and improved economic growth, but a growing literature (Smil, 1984; Komarov, 1978), suggests that they now show severe symptoms of environmental abuse. The majority have adopted western technology uncritically and have failed to give sufficient attention to the limits of nature in their economic planning. Their mistakes can be traced to the lack of a developed ecological perspective in Marxist ideology and to the growth of bureaucracies which exploit people and nature in their own interests. While any analysis should recognise the wide differences between socialist states, acknowl-edging China's experiments with communal organis-ation and radical technology for example, there is clearly a need for socialist planning to incorporate an ecological dimension.

In the core states, environmental problems result from the need to maintain profitability and political stability. Here, consumer societies are based on 'a treadmill of production' (Schnaiberg, 1980) which establishes ever more distorted wants and satisfies them with ever more damaging withdrawals and additions to the natural environment. Consumerism gained the support of capital, workers, and the state, for it yielded increased profits, living standards, and taxes. Firms, governments, and individual households, have all become addicted to patterns of growing production and consumption (Roberts, 1979). The political consequences of the slowing of the treadmill, with the onset of recession, have therefore been severe.

The recession of the 1970s and early 1980s was a product not only of capital over-accumulation but also of problems of reproduction. The post-war boom saw the acceleration of the treadmill in the core states, to counter falling profitability, but this meant quickening rates of resource depletion and environmental damage in much of the world. Capital was therefore faced with rising costs of raw materials and increased charges for reproducing such elements of the environment as clean water, previously free (Gorz, 1980). Its costs were also increased as pressure from a newly emerged environmental movement brought tighter controls over the use and pollution of nature. Meas-ures to protect environmental support systems had to be negotiated within the world's political systems.

The politics of world economy

Set in relation to the three-tier structure of the world economy is a three-tier political system consisting of local government, nation states and the realm of inter-national politics (Wallerstein, 1984). Decisions in this system regulate activity within the component parts of the world economy and it is often perceived as an effective instrument for resolving such problems as poverty, armed conflict, and environmental abuse. However, further consideration does suggest that existing political systems are generally capable only of ameliorative or reformist action and that their capacity for this is currently in decline.

The rise of capitalism saw the rise of the nation state; an institution for the collective management of the affairs of the ruling class within a particular terri-tory. The state was needed to impose some order and co-operation on economic and political life within its borders and so provide the ground rules for compe-tition between capitalist enterprises (Johnston, 1982). It also expressed the collective power of its rulers and enabled the competitive seizure of territory and people elsewhere in the world. Many states were set up in self-defence against such imperialism and some are still carrying out a form of internal colonisation designed to consolidate their territory and power. In those states where worker's parties have gained control of the state and attempted to create socialist states, these have generally failed to realise their promise of real economic and political democracy.

The modern world consists of around 200 nation states, each containing a sector of world economy and displaying one of a large number of forms of government (Finer, 1974; Hague and Harrop, 1982). Government is the major agent of the state, a short-term mechanism for carrying out its day-to-day busi-ness and promoting its long-term goals. Government action can, however, only be understood by reference to a theory of the state which separates it from government. The development of such theories has been one of the growth areas of the social sciences and political geography in recent years (Gamble, 1982; Johnston, 1982; Short, 1982). The key debate has been between liberal and radical theorists (Kliot and Waterman, 1983). Liberals separate economic and political life and employ pluralist theories of a neutral state, while radicals regard the economic and political as complementary aspects of one overall process, and use Marxist theory which regards the state as an instrument of the dominant class. Debate among radicals has centred on the need to avoid a narrow economism, which allows the political sphere no autonomy from the economic, and to explain the wide variety of states, each with different forms of political life and government, within the world system.

Nation states are the local authorities of the world system, enabling local capital accumulation and providing a platform for local capitalists to operate in the world market. Since they have different histories of incorporation, widely different populations and fragments of the total economy, and are differently affected by cyclical and secular trends over time, we should expect great variety in their form (Taylor, 1985). The political will attain greater autonomy from the economic in some states at some times, but this should not distract one from the modern state's core functions, of aiding capital accumulation, and legitimating the prevailing economic system. The global scale of capital's operations and the current need for economic restructuring, means that an increasing number of states find these functions contradictory. They must ally themselves with neocolonialism to attract investment and employment, but at the same time they must set themselves against neocolonialism if they are to protect other jobs and investment and so maintain the support of the people. As the state loses its bargaining power and room for manoeuvre, it tends to become more repressive.

The political stability of core states has been based on their strong place in world markets and consequent ability to pass on surplus to their peoples. The postwar boom enabled the growth of welfare and sustained forms of liberal democracy in which the political did gain greater autonomy. As growth turned to recession, the state acted to aid restructuring and this autonomy was reduced (Harrison, 1978). Welfare was cut back, the policies of social democracy changed to those of the New Right, and social consensus was replaced by social conflict.

In the peripheral states, a lack of economic surplus means that politics is often based on coercion and a strong state. Military rule has proven a popular means of sustaining the interests of local and international capital under forms of neocolonialism, and where popularist governments have gained power, their attempts at self-reliant development have often been subverted by internal tensions and bureaucracy, and the power of international financial institutions. Nationalism has played an important part in the politics of both peripheral and semi-peripheral states.

It is in the semi-peripheral states that the balance between coercion and consensus is often most delicately poised. If the state is to accumulate capital and climb into the core, it must put accumulation before consumption by its people. The potential for unrest and class struggle is therefore strong, and dictatorships are common. The costs of coercion are generally lessened by governments adopting the mobilising strategies of fascism, communism, or nationalism. The central bureaucracies of 'actually existing socialist

states' have used their own version of the treadmill to maintain public support and finance the arms race (Bahro, 1978). 'Nation before self' has been a continuing theme in the socialist states and the need for more rapid accumulation underlies current political change in China.

Within the various nation states are local political and administrative units. In advanced liberal democracies such as Australia and Britain, there are often three levels of government; the trilogy serving the same stabilising function as the threefold division of the world economic and political order. The local state develops its own priorities and bureaucracy, and its relations with local capital may set it in competition with national or international interests.

As the number and complexity of commodity chains have grown, individual states have sought to control the flows of capital, materials, and labour across their borders, and to shape world markets in the interests of local enterprises. The international political system provides the ground rules for such competition by legitimating and constraining sovereign states. It uses a framework of international law and treaties, much of it embodied in the United Nations system, to impose limits on the economic, political, and military behaviour of its constituent members. The political relations between states mirror the economic relations found in the global division of labour. Strong states are able to shape world trade to their own advantage and recreate new peripheral zones, using force if necessary. Weak states have very little power, their sovereignty often being little more than a token identity. The strongest states rely heavily on covert power which stems from their structural position in the world economy and their ability to determine and manipulate inter-state agenda setting and 'non-decision making'. Rarely will they need to resort to actual use of force, and their considerable power means that they can afford to appear liberal in nature. It is the weaker states which are often authoritarian and given to displays of overt power.

Consideration of the politics of the world economy suggests that the modern world is characterised by two kinds of politics. Within states, the basic struggle between the classes, at national and local levels, has been made more complex by the rise of other oppositional groups seeking separate identity or pursuing single issues such as peace, women's liberation, or ecologically sustainable development. Across states, international politics is characterised by the struggle for economic and political power between different groups of the world's ruling class. States continually enter and leave pacts and alliances in pursuing shared aims and it is the competition between these groupings which sustains the arms race and poses the ultimate global threat.

Environmental politics

In seeking to reduce the environmental damage which results from the workings of the world economy, environmental pressure groups seek to engage the governments of nation states and international political agencies. They take on the state because it is generally a major owner and user of land, plays a key role in regulating land use, and is regarded as the only body capable of enforcing environmental controls (Johnston, 1982). Studies of the environmental movement in the liberal democracies of the core help us to understand its class background (Cotgrove, 1982), the ideologies and utopias which guide its activities (Sandbach, 1980; O'Riordan, 1976), and the different ways in which its constituent groups engage the political process (Lowe and Goyder, 1983). These strategies include appeal to elites, electoral methods, links with trade unions, and community action (Martin, 1984): see Figure 2.3. Lowe and Goyder's work shows that environmental groups vary in the resources at their disposal, in their relations with

Figure 2.3 Protestors block the gates to the proposed low-level nuclear waste dump at Elstow in Bedfordshire. Direct action is one of the strategies used by environmental groups to influence the political process (Photograph: Format/Roshini Kempadoo)

government, parliament, and the media, and in their links with one another. Their tactics and level of success can largely be explained in terms of the theory of the state they overtly or covertly adopt.

Johnston (1982) and Sandbach (1980) relate environmental politics to alternative theories of the state. Pluralist strategies rely on mobilising public opinion, using the electoral system, and making use of such consultative mechanisms as public inquiries. They are often successful in protecting the interests of the already privileged, but reflect an essentially benevolent view of the state, a fragmented view of power, and a reluctance to recognise the class character of environmental issues. Those who see power as unevenly shared and lying with established groups are more inclined to adopt what Johnston terms corporatist strategies. Recognising that much debate is closed and that decision making is not democratic, they seek to get issues on the agenda and reform political procedures. Such strategies have led to a growth of lobbying, demands for greater freedom of information, and proposals for changes in the planning inquiry system. Radicals doubt whether pluralist or corporatist strategies can have much impact. Since the state acts in the interests of the capitalist system as a whole and has certain underlying imperatives, it can make only occasional concessions to environmentalists. These will be necessary to maintain its legitimacy, and while some have had major beneficial results, especially for human health, they have rarely harmed capital as a whole. The managerial activities of the state can only shift the balance of power between capital and other groups within certain limits (Blowers, 1984; Wilson, 1983). In times of recession, these limits are reduced and what environmental concessions are granted are likely to be at the expense of the already poor. In this situation radicals employ labour-based and grass-roots methods to relate environmental issues to the concerns of ordinary people, to challenge the state directly, and to give people a sense of their own power and of alternative futures (Martin, 1979; Roddewig, 1978).

The global dimension of such issues as desertification, acid rain, and the future of Antarctica, means that there is increased pressure for supra-national action. There is now a proliferation of international organisations concerned with environmental management and conservation and they police a growing number of international agreements and regulations (Boardman, 1981; McCormick, 1985). The main agencies are inter-governmental organisations such as the United Nations Environment Programme (UNEP) and the European Economic Community, and non-governmental organisations (NGOs) such as the International Union for the Conservation of Nation (IUCN), and the World Wildlife Fund (WWF). Much of their work is done through negotiation and international diplomacy but NGOs may resort to other tactics as Greenpeace does in its efforts to ban whaling. Until 1980, the actions of these agencies were largely reactive and ad hoc but in that year the WWF and IUCN launched the World Conservation Strategy designed to persuade governments of the need for national conservation and development programmes. By that time the initially hostile and suspicious attitudes to conservation of many peripheral and semi-peripheral states had mellowed (Hornby, 1985), but the priorities of the international political system and national sovereignty remained significant obstacles to the implementation of what were essentially liberal reforms.

Within the international political system, ecologically sustainable development is not a significant agenda item. International politics remains dominated by East–West rather than North–South issues and UNEP lacks the power and resources of a UN agency. It is merely the environmental conscience rather than the environmental programme of the United Nations (Redclift, 1984), and many states fail to fund it with international taxes as they are supposed to do (Earthscan, 1982). International laws and regulations on environmental matters are frequently ignored by nation states who put their own interests and sovereignty before the common good. Economic and political competition within the inter-state system generally acts against the co-operative solution of global problems.

An alternative world order

Our examination of the world economy and its related political systems suggests that 'global' problems have their origins in economic and political structures that work in the interests of a minority of the world's people. These structures are increasingly opposed by groups and nations seeking to satisfy their basic needs through varying forms of collective self-reliance. They seek to sever existing links of economic, political, and cultural dependency, to mobilise fully their own capabilities and resources, and to strengthen their collaboration with groups pursuing similar development goals. Such change is to be achieved from below, by raising people's consciousness of their own oppression, mobilising their resultant desire for change, and then confronting and transforming existing social structures. Self-reliant development takes varied forms but has the common theme of extending economic and political democracy. This is a theme also associated with socialism.

While the majority of existing socialist societies reserve power for a minority, and are often authoritarian and anti-democratic, real socialism requires the social control by ordinary people of economic production, and the reshaping of society. It would develop collective self-reliance by transferring land and technology to communal ownership, ensuring a high degree of material and social equality, and by giving workers and citizens real control over their workplaces and communities. A degree of planning and co-ordination from above would still be necessary but, by devolving economic and political power to smaller units, people would lose the sense of alienation and powerlessness they currently feel. In these conditions, social criteria would replace market criteria in determining economic production and distribution with consequent gains for both welfare and environmental well-being. There would be real incentives to conserve energy and materials, to adopt appropriate technology, to reduce pollution, and to slow the treadmill by producing a different mix of goods and services, many for public rather than private consumption (Roberts, 1979; Gorz, 1980). In such a society, everyone would be found mental and manual work to do and, with the slowing of the treadmill, there would be more time for personal development and mutual aid. Societies in the periphery have much to teach us about such forms of development.

Visions of such a socialist society are not new (Pepper, 1984). They have been rediscovered and revised in recent years, and there has been a growing awareness that attempts to implement such change will remain utopian unless co-ordinated and directed at the whole of society (Bahro, 1982; Williams, 1982). Barratt Brown (1984) provides a framework for an alternative, self-managing, socialist political economy and, with others (Harris, 1982; McNally, 1980), advocates an associated form of internationalism. This is based on a world federation of people's states, each a self-managing democracy. Following a radical reduction in inequalities between countries, and the replacement of international competition by co-operation, this new international order would be capable of solving problems such as those affecting the global commons.

Composite struggles to establish self-management and the type of socialist society I have just described are already under way. The new municipal socialism in Greater London, the Chipko movement in the Himalayas, the Wilderness Society, the Movement Against Uranium Mining in Australia, Solidarity in Poland . . .: all are attempts to bring about fundamental change in the existing order. They show that collective self-reliance is possible and that the seeds of a new society are here in our midst: see Figure 2.4. They can also be seen in education.

Figure 2.4 Wandsworth Community Transport Dial a Ride project: an example of collective self-reliance aided by the Greater London Council (Photogragh: Photo Co-op/C. B. Hughes)

Teaching geography for a better world

The development of the world economy and the growth of nation states were facilitated and legitimated by the spread of compulsory schooling. Schooling served to reproduce a graded and suitably skilled workforce, and to instill beliefs and values supportive to dominant economic and political interests. I have examined school geography's continuing role as an agent of social reproduction elsewhere (Huckle, 1983, 1985a), and have also looked at the way in which geography lessons conceal the true causes of environmental problems (Huckle, 1985b). Gilbert's analysis of geography textbooks provides us with further insights (Gilbert, 1984), as do many of the articles published in *Contemporary Issues in Geography and Education*.

Fortunately, school geography is heir to other traditions and is capable of being used to develop pupils' critical awareness of existing social structures and their ability to engage and transform society (Donelly, 1980, 1984). The vision of early socialists, including socialist geographers, was one of poly-technic education (Castles and Wustenberg, 1979). It would provide a practical and theoretical understanding of work and the economy, and a critical grasp of the social relations under which these take place.

Schools would seek to produce fully developed individuals, capable of productive work, and of understanding and controlling both the present and future shape of society. Such socialist education would be democratically run and would involve pupils in the everyday work, life, and decisions of the community. This would enable them to understand the foundations and workings of society, and experience the complementary nature of knowledge and experience in realising social goals. While the ideals of socialist education have been applied in some peripheral states, they were largely forgotten in the advanced capitalist countries, such as Britain and Australia, during the post-war economic boom. During this period, socialists generally settled for liberal or social democratic notions of education, designed to provide greater equality of opportunity within existing structures. The onset of recession, and attempts to restructure education in capital's interests, have, however, led to a renewed examination and advocacy of such ideals (Sharp, 1980; Sarup, 1982; Harris, 1982). What might they involve now that we are living in a global society?

Taylor (1985) provides diagrams (Figure 2.5) of the three-tiered structures of the world's economy and political systems described earlier in this article. These suggest that most people are unable to relate the causes of everyday events to the logic of these world systems because so much of what they are taught and told is centred on the nation state. By separating everyday experience from reality, the local from the global, the nation state acts as ideology. It denies people the ideas to make sense of the world and effectively places problems beyond their reach. The needs of global accumulation are experienced locally in such forms as unemployment or pollution, but they are justified nationally for the ultimate benefit of interests organised internationally. The environmentalists' catchphrase 'Think globally ... act locally' can be seen as an attempt to counter the ideology of the nation state which has implications for geography teaching.

Taylor's diagrams would suggest that we use commodity chains to relate pupils' local experience to global realities. The banner proclaiming 'Say No to Nirex Nuclear Dump' on top of County Hall in Bedford expresses the indignation of the normally conservative inhabitants of an English county now faced with the shallow burial of low-level nuclear waste. They are threatened with even closer links to the nuclear fuel cycle: a global commodity chain which sustains both nuclear power and nuclear weapons (Falk, 1982). It is clearly in the interests of certain transnational corporations and the world's most powerful nation states, and is supposedly regulated by a complex network of national and international controls. The proposed dump is justified in terms of national energy policy and the actions of some local environmentalists

in opposing it are similar to those of countless other groups around the world seeking greater control over their own lives and environments. The banner can be seen as a symbol of an alternative future yet few who look up at it are aware of these connections or of the challenges and possibilities it represents. Making pupils aware of such things is surely the major part of teaching geography for a better world.

While 'turning on the light' links school pupils in Britain to a nuclear power station and the network of relationships just examined, the consumption of other goods and services links them to other environmental issues and sectors of the world economy. A tin of corned beef links them to rainforest destruction in Brazil, a package holiday links them to coastal pollution in Yugoslavia, their parents' tax bill links them

Figure 2.5 Everyday experience and reality in the three-tiered structure of the world economy and political systems (Taylor, 1985)

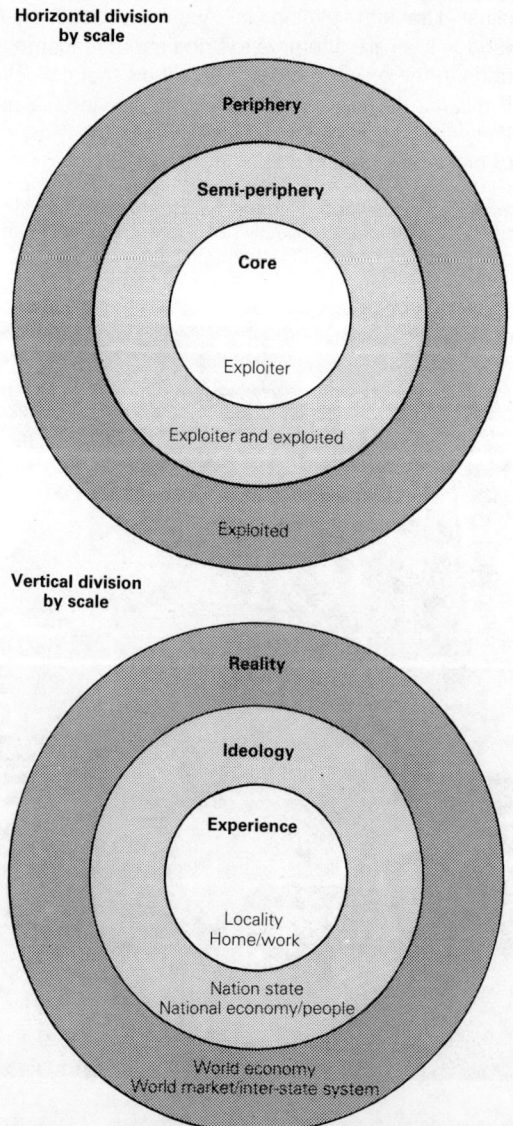

Horizontal division by scale

Periphery

Semi-periphery

Core

Exploiter

Exploiter and exploited

Exploited

Vertical division by scale

Reality

Ideology

Experience

Locality Home/work

Nation state National economy/people

World economy World market/inter-state system

to the arms race and the pollution of Lake Baikal in the USSR, and a pair of football boots links them to the fate of kangaroos in Australia. Understanding these issues means relating them to the political economies of nation states as structured by their history and place within the world economy. It means considering the policies of national governments to solve the issues and the policies being put forward by opposition groups. Other commodity chains link us to transnational environmental issues and provide opportunities for teaching about international politics. Still others link us to struggles for change from below and allow us to teach about possible social alternatives. Clearly a curriculum, based on a considered selection of local experiences and related commodity chains, would enable the teacher to sample a representative range of environmental issues, political economies, and global conflict formations (Galtung, 1975). Such a curriculum will be published as part of the World Wildlife Fund's *Global Environmental Education Programme* from 1987.

In developing global citizenship through geography, teachers could learn much from the Programme for Political Education and its concept of political literacy (Crick and Porter, 1978). McElroy (Chapter 3 of this book) provides geography teachers with an excellent summary of the possibilities, so I intend to relate my proposals to Porter's restatement of the four objectives of the political literacy approach, and his consideration of its inevitably radical nature (Porter, 1981).

1. Political literacy involves acquiring propositional knowledge about politics; developing an understanding of basic concepts, ideas, issues, and the way in which existing political systems work in theory. Such knowledge provides the foundation for a consideration of environmental issues, and geography teachers are well placed to provide it in the area of environmental politics.

2. Political literacy requires procedural knowledge, or know-how, which we can develop through case studies, simulation games, and real involvement in local issues.

3. Political literacy seeks a critical stance towards propositional and procedural knowledge and a readiness to examine and evaluate alternative political systems. This is crucial in the light of the type of curriculum outlined above. Developing this constructive scepticism would involve an examination of environmental management and politics within a range of nation states, with different forms of government, variously located in the world economy. It would also require pupils to question the efficacy of national and international agencies set up to protect the environment, and would allow

them to assess critically the beliefs and policies of groups seeking either reform or radical change. For older pupils, this would mean some consideration of the different theories of the state now so central to political geography. This objective is contrary to much of existing political education in school geography which presents liberal democracy as necessarily benevolent and in everyone's interests, and fails to deal adequately with alternatives in an open and critical way.

4. Political literacy should allow for the application of knowledge and constructive scepticism to everyday contexts and issues. Possibilities for pupils to test their developing political literacy in a widening context are central to the curriculum outlined above.

Porter describes a programme of political education reflecting all four of these objectives as having 'essential radical implications and imperatives' (Porter, 1984). He does not equate radical with socialist but his review elsewhere (Porter, 1983) of the forms of political education resulting from different social and political philosophies makes the socialist foundations of radical political education quite clear. It derives its aims from a theoretical (structuralist) analysis of society and seeks to provide pupils with a critical understanding of that society, their life chances within it, and a knowledge of the alternatives. It emphasises learning by doing, which requires analytical skills for reflecting on actions, and participatory and organising skills for action itself. Its values are collectivist and democratic in a socialist sense.

A similar philosophy is reflected in what Kemmis, Cole and Suggett (1983) term the socially critical school. They see such schools as aiding the transition to new forms of society by preparing pupils to participate in social, political, and economic change. Schools would become part of adaptive communities, helping them to research and create viable future lifestyles from below. They would expose irrational and unjust processes in the world and demonstrate how a just and democratic society might work. They would encourage self-reliance and collective decision making, and would co-operate with social movements for change within their communities. The curriculum would be negotiated with local people, would construct useful knowledge through reflection and action on issues affecting their lives, and would consequently involve active and experiential ways of learning. The teacher would be a co-learner and co-ordinator, involved in community life and fulfilling a leading role in convincing people that together they can change the world. The Joint Working Party is again careful not to describe its proposals as socialist, but they clearly owe much to the socialist tradition and are a very necessary part of creating an alternative world society.

The choices before us

As the crisis deepens, there are clear attempts to restructure schooling as a more effective mechanism of social reproduction and control (Freeland, 1985). The climate would not appear receptive to new radical initiatives by geography teachers, but our pupils' growing resistance to conventional offerings, and the rhetoric of 'the new vocationalism' provide us with significant opportunities to exploit. Requests to raise pupils' economic and social awareness, and to better equip them for work, allow us to introduce elements of real polytechnic education. At the same time appeals to break down the barriers between schools and 'the real world' allow us to form new links with community groups engaged in other forms of political education (Sharp, 1984). The transition to socialism involves a number of related tasks: establishing social control of production, providing an alternative culture, reconstructing the political movement, and countering attempts at co-option by existing interests (Connell, 1980). Schools cannot, of themselves, produce a 'better world' (Pepper, 1984), but they can help by rendering the process of social reproduction more open and democratic. Forecasts of alternative futures make the choices now facing us stark and clear (Stretton, 1976; Gorz, 1985). We can continue to allow a minority to run the world in its interest and therefore continue to be subject to the oppression, injustice, and mounting threats which this involves. Alternatively, we can work with others to reclaim the world and bring about the social revolution which new technologies now make a possibility rather than a utopia. As the study of people's active construction and transformation of their physical and social environment, geography can become a collective exercise in reclaiming our stolen humanity and reconstructing society (Harvey, 1984). That surely is what teaching geography for a better world should be all about.

3 Learning geography: a route to political literacy

BARRIE McELROY

Geography plays a major role in many of the issues and decisions that affect society, the environment and the resultant spatial forms. It is the nature of that contribution which is brought under scrutiny in this chapter. While we sometimes used to claim that the models, theories and explanations of geography are objective, it is not usually difficult to demonstrate the values that underlie them. It can be argued that, historically, geography has served the privileged of each age, from the voyaging merchants of yore to the modern industrialists.

When we teach geography in schools, we generally teach those topics and models that are of significance to the powerful elites, and ignore the aspects of life and space that are more important to the general public. The issues that we study are often remote from the real experience of life of most of the students, and the explanations, analyses and models used disregard factors of relevance to them.

This chapter does not address itself directly to the problems of academic and research geography that are created by the apparent neglect of major human, social and environmental factors during much geographical model building. Since the 1970s there have been plenty of studies by behavioural, human-istic and radical geographers that expose the narrow stance of much of positivist spatial geography. One must hope that in the future all approaches to teaching geography will take a more balanced view of social process and spatial form.

Through the late 1960s and most of the 1970s it was often assumed that school geography should reflect current academic geography. Indeed the most valuable progress in school geography stemmed from the conceptual revolution in geography and new learning theory. Unfortunately this attention to academic geography as the major source of objectives for teaching geography has meant a neglect of the needs of children as they develop into the potential decision makers in society. In fact geography rarely gives them much idea about how the decisions are made that affect the social and economic processes and the related spatial form of their world.

Even less often does it show them how they can become involved in the making of those decisions. Neither the explanations and theories of geography nor our teaching give the average citizen or student much understanding of how power is exercised in decision making and how they might share in that power.

In statements about the purposes of schools much is said about teaching children the knowledge and skills necessary for them to be able to have greater control over their own life chances. While detachment may be an admirable procedural value for research, it is not so appropriate for learning where participation in life is the constant goal. Effective participation grows from awareness, knowledge, and the appropriate skills, including one's understanding of the inclination to use political skills.

Implicit in the many general statements on the purposes of schooling is that education will result in changing the human, physical, social and economic environment for the better. At the same time some questions are not addressed. What kind of changes? Where should these changes occur? Better for whom? Who has the most say in decisions about change? The answers to such questions are generally implicit in the actual practice of schooling.

Can the current moves to improve the general literacy of school children result in their having greater influence over their own chances in life? Through improved literacy they may come to believe more fervently in the oft-repeated cliché about their right to a voice in their own destiny. But can it give them the political power to make changes? An effective literacy process must go far beyond a simple facility with words to probe the very relationship of people with their world (Freire, 1972).

The literacy process

The strong and obvious similarity between this view of literacy and the major people–environment paradigms of geography is inescapable. It provides an apt meeting place between the nature of the discipline and the processes of learning and living. If we believe that literacy goes way beyond basic encoding and decoding it is not hard to accept Freire's expansion of the definition to speak of it as a 'human act implying reflection and action' (Freire, 1972).

The literary process described by Freire requires this combination of thoughtful participation which he calls praxis. People must be able to participate consciously in transforming their world by their thinking, their words and their deeds. Literacy means that the participants are aware of how they can be involved. It is an 'act of knowing' and not just of the intellect but of how to act in the world.

While geography as it is frequently taught seeks to help students to *know* the world at an intellectual level it often ignores the *action* as the natural and necessary complement to *reflection*. It is generally accepted that all decisions affecting the social and economic processes and subsequent spatial patterns of our world are taken by remote groups of an elite 'them' and that 'we' rarely have any role to play except at the most trivial and personal levels.

If the study of geography is going to involve students in knowing their world by a process of praxis then geography teachers have a responsibility to teach them how to participate in the decision making that transforms their world. This will involve more than just a good grasp of geographical knowledge and skills, and will include the sound development of political literacy.

Political literacy

While political education is generally about:

> what differing viewpoints are held, who holds them, why, in what context and with what constraints (Crick and Porter, 1978)

the definition of literacy suggested above means that political literacy is more than this. As the central concept of the Hansard's Society's 'Programme for Political Education' Project, political literacy is defined as knowing:

> what the main political disputes are about, what beliefs the main contestants have of them, how they are likely to affect you and me

and to be:

> likely to be predisposed to try to do something about the issue in question in a manner which is at once effective and respectful of the sincerity of other people and what they believe. (Crick and Porter, 1978)

If we can include a wider range of scale than 'the main political disputes', this can serve as a useful definition of political literacy for geography teaching. For effective involvement in a dispute of any kind, from those at home to those of international scale, the politically literate person needs considerable knowledge of the issue, the people involved, their policies, and a range of possible alternative actions. A politically literate person will also manifest certain procedural values that allow others a similar voice. That person will also be able and inclined to use the knowledge and skills he/she possesses in effective and socially responsible ways (see Figure 3.1). The politically literate are characterised by:

> what they know, their attitiude to what they know and their skill in using what they know. (Crick and Porter, 1978)

The development of political literacy while teaching geography, or any subject, must focus study on issues characterised by disagreements and the resolution of conflicts. In the first instance children ought to examine the everyday political issues in which they are involved. It is through the study of these that they may begin to comprehend and practise the knowledge, skills and attitudes that are essential in the larger political arena.

The concepts of political literacy

This chapter makes no attempt to assay the whole range of possible fundamental political ideas and concepts. The twelve concepts suggested by Crick (1978) refer to government, people and the relationships between them. These concepts (for example, power, force, law, natural rights, freedom and welfare) are not equally basic to most political issues and this limits their value as a collection of concepts for teaching.

In particular many of these concepts are more commonly associated with national rather than local or homely political issues. Teachers need to concern themselves with the principles and concepts that are likely to be involved in all political issues no matter what the scale. Students can best recognise the various political concepts where they first see or engage in them, at home or in the local area.

Perception of issues

Recognition of conflicts and different policies
What do different people say needs doing?

Relevant knowledge	**Self-interest and social responsibility**	**Action skills**
For example:	For example:	For example:
Knowledge of who promotes what policies		Experience of conflicts of values and interest in home and everyday life
Scepticism about factual claims and knowledge of alternative sources		
Alternative ways of looking at things		Experiences of participation, debate and decision making in home, school, etc.
Knowledge of customary and alternative ways of settling disputes		
Knowledge of the appropriate ways and means of influence for particular purposes		Insistence on taking part and being heard in home, school, etc.
Knowledge of alternative types of societies and of the ways and means associated with them		Making real choices in school work generally and using independent study time, etc.

Under **Self-interest and social responsibility**:

Effect on oneself	Effect on others
Ability to express one's own interests and principles	Ability to perceive the interests and principles of others
Ability to offer justifications and reasons for pursuing one's own interests and ideals	Ability to understand the justifications and reasons of others

Realistic political judgements

Effective political participation

Political democracy in action

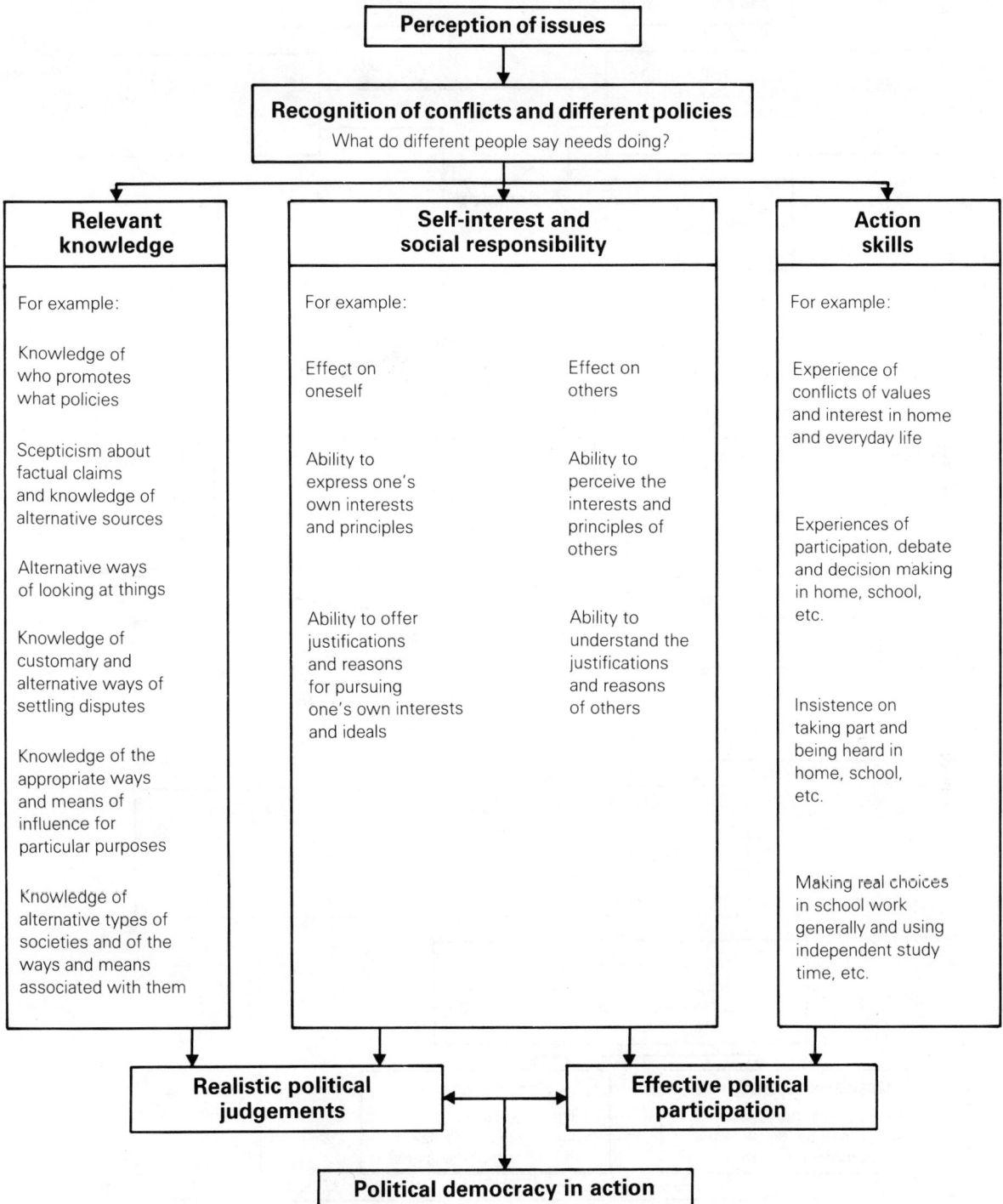

Figure 3.1 A model of political literacy (after Porter, 1979)

Conflict

The basic political problem arises from disagreement between group members with differing interests and beliefs over:

Goals *Attitudes* *Methods* *Results*	adopted in allocating scarce resources, using the environment, locating industry, etc.	

Either   Or

Principles and value preferences

A decision

A choice made between competing alternatives or policies proposed by different members of the group.

through

The exercise of power

The ability to achieve intended results.

Force
Achieving intended results by use of threat of physical sanctions

Manipulation
Achieving intended results by control of information

Authority
Achieving intended results by respect position or moral right

Influence
Affecting the achievement of intended results

Reason
Achieving intended results by argument

Responses to the decision

Compliance
Conforming involuntarily to the demands of others

Consent
Voluntary acceptance of a decision made by others

Dissent
Disagreement with the goals, values, methods or outcome of a decision

Order
When expectations are fulfilled and calculations can be made without fear of changing circumstances

Disorder
When uncertainties are so numerous as to make calculations difficult and even impossible

Rules
Principles based on experience which are designed to direct the group's actions and to which members are intended to conform

Representation
The claim for the few to represent the many because they embody some external attributes

Participation
The opportunity to take part in and have a say in the making of decisions

Patterns of decision making

Autocratic   Oligarchic   Democratic   Anarchic

Value preferences
e.g. critical stance; willingness to give reasons; respect for evidence; openness to change; fairness; freedom; tolerance; equality.

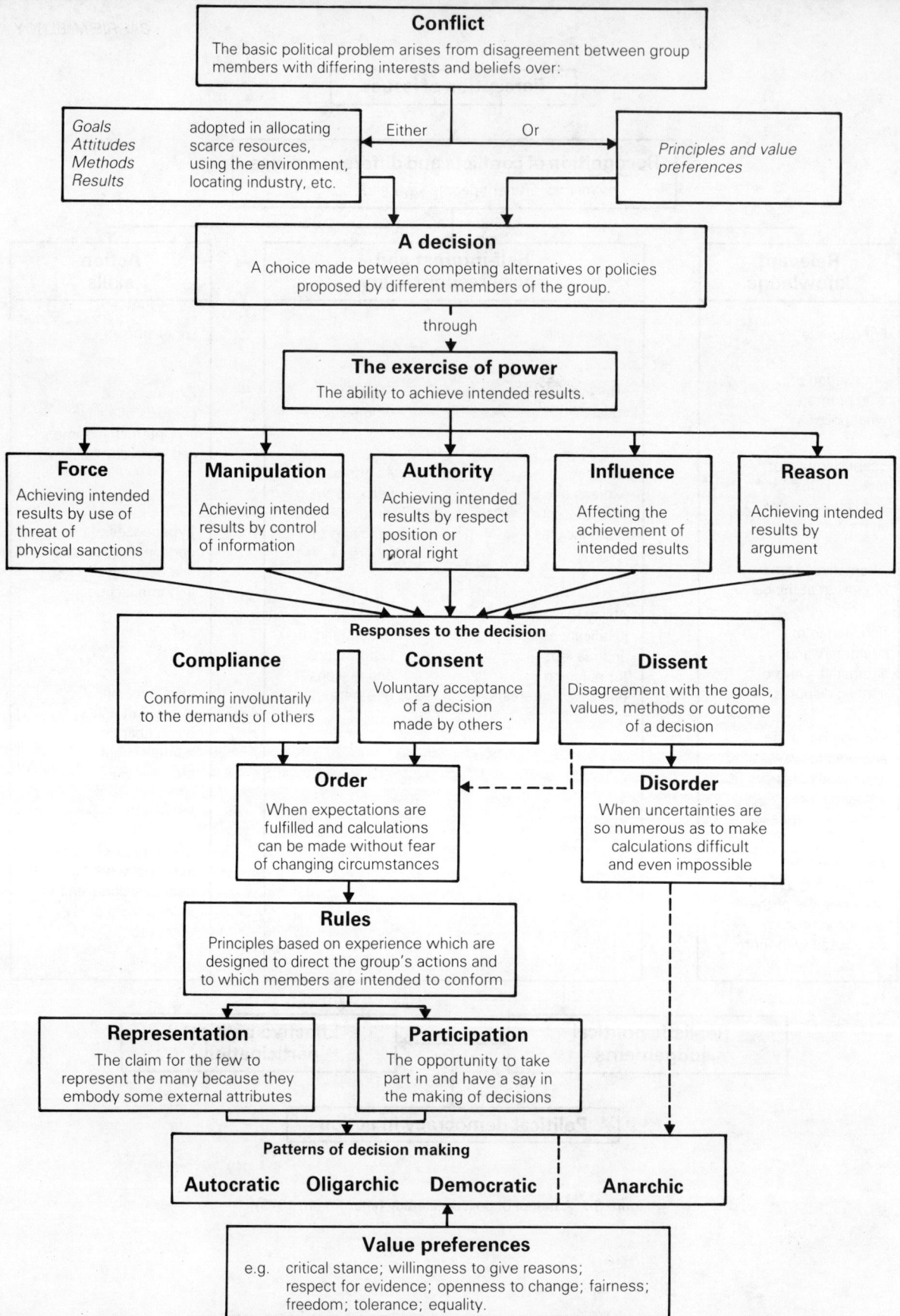

Figure 3.2 Political concepts: network of political decision making through the exercise of power (after Stradling, 1978)

Unfortunately, they are often first introduced on too remote a social or geographical scale.

The fundamental political concepts derive from conflicts of interest between people seeking diverse goals and from the ways such conflicts are resolved. They are concerned with the questions of Who? What? Where? When? How? and Why? while the issue of allocation of such things as resources, space, places and tasks is negotiated. They relate to the means of negotiation and settlement, and to the principles (for example, equality, freedom) that should control the parties involved in the action.

Stradling (1978) suggests that no matter what the scale of the political problem, decision is sought through the exercise of *power*. The various responses to such a decision can be traced through varying degrees of acceptance to reveal patterns of resolution ranging from anarchy to autocracy. Various procedural values also become manifest in such an analysis. The web of interdependent concepts thus derived is fundamental to most political activity (Figure 3.2).

While many other concepts, such as representation, must inevitably be learnt, most of them grow out of an understanding of the practice of political power and its direct consequences. In the case of a disagreement over a territorial expansion one can identify the way in which that conflict was or can be resolved by using Figure 3.2 to analyse the political activity. This holds whether the territorial dispute is between siblings over the shared space in a bedroom or the international argument over Palestine.

Each of the political concepts may be examined at increasing levels of abstraction, generality and complexity as they are met through a series of carefully chosen political issues in a spiral curriculum. This is also true of the geographical concepts in those same issues. It is possible to illustrate the development of the basic decision-making concept of the exercise of power in a spiral of various contexts as in Figure 3.3.

Figure 3.3 The concept of power: a spiral development (after Stradling, 1978)

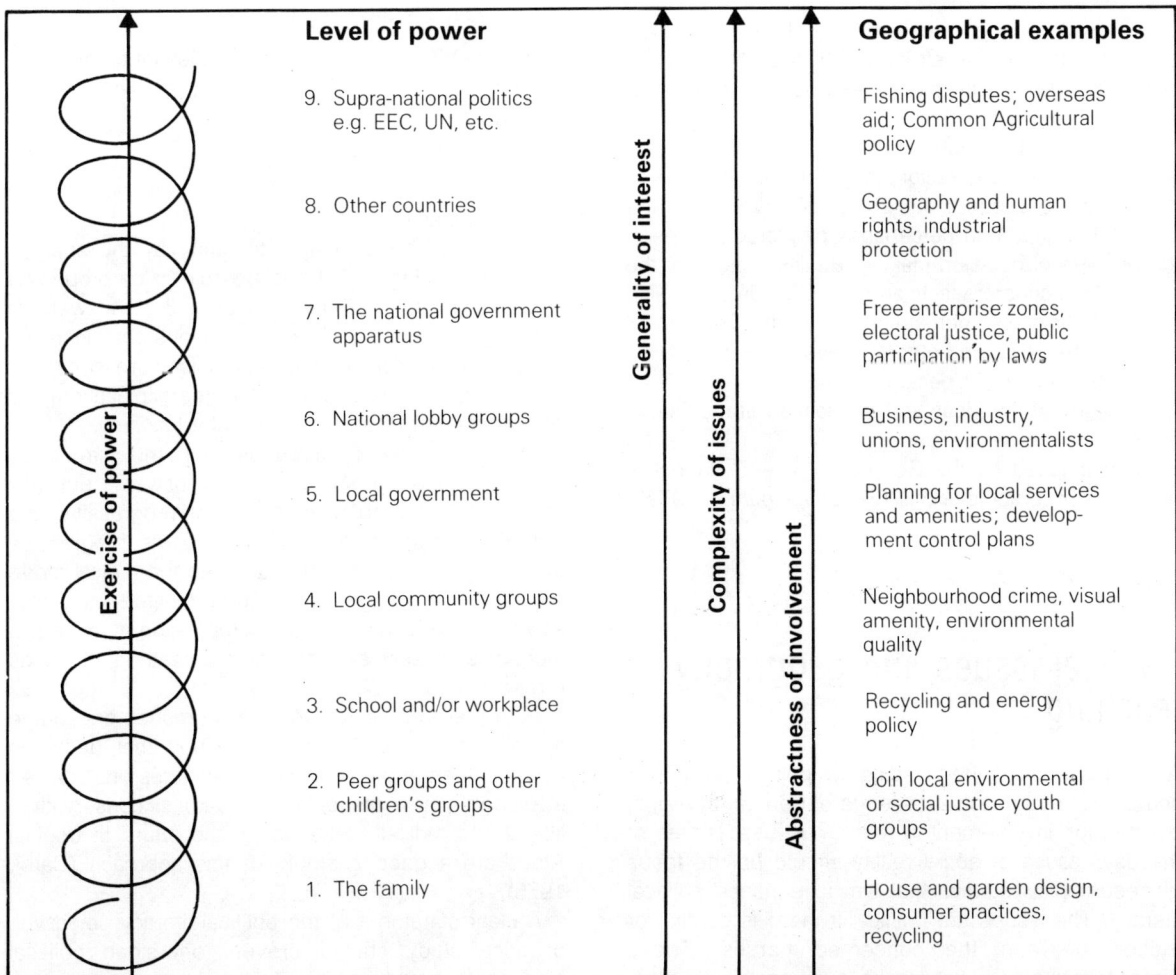

Level of power	Geographical examples
9. Supra-national politics e.g. EEC, UN, etc.	Fishing disputes; overseas aid; Common Agricultural policy
8. Other countries	Geography and human rights, industrial protection
7. The national government apparatus	Free enterprise zones, electoral justice, public participation by laws
6. National lobby groups	Business, industry, unions, environmentalists
5. Local government	Planning for local services and amenities; development control plans
4. Local community groups	Neighbourhood crime, visual amenity, environmental quality
3. School and/or workplace	Recycling and energy policy
2. Peer groups and other children's groups	Join local environmental or social justice youth groups
1. The family	House and garden design, consumer practices, recycling

Exercise of power · Generality of interest · Complexity of issues · Abstractness of involvement

Geography and political literacy

Questions to do with social and economic structure and the access to political power are implicit in many geographical studies. Relative access to and control over space, resources and the environment are posed, if often neglected, during studies of urban morphology, energy, transport, or the Third World, for instance.

Geography since the 1960s, in seeking powerful scientific models of description, has used generalised theory and lost some of its power of explanation of the particular. Positivist science largely ignored the socio-political inputs into decision making except as fine tuning or as a criticism of reality where it did not neatly match the predictions and assumptions of the model.

Newer approaches to geographical research such as the behavioural, humanistic and radical probe the human, social, political and economic origins of spatial form. So far these have had little impact in schools. Schools and geography have generally, if unintentionally, supported the contemporary status quo. It behoves geography teachers who genuinely wish to open a wider range of optional life chances for their pupils to identify less strongly with the elites and to sympathise more with the general public whose children we teach (Gill, 1980).

Students of geography must learn to appreciate the value bases and perceptions of the disadvantaged as well as the privileged; the powerless as well as the powerful. Values and perceptions play crucial roles in the process of decision making. Reality is not just the assembly of concrete facts and objective data, but also of the participants' perceptions of them. They must consider their own and others' views of the facts. This demands a model of pedagogy that ensures both an examination of the ideas and clarification of the values evident in the issue under study. The Route for Enquiry mapped by the Geography 16–19 Project is one attempt to achieve this (Schools Council, 1979).

Political issues and geography teaching

Awareness and understanding of political concepts come not through the knowledge of general systems, but through involvement in relevant issues. Issues of the day, issues of social reality should be the focus of geographical studies that aim to enhance political literacy. The issues are political if there is conflict or friction between the concerned parties. These disagreements are likely to be over goals, attitudes,

methods or results (Figure 3.2). Normally consensus will come only after controversy.

Most such studies of geographical/political issues are inseparable from a consideration of social justice like the equitable distribution of services, goods, or quality of environment. The social and political processes are frequently imaged in spatial form and so disputes are often focused on territories, frontiers, places, access and similar geographical concepts.

If geographical issues of a political nature can be recognised by the associated conflict then those for study should be carefully selected. The main and obvious requirement is that they are of significant concern to people. This may mean at an individual and personal, or at a national and public level.

Stradling and Porter (1978) suggest five ways of selecting such issues. Three things that can help choose broader-scale issues fairly objectively are:

1. national opinion polls,
2. media at the national or local level, and
3. materials issued by political groups.

At the more subjective level in the realm of the politics of everyday life they suggest:

4. teachers' judgement of issues relevant to the class, and
5. selection by the pupils.

However the selection is made, the issues must be appropriate and manageable in the defined terms of political literacy.

They must be amenable to study by the analysis suggested in Figure 3.1 and be able to be probed by questions such as those in Figure 3.4. Answers to these may reveal political implications that increase understanding of locational choice, reasons for relocation, contrary views of resource exploitation, and other common issues in geography teaching.

The pedagogy required is not the structured classical mode that seeks 'correct answers', but may more happily combine elements of progressive and radical approaches. Put over-simply the progressive mode uses a dilemma approach and the radical mode suggests that one gets involved in transforming reality as well as thinking about it. A combination of these two modes is closely akin to Freire's method of praxis (Freire, 1972).

Both the progressive and radical modes encourage a dialectic approach (Vogeler, 1977) that demands consideration of the policies and attitudes of all parties involved in the issue. Hans Carol's conservative, liberal and radical scenarios for the future of tropical Africa are a good example of this approach (Carol, 1975).

A clear statement of the political literacy objectives of each study should prevent one-sided political stances. It should also help to avoid the equally poten-

	Relevant knowledge		Self-interest and social responsibility			Action skills
Reflection	Who stands for what?	Where is this issue decided?	How can one make oneself felt?	How would I be affected?	How would others be affected?	What big disputes have I seen, in family, friends, school or in the neighbour-hood?
Analysis	Shouldn't I take this issue with a pinch of salt? Where else can I find out anything about it?	How is this dispute settled? As things are, what's possible?	How can one make oneself felt on this particular issue?	Can I put down what it means to me and how I think about it?	What does it mean to other people and what do they think about it?	What big disputes have I been involved in?
Action	What other ways are there of thinking about it?	Is it fair? Is there another way of doing it?	How is it done elsewhere?	How can I convince someone else that what I want to do is fair?	What sort of case do others have?	Do I know how to influence decisions?

Figure 3.4 Political literacy: some questions for students
(after Crick and Lister, 1978)

tially dangerous consequences of otherwise unrecognised ideology implicit in a particular study.

Teaching for political literacy

Political literacy, as defined here, demands certain teaching approaches, or rather it precludes common expository methods. One needs to be alert to the implications of particular teaching styles.

Teacher-dominant styles not only cannot develop political literacy, but may considerably harm it. Crick and Porter (1978) refer to a lesson closely based on all the elements of political literacy (Figure 3.1), including comments on the alternatives and how they might affect the students, 'but all this is a sprightly lecture to an inert and uninvolved class'. Schools might simply legitimise the status quo by the uncritical analysis of establishment-approved models in geography like those of Weber and Burgess. While schools cannot transform society themselves, they may educate people who can have some effect. 'School knowledge' cannot result in education for the practice of political literacy, but only 'real' knowledge gained from contact with real issues may.

Geographical education which seeks to develop students who will be 'active in society' should aim at raising questions and building confidence and skills in using political judgement. This can only occur when students participate fully rather than nominally. There is a logical absurdity in using methods that deny the basic tenet of political literacy, namely involvement in political judgement and action (Figure 3.1).

Any methods that prevent a full survey of all possible alternatives tend to view political literacy as commodity knowledge and skills. Whether intentional or not such restrictive approaches are forms of indoctrination. While the teacher may be professional and responsible, attempting to maintain a rational, sensible approach, this cannot ensure a lack of bias. The best way of avoiding indoctrinating this bias is to cover the widest range of views available and to allow students the freedom of inquiry and participation that removes the threat or actuality of control. Consequently political literacy cannot be taught directly, nor through abstract examples, but can only be learnt through an examination of an involvement in real and relevant issues.

The teaching of political literacy requires particular ways of considering knowledge, skills and attitude objectives. It demands special modes of awareness and understanding. These go beyond the propositional and procedural to encompass the critical and reflective modes of thinking and behaviour that are exemplified in Freire's idea of 'critical consciousness'.

Knowledge

Propositional knowledge involves not only the ability to recognise and recall the necessary information, but also being able to argue from the evidence to substantiate beliefs. Generally the growth of propositional knowledge is fairly rapid. Some of these kinds of knowledge are listed in Figure 3.5. For example, students, within the context of appropriate issues should understand the evidence used by uranium-mining lobbyists, or the arguments of local residents who oppose the location of a new hotel. Most important from the list of knowledge objectives (Figure 3.5) for the growth of politically literate students is that of the understanding of basic political concepts.

Skills

Procedural knowledge requires both an understanding of how something might be done and the ability to perform the activity. Such performance is characterised by conscious awareness of how it is done, and the ability to repeat, improve or adapt those skills to varying conditions. Examples of such skills (Figure 3.5) are how to use committee agendas to gain

---

A. KNOWLEDGE

The politically literate person should have some understanding of:
1. the structure of power;
2. customary ways of taking decisions and settling disputes;
3. alternative ways and means of making decisions and settling disputes;
4. where the resources (money, goods, time, space, etc.) come from and how they are allocated;
5. alternative ways of allocating resources;
6. the main political issues and disputes;
7. who promotes what policies, goals or values and why;
8. the nature of political disputes and issues and their causes;
9. how these political disputes might affect oneself and the groups to which one belongs;
10. how these disputes affect other people and the groups to which they belong;
11. how to influence the decision-making process in a given context including knowledge of alternative means of influence and their relative appropriateness for particular purposes;
12. basic political concepts;
13. how to obtain information which one lacks.

B. SKILLS

Political literacy includes the ability to:
1. interpret and evaluate political information and evidence;
2. organise information through basic political concepts and generalisations;
3. apply reasoning skills to political problems and construct sound arguments based on evidence;
4. perceive consequences of taking or not taking specific political actions in given contexts;
5. express one's own interests, beliefs and viewpoints through an appropriate medium;
6. participate in political discussion and debate;
7. perceive and understand (if not agree with) the interests, beliefs and views of others;
8. exercise empathy (to imagine what it might be like in someone else's shoes);
9. participate in group decision making;
10. effectively influence and/or change political situations.

C. ATTITUDES

These are the kind of values to be encouraged through political education:
1. willingness to adopt a critical stance towards political information;
2. willingness to give reasons why one holds a view or acts in a certain way and to expect similar reasons from others;
3. respect for evidence in forming and holding political opinions;
4. willingness to be open to the possibility of changing one's own attitudes and values in the light of evidence;
5. to value fairness as a criterion for judging and making decisions;
6. to value the freedom to choose between political alternatives;
7. toleration of a diversity of ideas, beliefs, values and interests.

Figure 3.5 Objectives in teaching for political literacy (after Porter, 1979)

political advantage or how to organise a pressure group. The growth of procedural knowledge and action is normally a slow process.

Most commonly, despite our bold claims to teach geography for a better world, we neglect the last two skill objectives on the list. These action skills of participation in group decision making, and the ability to influence and/or change political situations are essential if our students are to become truly politically literate. Without them the objectives of our geography teaching that seek action in society remain impotent. Porter (1979) claims that 'the ultimate test of effective political education lies in creating a proclivity for action'.

Critical reflection and action, or praxis, is the third but related mode of awareness necessary within a sound education for political literacy. Acceptance of the definition of political literacy used in this paper means that we must educate for a 'critical conscious- ness' that encourages reflection, questioning of evidence, consideration of alternatives, revelation of implicit assumptions and an intention and ability to participate. This 'act of knowing' includes critical reflection on and active participation in an issue (Freire, 1972).

Attitudes and values

A general list of the kinds of attitudinal objectives that may be achieved through the study of particular political issues is to be found in Figure 3.5. It is in this area that students most readily recognise a clash between theory and practice. If we are to teach geography for a better world by educating politically literate students, our classes and teaching methods must reflect these attitudes. As schools are normally politically and socially conservative institutions the openness and freedom of such an approach is often found to be quite threatening. This is especially so if the issue being studied is an appropriately relevant local issue. It may even call for students to examine critically the evidence and arguments of the power-brokers within the school, local government or busi- ness interests. Consider, for example, the issue of students parking in the staff car park. If we allow students the freedom to become actively involved it is quite possible for some less tolerant political faction to take umbrage and to seek to exercise whatever political power they can muster.

While this may provide fascinating material as a political study in itself the relatively powerless students need to be protected by sensible planning and sensitive handling of the study. That of course high- lights the obvious need for geography teachers who themselves manifest the knowledge, skills and attitudes of political literacy (Figure 3.5).

Strategies

The strategies for teaching geography for politically literate action in society must take regard of several principles. These derive from the definition of literacy that demands active involvement and reflection.

Teaching strategies must encourage the questioning of a range of facts, opinions and policies. This means that there must be time to think, time to debate, time to probe further. Growing concepts and skills need the good use of language and participation in political debate, and these cannot be rushed (Slater and Spicer, 1980).

Participation must be a real opportunity to act and not one of the bogus or token participation rungs on the ladder in Figure 3.6. The concepts, skills and procedural values of political literacy will only be prop- erly grasped when students learn them by using them.

Preparedness to take carefully calculated risks is required by these teaching methods. Teachers must have faith in themselves, and their own professional integrity and political literacy. They have to trust their students and believe in their strategies. Geography teachers already use teaching strategies that should allow the participation and reflection necessary.

Geography teaching is renowned for its use of direct

Figure 3.6 A ladder of public participation

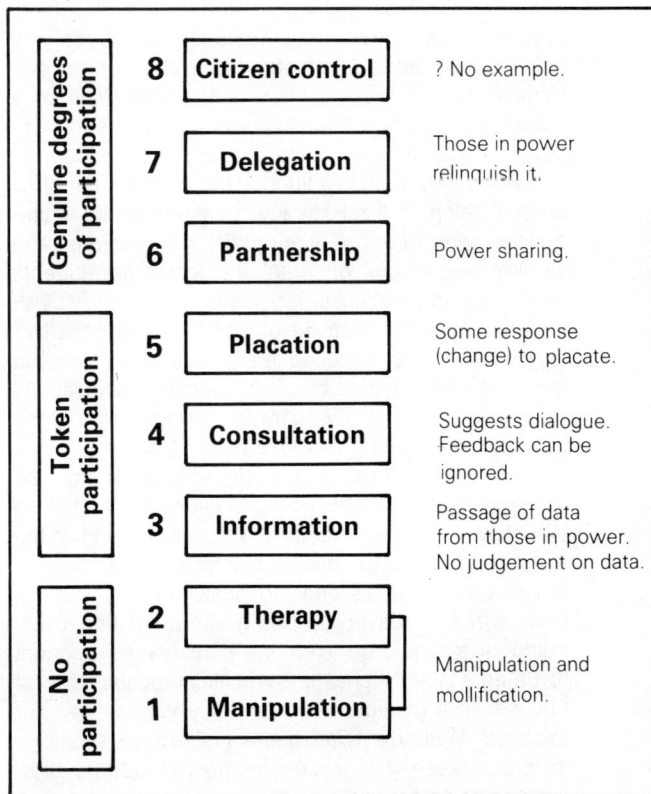

(field) and indirect (classroom and practical) methods of studying issues in the world. *Field methods* include place usage counts, movement mapping, vegetation study, land-use surveys, interviews, environmental appreciation studies, perception surveys and so on. *Practical activities* include the use of maps, aerial photographs, environmental impact reports, planning reports, historical documents, Council minutes, media surveys, mental mapping, and model building, among others.

The direct methods are obviously best used to study local issues, and the indirect to study remote reality where the issue is largely inaccessible to direct involvement because of distance or the nature of the issue. Often a suitable mixture of both is desirable.

A good geographical study can only achieve political literacy objectives when the normal study techniques are practised within a framework of political decision making. This is the crucial characteristic of a study for political literacy.

How many thousands of school litter surveys or nearby traffic counts have geography students done in recent years? Unless these are undertaken in an attempt to achieve agreed political ends, such as the alteration of student playground clean-up rosters or the provision of a controlled pedestrian crossing, how much have they learnt about the political processes that cause the phenomenon under study?

Through a study of the media, fieldwork and interviews with representatives of the groups involved, students may come to understand the issues and policies involved in a dispute, say over the proposed demolition of a historic building to make way for a supermarket. They should have the freedom to become involved if the issue is of appropriate interest. It is when they seek to influence the decision that they best develop political literacy. Lessons about manipulation, pressure, collusion, policy concessions, and varying perceptions of 'truth' are learnt as students play a role in negotiating a decision.

Sometimes the exercise of power is too covert or subtle to be easily exposed in such a study. The issue itself may be inaccessible. It is then that simulations may recreate the spirit of participation and expose the political means being employed.

The machinations underlying disputes can be revealed best by establishing conditions in simulations that allow much freedom for the varied aspects of the exercise of power to develop naturally as the students reflect on their goals and the best means of getting their own way (Laver, 1979). While some firm overriding laws should be fixed, the particular rules ought to be amenable to change by political means. One of Laver's laws of simulation games ensures this. For instance Walford's *Caribbean Fishermen* (Walford, 1973), because of its loose structure, can readily allow a range of political activity.

Topics for investigation

The study of geographical topics that involve disputes about the allocation, location, relocation, or use of space, places and environments on the surface of the earth should include political literacy objectives. Only a few examples of such topics are mentioned in this chapter. However, Chapter 4 explores in detail how one issue, the conservation of the Daintree rainforest, may be developed in the geography classroom according to the principles outlined earlier. Topics like these not only can be used to develop political literacy, but must be if students are not to get an unrealistic view of how geographical decisions are made.

Local and human issues are emphasised here because it is at this level that students first begin to comprehend and develop some skills in the use of political power. Geography teachers should make no apology for using the local area as a major source of issues.

My class of 15 year olds was concerned about the lack of football grounds where they lived. During a general community survey of the provision and perception of needs for services and recreation facilities they were dismayed to encounter some strikingly different points of view. Some residents most of all wanted a police station to help control youths like those conducting the survey, others wanted local health facilities, some desired clubs for the aged. By the time the class presented its findings to the local Council they were able to mount a strong argument for improved football club facilities that would be supported by people in the community with disparate interests. While their political participation was minimal, the exercise had enough reality for them to have learnt some valuable lessons about political influence and opportunism.

There is never a lack of local issues near a school. Our students have been able to study actively disputes over the attempted closure of roadside vegetable market stalls. There was also a vigorously opposed attempt (one man was sent to jail) to open a large local vegetable market run by the growers in opposition to the traditional central wholesale market. Another dispute was the thwarting of an attempt to build another major shopping complex by a national company. The opposition came from the unlikely alliance of heritage conservationists and local business people who ironically had proposed a similar plan a few months earlier.

We also had a local frontier dispute. Neighbouring Councils were in conflict over the upgrading of a ford and building of a footbridge on their river boundary (Figure 3.7). Local residents and the Education Department were also involved as move and countermove were made in a Gilbertian chess game of political geography. A group of well-organised resi-

Figure 3.7 A river boundary dispute (Photograph: Barry McElroy)

dents to the north of the river prompted the building of the footbridge so that their children could cross the river safely on their way to a new school on the south side. The local government to the south agreed to the footbridge in return for the upgrading of the ford. Once the footbridge for their children was complete the plans to improve the ford were thwarted by the residents living on the road leading north from the ford. Their close spatial association and political skills developed during the earlier issue meant that they were a far more effective lobby than the dispersed motorists who used the ford and road.

Webb (1979) describes a 'sweat equity' housing project at his urban studies centre in Nottingdale where the students learnt not only all the skills related to building, but also the political skills needed to get their own accommodation in the face of vigorous and practised opposition.

Geography teachers must seek studies of novel and relevant geographical/political issues. A geographic study of unemployment could be used to balance the usual study of industry and commerce which is really a geography of the employed. There is no end to the possibilities. What of issues relating to race, class or gender? What of war and peace? Why do we often avoid these in our geography classes when geography has so much to offer when seeking explanation of major human issues and resolution of conflicts?

The environment can provide a rich source of issues, not only raw data as is often the case. Waste disposal studies are relevant. Some of my students once became politically embroiled accidentally by tracing back the oil that was polluting their favourite swimming-hole in a small river. One photograph in the local press of the apparently guilty storm-water drain brought howls of denial from a major car manufacturer who had not even been accused.

How can we help our students to study responsibly the uranium-mining issue? What about environmental-action organisations? Are they serving only the middle-class elites? What about the workers?

Planning issues can be probed by examining locational aspects. Often a mixture of real and simulated study is useful. A class can prepare its own full plan, say for the re-organisation of parking in a town centre, and then present it to the parties involved.

Let a class draw up submissions to a city transport plan, or National Park plans. They may discover how some politicians make the decisions first and then do some research.

Simulation games such as *Millersburg* from the American High School Geography Project help reveal the politics and personalities behind many geographical decisions.

Equity geography. What are the politics involved in the unequal distribution of wealth and life chances in cities (Gill, 1980) or between rich and poor nations? Refugees are a particular class of immigrant. Where do they come from? Why do they come? Survey all the viewpoints on energy and transport including those of the more radical thinkers.

Figure 3.8 Who controls a vital river resource?

Resource allocation studies involved questions of who gets what, where and why? Space, both in terms of quantity and quality, as a commodity is the basic issue of most political geography whether in the homely scale of shared bedrooms or between states (for example, Jordan v. Israel, River Murray in Australia (Figure 3.8)).

Scarcity, real or manipulated, is worth studying (for example, petroleum, copra, sugar). The issues of production, transport and marketing and who controls them are pertinent studies. Similarly, resource usage is a worthwhile issue to study. Where is electricity used? Who uses it? Who pays for it?

Geographical theory and models. What are the explicit and implicit assumptions of the economic, social and geographical models we teach? Are they realistic now? Were they ever? What of Weber? Christaller? Burgess? (Bradford and Kent, 1977; Kirby, 1981). Do we teach them the full title of Rostow's political manifesto? Do we let them discover that the demographic transition model does not hold for many European countries, let alone Third World countries (Teitelbaum, 1975)?

Conclusion

Education is a part of the social process that reproduces society in geographically identifiable forms and relationships (Gill, 1980; Willis, 1977). The teaching of many of the theories, models and explanations of geography, and the student's too-ready acceptance of them as true, proper or inevitable, are a part of this process. What is taught and the way it is taught may simply reinforce the status quo.

The perpetuation of this cycle of social process and geographical form is rarely intended by individual teachers, but the result is none the less very conservative. It is the contention of this chapter that a more open approach to teaching literacy can help liberate students from primarily intellectual study to have a more active and politically effective say in their world.

Political power has to be a legitimate aspect of study and involvement if students are to develop as politically literate persons. This has consequences for the power-brokers in schools as well as the wider community. Political activity is encouraged to a degree, but sometimes when it begins to become effective it is found threatening.

It is ironical that the very success of political literacy education is what draws the most opposition. Politically literate students are seen as a threat to the established order of power and control. Hence potentially successful political action may be vigorously resisted while ineffective participation (Figure 3.6) is lauded.

'Save the whale' or 'Save the seal' campaigns have been sufficiently remote and innocuous to be approved in our schools. The organisation of politically emasculated student 'parliaments' has been encouraged, while the growth of student 'unions' has often been hysterically denounced.

I draw attention to the opposition to political literacy education, not to discourage, but to warn teachers to tackle such studies in a thoroughly professional and effective manner. Teachers may thus avoid being unwittingly pushed into always handling trivial or politically safe issues. For if we do we may as well give up any attempt to improve our students' political literacy.

It is often claimed in statements about schooling that it is the function of education to open minds, but surely it must go beyond this. In fact, unless there exists the possibility and predisposition for action, then our claim to be teaching geography for a better world is very hollow.

If in geography teaching we neglect to develop the students' political literacy, by the topics we teach and the way we teach, we are stifling their voices in determining their own destinies.

Section B

Section B

4 The Daintree rainforest: developing political literacy through an environmental issue

JOHN HUCKLE

The area provides a living museum of plants and animal species in what is one of the few remaining examples of undisturbed coastal rainforest in the world. (Hon. Sir Johannes Bjelke-Petersen, Premier of Queensland)

. . . one of the most breathtaking wild areas in the world; unbelievably beautiful, unbelievably interesting. There are birds, mammals and plants there that are unique. Beyond any dispute, it is a treasure. (David Attenborough, BBC television naturalist)

Australia is the only place in the world where the two highly complex environments of rainforest and extensive coral reefs are found adjoining one another; and Cape York is the only large area where these two adjoining environments are found in their pristine state. (Professor Des Connell, Griffith University)

The wilderness should be there for North Queenslanders, it should be there for people all around Australia, it should be there for everybody around the world. It should be there for the inhabitants of that wilderness, our fellow creatures on this planet . . . if we don't have the humility to consider our fellow creatures in nature, be they trees, be they living in trees, even the forest floor, there is no hope for us as part of the balance of nature. (Dr Bob Brown, Wilderness Society)

Chapters 2 and 3 suggested that teachers seeking to teach geography for a better world should develop their students' political literacy through a consideration of issues arising from the social use of nature. In the mid-1980s, proposals to develop land in north Queensland, Australia, provoked protest from environmental groups concerned to protect Australia's surviving rainforests. The ideas which follow provide geography teachers with a practical way of considering what constitutes political literacy with regard to two aspects of this environmental issue: the conflicts surrounding the building of a road from Cape Tribulation to Bloomfield; and the proposed declaration of a Greater Daintree National Park. Following the Southwest Tasmania debate in the 1970s and early 1980s, these proposals became an issue of major debate (Figure 4.1). Reconciling the conflicts over the Daintree rainforest has engaged local, state and national governments and caused a further examination of Australia's obligations as a signatory to the World Heritage Convention. The Daintree issue clearly illustrates the operation of environmental politics at a number of levels and provides teachers with rich resources for developing the components of political literacy outlined in Chapter 3.

Readers may find it most useful to work through the suggested activties in this chapter with one or two colleagues or at a departmental meeting. The activities invite you to interact with a variety of resources, to relfect on them, and to make decisions about planning a teaching unit on the Daintree issue so that the objectives of political literacy are fostered.

The Daintree rainforest issue: a workshop for teachers

1. Review the ecology of the Daintree region and the political conflict over developments in the Cape Tribulation National park and over proposals for a Greater Daintree National Park. This could involve using some of the following resources:

- The Daintree audiotape from the Rainforest Information Centre, PO BOX 368, Lismore, Australia 2480 ($Aus 7.00)

The Cairns Post

Stop the road

THE Douglas Shire Council should call an immediate halt to work on its proposed road to link Cape Tribulation with Bloomfield.

In the short term, the council can achieve little else but confrontation between its workforce, police and conservationists by going ahead with the work before the approaching wet season.

It would be a waste of public money to bulldoze a road which most likely will become nothing better than a quagmire when the monsoon rains fall during the ...

us, and not the sole responsibility of the Douglas Shire Council to do with it as it wishes.

Evidence of damage being done already came yesterday when the National Parks and Wildlife Service closed the area north of Cape Tribulation to campers until further notice.

The service's Cairns regional director, Mr Peter Stanton, said the action was taken to avoid injury to campers because the construction of the road had destabilised the steep slopes behind ...

Treetop protest stops dozers

From ADRIAN McGREGOR at Cape Tribulation

Two blockaders stopped bulldozers from road building in Cape Tr... yesterday... ing them... the bulldo...

At midda... workmen f... zed and a l...

Six arrested in rainforest blockade

By BRONWYN CRAN

... north Queensland ... conserva-...

... have condemned ... saying it

and members of the Rainforest Conservation Society, the Wilderness Action Society and the Wildlife Preservation Society mounted the blockade.

were expected to arrive from southern cities today.

About 12 conservationists travelled by boat to Bloomfield yesterday to reinforce the blockade there, they said.

The Douglas Shire Council wants to build a 26 kilometre ...ough the wilderness to ...ern part of the ...

The Queensland Government last Monday gave the council permission to deviate from the gazetted path of the proposed road.

A member of the Wilderness Action Society, Ms Denise Coleman, said yesterday she believed pressure was being exerted on the Douglas shire council by real estate developers owning land north ...

Battle of the virgin rainforest

From Cairns, heading towards the northern tip of Australia, the coastal highway passes through the green sugarcane farms of Mossman and comes to the Daintree River.

From there, you are on your own with a challenge. You are in the Cape Tribulation National Park, the largest remaining area of virgin rainforest in Australia.

And there are only four-wheel-drive tracks to lead you further north, eventually to Cooktown.

... where else in Australia do great forests come down to the coast ... they do at the Daintree ... ... Daintree area is rega... ...ists as a living ...

More than 250 millimetres of rain at Queensland's Cape Tribulation National Park has halted the controversial bulldozing of a road into the virgin rainforest. Despite that, the number of protesters will probably treble this weekend with ...

tree species recently discovered have not yet been named.

The Daintree forests are ... fauna. They are the h... tree kangaroo ...

the arrival of three busloads of conservationists from other parts of Queensland and other States. Here JOSEPH GLASCOTT, Environment Writer for The Sydney Morning Herald, looks at the forest and the fight ...

ported ...

Councillor Tony Mijo, of Douglas Shire Council, says far more people will be able to enjoy the beautiful rainforests if the road is built.

Conservationists point out that a four-wheel-drive track connects Daintree with Cape Tribulation.

Then a 34-kilometre walking track proceeds to Bloomfield in the north.

The Cairns and Far North Queensland Environment Centre save the track ...

Cape road is illegal: society

THE controversial Cape Tribulation-Bloomfield road now being cut through a national park was unsurveyed and illegal, it was claimed in Brisbane yesterday.

The Queensland Rainforest Conservation Society president, Dr Aila Keto, said it was also a contradiction of the commitment by the Premier, Mr Bjelke-Petersen, to safeguard what he described as one of the few undisturbed coastal rainforests in the world.

She said the legality of the Queensland Government-backed Douglas Shire attempt to put a 40 km road through national park rainforest between Cape Tribulation and the Bloomfield River would shortly be tested in court.

She would not say when and by whom the court action would be brought.

"We are keeping this one to ourselves," she said, "but our advice is that the road was started and work is continuing in defiance of the law which governs intrusions into national parks."

could or would be made before the land Cabinet met next Monday.

Earlier yesterday, a blockaders man, Mr Cliff Truelove, s... phone there had been a ... Tribulation between Dou... and workers, road co... ratepayers and protesters...

"At this meeting, Mr... National Parks Servic... supervisor, said the s... issued or was about to issue an ... der," he said.

"This would suit us fine if it... cludes bulldozer drivers as well ... ple."

Dr Keto said yesterday: "It i... liar that the Premier is apparent... ing bulldozers to run amok in an area which he described to a world wilderness conference ...

By environment reporter BILL ORD

Letters to the Editor

WEDNESDAY, DECEMBER 14, 1983

...adise lost

Very little of this letter is I write to remind readers of ... ...

Since we lost the Hayles boat rier we have been almost in the doldrums.

a tourist attraction and freight is made into a vehicular road.

I envisage beer cans and other strewn along the 32 km route is made into a vehicular road.

Cape Tribulation road issue

... our ... ... track from Cape ... only ...

Unique walk

Dr Keto said yesterday: "It i... SIR — I have been bushwalking in Australi and many overseas coun-

Chairm..., Mossman District Cane-growers Executive, Mossman.

Aptly named

SIR ... ...

POLITICAL CORRUPTION

Sir —

The Cape Tribulation road issue is nca... case of wanton destruction of the ... environment, it is indicative of the Quee... wide trend to disregard democratic pro... The National Party "puppet" Council Douglas Shire has highlighted not only its incompetence, but also its demo... negligence and political ... ... very de... ority simply to preve... anti-en...

Evans to check legality Cape Tribulation road

...eral, he said to pa... ...estigate... council to stop the project ...ensland set a dangerous precedent build a Dr Mosely said conserv... Tribula... would continue to bloc... area and were hopin... yesterday ... legal action in the ... ...formation on the Supreme Court. ...claims that the nation- "I am very disappo... ...ugh the nation... Government's deci... ...ea was "uncon... this area is one of ... ...legal." are on a list deve... ...of the Australian monwealth that a... Foundation, Dr ... Australia that w... wrote to the Minis... itage standard." ...ment and Home The Comm... ...asking the... sponsibility for ... ...der its de... tive. ...as disap... "They are... ...ot to halt the thoug... ...e of 28 po... tussle with... ...e areas. area of... ...orld Here... set a pr... **INTIMIDATION** the Douglas ... ...ment of planning an... ...mental crime".

PROPOSED ROAD TO BLOOMFIELD
CAPE TRIBULATION

COOKTOWN
- - - National Park boundary
Wilderness Area
MOUNT WINDSOR TABLE LAND
BLOOMFIELD
DAINTREE RAINFOREST
CAPE TRIBULATION

BLOOMFIELD
PROPOSED ROAD TO BLOOMFIELD
CAPE TRIBULATION
EXISTING ROAD TO CAPE TRIBULATION
NATIONAL ...

A&C 3.12.83

AUST 10

Figure 4.1 The Daintree rainforest issue (Gray *et al*, 1985)

- The tape-slide show, *Australia's Tropical Rain-forests*, produced by the Rainforest Conservation Society of Queensland for Environmental Audiovisuals, PO Box 311, Castlemaine, Australia ($Aus 33.00 filmstrip, $51.00 slides)

These resources could be supplemented with articles from *BBC Wildlife* (November 1984 and February 1985) and *The Ecologist* (Cohen and Seed, 1984), the summary on pages 52–3 and a map of the area (Figure 4.2) in order to develop a background understanding of the physical terrain, land use, ecology, resource management and development proposals for the area.

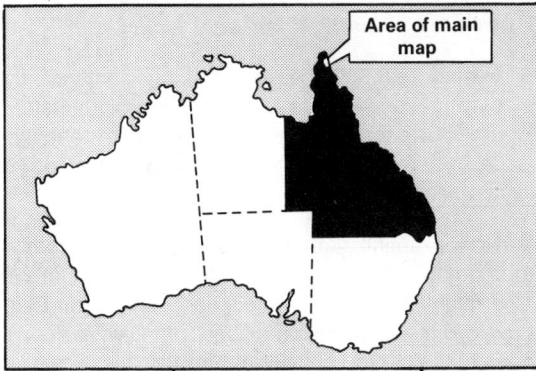

Figure 4.2 Proposed Greater Daintree National Park

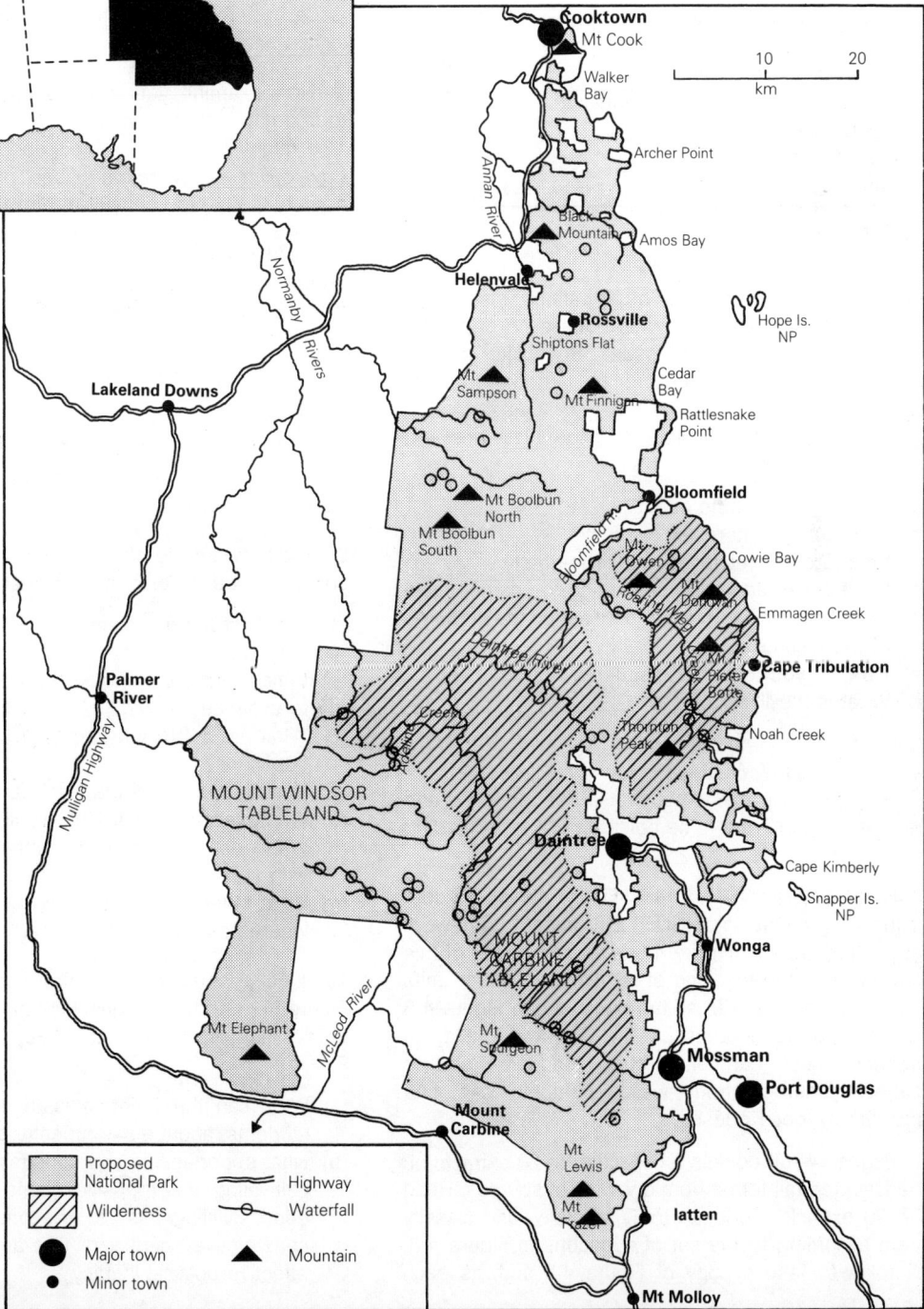

> **What have these to do with the Daintree rainforest issue?**
>
> World Heritage Convention
> George Quaid
> Public opinion
> Martin Tenni
> World oil prices
> Bi-centennial
> Greenies
> Arnie Pedersen
> Douglas Shire County
> Commonwealth Scientific and Industrial
>   Research Organisation
> Australian Conservation Foundation
> Joh Bjelke-Petersen
> Barry Cohen
> Australian Labor Party

Figure 4.3

2. Study the list of people, organisations, institutions and events in Figure 4.3. What does each one have to do with the Daintree issue? Speculate on the connections when these are not known or only partially known.

Consider your conclusions and formulate answers to these questions:

(a) What is the dispute about?
(b) Who are the interested parties?
(c) What are the reasons for their interest?
(d) What power and opportunities do the parties have to make their views felt and influence the outcome of the dispute?
(e) How do you think the dispute will be resolved?
(f) What is the likely outcome?

3. On reflection, how much do you think you know about this issue? What else would you like to know? Make a list of the things you would need to know and be able to do in order to be politically literate regarding this issue.

4. Study Figures 4.4 and 4.5. Figure 4.4 is a model of the Programme for Political Education's framework for political literacy. Figure 4.5 is an application of this framework to the teaching of issues. Curriculum units which give attention to all the questions in Figure 4.5 cover most aspects of political literacy – and, in preparing such curriculum units, teachers need to gather resources from which students can find answers to these questions.

5. Pages 54–60 contain a collection of 20 extracts on the Daintree rainforest from a variety of sources. Read the 20 extracts (coded A to T) carefully, and classify them according to the set of questions in Figure 4.5, as follows. Take a copy of Figure 4.5 and, as each

extract is read, mark its code letter on the appropriate part(s) of the chart. For example, Extract D entitled 'How you can help?' deals with avenues of influence and effective participation. Therefore it would be appropriate to mark boxes 6a, 6b, 7a and 7b in Figure 4.5 with a capital 'D' and, perhaps, boxes 6c, 6d and 7d with a lower case 'd'.

6. Having read all the extracts, and entered their identifying code letters on the appropriate parts of Figure 4.5, consider what you have learnt about the issue by referring back to question 3. Which of your initial questions remain unanswered?

7. Now examine your marked version of Figure 4.5 to find gaps in your understanding of the issue. What else might you need to know about the issue before developing a curriculum based on Daintree? What sources could you consult to find the answers?

8. Read Figure 4.6, which details the political background to the Daintree issues. It shows how many of the extracts on pages 54–60 (and many other resources) fail to reveal the economic and political structures which shape environmental conflict and take many components of political literacy for granted. Such resources often deal with 'newsworthy' trivia rather than underlying interests and social processes. This can make teaching environmental issues for political literacy difficult.

9. It is now time to consider how the curriculum unit could best be developed. Consider the following.

(a) Which of the questions in Figure 4.5 are the most important?
(b) Which questions should the curriculum unit seek to examine? Why?
(c) What is a suitable progression through these questions?
(d) What forms would the lessons take?
(e) What classroom activities would be suitable?
(f) What resources from this chapter could you use with your students?
(g) What other resources would be needed and from where could they be obtained?

10. Finally, refer back to the political concepts in Figure 4.4 and the consideration of environmental politics and environmental literacy in Chapters 2 and 3.

(a) What can the Daintree issue teach us, and our students, about environmental politics?
(b) what opportunities and constraints are involved in cultivating the propositional and procedural knowledge, willingness to become involved, and constructive scepticism that are so important for effective political literacy?

KNOWLEDGE		SKILLS		ATTITUDES AND PROCEDURAL VALUES
Propositional	**Practical knowledge and understanding**	**Intellectual skills**	**Communication skills**	
Within given political contexts (eg, the State, workplace, union, college, school, etc.) the politically literate individual should know something about: 1. the structure of power; 2. customary ways of taking decisions and settling disputes; 3. alternative ways and means of taking decisions and settling disputes; 4. where the resources (money, goods, time, space, etc.) come from and how they are allocated; 5. alternative ways of allocating resources; 6. the main political issues and disputes; 7. who promotes what policies, goals or values, and why.	1. Some understanding of the nature of political disputes and issues (whether they are about goals, values, methods or results) and their causes. 2. Some understanding of how these political disputes might affect oneself and the groups to which one belongs. 3. Some understanding of how these disputes affect other people and the groups to which they belong. 4. Knowledge of how to influence the decision-making process in given contexts including knowledge of alternative means of influence and their relative appropriateness for particular purposes. 5. A developing understanding of basic political concepts (conflict, decision making, power, consent–dissent, order–disorder, and rules). 6. Knowledge of how to obtain information which one lacks.	1. Ability to interpret and evaluate political information and evidence. 2. Ability to organise information through basic political concepts and generalisations. 3. Ability to apply reasoning skills to political problems and construct sound arguments based on evidence. 4. Ability to perceive the consequences of taking or not taking specific political actions in given context. **Action skills** 1. Ability to participate in group decision-making. 2. Ability to influence and/or change political situations.	1. Ability to express one's own interests, beliefs and viewpoints through an appropriate medium (oral or written). 2. Ability to participate in political discussion and debate. 3. Ability to perceive and understand (if not agree with) the interests, beliefs and views of others. 4. Ability to exercise empathy (i.e. to imagine what it might be like in someone else's shoes).	1. Willingness to adopt a critical stance toward political information. 2. Willingness to give reasons why one holds a view or acts in a certain way and to expect similar reasons from others. 3. Respect for evidence in forming and holding political opinions. 4. Willingness to be open to the possibility of changing one's own attitudes and values in the light of evidence. 5. Value fairness as a criterion for judging and making decisions (i.e. regardless of whether the outcome will personally benefit or harm oneself). 6. Value the freedom to choose between political alternatives (goals, methods, values, parties or groups). 7. Toleration of a diversity of ideas, beliefs, values and interests.

Figure 4.4 A framework for political literacy (Porter, 1984)

POLITICAL LITERACY involves				
1. Perception of issues and political problems and				
	a **understanding of:**	**b** **reflection on:**	**c** **fairness**	**d** **alternatives**
2. **Own** **responses**	How does this matter affect you – your rights, freedom and welfare?	What are your interests? What are your opinions? What are your rights, etc.?	Can you justify your opinions?	
3. **Others'** **responses**	How would others be affected – their rights, freedom and welfare?	What are others' interests? What are others' opinions? What are their rights, etc.?		How do others justify the opinions they hold?
4. **Procedures**	What are the circumstances in which the disputes occur?	How are they normally tackled? What are the rules?	What conditions help a successful solution to the problem? Are the rules fair/being applied fairly?	In what other ways could the problems be tackled? Could the rules be changed?
5. **Policies**	Who proclaims what policies? What right/authority do they have?	What are their interests and attitudes?	Where does information on these policies come from? How reliable are these sources?	Are there other sources? Are there other ways of looking at things?
6. **Influence**	How are people persuaded to act or change their minds?	Who has the ability to get things done?	Is this done fairly?	Are there other ways you can go about this?
7. **Effective** **participation**	How can you get your point of view across?	Will anyone else speak for you?	Are these methods fair?	Are there other ways you can go about it?
and: What issues have you seen at first hand? What issues have you been involved in? Are you experienced in getting your views across?				

Figure 4.5 Questions to be investigated in a political-literacy-oriented curriculum unit (Porter, 1984)

The Queensland State Government is pro-development, anxious to defend the state's rights, and much criticised for its record on democracy and civil rights. Premier Joh Bjelke-Petersen's National Party government remains in power in Queensland due to a gerrymander and has a long history of favouring the interests of graziers, real-estate developers, mining corporations and the Electricity Commission over environmental conservation. When the federal government refused Douglas Shire Council funding to build a road through Cape Tribulation, under the Bi-Centennial Road Funding Project, Queensland granted just enough money for a cheap and environmentally damaging road. It then declared the road construction to be 'works within a national park' so that National Park and Wildlife Service officers could order the arrest of blockaders.

The Australian Federal Government in Canberra is reluctant to use its powers to prevent further damage to Queensland's rainforests. Australia has signed the World Heritage Convention but the Hawke Labor government is reluctant to nominate Daintree for World Heritage listing. While it did this in the case of the Franklin River in Tasmania, and was able to stop development there under related federal legislation, it fears a political backlash in Queensland if it follows a similar policy over Daintree. The state Labor Party has requested federal environmental minister, Barry Cohen, to nominate the wet tropical rainforests for World Heritage listing, but he prefers a consensus approach based on a working party and likely financial aid to compensate for rainforest conservation and the restructuring of North Queensland's rural economy. Australia's trade deficit, linked to world oil prices, will be a key factor in deciding how much compensation the federal government can afford.

Douglas Shire Council supports development and growth as 'progress'. Following proposals for a national park at Cape Tribulation, recommended by the Commonwealth Scientific and Industrial Research Organisation, Australia's premier research body, as early as 1972, it gave its tacit approval to the illegal bulldozing of a road through the area and subsequently sought to remove significant areas from the park's gazettal. In 1983–85 it sought to complete the road at low cost and was much criticised for the resulting damage to the environment. The council claims the road is essential for access.

Private land developers such as Arnie Pedersen and George Quaid own large areas in North Queensland, including most of the private land around Cape Tribulation. Having abandoned cattle ranching they are anxious to sub-divide their properties and realise their value as real estate. Improved access is central to these plans and the developers have used their influence on Douglas Shire Council and the State government to advantage. Their local member, Martin Tenni, now Queensland's Minister for the Environment and Administrative Services, has strongly supported the road and has attempted to discredit the environmentalists' case with 'smear campaigns'.

Local residents' opinions on the road seem to be divided with large numbers uncommitted. The decline of primary industry means unemployment is over 20%. Developers offer jobs and prosperity and attack environmentalists as 'greenies' and anti-development. They, in turn, ask local people to support an alternative form of sustainable development with claims of more jobs in the long term.

Environmental groups such as the Australian Conservation Foundation and Wilderness Society believe that all remaining rainforests under control of the Crown should be held under National Park status and left inviolate. They have actively lobbied the state government to support gazettal of the Greater Daintree National Park, and have pressed the federal government to use its powers to stop the building of a road through Cape Tribulation. Such groups lack resources to oppose development in the courts and accuse the state government of continually changing legislation to favour the development lobby. Environmentalists, including many from other states, have engaged in direct action, or blockades, to stop the road. The environmental groups propose an alternative rural economy for Daintree based on plantation timber and tourism.

Adapted from Progress in Queensland: The Daintree Forest, *Arena*, No.69.

Figure 4.6 Major parties and their interests in the Daintree rainforest issue

The Daintree region: ecology and development

The wild tropical rainforests which blanket the mountain ranges and valleys between the Daintree River and Cooktown are precious and beautiful. Here along the coast is Australia's last major intact area (120 000 ha) of virgin tropical rainforest, contained within a 350 000 ha region of rainforest and associated vegetation.

Living fringing coral reefs and white beaches form the eastern margin. (South of Daintree many fringing reefs have been killed by siltation and pollution following land development.) Huge laurels, cottonwoods and frangipanni overhang the beach on the edge of the rainforest.

From the coast the rainforest climbs abruptly over 1000 metres to the giant boulder outcrops of Thornton Peak and Pieter Botte. The Roaring Meg Creek silently gathers its headwaters in this granite upland before crashing seawards in spectacular falls.

Beneath the forest canopy is a clear understorey with knotted lianas, and a profusion of small trees, palms, fungi, vines, ferns, mosses, and leaf litter. Buttresses protrude from the forest giants, often covered with flower or fruit. The still blue pools of the unpolluted creeks abound with jungle perch, turtles, crayfish, water snakes and eels. Everywhere there is an intensity of life.

Flora

The Daintree–Cooktown region may hold the key to unravelling the origin of flowering plants on Earth. Eight of the world's 14 primitive plant families are represented here by plants such as *Idiospermum australiense* and *Austro balieya scandens*. Botanists regard the area as a living museum, and believe that, within the area, forest has existed continuously for possibly more than 100 million years.

The proposed Greater Daintree National Park contains a range of plant communities including lowland and montane rainforests, wet and dry sclerophyll forests, mangroves, fan palm and melaleuca swamps. The diversity of plant species and associations in the area cannot be equalled anywhere in Australia. Scientific study in the area has barely begun and as many as 10–11% of the species are as yet unnamed.

Fauna

The Greater Daintree forests are a refuge for many animals, some rare and others occurring only in this region, whose habitats are suffering accelerated destruction. Bennett's tree kangaroo is found nowhere else in the world. Much of the fauna is undescribed or awaits detailed study. Intriguing creatures such as the cassowary, the Cairns birdwing butterfly, Boyd's Dragon and the Giant Atlas moth live here. Twenty species of bats have been recorded.

The daytime forest resonates to the call of white-tailed kingfishers, rainbow lorikeets, noisy pittas and scrubfowl. A rain of seeds betrays the presence of Wompoo and Torres Straits pigeons in the canopy. The exuberance of life is expressed in the reckless flight of shining starlings, the hoodlum shouts of cockatoos and the colourful undulations of tropical butterflies.

As dusk deepens, the low swerving flight of swiftlets is replaced by the fluttering manoeuvres of bats. The darkened forest holds the furtive movements of possum, glider, quoll, native rat, mouse, bandicoot and the silent stealth of the amethystine python. The timeless calm may be shattered by the scream of a barking owl.

Wilderness

People have long sought peace and tranquillity in the wilderness. Today both wilderness and rainforest are diminishing rapidly; globally rainforest is disappearing at the rate of an area the size of Victoria each year (US Academy of Sciences).

The proposed Greater Daintree National Park contains two major areas of rainforest wilderness. The coastal wilderness stretches from the sandy beaches of Cape Tribulation to the Upper Roaring Meg Valley and Thornton Range. The Upper Daintree River forms the heart of the wilderness area to the west. Here a wide clear and swift stream, it flows through a steep sided valley fringed with rainforest.

Protection or devastation

These outstanding natural values have led to the area being listed as a National Heritage (in the National Estate Register), and to a recommendation by the International

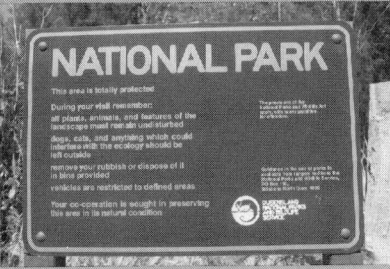

Union for the Conservation of Nature and Natural Resources for listing as a World Heritage.

The Queensland Government has reserved only 10–15% of the area as National Parks. These have not protected all the major freatures, the wilderness areas or the ecological integrity of the region.

In 1983 the Cape Tribulation National Park was violated by bulldozers in an attempt to construct a through-road.

The road

During December 1983, the Douglas Shire Council bulldozers pushed into the coastal wilderness in the Cape Tribulation National Park, funded with $100 000 from the Queensland Government. No preliminary survey was made of the road alignment. An 'Environmental Impact Statement'

prepared by the Shire Engineer made shallow mockery of the great scientific value of the region.

The Council claimed that the road was essential to provide short four-wheel drive access for the people at Bloomfield – yet it would shorten their drive to Cairns by only 5 km. Many Bloomfield residents were opposed to this road.

Queensland has a tradition of not permitting the construction of through-roads in National Parks and the State law expressly forbids such roads.

Blockade action successfully slowed the construction, but the Council completed the road in 1985, despite concerted action by many conservationists.

Other threats

The road is only the thin edge of the wedge of development in the wilderness and the Greater Daintree region. The Queensland Forestry Department has plans to log some of the remaining virgin areas outside National Parks if access becomes available. Tin miners are working in the area. Cane farmers and real-estate developers are anxious to expand their activities.

Conservation

The Greater Daintree National Park will protect an entire ecosystem, and provide opportunities for natural history study and outdoor pursuits. Gazettal of this Park would be a major step toward the conservation of the rainforests in the humid tropics of Queensland. It will ensure the area remains a 'crowning jewel of all of our natural wonders'.

The Great Barrier Reef which is situated immediately to the east of the area is already on the World Heritage List. Here we have a chance to protect one of the world's most magnificent scenic rainforests alongside the world's finest coral reef region. World Heritage Listing would confirm the international importance of the area and protect it if the State Government will not

face up to its responsibilities. The responsibility for nominating the area for the World Heritage List rests solely with the Federal Government.

Early in 1984, the Rainforest Conservation Society of Queensland was commissioned by the Australian Heritage Commission to prepare a report on the environmental value of the wet tropical forests between Townsville and Cooktown. The report was favourably refereed by four overseas environmental scientists as required for World Heritage Listing. One referee, Professor Endress of Zurich University, wrote:

The region is really a priceless and irreplacable possession of mankind[sic] as a whole. A disturbance and destruction of the tropical rainforest region of North Queensland would be a global fraud to the future of mankind as a whole. (Borschmann, 1984)

However, the Federal Government has been reluctant to nominate the area to the World Heritage List. Instead, it formed a Commonwealth Rainforest Working Party (comprising Federal and State Government, industry, union and conservation interests) to advise the Federal Government on policies for Australia's rainforests. This Working Party recommended a National Rainforest Conservation Programme. By June 1987 all States in Australia with rainforests were participating – except Queensland.

Adapted from Australian Conservation Foundation leaflets

Viewpoints on the Daintree issue

The following 20 extracts represent a range of viewpoints and newspaper reports on the status of the tropical rainforests of North Queensland, the political conflicts generated by the building of a road through Cape Tribulation National Park by the local Douglas Shire Council, and conflicts generated by the campaign for the declaration of a Greater Daintree National Park and the World Heritage Listing of the rainforests of the region. Each extract represents one or more aspects of political literacy that could be interpreted into a curriculum unit on these topics.

Read the extracts, perhaps working in a group to share the load. Mark the initial of each one on the appropriate part(s) of the model of political literacy in Figure 4.6.

Extract A

... Last December (1983) Douglas Shire Council suddenly started building a road from the north bank of the Daintree to the settlement of Bloomfield (pop. 600) on the other side of the national park. The shire lacked enough money for the project, the federal government – which had a conservation mandate dating from the aborted Franklin River dam in Tasmania – refused to help, and the Queensland government, personified by Premier Sir Joh Bjelke-Petersen who was itching for a fight, gave the shire just enough to assure that it would build the most damaging road possible, an unsurfaced track that was bound to cause mudslides when the rains came, barely a month after construction began.

David Helton (1984) Where the Franklin meets the Daintree, *BBC Wildlife*, November

Extract B

Real estate development threatens important areas of lowland rainforest. Just across the Daintree arguments raged in 1981 and 1982 over partially cleared rainforest lands with sugar interests and subdividers vying for the rights to exploit freehold lands. With road work having commenced in 1982, up to 3,000 hectares of land were being subdivided into blocks as small as one hectare. An area between Noah Creek and Cape Tribulation containing rare rainforest tree species was leased to tourist developers in 1981 without an environmental impact study being required. A 14,000 hectare national park was finally declared between the Daintree and Bloomfield Rivers in August 1981, but significant areas of land included in the original park proposal were excised from the gazettal. These included land fronting Cow Bay, one of the most attractive beaches in the entire region, and extensive estuarine channels, mangrove wetlands and an area of vine forests on sand ridges on the southern bank of the mouth of the Daintree River.

Ross Fitzgerald (1984) *From 1915 to the Early 1980s: A History of Queensland*, Brisbane, University of Queensland Press.

Extract C

In December 1983, a small number of conservationists gathered for a spirited defence of this forest. They physically blockaded the local council's bulldozers in a series of actions which confounded both workers and a strong contingent of police.

The month-long direct action campaign witnessed 40 arrests while conservationists successfully utilised the resources of the natural environment. They locked themselves high up in the trees, buried each other up to their necks in the path of the machinery, and suspended themselves from ropes between trees marked for felling. Police were forced to employ rescue equipment and a lot of work to extract and arrest the demonstrators. Hostility was succeeded by incredulity as police swung from trees and dug protestors out of the ground.

John Cohen and John Seed (1984) In defence of Daintree, *The Ecologist*, **14**(4).

Extract D

How can you help?

1. Write to the Prime Minister, the Rt Hon. R.J. Hawke, Parliament House, Canberra, ACT. 2600, urging his Government to nominate the area for World Heritage, and use its powers to stop any further development.

2. Write directly to the Hon. Sir J. Bjelke-Petersen, Premier of Queensland, Parliament House, Brisbane 4000, urging him to gazette the Greater Daintree National Park as proposed by the Australian Conservation Foundation.

3. Write to Councillor T. Mijo, Douglas Shire Council, Mill Road, Mossman 4873, urging the Council to abandon the Cape Tribulation Road, and co-operate with the Greater Daintree National Park proposal, which will provide a far greater boost for tourism in the Shire than the coastal road.

4. Write or (even better) go and see your Local Member about the issue.

5. Find out if you can help the Blockade. For information on what you can do, contact either the ACF, the Rainforest Conservation Society, the Wilderness Society, your Local Environment Centre, or ring Cairns (070) 51 1204 or (070) 51 1344.

6. Send donations to the Australian Conservation Foundation, 672B Glenferrie Road, Hawthorn, 3122, marked 'Daintree Account' (tax deductible).

Daintree Tropical Rainforest World Heritage Wilderness, a leaflet published by the Australian Conservation Foundation.

Extract E

The proposed road is only the thin end of the wedge regarding development in this splendid Greater Daintree wilderness. The Queensland Forestry Department has plans to log virgin rainforest as access becomes possible; tin miners are working nearby. Real estate developers (who have been carving similar lowland rainforest into two acre residential blocks nearby) are anxious to expand their activities.

John Cohen and John Seed (1984)
In defence of Daintree,
The Ecologist, **14**(4).

Extract F

Police, a shire council chairman and a government minister have called on supporters of the proposed road through the Cape Tribulation road to 'cool it' in their attitude to environmentalists.

Cr Tony Mijo, at a meeting yesterday between Douglas Shire officials and police, expressed concern over local ratepayers who wanted to "throw the greenies into the sea".

And Mr Tenni, the Environment Minister, today pleaded with the road's supporters not to resort to vigilante tactics.

"I've heard reports of up to 750 people from Cooktown and Bloomfield and 1000 or more from Mossman and Daintree going up there with pickhandles," he said.

"That's the last thing we want. They should stay right away from the area."

He said ratepayers in the Douglas shire were "extremely angry" with environmentalists.

"They have paid rates for a road and the greenies are digging holes in it," he said.

"You can understand why they're put out. But we don't want people taking the law into their own hands."

But North Queensland police today appealed to people to stay away from the Cape Tribulation road construction site.

'Protesters see red at Greenies',
Courier Mail, 25 July 1984.

Extract G

I have learned with utter disgust that the Federal Government, through their various agencies have been accepting the opinions of a few unqualified people to deprive the Douglas Shire Council of road development funds for the road between the Daintree River and Cape Tribulation.

From the information I have received from these Canberra bureaucrats it appears that they are prepared to influence their gullible government into depriving the Douglas Shire Council of job creation funding without even visiting the area prior to making their decision.

In fact, the Council was not consulted but the decision was made at the instigation of the environmental lobby. Prior to the advent of the current Federal representation the Shire was receiving approximately $40,000 through the Main Roads Department for road development north of the Daintree River and unless the decision is reversed this has come to an end.

I am sure council workers are learning that it does not pay to live in a green area that holds the attention of job-destroying stirrers.

Douglas Shire Council Chairman,
Tony Mijo, From the chairman's desk,
Port Douglas and Mossman Gazette,
15 December 1983.

Extract H

Council says:

At a public meeting in Port Douglas on October 6th, 1983, at the Shire Hall, local councillors outlined many humanitarian, community-spirited reasons for building their 4WD track:

The old and infirm: access was needed to allow car-bound people to see the beauty of the forest. Why should this treasure be available only to the fit hiker, they asked? The fact that there is already 38 km of dirt road cutting through what was much more spectacular rainforest, before the disputed area is reached, was ignored, and at this stage the Council was saying that it was to be only a 4WD track which gave the sentiment less credibility.

The missing link: it was considered natural, inevitable, that development would sooner or later link Mossman, the Bloomfield River district, and Cooktown by a coastal road. When asked why the CREB track – only 10 km longer and inland, could not be upgraded, the reply was that it would cost too much to survey. There was no need to do a survey in the National Park.

Defence: this brought hoots of laughter from a hall full of more than 100 people. The Army uses Timber Reserve 165 for training exercises, but declined the invitation to build the road. Field Marshall Mijo appears to feel part of his shire's job is forward defence of the north.

Drugs, defectors and refos: the road would allow better mobility against drug runners, illegal immigrants. They didn't mention cattle duffers, or illegal net fishermen. It's easy to whip up fear of illegal activities up here. But surveillance planes already fly over almost every day. The shipping channel is close to the coast – a drop-off point for contraband? If so, the baddies would certainly appreciate a road to make a quick get-away, not with back packs, but with semi-trailers.

Don Gray et al. (1985) *The Trials of Tribulation*, Port Douglas, Wilderness Action Group.

Extract I

Sir, I fully agree with the letter by Councillor Greg May about the road from Cape Tribulation to Bloomfield. I would also like to ask some questions:

1. If siltation from this few kilometres of road is going to destroy the reef along this part of the coast, why hasn't the reef been totally destroyed south of Cairns already?

2. Why can Greenies have a sawmill and planing machine and also a special trailer for transporting logs of 2 to 3 tonnes weight? This trailer was seen south of the Daintree River at least once.

3. How many of these protestors are genuine ratepayers in the Douglas Shire and derive a legal income from their land?

4. Why should Greenies and tourists from other states and countries be able to sign a petition saying 'No'. The people of Bloomfield and Cooktown cannot have a road along to the coast to Mossman (less than 100 kms). They must travel 200 kms around the Mulligan Highway.

5. How many of these areas are the last remaining pieces of rainforest in the state? Logging in the timber reserve near the Palmerston Highway was said to be the last remaining piece of rainforest in existence. Road work in the Palmerston was also said to be destroying the last bit of rainforest in the country. Windsor Tableland was also the last unique rainforest in the country. Now it is Cape Trib's turn. I guess if the Forestry Dept decided to log part of the timber reserve on Barretts creek, it would be the next 'last'.

I often wonder what some of these scrub dwellers live on? Perhaps scrub hens, scrub turkeys & pidgeons, all protected species go into the stew pots. I guess they must be poor hunters because I have never seen a fat hippy.

Finally I am not against National Parks. I thoroughly enjoyed visits to The Open Plains Zoo Dubbo, Warranganba Lion Park, Bullens Animal World, Taronga Park and even our few small local ones in the North. I am sure a small area used by a road is not going to destroy this park, but motorist (and walkers) please carry your empty containers out of the park to rubbish collection points. If the Greenies and hippies don't want the general public in the area, what is it that they have to hide? Also what right have they got to live there?

Many thanks to the editor for the space.

Yours sincerely,

Letter to the Editor, *Port Douglas and Mossman Gazette*, 15 December 1983.

Extract J

Only one kilometre of genuine, well-developed primitive rainforest of world significance would be affected by the 30 km road through the Cape Tribulation National Park, the National Parks Minister said yesterday.

He said this information was contained in a report he studied last week and "confirmed once and for all that the road was not destroying a significant quantity of rainforest that was unique and of international interest".

The report was prepared by an officer of his department 'who was highly regarded and had an intimate knowledge of the area'. He would not name the officer or give his qualifications, except that he was a 'senior scientist'.

Mr McKechnie also refused to release the report or make it available for perusal and would not allow his officer to debate with other scientists who disputed his findings.

When asked if he thought the public would accept details of the anonymous report rather cynically, Mr McKechnie said he hoped people accepted him at his word, as he never told lies.

He said the road would be built because the State Government originally made an agreement with the Douglas Shire Council that it would approve the road when the Cape Tribulation area was declared a national park.

"The main reason is to give the people of Douglas Shire better access to Mossman," he said. "I do not accept that the road going through would do any particular damage to the area.

"I am not in favour of having one more inch of Queensland on the World Heritage List."

The report said that for approximately 11 km through the park, the road would cut through young rainforest types which were less than 70 years old and eucalyptus, melaleuca and wattle forests.

"These areas, although often lush in appearance, are relatively poor in species," Mr McKechnie said.

"Left-wing ALP members led by the Opposition Leader, Mr Wright, have been engaged in a campaign designed to mislead people about the effects of the road."

The report also dispelled any argument that the park should be included on the World Heritage List, he said.

Tony Koch (1984) Only 1 km of rainforest in northern road: McKechnie, *Courier Mail*, 24 July 1984.

Extract K

Queenslanders must be wondering if the National Parks Minister, Mr McKechnie, is one of those people who can't see the north Queensland rainforest for the trees.

His latest justification for the bulldozing of a track through the Daintree forest from Cape Tribulation to Bloomfield – that only one kilometre of genuine, well-developed rainforest of world significance is involved – has angered conservationists and bewildered neutral observers.

And his statement that he is not in favour of having one more inch of Queensland on the World Heritage List shows scant regard for future generations.

The fact is that only one region of Queensland – the Great Barrier Reef – is on the World Heritage List. If Mr McKechnie has his way, no mainland asset will ever achieve that status.

These are curious attitudes for a Minister administering our National Parks to adopt. And they seem to fly in the face of the statements made in the name of the Queensland Government only three years ago when the Cape Tribulation National Park was declared.

The Government suggested then that it was doing a wonderful thing for posterity in preserving what it described as 'a fantastic area of lowland rainforest'.

Mr McKechnie apparently fails to recognise the importance of the Daintree forest in relation to the Great Barrier Reef. The reef and the forest are so close in the Cape Tribulation–Bloomfield region that the two organisms are symbionts.

It seems extraordinary that the unnamed scientist who Mr McKechnie suggests has given the all-clear for the track has not recognised this basic point.

Editorial: The trees and the forest, *Courier Mail*, 25 July 1984.

Extract L

CANBERRA. – The Government will not intervene to stop the Cape Tribulation road.

Cabinet yesterday decided not to nominate the Daintree rainforest area in North Queensland for the World Heritage List.

The Government feared Queensland would wage a states' right campaign during the Federal election.

Instead, the Government is understood to be ready to offer Queensland $1 million under a joint conservation management plan for the area.

The Australian Heritage Commission in a report to the Government yesterday recommended the Daintree nomination, saying the region was unique. The Australian Conservation Foundation has called on the Federal Government to protect the region . . .

It was World Heritage Listing which allowed the Federal Government to stop the Franklin Dam in Tasmanian wilderness.

The Heritage Commission's Daintree report was prepared by the Queensland Rainforest Conservation Society and backed by a panel of international experts.

The Opposition spokesman on the environment, Mr David Connolly, said the Environment Minister, Mr Cohen, was trying to stifle Parliamentary debate by refusing to release the report.

It is understood Mr Cohen believed a confrontation with Queensland under World Heritage powers would have ended in the high Court with no guarantee of a Commonwealth victory . . .

The chairman of the House of Representatives standing committee on the environment, Mr Peter Milton, yesterday welcomed the management plan proposal.

Mr Milton and the other Labor members of his committee recently called for negotiations with the Queensland Government for a moratorium on construction of the road and development of a proper management plan.

But the majority committee view was that the Federal Government should retain the option of using its powers under the World Heritage Properties Protection Act to intervene if necessary.

Mr Milton said he accepted the need for the guarantee to Queensland that the Commonwealth would not unilaterally nominate the region for World Heritage status because of the political realities.

Political ploys means no Cape road intervention, *Courier Mail*, 12 September 1984.

Extract M

It is difficult to reconcile the above legal analysis with the Minister's statement that responsibility for Cape Tribulation lies with the Douglas Shire Council and the Queensland Government.

The Federal Government's stand shows that it has not grasped the outcome of the Dams decision. South West Tasmania was not an isolated case.

The Commonwealth has substantial powers to act in environmental matters. Speaking in terms of playing the States not to take environmentally harmful action is just a variation on the 'States' rights' excuse of the former Fraser Government.

The Commonwealth Government must stop thinking that it was lucky (or unlucky) to win the Franklin Dam case. The Government will be rightly accused of political opportunism for opposing environmental destruction in South West Tasmania, unless it is prepared to take decisive action in other cases where a unique environment is threatened.

Elizabeth Ward (1984) The Commonwealth has legal responsibilities for Cape Tribulation, *Habitat Australia*, **12**(2) (April).

Extract N

The situation with respect to the Cape Tribulation road is different. While many people are saying the area is of World Heritage quality, the fact is that it is not on the World Heritage List, and it has not been considered for entry on the list by the Commonwealth Government, which is the appropriate body to nominate it. The Commonwealth Government receives advice on world heritage matters by a special program committee of officials representing relevant areas of Government administration, including the Australian Heritage Commission. I am informed that a number of places, including the Cape Tribulation area, that might be nominated in the future by Australia for the World Heritage List are being considered by the group.

When the Government receives the advice of the special program committee it will consider the matter. Before making any decision on the nomination of any properties to the World Heritage Committee the Government will consult fully with the State or Territory Governments concerned.

I will conclude by re-affirming the Government's commitment to developing policies which will provide a balance between economic, ecological and recreational needs in relation to Australia's forest resources. To this end, and particularly when faced with sensitive issues such as Cape Tribulation, we will strive to achieve consensus with all interested parties, rather than pursue the interventionist approach so readily advocated by Ms Ward.

Hon. Barry Cohen (Minister for Home Affairs and Environment) (1984) Environment Minister explains his 'consensus' approach to the future of Cape Tribulation, *Habitat Australia*, **12**(4) (August).

Extract O

The federal government, meanwhile (Dec.–Mar. 83/4), had supported the conservationists about as unenthusiastically under Bob Hawke and the Labor Party as it had during the Tasmanian battle under Malcolm Fraser and the Liberals. Led by the Australian Conservation Foundation and the Wilderness Society (nee Tasmanian Wilderness Society), the conservationists' main legal tack was to have the area nominated as a World Heritage Site, but the federals refused to do this on various weak constitutional grounds that everyone thought had been discredited after the Supreme Court defeat of the state of Tasmania on the dam issue.

Impatient with federal inaction, the Australian Heritage Commission asked the Rainforest Conservation Society of Queensland (RCSQ) to prepare its own report on Daintree and this was released in September and accepted as 'rigorous, comprehensive and relevant to World Heritage criteria' by four international experts.

David Helton (1984) Where the Franklin meets the Daintree, *BBC Wildlife*, November.

Extract P

In November (1984), Bellamy returned to Australia to try a different publicity routine to help save the wet tropical rainforests of North Queensland, home of the world's richest collection of primitive flowering plants.

With not a policeman in sight inside the crusty but highly respectable Brisbane Town Hall, Bellamy opened his three-city Australian lecture tour by dropping to his knees centre-stage, before more than 1,000 people, and begging, literally begging, the state premier, Sir Joh Bjelke-Petersen, to agree to the nomination of the forest to the UNESCO World Heritage List.

Bellamy said he, like the premier, was a Christian, and he wanted Sir Joh to remember God's commandment to man to have dominion over the earth and its creatures. "But dominion is not sending anything to its extinction, and what we are looking at is a world in which 1.5 million species – or about a quarter of all known life on earth – will become extinct at the hand of man by the end of the century."

'The forests of North Queensland are much, much, more important than the Franklin River', Bellamy told his audience, 'so much more important it is hardly possible for me to believe what I have seen happening up there, with the road building, the foresters and the real-estate development'.

Greg Borschmann (1985) Rainforest politics, *BBC Wildlife*, February.

Extract Q

According to environment minister Barry Cohen, the Australian government has accepted that 'it now looks likely that the wet tropical rainforest region is of World Heritage value and ought to be on the list'. But the government has been told to 'go jump in the lake' by Queensland, which administers the state forests, crown lands and national parks that make up most of the region.

The December elections safely returned the Labor Party (although with nothing near the landslide majority anticipated), but the Federal Government has not abandoned its low-key conciliatory approach to Queensland or used its powers to lodge a World Heritage nomination without that State's support.

Greg Borschmann (1985) Rainforest politics, *BBC Wildlife*, February.

Extract R

Some points to consider
The rainforests contain fully half of the ten million species of plants and animals on earth – the very womb of life. The continued evolution of life on this planet depends on the survival of the genetic materials that these forests contain.

The continued existence of the rainforests beyond the first few years of the next century is in doubt unless action is taken immediately. In Australia, as in the rest of the world, lowland tropical rainforest is the richest, most diverse and most threatened rainforest type.

Australia, as the only developed country to contain tropical rainforest, has the moral duty to show the way to those poorer nations which will have to take steps to preserve their tropical rainforests if the genetic future of the earth is to be maintained.

Rainforest Information Centre (1985) *World Rainforest Report*, No. 3, Lismore.

Extract S

Small change for rainforest

At 3 pm on Tuesday 17 June, 1986, Federal Environment Minister, Barry Cohen, announced the funding of the long awaited National Rainforest Conservation Program. Originally proposed in October 1985, as an alternative to World Heritage Listing, Cohen's "Masterplan" languished for seven months before gaining Cabinet funding. The Canberra piggy bank is to be raided to the tune of $22.25 million.

The effectiveness of the National Rainforest Conservation Program depends on agreement being reached with the states. Discussions between the Australian and Queensland Governments will sorely test the negotiating skills of the federal government. Taking the view that confrontation will not benefit the rainforest, five of the seven aims of the Program are non-contentious. Only two items come close to the real issue.

A survey, a study and research are proposed to identify rainforest needing reservation, and to ascertain the potential for tourism. The planning, management and building of visitor centres in national parks are targetted for Commonwealth funding. Sounds wonderful, but it could be shutting the stable door after the horse has bolted!

The two strategies that have any chance to protect trees and not just stumps, are the proposed purchase of private rainforest for parks, and most importantly, funds for the establishment of timber plantations on land already cleared.

While buying private rainforest for parks is great in principle, the economics are dubious; $22M would buy only 890 hectares at current prices for real estate at Cape Tribulation.

The majority of the threatened rainforest doesn't have to be bought, over half a million hectares is locked up in State Forests and Timber Reserves, already owned by the state government. The Queensland Forestry Department is keen to expand their plantation estate. This is where the bargain has to be made. The last virgin and key endangered sites have to be spared from the axe. Then we can afford the luxury of more studies, surveys and research!

Goeff Smith (1986) Small change for rainforest, *Wilderness News*, **7**(6).

Extract T

Queensland rainforest nomination

On 5 June 1987, simultaneous with the release of this publication, the Government announced a major initiative concerning conservation of the Wet Tropics of North-East Queensland:

"The Prime Minister and the Minister for Arts, Heritage and Environment the Hon. Barry Cohen, said today that the Government would immediately proceed towards nomination of the Wet Tropics of North-East Queensland to the World Heritage List. As part of the process the Government will be consulting with the Queensland Government and parties with interests in the region and will invite submissions to be made within a period of three months. This process is necessary as a nomination would need to be made by 31 December 1987 for consideration by the World Heritage Committee by the end of 1988.

Discussions with Queensland concerning rainforest conservation have proceeded for ten months. The Government has made a generous and reasonable offer of funds from the National Rainforest Conservation Program in the expectation that Queensland would enter into acceptable rainforest conservation arrangements particularly for cessation of logging.

The discussions with Queensland have been conducted in a cordial and frank manner. Unfortunately Queensland still maintains that rainforest logging should continue. This has left the Government with no choice but to consider nomination of the Wet Tropics for World Heritage listing.

The Government is determined that the outstanding values of the region be protected. The Government is sure that its actions will bring home to the Queensland Government the need to change its approach to management of the region.

In considering nomination of the Wet Tropics the Government will formally consult the Queensland Government about the decision and, by a process of correspondence and advertisements placed in the national and regional press, will also invite the views of other organisations and individuals with interests in the Wet Tropics.

Any views put to the Government in this process will be given careful consideration before any nomination is made."

News release by Hon. Barry Cohen (now Minister for Arts, Heritage and Environment), 5 June 1987.

5 Teaching for human rights in geography

JENNY BURNLEY

Critics of today's radical humanistic teaching allege that it is sabotaging Christian ethics, society's morals and traditional educational skills. Yet, for many students, traditional education has little relevance to their experience, needs or future lives. By contrast, education for human rights involves much more than transference of knowledge (teaching by telling: see Figure 5.1). It leads to a critical awareness of the *real* world: not the vocational real world – preparation for which, some traditionalists say, should be our chief concern – but the political, economic, social and cultural real world in which we all live and interact. Such education cannot be value-free; indeed no education is. The school system embodies many values: principles of co-operation, power and authority, justice and injustice. School is only one way in which students absorb values and attitudes, but it can be of critical importance in teaching them to understand the links between injustice, inequity and conflict on the domestic, national and international scenes.

Figure 5.1 Teaching by telling: education *against* human rights (Source: Freedom from Hunger Campaign)

Teaching for human rights

The United Nations Universal Declaration of Human Rights (1948) and the European Convention on Human Rights and Fundamental Freedoms (1951) are comprehensive and explicit statements which assert the equality, dignity and, by correlation, the responsibilities of all people. While the UN Declaration is only a statement of intent (though globally agreed upon), the European document is legally binding and enforceable. Both documents delineate the basic entitlements of every human being, regardless of race, gender, religion or nationality. The rights asserted are not absolute – rights must walk hand-in-hand with responsibilities – but they are designed to protect people from unfair treatment.

It is not enough to teach *about* human rights. To avoid structural hypocrisy – where what you are teaching is patently at odds with how you are teaching ('today we are going to talk about freedom of expression: shut up in the back row'), or ('if that note you're writing is so interesting, you can read it out to the whole class; by the way, the subject of the next lesson is privacy') – one must teach *for* human rights. This means exploring the values implicit in rights, and developing educational strategies which will deal with more than facts. Experiential teaching and learning allows students and staff to analyse the reasons for particular human values, and the relationships such values have in our interpersonal lives as well as in our interdependent world.

By careful study of reasons for human rights we learn that upholding them needs awareness and involvement: that is, responsibility. Educationalists argue for many fundamental skills: the ability to think rationally, to argue logically, to examine ethical dilemmas. All such skills are necessary to human rights education. There is a real need in schools to identify with the *process* of learning. Schools are generally hierarchically structured with limited student participation in decisions which affect them. Teachers could begin by trying to develop their school or classroom into one where human rights values are practised and promoted. From there they can look outwards to the community and globe.

The place of geography

Opportunities

Within a school's curriculum, geography must take a principal responsibility for human rights education. Geography has the advantage of being inter-disciplinary with a global vision, spatially and thematically. Yet, often, little systematic teaching of rights and peace issues occurs. There are suitable themes (development, militarisation, resource management, demography, political and economic systems), and skills objectives (systematic collection and recording of data, analysis, inference, interpretation), together with the concepts of interaction, spatial justice, culture, community and change.

What then are some human rights issues for geography students to explore? Here are eight possibilities. The references in brackets are to maps from *The State of the World Atlas (SWA)* (Kidron and Segal, 1981) and *The New State of the World Atlas (NSWA)* (Kidron and Segal, 1984) which are excellent resources for triggering enquiries in this area:

1. *The right to live.* The geography of life expectancy and infant mortality (*SWA* map 45).
2. *The right to health.* The geography of diet, nutrition and disease (*SWA*, maps 14 and 39), access to safe water (*NSWA*, map 46) and medical services (*SWA*, map 45: *NSWA*, maps 24 and 40).
3. *The right to be human* by having an appropriate standard of living and life quality. The geography of income distribution (*SWA*, map 43; *NSWA*, maps 21, 22 and 38), educational provision (*SWA*, maps 29 and 46; *NSWA*, map 41), welfare provision (*SWA*, map 48; *NSWA*, map 43) and housing (*SWA*, map 50; *NSWA*, map 46).
4. *The right to freedom of information and expression.* The geography of newspaper, radio, television, telephone and mail services (*SWA*, map 47; *NSWA*, map 42) and freedom of speech (*SWA*, maps 31 and 33; *NSWA*, maps 25 and 27).
5. *The right to equality* without discrimination on the basis of gender or racial background (*SWA*, maps 41 and 63; *NSWA*, maps 35, 54, 55 and 56).
6. *The right to participation* in the political processes in one's own country. Political geography, geopolitics and the geography of prisoners of conscience (*SWA*, maps 7, 27, 56 and 57).
7. *The right to depart* if one feels unsafe or oppressed. The geography of refugees (*SWA*, map 32; *NSWA*, map 26).
8. *The right to work.* The geography of employment and unemployment (*SWA*, maps 40 and 52; *NSWA*, maps 34 and 37), working conditions (*SWA*, maps 41 and 42; *NSWA*, maps 35 and 36) and overseas workers (*SWA*, map 38; *NSWA*, map 32).

Relationships exist between many of these of course. The English geographer, Peter Taylor, explained the relationship between the right to economic and social well-being, the right to work and the right to freedom from oppression in a letter to the *Guardian* at the height of the Falklands/Malvinas War (see Figure 5.2).

Difficulties

Despite these opportunities for committed geography teaching, there are a number of difficulties to be overcome. In the media, much has been made of the 'watering down' of traditional disciplines, of 'Mickey Mouse' courses, of the '3 Rs with their backs to the wall'. Many social science courses are seen as intellectually weak 'soft options'. Vociferous criticisms against changes to traditional disciplines appear frequently in the media, hitting out especially at education for peace, human rights, personal development and geography development, with comments such as 'yet another catastrophe', 'blatantly political motives', 'absence of any sort of intellectually acceptable content', even 'do-it-yourself illiteracy'.

The teaching profession is conservative, and the obstacles faced by innovative teachers are endless ('the timetable doesn't allow it', 'we don't have the textbooks for it', 'we've always done it this way'). Pressure to revert to traditional content and methods defeats some. The insecurity involved with 'going it alone' defeats others. Lack of time for devising learning materials, thinking through methodologies, establishing assessment procedures and re-examining all of these in the light of outside evaluation drives many back to less-demanding options.

The topics covered in human rights and peace teaching are sometimes criticised because they are political and controversial, and therefore thought to be unsuitable topics for children. This suggests that knowledge of our rights is not good for us, and that understanding the causes of conflicts and alternative methods of resolution is not 'education'. Relevance is not seen as a proper concern of education. Yet most students seem to regard environmental issues, poverty, military affairs, human rights, economic and social structures as *basic* to their understanding of what is happening in the world, why, and *what their place is in these issues*. We know that students'

Sir, – Why has Argentina got such a nasty government? Is it that the people of Argentina are more excitable than we British, so that they cannot sustain a healthy democracy like us? Or perhaps it is not the fault of the Argentines at all.

If we look at the geographical distribution of repressive regimes around the world, we see that they are not just located anywhere. Rather they are found in those parts of the world with lower material standards of living, leaving liberal democracy to be enjoyed only in rich courtries like Britain.

In the First World enough material resources are available for dominant classes to rule without repression, i.e. the dominated classes are bought off. In Second and Third World countries, dominated classes cannot be bought, leaving repression as the only alternative.

Hence it is not racial accident that Argentina has a repressive regime and Britain is democratic. The particular nastiness of the Argentine government – like that of its Chilean neighbour – results from its dominant classes being faced by an unusually strong labour and left-wing political organisation. Such an exceptional challenge has required an additonal quota of repression.

An important corollary is that Third World elites – such as Argentina's dominant class – although acting in their own self-interest, are also carrying out policies to the First World's general advantage. Their repressive regimes keep down labour costs so that even more of the world's material resources end up in First World pockets.

Since it is the First World powers which have developed and nurtured this international system, it is *us* who are ultimately responsible for *their* repression. This is the shabby basis of our moral and democratic superiority.

Invoking democracy as a banner for battle sets a dangerous precedent. It means that any military action by a rich country against a poor country can be portrayed as democracy versus tin-pot dictatorship, and so diverts attention from the plight of the Third World.

The real tragedy of Argentina is to be found in the slums of Buenos Aires, not on the Malvinas.

Your sincerely,

Peter J. Taylor,

Department of Geography,
The University of Newcastle upon Tyne.

Figure 5.2 The geography of human rights explained (*The Guardian*, 14 June 1982)

literacy and numeracy has not been adversely affected by the teaching of such issues – indeed, rather the reverse. However, the teaching of such world 'problems' can be done in two ways: by distancing (the terrible problem of poverty 'over there', the bland reporting of coups and conflicts), or by placing these problems in their political settings. If teachers omit the politics as 'irrelevant', they are not teaching students to become sensitive to the real world.

Human rights in school

It is not from teaching alone that values are transferred. As Goethe wrote 'the highest cannot be spoken, it must be acted'. The dichotomy between what is being transferred as knowledge in the classroom and what is being transferred as values by the 'hidden curriculum' can lead to rejection of all human rights teaching as yet another manifestation of adult inconsistency. Staff–student relationships, respect for individuals, authority structures and discipline methods: these are all part of 'values' education (see Figure 5.3). If the concepts of justice, interdependence, non-discrimination, and freedom of expression are to be valid as *content*, they should be equally apparent in general school organisation and interpersonal interactions at classroom level.

Teachers have a formidable responsibility in introducing human rights education. Half-hearted attempts will collapse in the face of opposition. Our teaching practices need to be clearly formulated and openly stated or we may face opposition that will not only be strong, but lethal.

Figure 5.3 Non-violent power at school (Source. Freedom from Hunger Campaign)

"I'm glad you young people have seen fit to protest non-violently. It shows you're civilised.. Now get out."

Practical activities

The following activities illustrate a range of approaches to the teaching of human rights issues and, in some cases, allow for the development of materials for classroom use. Most exercises are designed for use with 12 to 16 year old students. The activities are divided into four groups:
- Human rights
- Freedom of conscience and expression
- Racial discrimination
- Discrimination by gender

Human rights

Activity 1: Signs of the times

In this activity students are asked to imagine they are living in one of two different environments: a major western city; and a city in a society where it is well known that human rights are denied to the majority of the inhabitants (for example, South Africa). Students make suitable 'street' signs to illustrate violations of any human rights in each of the environments (see Figure 5.4).

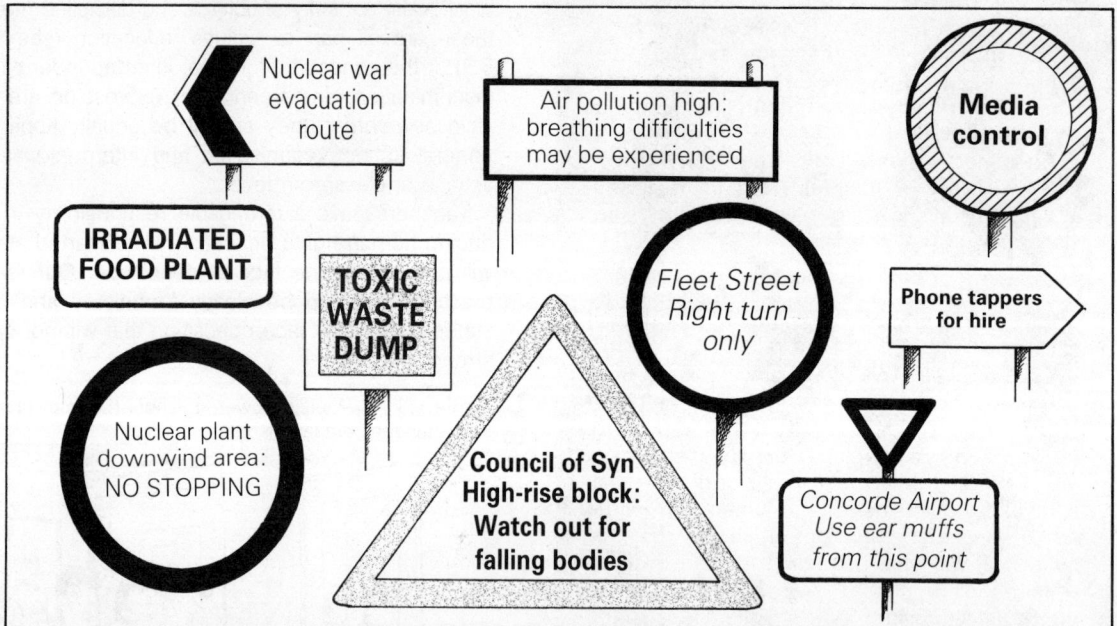

Figure 5.4 Human rights 'street' signs

Instructions

Prepare wall displays of photographs, maps and newspaper articles to create a collage impression of each of the two environments. Divide the classroom (and the students) into two, using one half for each city; tell the students that they are to imagine they live in that city. Talk about the difficulties presented by the human environment and its organisation and get the students to develop a list of ideas from which 'street' signs can be constructed. Ask students to relate the signs to the wall display, re-arranging it as necessary.

Follow-up

This activity can be related to an understanding of the provisions of the UN Declaration of Human Rights. Are rights 'relative'? Are some infringements regarded more seriously than others?

Activity 2: A right is. . .?

What does the word 'right' as in 'human right' imply? Have a brainstorming session to see what understanding the students have. Do they think there is a relationship between rights and any of these:

- justice
- responsibilities
- assumptions?

- impartiality
- morals

- demands
- freedom

You may need to teach new words: for example, if students say 'give people a fair go', or a 'square deal', introduce the nouns 'equality' and 'impartiality'.

Once a vocabulary is well established, students can have great fun with the use of the word 'right' in the English language:

- stand on one's right
- divine right
- serve one right
- loss of right
- righteous
- to be rightly served
- the right hand of friendship
- to turn to the right
- in one's right mind
- a Bill of Rights

- by right of
- claim one's right
- have the right to
- to be right-minded
- to put/set to rights
- to be the rightful owner
- right about
- to keep to the right path
- a step in the right direction
- to right itself

Activity 3: The Universal Declaration

If possible buy a wall chart of the Universal Declaration of Human Rights (approach the United Nations Association in your capital city). With younger students you may prefer simply to use the key headings, or to simplify them further. For example:

- Freedom, Life, Equality   To be treated the same
- Social & Economic Issues   How we live and what we do
- Legal Issues   The law and me
- Nationality & Government   My country and how it is run

Alternatively, a graphic summary such as Figure 5.5 may be used.

The Universal Declaration of Human Rights

What it is:

It's a "common standard of achievement" for all people in all nations – a declaration that universal human equality and dignity are goals for all mankind. It was signed by the General Assembly of the United Nations December 10, 1948.

What it does:

It commits all member nations to work towards this goal, as elaborated in the declaration's 30 articles. It gives people a list of basic needs and reasonable expectations and provides an internationally accepted reference point for victims of human rights violations. The Declaration also provides a useful starting point for enforcing human rights reforms.

What it says:

that everyone

- is born free and equal in dignity and rights.
- has the right to freedom of thought, opinion and expression.
- has the right to work, to rest, to health, to education, and has duties to the community.

that no-one

- shall be held in slavery, subjected to torture or to arbitrary arrest or interference.

that all

- are equal before the law and entitled to its protection.

Figure 5.5 A student summary of the Universal Declaration (Source: *New Internationalist*)

Instructions ⟶

Ask the students the following questions.

1. What would they write as a human right under any of these headings?

2. On what grounds did they make their choice? Do they have knowledge to substantiate their 'choice' or are they expressing an opinion? What is the difference?

3. Would gaining their chosen 'right' cut across anyone else's right?

4. Could the social and economic rights (of health care, adequate food and clothing, housing, education, the right to work, to leisure, to choose a religion, to social services) be provided by any government, of any political system? What do the students know about (as opposed to holding opinions about) how different governments allow or deny such rights? Why do some countries deny rights? Which countries? Do we get media reports about human rights abuses in some countries more than others? Is there any country where abuses might not happen? What about our country?

Activity 4: Off the planet

Instructions ⟶

1. Pre-teach vocabulary such as democracy, vote, rights, responsibilities, political party, election.

2. Tell the class to imagine they have been isolated on a remote space station. They are the only inhabitants and they have to live there for an indefinite period of time. There is no problem with the air or with the immediate supply of provisions, but people will need organisation. How will rules be devised? What is consensus? What is the democratic way of establishing the majority wish? How could we do this?

    You should be an equal member of the space society with the same rights and responsibilities as the students. Let the students have their say. Do not try to use your extensive knowledge of the workings of a society to interfere with what they may create.

3. Once the process is understood, you can move on to getting the students to create the rules themselves. Use the following discussion points. What types of rules will be needed? What do we need to control and why? What about rights of the people? Do we have rights? Are all our rights the same or do rights differ according to our age? If so, is this how society has always been structured? Why might this be so? For example, if it is your right not to be beaten, tortured, or imprisoned as a punishment on the station, is it your responsibility not to provoke? What ways will the space stationers use to punish people who do not obey the rules you have collectively made? During punishment do people still have any rights?

4. Get students to compare what they created on the space station with the ideas they have about what goes on in society. Are they clear about the rules of the society? Who makes the rules? Are the rules fair and just to all people? Did everybody participate? Does everybody's voice get heard in democracy? Can students think of any ways in which something they disagree with could be improved? If they do not like the way things are done, they have to think further and try to find alternatives.

Follow-up ⟶

This exercise could then be compared with the workings of a society in which people are not free to make decisions. Again, pre-teach the vocabulary: repression, oppression, injustice.

Try to establish the students' preconceptions of a repressive society. They may identify this with a particular state or series of states in their world. How did they establish this impression? Do they have any knowledge on which to base what they are saying? How could extra knowledge be gained? Get students to create a comparative chart to show the type of society they think would be desirable and the one they would oppose.

Activity 5: Repression

Ask the students if they can envisage a situation in which they set out to deny one of the human rights to their colleagues? Some classes may feel sufficiently 'strong' to be able to form a circle of students and have one volunteer to remain outside the circle. The circle presses tightly together constantly preventing the volunteer from entering or passing through. How did the volunteer feel? How did the members of the circle feel? Or students may like to prepare a chart of any denials of human rights which they observe in their immediate society. Use this as a basis of discussion.

You may like to play the simulation games, *Repression* or *Apartheid*. Both are available from: Coral Broadbent, Cabbage Tree Publication, PO Box 17–530, Sumner, Christchurch, New Zealand ($NZ25.00 each).

Repression is a general human rights game about situations which exist in many countries today. There is an alternative version which specifically deals with the rise of Nazi Germany 1930–1945. The game has been designed to increase awareness of the whole concept of human rights and to confront players with the situations and more dilemmas faced by those living in the totalitarian state. I suggest several staff or parents get together to play the game before attempting it with students. It is best suited to older students.

Apartheid is a historical learning experience game set in South Africa 1910–1966. It deals with human rights experiences of black South Africans and leads to discussion of present-day difficulties and changes. It is a very powerful and effective simulation game for 13 to 17 year old students.

Freedom of conscience and expression

Activity 6: I accuse. . .

Preparation ⟶

This role-play activity takes the form of a debate about the punishment of human rights abusers. Divide the class into five groups and give each one a copy of one of the role cards in Figure 5.6. Each group must choose a member to act as the role player (speaker) while the others can be involved as assistants, supporters and advisers. If the class is very large it may be better to divide it in two and have each half act out the role play separately.

The President of Atitagain

This person has been democratically elected and is untainted by the previous regime. S/he is a popular figure, travels widely throughout the country, 'a person of the people' who talks constantly of 'bringing the nation together', of 'reconciling differences', of 'forgetting and forgiving'. The President would prefer that none of the offenders is brought to trial for most were only carrying out orders. The President believes the 'top' people could be brought before the courts – the people who issued the orders – and s/he agrees to support a bill which demands only this.

The President can be assisted in preparing his/her case by several Ministers and Departmental Advisors: for example, from the Law Office and the Department of Defence.

The spokesperson for the League Against Repression and Torture (LART)

The League has gathered volumes of evidence against specific members of the military. LART points out the apparent willingness of officers to carry out orders and is also fully aware of the fact that the 'top' people, who conceived the various forms of repression, are now mostly dead or abroad. LART is strongly pressing for legislation which will allow all alleged offenders to be tried in the civil courts.

The LART spokesperson can be assisted by survivors of the repression and their relatives, who share their files of information with members of the general public.

A military Chief of Staff

In his full dress uniform what an imposing figure he cuts! He is a 'survivor' – he was fully involved with the previous military regime but managed somehow to 'keep his hands clean' of charges of torture and repression. When the military government was overthrown, he rose rapidly to his current position: one he does not wish to lose. He speaks freely about the army's role in maintaining democracy. While it is rumoured that he has been paid to keep quiet about some of the workings of the previous regime, there is no proof of this. He speaks freely, is popular with many of the present government Ministers and with his junior officers. It is in his interests that no law allowing the trial of human rights offenders is passed. His junior officers have warned him they will not permit such investigations.

The Chief of Staff may be assisted by other Chiefs from various branches of the military and by junior officers.

A member of the dominant left wing faction of the Opposition

This political faction wants all the alleged abusers of human rights to be tried. It is looking for justice, impartiality before the law, people's rights – or so the faction's posters claim. For justice to be rightly served, all alleged offenders must submit to a fair trial.

There is a free press in Atitagain now and polls show that the majority of the people favour passing a law to allow all alleged offenders to be brought to trial. It is in the left's interest to be seen to support the wishes of the people. This person may be assisted by others of the faction.

One who was tortured under the orders of the previous military regime

This person, though a member of the LART, has received special permission to present his/her case in parliament. So horrifying were the experiences that LART and the left wing felt that these should be made a matter of record. This person had exercised the democratic right of freedom of expression. Criticism of the excesses of the military government included:

- resistance to compulsory military service.
- exposure (in conjunction with many journalists) of the luxurious lifestyle of the Generals, while many people were very hungry.
- organisation of like-minded students into protests against the loss of democratic rights.
- speaking against the military's denial of free speech and their control of the mass media.

Figure 5.6 Role cards for the simulation 'I accuse . . .'

Scenario ⟶

The military government of Atitagain was overthrown three years ago. Democratically organised elections were held and representative democracy was restored. However, during the years of military control, there were many abuses of human rights. People who protested against these abuses were arrested, tortured or even 'disappeared'. It was not until the change of government as a result of popular pressure ('peoples' power') that the perpetrators of various abuses could be charged in civil courts.

A proposal for a trial of human rights offenders is going to be debated in parliament. Many demands for punishment of human rights abusers (mostly members of the military) are being made. Polls show that at least 70% of the people want the offenders to face the civil courts. However, the army is in a state of unrest and the Chiefs of Staff of various military branches have approached the President, saying that it would be difficult to control the unrest among the military if offenders from the past were to be tried.

Instructions ⟶

Each role player (with the help of his/her group) prepares a case to place before the parliament and the people. LART supporters write and display graphic photographs and stories — many of which are carried by the newspapers, copies of which are available. Members of the public (non-role players) can approach or be approached by any of the five role players, before the debate begins in parliament. Each role player attempts to influence as many of the public as possible.

Finally, a time is decided for the five role players to present their cases before parliament and the people. The debate takes place and a vote is taken to decide the outcome.

Activity 7: Human rights legislation

Discuss with the students the following list of some of the techniques that countries use to prevent or silence opposition.

- Detain people for years, without charge or trial.
- Banish people.
- Subject people to physical torture to intimidate or force 'confessions'.
- Run false trials, using made-up evidence in order to obtain a conviction.
- Make release of a prisoner conditional upon the prisoner 'confessing'.
- Use of mind/personality altering drugs and then committing people to mental institutions.
- Barring people from practising their skills — for example, stopping lawyers from practising — preventing them earning a living.
- Control of the media so that only the government viewpoint can be made public.

Instructions ⟶

Give the students the following assignments.

1. Which Articles of the 1948 Universal Declaration of Human Rights would be violated by such methods?

2. Study maps in the *State of the World Atlas* and the *New State of the World Atlas* to see which countries have the worst records for such practices. Use other maps in these atlases to see if you can explain why these countries have such bad practices.

3. See if you can draft a piece of legislation about any one of these methods. Remember even some democracies have such legislation. Give your legislation a title, for example The Internal Security Act, The Interrogation Act, The Media Control Act . . .

4. Now see if you can draft a law banning such a practice.

Activity 8: The rights of children

Discuss with the students the fact that it is not only adults who suffer through injustice in the legal systems. Children have gone missing after their parents have been seized by security forces. Very young children have been put up for adoption. Others have apparently been killed. Grandparents have searched for the children, usually in vain.

Instructions ⟶

Give students the following assignment.

Imagine you live in a police state. Your parents oppose the regime and, although you are very young, you have attended political rallies with your parents.

One weekend security police burst into your home where your parents are leading a meeting of 'dissidents' (people who express views against those of the government). One minute all was peaceful discussion – the next . . .

Using factual information as a basis, construct a story about what might have happened next. Give all your characters names and ages; build up a profile of them; try to 'walk in another person's shoes'.

Activity 9: The geography of torture

Preparation ⟶

Get students to research methods of torture in the past. For example, in the UK the following methods have been used:

- The rack (the last recorded use was 1680)
- Pilliwinks and thumbscrews
- Burning at the stake
- Execution by axe or hanging
- The Scavenger's Daughter – it crushed the body instead of stretching it (as the rack did) and was mainly used in the sixteenth century
- Manacles or gauntlets – locking the wrists of the victim in a pair of iron fetters, joined by a bar which was hooked to a staple, leaving the prisoner suspended
- Spiked collars for the neck together with lead collars and jongs – a collar attached to a post in a public place
- Bilboes – shackles which prevented a prisoner from walking
- Scold's bridle – an iron frame for the head with a serrated iron tongue inserted into the mouth.

Obtain a report entitled *Torture in the Eighties* from Amnesty International. It should also be available from local libraries.

Instructions ⟶

1. Discuss the following with the class. Can we judge what was done in the distant past by the standards of today? What about the recent past? Have students heard or read of any forms of torture being used during any wars this century?

2. Using information from Amnesty International on what methods of torture are in use in what countries today, get students to map the distribution of countries where Amnesty International has reported torture to be used.

3. Give students copies of the letter to the *Guardian* by Peter Taylor (Figure 5.2) and ask them to use it to explain the pattern on their map.

4. Compare a historical account of the force feeding of suffragettes during the early twentieth century with this 1980s account (class discussion).

> *A dissident, a political activist, deprived of freedom by his government, was subjected to physical torture and mental abuse. During forced feeding he was handcuffed to his bed. The feeding tube, forcibly inserted, was covered with a corrosive substance. The dissident accuses the state medical service of abuse of medical ethics in so assisting the state in its repression of freedom of expression.*

Activity 10: Prevention

Instructions

Have a brainstorming session to think up ways in which:

- torture
- imprisonment without trial
- imprisonment for political or religious reasons

could be prevented altogether. Is it possible to legislate guarantees against injustice?

Activity 11: National rights

Scenario

The small country of Btirh is experiencing rapid population growth: up to 4% per year in urban areas. There is massive rural-to-urban migration as adverse physical conditions (increasing acidity, locust plagues, lack of vegetation cover and resultant soil erosion) drive many from the land. Repeatedly over the past decade, Btirh has requested and received food aid from its ally, a major nation.

The government of Btirh encourages all manner of birth control methods. Abortion is legal, and is the most widely used method, because contraceptives often cost more than people can afford.

The major donor nation now officially expresses its intention not to assist nations who use abortion as a method of population control. This policy will be implemented immediately. Btirh is in a famine situation.

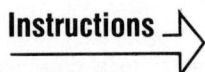

Instructions

Ask the students the following questions.

- What do you imagine will happen?
- Who might apply what kinds of pressure?
- Which country has greater bargaining power, and why?
- Do you know any occasions when situations such as this one have occurred?

Activity 12: Race and ethnicity

Preparation ⟶

Write out on card, for display, the first section of Article 2 of the 1948 Universal Declaration of Human Rights. Emphasise the word 'race', and underline as illustrated.

'Everyone is entitled to all the rights and freedoms set forth in this Declaration without distinction of any kind, such as RACE, colour, sex, language, religion, political or other opinion, national or social origin, property, birth or other status.'

Instructions ⟶

Discuss the following with the students.

1. Why might race have been placed first in this list of possible areas of discrimination?

2. What do the students understand by the word 'race'? Are there different races of people or is there only one race: the human race? How do we use the words 'race' and 'ethnic group'? What does the dictionary say about the meaning of these two words? Will students need to revise the way they use them?

3. How are these words commonly used:
   - in our immediate community?
   - in our country?

Activity 13: Racial discrimination

The 1965 UN Declaration on the Elimination of all Forms of Racial Discrimination, Article 4 reads:

... condemn all propaganda and organizations which are based on the ideas of theories of superiority of one race or group of persons of one colour or ethnic origin ... or which attempt to justify or promote racial hatreds and discrimination in any form ...

Instructions ⟶

Discuss the Article with the class then organise the following student activities.

1. Discuss whether there are organisations in your own country which discriminate against people on grounds of alleged superiority of whites over blacks.

2. Survey newspaper articles for evidence of racial discrimination.

3. There is a difference between voting for a UN Declaration on Human Rights at the UN, and ratifying the covenants so as to guarantee such rights to its citizens in a legal and binding way. Get students to research when the UK voted on the UN Declarations on Race or Human Rights and whether they have ratified such decisions at home.

4. Obtain large-scale street maps of your local area. Discuss whether there is any particular concentration of any ethnic group in any particular area. If so, why, and over what period of time, has this occurred? Has there been any sequent occupancy, with different ethnic groups occupying the same area at different times? Do a detailed street analysis of some areas to show the importance of support services for ethnic groups: for example, shops selling special foods, religious institutions, professional offices. Comment upon the accessibility to public transport, the availability of public areas (libraries, recreation centres).

Activity 14: Prejudice

A prejudice is a bias, a pre-judgement, a pre-conceived opinion. Most of us have learned some prejudices even though we often deny that this is so. We hear prejudice expressed in many ways, for example:

- Young people today are worse than those of previous generations.
- Women are not equal to men.
- They should not let (named ethnic group) come into our country as immigrants.
- If they're poor it's their own fault.
- Black and white will never be equal.

Prejudiced opinions are usually expressed negatively. They are opinions often maintained through ignorance or stubborn refusal to change.

Instructions ⟶

1. Have the students make a chalkboard list of prejudiced opinions they have heard expressed.

2. Critically examine selections from the statements and discuss how the true facts could be obtained.

Activity 15: 'This flat would be unsuitable. . . .'

Scenario ⟶

A mixed-race couple (the wife is white) have been flat-hunting for weeks. The wife is pregnant and the landlord has said that the couple must leave their bed-sitter by the end of the month as no children are allowed. Many suitable one-bedroom flats have been advertised in the newspapers and in estate agents' window displays, but when the couple go to see the properties they are told that the flat has already been let; it would be unsuitable for a child; or the owner has decided against renting.

It becomes apparent they are facing discrimination because of colour. The wife suggests she visits the next place on her own. Her husband says . . . . They discuss . . . . and agree to . . . . When the next flat is seen . . . .

Instructions ⟶

1. Have the students write several possible endings for this story and act them out.

2. Do the students know of similar cases in their area? Are particular groups singled out for discrimination? Are particular reasons used by people as a basis of discrimination? When racial discrimination occurs, does it lead to any spatial result?

Activity 16: Stamps against racism

1971 was the International Year Against Racism (International Year for Action to Combat Racism and Racial Discrimination). During that year over 40 countries issued stamps to highlight the campaign. Ask the students to design a stamp which, through its use, could increase people's awareness of the issues of racism and racial discrimination. The message has to be very concise on a stamp: students must think about what wording to use.

Activity 17: Teacher's pet

Instructions ⟹

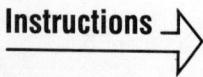

Have the students consider the following story.

> In your class there is a girl who has recently arrived in your country. She speaks some English (as it is taught in her country of origin) but it is much easier for her to converse in her own language. None of the class speaks this tongue but one of the teachers does.
>
> At first, when your class teacher introduces the new girl and explains a little about her background, you try to include her in your activities. But more and more she hangs around the teacher to whom she can speak her own language. She waits outside the staff-room at interval and lunchtime. The rest of the class get tired of trying to be nice to her, and begin to ignore her.
>
> This girl's language is one of the languages you study in the first year of secondary school. She starts to bring small presents to the language teacher and they have many conversations between themselves, sometimes while the class is going on. Most of the rest of the class are really struggling with this language. The new girl, of course, tops the class.
>
> Some of you start to call the new girl 'teacher's pet'. The girl becomes more isolated from you and never speaks to your group at all. But the teacher who speaks her language is about to leave to have a baby. The language classes will be discontinued.

Discuss the following with the students.

1. What action will you and your class take now?

2. Is there a possibility that the girl could become less isolated because of actions you could take?

3. Should the girl be left on her own?

Instructions ⟹

Have the students consider the following story.

> You belong to a distinctly different ethnic group. Your skin colour makes you stand out in a crowd. Travelling to school by train you are often jostled, white students order you out of a seat and throw your school bag around. You are an excellent student at school, though you feel that the teachers regard you as 'different'.
>
> One afternoon a group of white students beat you up on the station platform. Included in that group was one of the students from your class. Nothing but discrimination had provoked the attack, as you tend to be rather quiet and don't mix with people easily – whether of your own ethnic group or of others.

Discuss the following with the students.

1. What actions would you take at home and at school?

2. What organisations exist to help people in your situation? Do these organisations work effectively? Why or why not?

Activity 19: Stereotypes

We have built up images of what people from other places are like from a whole range of sources. Television is important, so are parents' comments, and the attitudes shown in the books we read (see Hicks, 1981). A fixed image of any group of people is called a stereotype: 'All (X-group) are dirty'. But, of course, all X's are not dirty. Maybe none are.

Instructions

Discuss the following with the students.
1. Could people overseas have built up stereotypes about white people from this country? What words might be used to express their stereotypes?

2. What stereotypes have the students heard about ethnic groups in this country? Do such stereotypes translate into prejudices? Are they based on fact or opinion? What do the students do when they hear stereotypes or prejudices expressed against an ethnic group?

Activity 20: Quick quips

Instructions

Ask students how they feel about such statements as these.

- All Germans were Nazis.
- Never trust a Jap.
- Russians are dour and hardworking.
- Striking is the British disease.
- All Chinese are clever.
- '. . . One may dislike, or even hate, a nation without hating or disliking an individual of that nation.' (Henry Lawson).
- 'Two Wongs don't make a white.' (Arthur Caldwell, Australian Minister for Imigration, 1947.)

How many people of a certain nationality would you need to know to test whether a stereotype is true or not?

Activity 21: Slavery

Preparation

Before the main activity, have the students research the Africa–North America slave trade and discuss the racist assumptions on which it was based.

Instructions

Students take their chance on being slaves for a day. In a large bag put a 'ticket' for each student. For a class of 30 make 27 tickets black (for slaves) and 3 white (Europeans). The Europeans can be given roles: slave shippers, auctioneers, cotton merchants, for example. Let the students play their roles for the day, or part of a day.

Discrimination by gender

Activity 22: Occupational expectations

Instructions ⟶

Obtain a selection of newspaper job advertisements and examine whether they request either male or female workers or whether gender is not mentioned. Discuss the following with the students. .

1. Should it be necessary for gender to be written in an advertisement? Do the students see some occupations as being 'male' and others 'female'? Which occupations? How do they react to the idea of:
   - a female pilot of an aeroplane
   - a female truck/train driver
   - a female car mechanic?
   - a female surgeon
   - a female road-sweeper

   Think of others to add to this list. Get the students to help.

2. Critically examine the reasons students suggest for their approval or disapproval of women in various occupations.
   - Would their answers be applicable in other societies: Eastern or Western, developed or developing?
   - Compare the workplaces of women in your country with (say) the Soviet Union, India, or the USA.
   - Are any differences apparent?
   - What allowed these differences to develop?

3. What is a 'status position'? Are women equally represented in these jobs?

4. Where are the locations of 'women's jobs' compared with where families live in your town?

5. Do a local area survey of the location of child care centres. How does the provision of child care influence women's access to work?

6. In a one-car family, the car tends to be the man's. Women use public transport more than men. What problems do women with children, push-chairs and groceries have in using public transport?

7. We often hear the phrase 'only a housewife'. Discuss with the students, the jobs a housewife does, and make a list of them. Do students think the phrase should be used? Do people say 'only an engineer' or 'only a doctor'?

8. Have the students bring a selection of teenage magazines/comics to school. Discuss whether the images presented are sexist.

9. Discuss whether there is any work which should be exclusively female? Why? Or why not?

10. Discuss whether it should be necessary to legislate to prevent discrimination by gender in the workplace? Why?

Activity 23: Nobela's story

Have the students consider the following story.

> Nobela lives in a small village. Her husband used to go to South Africa to work as a migrant labourer in the mines, but now he is dead. Nobela had her first child before marriage, thus proving her fertility. She was fortunate that her man married her. While he worked in South Africa, she tended the farm, bore the children conceived during her husband's holidays, and looked after his parents. Now he is dead from tuberculosis and she is left with four children.
>
> The drought has come to Botswana and the cattle die. Nobela's sons are not old enough to plough her land, even if she had cattle. Nobela is prevented by tradition from ploughing it herself. If the rains come she will have to rely on help from a male relative or neighbour. If the rains do not come she will have to endure even worse poverty.
>
> Nobela hires herself out as a farm labourer – she and her older children can work at scaring birds, gathering fuel or collecting water – for a few cents a day: enough to buy food.
>
> If the rains do not come, people will not hire casual workers, and the price of food will rise.
>
> Next to Nobela's farm is a rich farm. Cattle have been fed by hand during the drought. Watering systems have kept some grass alive. This farm is owned by a rich man who lives in the capital, Gabarone. In Botswana, 10% of the population own 90% of the cattle.
>
> Nobela has two daughters and two sons. The boys spend most of their day in play, now the cattle and goats are dead. In the past they had meat and milk to supplement their diet and they are not yet too thin. The girls help Nobela with the household chores. Girls are considered less important and have less to eat. The baby is pitifully thin.

Give the students the following assignments (with guidance from you).

1. Look up in an atlas the location of Botswana and South Africa.

2. Research details of various development indicators (such as gross national product) in Botswana. Relate these to the migrant labour system.

3. Investigate the infant mortality statistics for Botswana. Are Nobela's children likely to survive?

1. Which international agencies provide help for drought-stricken countries? How is the aid distributed? What problems arise?

2. For children to have normal growth and mental development, and disease resistance, they need proper nutrition. The weaning period is the crisis point for many children in developing countries. What advantages does breast-feeding offer over artifical feeding? What foods would be available in Botswana for infants after weaning?

Activity 24: An international affair

Instructions ⟶

Have the students consider the following situation.

You are a girl of Indian origin who has lived in Britain since early childhood and is now in the first years of secondary school. Dating is common and a boy has asked you out, to go to see a film one evening. When you ask for permission at home, your father makes it perfectly clear that in your culture no decent girl goes out unaccompanied with a boy. You protest that you all live in Britain now, and these are British ways. You're a UK citizen. Every other girl in the class is allowed out. You'll be home by a stated time.

"Please Dad, don't make me stick out as different from the other girls. The boy will come to the house first, and you, Dad, can meet him."

Your father remains adamant and your mother supports him.

You are the third child of the family. The older brother is unmarried and lives at home. Your older sister was married at 18 and did not finish school. She now has a child and you feel she does only what her husband allows. For your own sake, and for that of your younger brothers and sisters, you wish to change your parents' attitude.

Discuss with the students how they would go about doing this.

Activity 25: Women and planning

Scenario

There is to be considerable re-development of a depressed section of the city: an area close to the central business district, with excellent public transport and with many already established educational, recreational and craft/industrial facilities close by. The areas immediately adjacent have a high population density. The depressed section contains nineteenth-century terrace houses which have become a fire and health hazard. They are uninhabited, except by some 'down and out' squatters.

The local council proposal is to demolish the houses and put up new buildings which will extend the available space of a nearby industrial arts complex. This section would house improved facilities for teaching metalwork and technical drawing, and would also provide space for computer technology. Town planners have allowed for open space as formal gardens and lawn.

This plan has been on display for some time. At the council meeting, when it will be put to the vote, a Womens Collective group arrives and attempts to delay the vote. Representatives of the Collective claim that women's activities have been ignored, that the formal gardens should be creative play space (with junk dumps from which children can make their own items) and that, instead of funding (with government assistance) new buildings, the council should be putting its money into low rental accommodation and child-care facilities.

Instructions

Get students to develop this scenario further and discuss the geographic implications of inner-city planning. Who has 'rights'? Are any one group's 'rights' paramount?

Conclusion

Given how important the kind of teaching described in the above activities is, why does it not get the attention it deserves? One impediment is the fear that teachers will 'preach' and that any teaching for human rights will become a vehicle for student indoctrination. But then who would make the case for teaching *against* human rights?

The UN Declaration is a globally accepted statement, and many nations have committed themselves to establishing school courses which follow the UNESCO recommendation concerning education for International Understanding, Co-operation and Peace, and Education Relating to Human Rights and Fundamental Freedoms (November 1974). Such courses have a global perspective, deal with human values, rights and responsibilities and attempt to develop an understanding of the necessity for international solidarity and co-operation.

Human rights education is geopolitical education. It encourages critical awareness of our world, an awareness that we should be pleased our children have the chance to obtain. And political illiteracy is of no value in a democracy. Human rights awareness is not a form of subversion. It is a legitimate part of everyone's education.

6 Teaching geography in a multicultural society

LEONIE DAWS

Introduction

An understanding of the place of minority groups in the study of geography may be acquired through an exploration of the issues of multicultural education and anti-racist teaching as they impinge on the theme of teaching geography for a better world. Implicit in this brief is the need to come to terms with the experience of minority groups, particularly those defined by ethnicity and race. Other chapters in this book address issues relating to women, the Third World and human rights. There are clear parallels and significant overlap between those issues and the study of minority groups.

At the outset it is necessary to define the intersecting points between the three relatively distinct areas – multicultural education, anti-racist teaching and geographical education – to determine their relevance to creating a better world through teaching geography. This will serve to sharpen the focus for this chapter. This focus can then be used to examine implications for teacher education, curriculum development and classroom practice.

While this chapter draws extensively on the Australian experience in making its case, its conclusions are applicable to similar societies such as the USA and Canada which, like Australia, have been derived from, and have continued to draw on, British cultural patterns and social institutions in the development of a dominant culture. It is seen as particularly relevant to the British experience since the Second World War which has included extensive immigration from Commonwealth countries with ethnic and racial groups quite distinct from the dominant Anglo-Celtic groups within Britain.

Multicultural education and geography in a multicultural society

Australia is unarguably a multicultural society today, and has been so at least since the first major wave of European immigration in 1788. It has not always been seen as such by members of the dominant cultural group, those of British origin, who have variously pursued policies of exclusion or assimilation; the former policy seeing Aborigines forcibly removed to isolated reservations, and migration restricted to those of a similar cultural background to the dominant group, while the latter policy tried to require both Aborigines and migrants to conform with the values and expectations of the dominant group. It is only since the 1970s that there has been growing official recognition of the validity and right to existence of a variety of cultures within Australian society in a policy which has come to be called multiculturalism.

Multiculturalism has developed at least three sets of ideals in relation to education: promotion of intercultural understanding and communication, the maintenance of the cultural-linguistic heritage of non-Anglo-Australian groups; and the achievement of equal occupational and social opportunities for children and adults from non-English-speaking backgrounds (Australian Ethnic Affairs Council Committee on Multicultural Education, 1979). The Australian Ethnic Affairs Council advocated an approach which brought each of these aspects together.

The multicultural nature of the society around them, and the implications of that for education, are issues which have exercised the minds of geographers in

Australia for at least a decade (Davey, 1978; Emery, 1980; Curriculum Branch, 1983; Fraser, 1985a). In 1978, Davey presented a paper to The Sixth National Conference of the Australian Geography Teachers' Association where he identified eleven specific ways in which geography teachers could contribute to multi-ethnic (multicultural) education. They ranged from using case studies from source areas of ethnic groups, to ensuring that all information is accurate, authentic and current. Emery made a similar plea to the Seventh National Conference in Adelaide in 1980. He proposed the inclusion of a unit on culture and geography, and provided an outline of such a unit.

In Britain, the recent Department of Education and Science publication, *Geography from 5 to 16*, (Department of Education and Science, 1986) emphasises the contribution of geographical education to the study of human and social behaviour and circumstances. Geographical studies, it claims, should aim to help pupils to:

- *appreciate the variety of physical and human conditions on the earth's surface,*
  . . .
- *appreciate the importance of geographical location in human affairs and understand how activities and places are linked by movements of people, materials and information and by complex economic, social, political and physical relationships;* [*and*]
- *appreciate the significance of people's beliefs, attitudes and values to those relationships and issues which have a geographical dimension.*
  (Department of Education and Science, 1986)

Such a view of geographical education demands the inclusion of material drawn from a variety of cultures. Furthermore, it encourages curiosity about the impact of geographical factors on different groups of people. *Geography from 5 to 16* is quite explicit about the inclusion of a multicultural perspective in the teaching of geography. In the context of discussing cross-curricular issues of themes which schools need to address it is argued that:

> *. . . fundamental is the need to ensure that geographical learning offers equal interests and opportunities to girls and boys and that it prepares them adequately for adult membership of a multiethnic and multicultural society.*
> *(Department of Education and Science, 1986)*

Gill takes the notion of geographical education for a multicultural society a step further when she argues that 'The content of education is not politically neutral' (Gill, 1985). She acknowledges the explanatory

function of geography, stating that it has been largely neglected in favour of pure description in the past. Gill points out that 'An understanding of important political issues must underpin geographical education if explanations of spatial patterns are to be meaningful' (Gill, 1985).

In Britain, and more recently in Australia, there has been growing concern that multicultural education programmes are failing in their intention of promoting greater understanding of, and empathy for, other cultures and lifestyles (Lippman, 1984; Murray, 1985; Pettman, J., 1983, 1984). The precise reasons for this failure are not clear. It may be quite simply that multicultural approaches to education generally, and geography specifically, have not been implemented to any significant extent, or at least have not been implemented effectively.

But the explanation may be even more serious. Murray (1985) points out that multiculturalism has failed to check the increase of racist violence. She argues that it has served to mask the institutional racism of the very fabric of British society: that it has both diverted attention away from this fact and has at the same time reduced the ability of the minority groups to resist this racism by splitting them into specific racial groups, and focussing attention on the 'problem' of minority group identity.

Anti-racist teaching and the geography teacher

In Australia and Britain racism is fairly generally decried as unacceptable. Legislation makes discrimination on racial grounds unlawful in a variety of circumstances including education. There would be little opposition in either country to the notion that geographers should avoid teaching in a manner which supports racism.

However, arguments such as Murray's against multicultural education and in favour of the stronger notion of anti-racism teaching, may not find such wide endorsement. Racism conjures up notions of extremism which would not normally be considered part of the average geography classroom.

Teachers need to reflect carefully on what racism actually means. Racism is the net effect of institutional and individual attitudes and actions, whether intentional or not, which serve to create and maintain the power, influence and well-being of white people at the expense of other racial groups. Its effect is 'to relegate and condemn black (and Asian) people to the poorest life chances and living conditions, the most menial work, and the greatest likelihood of unemployment or underemployment.' (Geographical education for a multicultural society: An introduction, 1983).

The question is whether Australian or British geography teachers agree that their societies are racist. There is much scope for geographers to use their own discipline to determine this. An initial step could be to determine whether or not population statistics and demographic distribution patterns indicate the existence of conditions which are the product of racism, such as those listed in the preceding paragraph. The Inner London Education Authority (ILEA) has amassed a stark series of data confirming the existence of such patterns within the boundaries of the Authority, (ILEA Centre for Anti-Racist Education 1984b). This should challenge others to research patterns and indicators of racism in other geographical locations. One small step in this direction was demonstrated at the Twentieth Conference of the Institute of Australian Geographers where Wundersitz and Gale presented a paper investigating the differential patterns of offending Aboriginal youths and the differential treatment meted out to them in the Australian criminal justice system (Wundersitz and Gale, 1985).

In addition to such evidence of the existence of racism, there is also growing evidence to suggest that geographical education is an unwitting vehicle for racist attitudes and contributes to the unthinking maintenance of racism as a way of life (Wright, 1983a; Gill 1983a, 1984; Bunge, 1984; Cook, 1984; Fien, 1984; Brazier, 1985). Perhaps the most telling account is Bunge's article which was first published in 1965. In choosing to republish it Bunge commented that little had changed in American geography teaching in the intervening 19 years! From the evidence presented by these writers it is clear that through the selection and omission of areas of content, through the textual materials which are available to use, and through their own unintentional actions within the classroom, many geography teachers are almost certainly contributing to the cycle of racism.

If these arguments are valid, then perhaps we do need to explore the notion of anti-racist teaching in the context of geography. Pettman writes:

> Anti-racist teaching aims to better equip people to recognise and combat racism in its various forms. It often begins as a particular strategy for revealing and modifying the widespread but often unconscious or unintended racism of individuals, for example through racial awareness training. It can also incorporate a commitment to identify and oppose racism, not only in individual attitudes, but also in the way institutions work and social relations are structured in our society.
> (Pettman, J., 1984)

Gill expands on this in relation to geography:

> If schooling is to take seriously what knowledge the child brings to school . . . it must recognise and respond to the knowledge brought by the child of a white racist family. Teachers must be prepared to work from that towards a different perception of reality which recognises the reasons for prejudices and locates the cause of problems like unemployment, inadequate and overcrowded housing, poverty and its experiential consequences not within the individuals who suffer from them, but within an explanatory framework which separates the **causes** from the effects of social inequality. [Bold type shows her emphasis] (Gill, 1983a)

A geography syllabus such as that recommended in Geography from 5 to 16, which seeks to help pupils to:

- appreciate more fully the significance in human affairs of the location of places and of the links between places, and to develop understanding of the spatial organisation of human activities (Objective 4). . .
- develop a sensitive awareness of the contrasting opportunities and constraints facing different peoples (Objective 6). . .
- develop an understanding of the nature of multicultural and multiethnic societies and a sensitivity to cultural and racial prejudice and injustice (Objective 7). . .
- gain a fuller understanding of some controversial social, economic, political and environmental issues which have a geographical dimension, reflect on their own and other people's attitudes to these issues and make their own informed judgements (Objective 8). . .
- (and) act more effectively in the environment as individuals and as members of society (Objective 10). . .
(Department of Education and Science, 1986)

is well positioned to question racist assumptions and to promote anti-racism.

Teaching geography for a better world?

It has been argued here, and elsewhere, that geography is a suitable vehicle for multicultural education, and that it is equally well suited to anti-racist teaching. The question which remains is one of values and of vision: which way of teaching geography really leads to a better world?

If we accept the analysis that Australia, Britain and other similar societies are multicultural and multiethnic, then some elements of multicultural education must be a component of teaching geography. These would include the provision of accurate information about the variety of ethnic and racial groups represented in society, and particularly the fostering of secure and positive personal and cultural identities for each of the young people in our care.

If we also accept that these societies are racist, and that all forms of racism should be opposed, then we must also undertake some form of racial awareness programme. We must be equipped to recognise and combat racism, and have an appropriate framework for separating cause from effect in social inequality. Without this informed awareness we are in no position to make effective curriculum decisions, to select relevant resources, or to monitor our own performance in the classroom.

Developing these notions in practice is clearly an ongoing task requiring both staff development and curriculum change. The activities proposed here should offer some insights into the practical implications of the views presented in this paper.

Activities

The following principles, derived from issues identified in the discussion above, have shaped and informed the selection of activities presented in this section:

- Geography is concerned with appreciating the variety of physical and human conditions on the earth's surface and the importance of geographical location in human affairs. It is also concerned with appreciating the significance of people's beliefs, attitudes and values to those relationships and issues which have a geographical dimension, and with acting more effectively in the environment as individuals and as members of society.
- There is a political dimension to the explanation of spatial patterning which has not always been fully understood or acknowledged.
- In exploring the various dimensions to the study of geography, including the political, we must take full account of the impact of our own culture upon the phenomena being studied, and upon our interpretation of those phenomena.
- To understand fully the impact of our own culture we must be aware of all the elements of racism, and our own part in the continuing role of racism in society.

With these principles in mind, three activities are presented.

The first activity, *Teacher, teach thyself!* presents a framework for a programme of professional development which could be undertaken at either the pre-service or in-service level of teacher education. This framework for developing teachers' awareness of racism is based on Katz's work, presented in *White Awareness: Handbook for Anti-Racist Training* (Katz, 1978). While the programme could be used with teachers from any discipline, it has an emphasis on awareness of issues directly relevant to teaching geography.

The programme is divided into three stages of awareness, *This Thing Called Racism, Confronting the Reality of Racism*, and *Developing Action Strategies*, and involves nine sessions in all. The sessions are of varying length and could be used either as part of a continuing series of geography department meetings, occasionally requiring an extended time period, or as an intensive programme undertaken over one and a half to two days.

Particular reference is made to the experiences of the Australian Aborigines as an example of a minority group. Resources and data relevant to significant minority group experiences in other societies may be substituted readily.

One session of this programme, *In the nation of . . .*, is presented in detail in Figure 6.1 to show the possibilities for translating these staff development activities into classroom activities for senior students.

The second activity, *The geography curriculum through racist-coloured glasses*, guides teachers in detecting unintended racism in the geography curriculum, and in planning either to eradicate it or to provide a counterbalancing view.

The third activity, *The minority experience*, (developed by David Hicks) provides a simulated experience to help students to understand the nature of the minority experience. It could be used profitably in conjunction with the simulation presented in Activity 1, *In the nation of . . .* either as a preparatory experience if students are not familiar with the issues of racism, or as a follow-up activity to extend students' insights into the effects of racism.

Activity 1: Teacher, teach thyself!
A framework for a professional development programme

Stage 1: This thing called racism

Session 1: Is it just prejudice?   (30 Minutes)
Small group activity which examines definitions of prejudice and develops a common definition for use by the whole group.

Session 2: In the nation of . . .   (120 Minutes)
A simulation designed to assist participants to ident-ify the key elements of racism, and to discover how racism functions in our society. (This activity is presented in Figure 6.1.)

Session 3: Defining racism   (30 Minutes)
Using a similar format to Session 1, participants develop a definition of racism to be used by the group, and clarify the differences between racism and prejudice.

In the nation of . . . : a simulation

Objectives ⟶

1. To identify the key elements of racism.

2. To discover how racism functions in our society.

3. To explore the relationship between racism and the distribution of geographical phenomena.

Materials ⟶

Large sheets of paper, felt pens, masking tape.

Instructions ⟶

1. Divide the participants into small groups of four to six. Give each group sheets of paper and felt markers.

2. Ask the groups to design a racist nation. Have each group describe its nation on paper. It can be blatantly racist or subtly racist. Ask groups to make sure they describe.
   (a) the population statistics and distribution (including breakdown by racial groups);
   (b) the geographical features;
   (c) the distribution of natural resources;
   (d) the nature and location of industries;
   (e) who makes decisions;
   (f) how decisions are made;
   (g) who has control of money;
   (h) who sets up formal policy for the nation;
   (i) who sets up the informal policy of the nation;
   (j) the role of various institutions – schools, churches, businesses, media, social organisations, recreational facilities.

3. Pin up the sheets of paper and ask each group to share its nation with the whole group.

4. Reactions, discussion. Points raised should include the following.
   (a) What are the key elements that make your nation and all the others racist? List these elements separately on a sheet headed 'Racism is . . .'
   (b) What interaction is there between the geographical features of your nation and the way that racism is manifested there?
   (c) How different is the nation you have just created from your own country?

Figure 6.1 In the nation of . . . : a simulation

Stage 2: Confronting the reality of racism

Session 4: How racism functions   (45 Minutes)
Kinds and levels of racism are presented in a 10-minute mini-lecture. The group then explores inconsistencies between ideology and behaviour in their own society.

Session 5: Middletown State High   (60 Minutes)
This simulation is designed to help participants understand some of the dynamics of institutional racism by experiencing how racism oppresses people. Participants should also begin to understand the role of power in white racism.

Session 6: Institutional racism and the Aborigines   (90 Minutes)
Video material and discussion are used to present some facts about racism in Australia and to highlight basic inconsistencies between Australian ideals and behaviour.

Session 7: Some perspectives on institutional racism   (45 Minutes)
The effects of institutional racism on Aborigines and other minority groups is further clarified. Participants are exposed to an Aboriginal perspective on racism through audiotapes and print material.

Stage 3: Developing action strategies

Session 8: How do I wish to respond?   (45 Minutes)
This session uses prepared worksheets to assist participants to assess their personal commitment to the concept of combatting racism, and serves to begin to generate ideas about actions which they might take.

Session 9: Strategy and action planning   (60 Minutes)
Using the ideas generated in the previous session, participants define and develop a specific action project to deal with racism in their own teaching and/or in the curriculum itself.

Activity 2: The geography curriculum through racist-coloured glasses

Objectives ⟶

1. To analyse the existing curriculum in terms of the ways in which racism is communicated or endorsed, albeit unintentionally.
   (a) To explore the values communicated through the use of language.
   (b) To analyse the messages conveyed through illustrations.
   (c) To assess the balance of information and perspectives presented through particular selections of content and material resources.

2. To determine what action needs to be taken to remove or counteract racism in the curriculum.

Materials ⟶

Large sheets of paper, felt pens, masking tape, copies of geography syllabuses, work programmes, textbooks, other audiovisual or print materials used in teaching geography.

Instructions ⟶

1. Divide the participants into small groups. Depending on the number of participants, the following group assignments are suggested:
   (a) language usage;
   (b) illustrations;
   (c) content selection.

2. Set each of the groups to work as follows:

(a) Language usage
- Sensitisation activity
  (i) Ask participants to make lists of expressions and/or sayings that contain the word 'white' (white knight, white as snow, whitewash, etc.). Then brainstorm lists of words or expressions that contain the word 'black' (blacklist, black sheep, black magic, etc.). Record these on large sheets of paper.
  (ii) Compare and contrast the lists. How many items in each list have positive connotations? How many have negative connotations? What are the positive and negative cultural values in terms of colour? What effect does language usage have on the self-image of white children and of children from other racial groups?
- Analysing language usage
  (i) Ask each group member to select a textbook or other printed resource and read two or three chapters, monitoring the language usage in terms of the cultural and racial values implicit in it.
  (ii) When this is completed, have the group prepare a summary of their findings, on large sheets of paper, for presentation to the larger group.

(b) Illustrations
Before beginning this task, group members should read the stimulus material provided.
 (i) Ask each group member to select a textbook or other printed resource and sample the illustrations presented in a significant section of the work (three or four chapters). Count the total number of illustrations and the number which portray racial groups other than white.
(ii) Note the characteristics and common activities attributed to each racial group (including whites).
(iii) When this is completed, have the group prepare a summary of their findings, on large sheets of paper, for presentation to the larger group.

(c) Content selection
Before beginning this task, group members should read the stimulus material provided.
 (i) Ask the group to choose a geography syllabus statement or work programme. Note the degree to which content is actually prescribed or merely suggested as an indication of choices which might be made.
(ii) Analyse the content selection in terms of its coverage of racial groups other than white British or Australian. Where other groups are presented, what is the focus of this presentation?
(iii) Group members should prepare a summary of their findings, on large sheets of paper, for presentation to the larger group.

3. After reports from each of the groups have been received, the whole group should discuss action which needs to be taken. Items such as the following should be considered.
   (a) Suggestions for interpreting, supplementing or modifying syllabus statements and/or work programmes.
   (b) Preparation of a list of recommended (and not recommended) textbooks and other resources.

(c) Suggestions for using racist resources as a basis for class discussion of racism.

(d) Development of a policy for purchases and use of resources.

Activity 3: The minority experience

David Hicks

Introduction

This simulation is an aid to exploring the experiences, past and present, of indigenous minorities that have been oppressed and marginalised by the activities of a dominant majority group. This case study is based on the native American situation but students are *not* told this until the end of the activity.

Objectives

1. To begin to understand the nature of the minority experiences.

2. To begin to understand the meaning of empathy.

3. To begin to understand the varying responses to minority oppression.

Instructions

Divide the class into groups of five or six students. Give each group a set of the 15 Minority experience cards (see Figure 6.2). The instructions are as follows.

1. They should lay the 15 cards face down on the table.

2. Tell the class that the information on the cards is not about someone else, but about *them* and *their* group.

3. Group members take it in turn to select a card and read it to the rest of the group. They continue until all the cards have been read out.

4. Each group discusses the following four questions in sequence.
One member acts as a scribe for the group. Teachers may find it useful to write the four questions on the chalk board or a worksheet.

   (a) How does it *feel* being in the situation described?
   (b) Select the three cards that best explain why you are in this situation. Briefly explain your reasons for choosing these three cards.
   (c) What are you going to *do* to change things?
   (d) Which *real* minority group does this information relate to? What clues are there in the facts?

Debriefing

1. The discussion questions should be debriefed in the order shown:

   (a) How does it *feel* being in the situation described?

   Elicit as wide a range of feelings as possible, from anger to sadness to despair. These could be shown on the chalk board as a continuum. Students could be asked to explain why different people and groups have reacted differently.

   (b) Select the three cards that best explain why you are in this situation. Briefly explain your reasons for choosing these three cards.

   Use this as a summary activity with a report from each group. Keep a record of which cards were selected. Pay particular attention to the reasons offered for selecting each card. Relate the selection of the cards to the range of feelings outlined in question (a).

(c) What are you going to *do* to change things?

Elicit as wide a range of outcomes as possible. These will match the feelings and may range from suicide and drinking to violent or non-violent revolution. Relate these to the feelings recorded on the continuum. Students should be encouraged to consider the constraints upon, and possible consequences of, their proposed courses of action.

(d) Which *real* minority group does this information relate to?
What clues are there in the facts?

Make a list of the minority groups suggested by the students and focus on the evidence used.

2. Tell the students that the cards described the experiences of the native Americans. Distribute Figure 6.3, *The Trail of Tears*, and have the students read it quietly. They then discuss it in relation to the 15 cards, with the goal of selecting the cards that explain the relationship between historical events, such as *The Trail of Tears*, and the native American experience today.

3. If the students have suggested Aborigines as the minority group described in the cards, a useful activity would be to ask the groups to sort the 15 cards into three groups: cards they think relate to Aborigines, cards they do not think relate to Aborigines and cards about which they are unsure. Class and library research should be used to clarify their ideas.

Extension activities

1. Which of the fact cards relate to 'objective discrimination' i.e. can be objectively qualified? Which relate to 'subjective discrimination' i.e. are hard to prove to outsiders?

2. Discuss the relative importance of objective and subjective discrimination to the minority experience.

3. Identify contemporary examples of the various responses of one indigenous minority to oppression.

4. Does real justice for minorities always require a radical change in the dominant group?

Reading

Brown, D. (1975) *Bury my Heart at Wounded Knee: An Indian History of the American West*, Picador, London.

Hicks, D. W. (1981) *Minorities: A Teachers' Resource Book*, Heinemann, London.

Johansen, B. and Maestas, R. (1979) *Wasi'chu: The Continuing Indian Wars*, Monthly Review Press, New York.

USPG, 'Testimony of Chief Seattle', slide/tape sequence, United Society for the Propagation of the Gospel, 15 Tufton Street, London SWIP 3QQ.

Wilson, J. (1980) The Original Americans: US Indians, Minority Rights Group Report No. 31, Minority Rights Group, 29 Craven Street, London.

MINORITY EXPERIENCE CARDS

THESE CARDS ARE TO BE REPRODUCED AND CUT OUT SO THAT EACH GROUP OF STUDENTS HAS ONE SET OF 15 CARDS.

MINORITY EXPERIENCE CARD 1
Income. Our average income per person is around £1500 a year, but much less in rural areas. This is much lower than the income of any other group in the country.

MINORITY EXPERIENCE CARD 2
Unemployment is bad, particularly outside the towns, where it may be as high as 40%. 18% of those who are employed have temporary or seasonal jobs only.

MINORITY EXPERIENCE CARD 3
Our land is poor and often badly eroded, with acute shortages of water. About 25% of it is more or less permanently controlled by other people.

MINORITY EXPERIENCE CARD 4
Genocide. 80% of our people have been killed by disease and warfare in the past. This has almost totally destroyed our culture.

MINORITY EXPERIENCE CARD 5
Crime. They say that crimes of violence in our community are 10 times more frequent than in the population at large. Vandalism and stealing are much less common.

MINORITY EXPERIENCE CARD 6
Heritage. We are proud of our history and cultural heritage. However, other people often consider them to be unimportant and inferior.

MINORITY EXPERIENCE CARD 7
Alienation. The many daily injustices we face make us feel alienated from the authorities.

MINORITY EXPERIENCE CARD 8
Racism. We are the victims of discrimination by people in the dominant groups of society.

MINORITY EXPERIENCE CARD 9
Housing. Approximately 90% of our housing is substandard. Sanitation is non-existent or so inadequate that it is a serious health hazard.

MINORITY EXPERIENCE CARD 10
Health. The incidence of communicable diseases is high. We are 8 times more likely to suffer from dysentry than the majority of the population.

MINORITY EXPERIENCE CARD 11
Education. Schools are often unrelated to our needs and generally controlled by outsiders. 45% to 62% of our young people drop out of school.

MINORITY EXPERIENCE CARD 12
Mining. Many large multinational mining companies are operating on our land extracting coal and uranium. We get few or any benefits from this mining.

MINORITY EXPERIENCE CARD 13
Accidents. Drink-driving accidents are the main cause of death. Also our suicide rate is twice that for the population at large.

MINORITY EXPERIENCE CARD 14
Self-esteem. We are constantly reminded by others outside our group that we are of little use to society. They tell us we are hopeless and worthless.

MINORITY EXPERIENCE CARD 15
Resignation. Our situation at the bottom of society makes us feel helpless, with little chance of controlling or changing our lives.

Figure 6.2 Minority experience cards

The Trail of Tears

In 1838 and 1839 laws were passed by the white American government taking away all the Cherokee lands. The army was then sent to round up all the Cherokee men, women and children at gunpoint. Those who resisted were killed.

In the autumn of 1838 12,000 Cherokee were forced to march west away from their land to Oklahoma. 4,000 of them died on the march. Eyewitness accounts of this still exist. Here is a description by Private John Burnett who was one of the soldiers taking part. He called it his 'Birthday Story', and addressed it to his sons and grandsons.

Children:

This is my birthday December the 11th 1890. I am eighty years old today ... The removal of the Cherokee Indians from their life long homes in the year of 1838 found me a young man in the prime of life and a private soldier in the American Army ... I saw the helpless Cherokees arrested and dragged from their homes, and driven at bayonet point into the stockades. And in the chill of the drizzling rain on an October morning I saw them loaded like cattle or sheep into 645 wagons and started towards the west.

One can never forget the sadness and solemnity of that morning. Chief John Ross led in prayer and when the bugle sounded and the wagons started rolling many of the children rose to their feet and waved their hands goodbye to their mountain homes, knowing they were leaving them forever. Many of these helpless people did not have blankets and many of them had been driven from home barefooted.

On the morning of November 7th we encountered a terrific sleet and snow storm with freezing temperatures and from that day until we reached the end of the fateful journey ... the sufferings of the Cherokees were awful. The trail of the exiles was a trail of death. They had to sleep in the wagons and on the ground without fire. And I have known as many as twenty-two of them die in one night of pneumonia due to ill treatment, cold and exposure. . . .

At this time in 1890 we are too near the removal of the Cherokee for our young people to fully understand the enormity of the crime that was committed against a helpless race, truth is the facts are being concealed from the young people of today. . . .

. . . . Murder is murder whether committed by the villain skulking in the dark or by uniformed men stepping to the strains of martial music. Murder is murder and somebody must answer, somebody must explain the streams of blood that flowed in the Indian country in the summer of 1838.

Somebody must explain the 4,000 silent graves that mark the trail of the Cherokee to their exile. I wish I could forget it all, but the picture of 645 wagons lumbering over the frozen ground with their cargo of suffering humanity still lingers in my memory.

Let the historians of a future day tell the sad story with its sighs its tears and dying groans. Let the great Judge of all the earth weigh our actions and reward us accordingly to our work.

Children – thus ends my promised birthday story. This December the 11th 1890.

Figure 6.3 The trail of tears (quoted in Porter, 1973)

7 Engendering a new geographic vision

JANICE MONK

One of the most stimulating experiences in geography is learning to interpret landscapes with a stereoscope and two aerial photographs taken from different perspectives. We see the flat landscape transformed into one with a new dimension of depth, a much more revealing and realistic image than that offered by the individual photographs. Contemporary research on women and gender relations likewise offers us the opportunity to create an exciting new vision in a curriculum that for too long has presented a view substantially confined to masculine activities seen through masculine eyes. Integrating a perspective that examines the world of women and the significance of gender not only adds a second view. It engenders a vision of a new geography that more truly represents the human condition and brings into sharp focus inequities that must be challenged if we are to progress towards a better world.

The growth of women's studies as a research and teaching field has been substantial in many countries since the early 1970s. Within geography critical feminist analyses have demonstrated how interpretations that presumed to deal with the generic 'man' omitted information on women's lives. New research has addressed such themes as the deleterious effects of development on Third World women and highlighted gender inequalities associated with the evolution of contemporary urban spatial patterns. We now have texts, journal issues, and articles that deal with teaching the new material (Drake, 1983; *Journal of Geography*, 1978; Mazey and Lee, 1983; McDowell and Bowlby, 1983; Monk and Rengert, 1982; Williamson-Fien, 1985; Women and Geography Study Group of the IBG, 1984), and some feminists have developed courses in geography based on the new scholarship, though mainly within higher education. Critical as such courses are, both for examining the new work in depth and to meet the needs of students with special interests in women's studies, they have little effect on the mass of students who continue to be presented with a curriculum that emphasises the public lives of men. Motivated by a vision of an inclusive curriculum that reflects the diversity of human experience and contributes to social change, feminist teachers have additionally, therefore, addressed the issue of developing a geography curriculum that integrates perspectives on women and gender in a comprehensive way (Monk, 1983; 1985).

A curriculum that presents the world through the eyes of both genders, like a stereoscopic perspective, does not readily come into focus for all of us. We cannot see why we should present the world from women's perspectives, or merge these perspectives into an integrated curriculum. Yet such revision is vital. The new feminist research clearly reveals that gender is crucial to experience. In addition, reflection on a few statistics demonstrates that, if we accept responsibility for teaching about values, then, in addressing issues of social justice and equity, we must focus on gender in our treatment of such topics as global economic development, poverty, and population growth and migration. We should ask why women, half the world's population, perform two-thirds of the world's work, yet are counted as one-third of the labour force, earn one-tenth of the world's income, and own about 1% of the world's property (UNA/USA, 1980), though they 'head' between one-quarter and one-third of the world's households (Buvinic, Yousseff and Von Elm, 1978).

Meeting the needs of our students also calls for recognition that they live in a world where increased numbers of women in the labour market and shifting roles for both sexes will require creative new approaches to social, economic, and political challenges. To make sensible, workable and humane public policy and personal decisions in future years, students need information about, and understanding of, both sexes. In addition, to develop self-respect, a sense of identity, confidence and competence, girls need to see women presented in positive ways. The same presentations will help boys to understand and respect women's ideas and activities. Thus, although we should examine gender inequities, our teaching should not confine women to roles as passive victims. Around the world women take diverse initiatives to express their values and concerns for humanity and to shape their own lives, ranging from the protests of British women at Greenham Common (see Figure 7.1), to the joint efforts of unskilled Indian women to gain access to credit (Jain, 1980), or Aboriginal women's organisations in Australia to fight for the preservation of women's sacred sites (Gale, 1985).

To rectify the limitations of our existing materials we must go beyond making superficial additions. Rather, we need to transform the curriculum by (i) revising the content to integrate gender as a variable wherever this is essential for describing and understanding the differences in men's and women's lives and for challenging students to think about the actions necessary to redress inequities; (ii) adding new topics that reflect the range of women's experiences seen from their viewpoint: and (iii) helping students to develop critical perspectives on existing materials and sources of data. To grasp the dimensions of this curriculum transformation, consider, as an analogy, the extent to which we would need to change our teaching were we to learn that the earth is, after all, flat rather than round!

Concepts for studying women and gender

Several concepts widely used in interdisciplinary studies of women and gender are valuable for geographers. The first is *gender* which refers to social experience in comparison with 'sex' which is a biological basis for distinction. A gendered perspective not only focuses on the categories of men and women, but examines the origins and implications of the relationships between them. It demonstrates how socialisation creates gender distinctions and reveals inequities that stem from patriarchal social organisation.

A second valuable concept is the *gender division of labour*, its variation within and across societies, its ecological, historical and ideological origins, and its consequences. Why, for example, is commercial export agriculture men's work in many African countries but farming for local food production women's work (see Figure 7.2)? Why do women account for almost 90% of sales workers in Ghana but only 1% in Turkey or Algeria (Dixon, 1981)? Why are 67% of Vietnamese immigrant women in Australia in the labour force, but only 37% of those from the Lebanon (Evans, 1984)? Activity 1 on page 98 suggests ways for using social statistics to explore the gender division of labour.

The ways *public and private space* are differentially

Figure 7.1 Women at Greenham Common demonstrate for peace

associated with men and women is another widely used concept in gender studies that can be valuable for geographers. In many societies the public sphere (and space) is identified with the male world of production, formal culture and power, and the private sphere (and space) with the female world of reproduction, domestic activity, and powerlessness. Neverthess, public and private worlds are clearly linked, as becomes obvious when we study how the spatial behaviour of women employed outside the home is affected by their concurrent roles as wives and mothers (Tivers, 1985). Further, the meaning and use of public and private space for men and women vary throughout the day and across cultures. Examination of such variations gives us insights into the ways cultural ideologies about gender shape spatial arrangements in the home or the city (Ardener, 1981).

In thinking about the relationships between public and private space we can profit from examining the economic concepts of *production and social reproduction*. How does work in the household that creates and maintains life (social reproduction) relate to production in the world beyond? What, for example, have been the consequences for the household economies of Turkish women in Western Europe and in Turkey of the employment of Turkish male guest-workers in Germany or the Netherlands (Abadan-Unat, 1977; Brouwer and Priester, 1983)?

Applying gender concepts in geography

The concepts outlined above have valuable applications in diverse approaches to teaching geography. They can help us gain insight into responses to the environment, show the influences of values and ideologies on spatial behaviour and patterns, and reveal the constraints within which we make choices. Most importantly, they are useful in our efforts to create a curriculum that fosters equity and positive social change. The examples below show how content might be changed both by introducing gender as a variable in the treatment of traditional topics and by including new topics that examine the previously invisible lives of women. They, and the range of practical activities in this chapter, have been included with a view to demonstrating not only the significance of gender, but also the diversity of women's lives as they reflect differences between contexts, cultures, classes, and stages of life.

Human–environment relationships

Gender is important in shaping our environmental values, the opportunities we have to make these

Figure 7.2 Most of the market traders in West African countries are women

values heard, and the actions we take in the environment. Several recent studies in the history of American attitudes towards the land show how gender relates to the visions people hold. Writing by white American men of Western European heritage reveals dreams of conquering and transforming the virgin land, or romantic visions of heroic scenery and preservation of pristine wilderness. Nineteenth-century women travelling from the east to settle the mid-western prairies, however, envisioned the land as a sanctuary for an idealised domesticity, and conceived the flowering prairies as a natural garden in which to place cottage homes (Kolodny, 1984). Twentieth-century women writers born in the arid south-west, Anglo Americans, Mexican Americans and American Indians have placed value on adapting to an environment of scarcity. When they write of the desert landscape as a woman they admire her strength and resistance to human transformation, or they see her as an old and wise woman who teaches us how to live. Rather than valuing empty and heroic landscapes they find beauty and meaning in the ordinary and everyday: the flower that survives in the asphalt parking lot as a reminder of the people who once lived on the site, the simple plastered adobe homes, or the peeling painted messages left by children on the walls of public housing projects (Norwood and Monk, 1987).

In another example, failure to consider how the gender division of labour varies across cultures has led Australian male scholars, politicians, lawyers, and bureaucrats to exclude Aboriginal women from consultations on land rights. These men have assumed that land ownership in Aboriginal culture is 'men's business', celebrated in their religious rituals. Yet women place high value on sites that are central to their sacred life, and Aboriginal women have had to organise protests to make their interests apparent (Gale, 1985).

Such failures to recognise or acknowledge the gender division of labour can promote or exacerbate environmental degradation. This can be clearly demonstrated by looking at the work of women in many Third World countries where they are primarily responsible for the production, processing, and storage of food, the collection of fuel and water, and the care of animals (May, 1981). The activities of colonial governments, and more recently of inter-nationally designed development projects, have made this largely 'invisible' work of women more difficult and the resources they require more inaccessible, and

Figure 7.3 (Cartoon: Centre for World Development Education cartoon sheet no. 3/UN Water Decade)

- BUT WHAT WILL WOMEN DO
IF THEY DON'T HAVE TO
CARRY WATER FOUR HOURS
A DAY?

© CWDE

helped to destroy the environment on which so many of their activities depend (Rogers, 1980). For example, deforestation for commercial timber or cash cropping has forced women to go further afield and spend more time in order to collect a diminishing supply of fuel, and this has encouraged them to use animal dung instead of wood, when the dung could have been used to fertilise the soil (Mahajani, 1976).

That many women are vitally aware of their depen-dence on the forest ecosystem is illustrated by the modern Chipko, a movement of village women in the Reni forests of Uttar Pradesh (Ummayya and Bandyo-padhyay, 1983). The Chipkos seek to prevent the activities of commercial logging contractors by hugging individual trees, protecting them with their bodies. Such actions have a long tradition in India, yet the importance of female interests in re-afforestation programmes has rarely been fully acknowledged (Bagchi, 1984) and the neglect has also forced women in rural India to take action to see that planting sites are brought nearer to their homes (Sharma, 1982).

Research in the United States on environmental quality issues that considers gender indicates the usefulness of the concept of public–private spheres. Women have been found more likely to engage in private behaviour to express their environmental concerns, by avoiding damaging products, recycling newspapers or conserving energy, whereas men undertake public activities such as attending meetings, contacting officials or writing letters to newspapers on environmental issues (McStay and Dunlap, 1983).

Interesting new material can be incorporated into the study of human–environment relationships if we turn to the private space in landscapes, considering interior landscapes of the home as places women have shaped in their roles as consumers, decorators, and practitioners of domestic arts (Hayden and Marris, 1981; Hess, 1981; Lloyd, 1975). Such interior land-scapes are traditionally excluded from geographic study, yet they are important in giving us a sense of place and personal identity.

The suggestions for classroom and fieldwork activi-ties on retail and advertising landscapes on page 99 provide ideas for exploring these concepts.

Studies of space use and design within homes also show how ideologies about gender roles are given landscape form. Thus we can look at designs that seclude women in private rooms within traditional Chinese or Iranian houses (Pollock, 1981; Khatib-Chahidi, 1981) or we can examine the evolution of designs of homes in our own cultures that reveal the changing nature of thinking about women's work in the house (Hayden, 1981; Hayden, 1984; Wright, 1981). Indeed, the topic of housing provides many possibil-ities for revealing the central role of gender ideologies in shaping the quality of life. Work on housing and homelessness in Britain, for example, shows how little

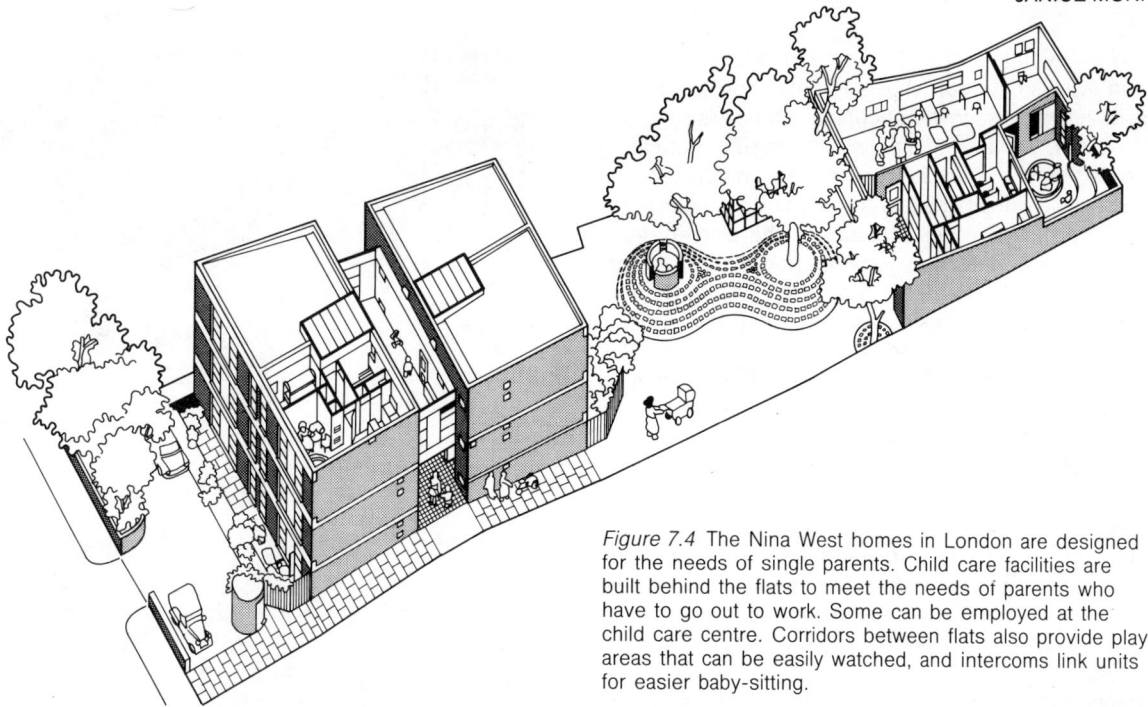

Figure 7.4 The Nina West homes in London are designed for the needs of single parents. Child care facilities are built behind the flats to meet the needs of parents who have to go out to work. Some can be employed at the child care centre. Corridors between flats also provide play areas that can be easily watched, and intercoms link units for easier baby-sitting.

affordable or quality accommodation has been provided by local authorities or the private sector for women who do not or cannot live in nuclear families supported by men (Watson with Austerberry, 1986).

Spatial relationships and spatial behaviour

Geography's basic concern with location means that an obvious way to integrate women and gender issues into the curriculum is to ask where the women are.

Much data, for example Sivard's *Women ... A World Survey* (Sivard, 1985), and many maps – indeed there is now a readily available specialist atlas, *Women of the World* (Seager and Olson, 1986) – now exist to show us where women are located and the spatial aspects of many issues concerning women's lives. The mapping activity on page 100 is a sample of the type of classroom exercises that can be prepared using such data.

But where are women in relation to men? What are the implications of these distributions? Such questions are critical for understanding contemporary changes in industrial location, for instance. Employers' policies of seeking out low-cost flexible female labour affect the global distribution of manufacturing by multi-national corporations, since they recruit young women in the Third World (Nash and Fernandez-Kelly, 1983). They are evident in changing patterns of regional development in Britain (McDowell and Massey, 1984) and in the suburbanisation of clerical work in American metropolitan areas (Nelson, 1986). In each case, new supplies of female labour are being tapped for low-paying jobs and other women are losing their sources of income. In some instances these changes reflect an internationalisation of the gender division of labour.

These examples indicate not only how information on women can be added to the curriculum but also show that we cannot adequately understand contemporary aspects of traditional topics *unless* we incorporate the gender dimension. The necessity for such revisions is widespread. Here I shall focus on examples that deal with human movement, including intra-urban travel in western societies and migration in the Third World.

Intra-urban travel and effective accessibility

Research demonstrates that women's daily travel behaviour in cities differs from men's (Fagnani, 1983; Guiliano, 1979; Hanson and Hanson, 1980; Hanson and Johnston, 1985; Howe and O'Connor, 1982; Madden, 1981). Women have less access to cars, use public transport more, make shorter trips to work, and have different kinds of destinations. They add trips for shopping and household errands to journeys to work, whereas men's non-work trips are principally leisure-related. These studies clearly show how gender roles shape travel and point out how women are disadvantaged as they rely on less convenient modes of transport while fulfilling dual roles as employees and housewives. Some scholars suggest that women choose to work closer to home to accommodate both roles. Others think occupational segregation directs women into jobs which are relatively ubiquitous spatially (primary school teaching, clerical or sales work, for example) and lower paying, so that they have less motivation and means to travel greater distances (Hanson and Johnston, 1985).

Work by Tivers (1985) on women with young children living in London shows in detail how a range of daily activities such as shopping, home visiting, use of parks, and participation in adult education programmes, as well as work in the paid labour force, are spatially constrained by the women's gender roles. She shows how other attributes of the women, such as their social class or type of housing tenure, interact with gender roles to create distinctions among women. Nevertheless, the striking aspect of her study is that it reveals how often gender overrides other variables more traditionally studied. Tivers collected her data by interviewing women about their attitudes and usual activities and by having them keep travel diaries and time budgets for one day. Her work suggests possibilities for class projects that could examine the spatial activities of various family members and of different types of families to explore how ideologies about gender and the gender division of labour in the family affect and constrain movement and access to services. Students could also be asked to propose spatial distributions of services that would serve women more equitably, and to question the appropriateness of gender roles that inequitably constrain women (Monk and Rengert, 1982).

Third World migration

The gender division of labour and the links between production and reproduction are helpful ideas for understanding patterns of male and female migration among Third World people. For example, in many sub-Saharan African countries migration from rural areas has predominantly involved men, whereas in Latin America women tend to outnumber men among migrants to cities (International Center for Research on Women, 1979). The gender divisions of labour in the two regions contrast markedly. In Africa, men were recruited for work in colonial urban centres and also left rural areas for the mines. Women had few opportunities in cities until recently, but had significant roles as farmers. Conversely, migrant women in Latin American cities generally work as domestic servants or sell goods in the streets and markets (see Figure 7.5). They have a lesser role in agriculture (Boserup, 1970). Young (1982) demonstrates how relationships between productive and reproductive work shaped such movements in Mexico. Monetarisation of the economy, development of roads, electricity and piped water supplies, and the introduction of manufactured goods displaced rural women's reproductive work (weaving, making clothes and pottery, and hand-grinding corn) but not men's agricultural work. Displaced women moved to cities to support themselves and contribute to family incomes. The activity on page 102 suggests ways for students to investigate migration movements in Mexico and it highlights the key role that gender plays in these movements.

Figure 7.5 (a) Many Latin American women who migrate to cities make their living selling fruit, vegetables, prepared food, clothing or other small items. Their stock is small, and profits are meagre. Often the women have to care for their children while they work. (b) Others work as domestic servants, cleaning, cooking, laundering, shopping and taking care of their employers' children. They work long hours for low wages.

Critical perspectives

The examples given to date show that we can revise the teaching of traditional topics by incorporating gender perspectives and by adding new topics that illuminate women's lives, thus providing students with an understanding of inequities and a sense that women make valuable contributions to society. A geography teacher sensitive to gender issues and concerned about social change also needs to foster in students critical perspectives that stimulate them to question received wisdom and give them the skills to analyse the values and assumptions underlying sources of information.

At the simplest level, exercises can be introduced that ask students to count the representation of women and men in pictures in their textbooks, to see who is presented as central or peripheral in such illustrations, and to look at whether they have been presented in active or passive roles. Language usage can be analysed in a similar way. Are workers always described as 'he'? Is the 'family farm' presented only as a unit where the farmer and his sons do the work and hand the property down the generations? Is much of the writing in the passive voice, so that sense of human agency is obscured? Several studies demonstrate that sexist biases of these kinds exist in geographic education materials (ILEA, 1984; Larimore, 1978; Monk, 1978; Slater, 1983).

More complex tasks are critical readings designed to reveal whose lives and values are being taken into consideration by the authors of a text or makers of a film. For example, does a chapter on population problems cover themes such as national population policies and the effects of changing health and birth-control technologies on population growth (issues in the 'male' realm of public politics and technology) but neglect to consider how women evaluate their options for support and status in society other than on the basis of the children they bear? Are chapters on the location of economic activities devoted to industries that employ mostly male labour, such as the iron and steel or automobile industries, or does discussion also focus on textile and garment industries, micro-electronics, and clerical work which are major sources of female employment? Are the implications of male versus female preponderence among employees incorporated into analyses?

Questioning sources of information is also important, particularly if we are introducing students to fieldwork. Who should be interviewed? Does one person really represent the household? What difference does it make if a person is interviewed by a member of the same or of the opposite sex? Will we learn what women think if our questions are all closed items based on a literature that has drawn on male experi-ence (Monk and Hanson, 1982)? What is measured by the statistics published in censuses or such indicators as gross national product? Important new resources such as Sivard's statistical and graphical treatment of women around the world (1985) and Seager and Olson's imaginative *Women in the World: An International Atlas* (1986) help us to develop critical perspectives on other data sources, provide up-to-date information on women, and show the kinds of themes that need to be included if we are to represent women's lives.

Conclusion

No geography that hopes to motivate students to create a 'better world' and prepare them to bring that world into being can presume it will achieve its goals if it leaves out half of humanity, fails to challenge gender inequities, and does not show women and girls as valid and valuable sources of information and important contributors to society. To 'engender' the new geography calls for a transformation of our vision, so that we see the world in stereoscopic perspective and create a curriculum that serves the interests of women as well as men. The task will require a substantial effort. The suggestions and practical activities in this chapter are offered to help those who would like to begin.

Activity 1: What counts?

Introduction ➜

Many social statistics available for teaching are inadequate measures of women's life experiences and status. Concepts such as household head, household income, employment, and unemployment as they are widely used mask the nature of women's roles, their work in informal and unpaid sectors, or the unequal division of resources in the household. By introducing students to critical evaluation of statistical measures we can help them to see the values inherent in 'objective' measures and begin to reveal otherwise hidden material about women. Lourdes Beneria (1982) has written an informative article on the ways women's work has been dealt with in statistics. A more detailed resource on improving statistical measures has been published by the United Nations (1984). The Venezualan data in Tables 1 and 2 illustrate the problems of learning about women's work from national censuses. Table 1 lists categories of work identified in a 1982 field study of 105 households on the Caribbean island of Margarita, a tourist resort and free port that is part of Venezuela. (See Monk and Alexander (1986) for more information on gender and employment in Margarita.) Table 2 is an English translation of the occupational categories used in the 1970 Venezuelan census.

Table 1 Village women's work, Margarita Island, Venezuela (1982)

Housework	Housework/seamstress (makes clothes)	Sells clothing on street in nearby town
Cleaner (in government offices)		Housework/works in small family store/makes parts of shoes
Weaves hammocks/seamstress (repairs clothes)	Laundress (operates from home)	
	Teacher	Sells clothing in store
Sells shoes	Street drink-stand operator	Clothing store operator
Housework/sells rabbits	Housework/sells corn	Maid
Shoemaker in home	School cook	Revendedore: retails clothing and housewares (purchased duty free) in streets and to private customers on the island and the mainland
Housework/makes and sells corn bread	Housework/operates small general store in home	
Chambermaid	Housework/rents space in home for small general store	
Housework/crochets portions of hammocks for small manufacturer	Raises chickens and sells direct to consumer	Local government official
Housework/sells soft drinks from home	Housework/operates small fruit and vegetable store	Housework/takes in male boarder
Housework/weaves hammocks		Housework/baby sitting

Table 2 Occupational classifications in the 1970 census of Venezuela

Professional/technical workers	Transport and communication workers
Agents, administrators, directors	Artisans and factory workers
Office employees and kindred workers	Service workers
Salespersons and kindred workers	Others, not identifiable
Agricultural, livestock, fisheries, hunting, forestry etc. workers	Unemployed (identified according to categories above)

Instructions ➜

Give students copies of Tables 1 and 2, then ask them to answer the following questions.
1. Try to assign each of the women represented by the information in Table 1 to one of the categories provided in the census (Table 2).
2. Which kinds of work are easy to assign?
3. Which kinds present problems?
4. How useful is the census list of categories for describing women's work?
5. How would you modify the census classification to give a better description of women's work?

Extension activities ➜

As a follow-up to this exercise, you might ask students to provide information on the work (paid and unpaid, part-time and full-time) of their parents. Then take the categories from your own census and see which of the forms of work identified by the students would be included. How many hours are required of part-time employment, for example, before this work is counted?

Activity 2: Whose place is this?

Retailers and magazine advertisers use landscapes in ways that convey messages about gender, thus helping to shape boys' and girls' views of appropriate roles and behaviour. Analysis of such landscape manipulation can enhance students' understanding of gender socialisation and lead them to question the appropriateness of images presented to them. Student projects have revealed that advertisers disproportionately portray men in active roles in outdoor settings and women in domestic settings, though the tendency to make these distinctions is less today than in magazines of a few years ago. Retailing landscapes vary in their gender orientation, but those geared to women are more likely to use soft colours and furnishings and floral decorations, for example, whereas those serving men use darker colours, tweedy textures, wood panelling, and dark or leather furniture. Age of intended customers also influences design, with little apparent gender distinction in landscapes designed to attract teenagers compared with those serving adults. The former often focus on energy, sportiness, neon and 'hi-tech' decorations.

The following two activities are designed to increase students' understanding of human–environment relationships and to develop skills in observation and analysis.

Shopping landscapes

As a homework assignment tell students to visit a shopping mall or centre. They should observe the landscapes of a variety of shops or departments within stores such as those selling women's dresses, menswear, bridal and maternity wear, sportswear, hardware, books, records/tapes, shoes; and barbers and hairdressers. In preparation you should discuss with them the elements of the landscape they can observe: for example, the use of colour, textures, lighting, wall and floor coverings, furnishings, space use, accessories, and signs. In the field students should record:
(a) descriptions of the landscape elements,
(b) whether the intended customers are male, female or both, and whether they are of a particular age group, and
(c) their personal reactions to each setting, for example like/dislike, comfort/discomfort.

Discuss their observations in class. What generalisations can they make about landscapes designed to serve men, women or those that are 'unisex'? Why do they think landscapes have been designed like this? Review their likes and dislikes, comfort and discomfort in the various settings. Why do they have these reactions? Do they think the distinctions they have observed are appropriate or inappropriate? Why? How would they change these landscapes?

Advertising landscapes

Ask students to bring to class advertisements from magazines that show males and females in various settings, indoors or outdoors. You many wish to specify the magazines to be reviewed and the number of pictures students should collect. In class, tabulate the frequency with which pictures of men only, women only, and mixed groups are shown in indoor or outdoor settings. What conclusions can be drawn from these tabulations? Ask students to describe the outdoor landscapes used as settings for each of the groups. Are men and women shown in active or passive relationship to the outdoor environment? What do these advertisements say about the kinds of places women and men belong and the ways they are expected to behave in different settings? Do the students think the advertisements are appropriate? Why? Or why not?

Activity 3: Mapping education

Introduction ⟶

Higher education opens doors to employment and leadership roles in a society. Which people get this education varies considerably between countries. Factors such as class, race and ethnicity, and rural or urban residence influence the situation, but in different ways in some countries than in others. Gender is a factor that has substantial influence on access to education. This activity is designed to make students aware of the significance of gender as a variable that shapes life opportunities, and to challenge stereotypes they might have about 'developed' and 'underdeveloped' countries. The activity also builds skills in making and interpreting maps.

Instructions ⟶

Table 3 shows the number of women per 100 men enrolled in higher education in the 20–24 year old age group. The figures come from material collected by UNESCO and the table was drawn up by Ruth Sivard (1985). Divide the class into groups and give each group a copy of Table 3. Ask the groups to use the information in the table to make a map, and then to discuss possible causes and consequences of the spatial patterns revealed.
After the maps are complete discuss the following issues in class.

1. In which countries are women *more likely* to be enrolled in higher education than men? Is this the pattern you would have expected? Why? Or why not?
2. In what general regions of the world are the ratios of women to men in higher education the *lowest*? What do you think some of the social, political, and economic consequences of this might be?
3. Are the ratios in 'developed' countries always higher than those in 'less developed' countries? How do the patterns vary? What does this suggest about (a) the relationship between women's opportunities and development, (b) factors, other than economic development, that might influence women's opportunities to participate in higher education?

Comments ⟶

You may wish to have students work in groups to classify the data to reduce time spent on the task. It takes a superior student working alone about two hours to find the countries in an atlas, categorise the statistics, and make the map. If you wish to focus on map making as an important aspect of the activity, discuss with students how to break the data into categories. For example, they could select class intervals that would include an equal number of cases in each category, or they could arbitrarily use value categories such as 0–24, 25–49, 50–74, 75–99, 100 and over. You should discuss the need to keep categories limited (e.g. 4–7 groupings). The class could use one categorisation system, or maps using different categorisations could be compared.

In using this exercise with students I chose to use the arbitrary categorisation noted above. The resulting spatial pattern revealed interesting questions about the relationships between education and development, political systems, and the roles of women and men in different cultures. Some of the patterns did not conform to our expectations. For example, we noted that ratios in some Latin American countries were higher than they were in the United Kingdom, the Netherlands, or Germany. Ratios in Switzerland and Japan were lower than in a number of Middle Eastern countries. Ratios in the Soviet Union were markedly different from those in China. You should also remind students that the data present *gender ratios* within each country. A map showing how many women in a country receive higher education as a percentage of its female population would reveal a different spatial pattern. If you are interested in global patterns of women's education at other levels, see maps and tables in Seager and Olson (1986).

Table 3 Female enrolment rates in higher education (Sivard, 1985)

	Number of women per 100 men		Number of women per 100 men		Number of women per 100 men
WORLD	74	Spain	83	**OCEANIA**	78
• Developed (28)	92	• Sweden	85	• Australia	84
Developing (112)	57	• Switzerland	48	Fiji	43
		• United Kingdom	60	• New Zealand	70
America (24)	82			Papua New Guinea	26
Europe (6)	82	**Eastern Europe & USSR**	101		
Asia (35)	47	Albania	92	**AFRICA**	40
Oceania (2)	31	• Bulgaria	113	Sub-Saharan Africa	28
Africa (45)	40	• Czechoslovakia	74	Other Africa	49
		• Germany, East	141		
AMERICA		• Hungary	107	Algeria	40
North America	107			Angola	..
• Canada	107	• Poland	123	Benin	21
• United States	104	• Romania	74	Botswana	86
		Yugoslavia	83	Burundi	43
Latin America	82			Cameroon	29
Argentina	103	• USSR	100	Central African Rep.	23
Barbados	90			Chad	14
Bolivia	50	**ASIA**		Congo	18
Brazil	116	**Middle East**	49	Egypt	54
Chile	72	Bahrain	62		
		Cyprus	80	Equatorial Guinea	10
Colombia	77	Iran	50	Ethiopia	31
Costa Rica	82	Iraq	56	Gambia	33
Cuba	85	• Israel	104	Ghana	17
Dominican Rep.	92	Jordan	72		
Ecuador	64	Kuwait	122	Guinea	28
		Lebanon	38	Ivory Coast	29
El Salvador	59	Oman	—	Kenya	29
Guatamala	37	Qatar	162	Lesotho	153
Guyana	107	Saudi Arabia	38	Liberia	34
Haiti	43	Syria	50		
Honduras	69	Turkey	36	Libya	30
		United Arab Emir.	93	Madagascar	54
Jamaica	73	Yemen, Arab Rep.	17	Malawi	26
Mexico	53	Yemen, P.Dm. Rep.	51	Mali	18
Nicaragua	58			Mauritania	23
Panama	120	**South Asia**	37	Mauritius	41
Paraguay	80	Afghanistan	22	Morocco	38
		Bangladesh	22	Mozambique	44
Peru	54	India	38	Niger	23
Trinidad & Tobago	67	Nepal	26	Nigeria	24
Uruguay	113	Pakistan	36		
Venezuela	91	Sri Lanka	62	Rwanda	20
				Senegal	34
EUROPE		**Far East**	59	Sierra Leone	19
Western Europe	76	Brunei	..	Somalia	20
• Austria	78	Burma	96	South Africa	..
• Belgium	80	Cambodia	—		
• Denmark	98	China	36	Sudan	43
• Finland	97	Indonesia	46	Swaziland	107
• France	85	• Japan	50	Tanzania	23
		Korea, North	..	Togo	23
• Germany, West	72	Korea, South	38	Tunisia	51
Greece	65	Laos	47		
• Iceland	57	Malaysia	64	Uganda	39
• Ireland	68	Mongolia	142	Upper Volta	32
• Italy	81	Philippines	120	Zaire	23
		Singapore	78	Zambia	18
• Luxembourg	40	Thailand	85	Zimbabwe	57
Malta	25	Vietnam	37		
• Netherlands	72				
• Norway	95				
Portugal	90				

• Developed countries   — None or negligible   .. Not available

Activity 4: Mexicans on the move

Introduction ⟶

Many studies of migration are inadequate because they fail to consider gender, discuss only male migrants, or assume that if women migrate it is because they move with their husbands. Recent research demonstrates, however, marked regional differences in patterns of rural-to-urban and international migration by males and females. These differences reflect gender distinctions in the division of labour and ideologies about appropriate gender roles.

This activity draws on research from Mexico (Rengert, 1981; Young, 1982) to show how the gender division of labour and changes in reproductive work resulting from economic development have created a situation in which girls between 10 and 19 years of age from poor families are more likely to leave rural communities for Mexico City than boys. Males who migrate from these communities are more likely to be in their 20s, come from families that are better of, and go to places other than Mexico City.

The activity is suitable for units on migration or development. It provides an opportunity for students to analyse written material and to empathise with the conflicts and complexities that people face in making decisions.

Instructions ⟶

Ask students to read the information on the Sanchez family (page 103), then divide the class into small groups and give each group the following assignments. When these are complete, organise a general class discussion of the answers.

1. Make a list of the Sanchez's children who have left San Felipe, and a list of those who have stayed. What ages were the children when they left?
2. What differences can you see in the migration patterns of the boys and girls?
3. If you were Teresa and Miguel, would you want Ricardo to stay in San Felipe or to leave? Would you send Carmen to Mexico City? What reasons would you give to each of them?
4. Imagine you are Carmen. Do you think you should go to the city like your sisters? Do you think you would have a better life in the village or in the city?
5. Imagine you are Ricardo. Try to persuade your parents why you should be allowed to leave.
6. How do you think opportunities might be improved in the city for Maria, Rosalinda, and Luisa?

Variation ⟶

As an alternative, you may wish to prepare a role-playing activity, using the reading material to develop roles for members of the Sanchez family as they try to reach decisions about whether Carmen and Ricardo should leave.

Figure 7.6 (a) A young immigrant to Hermosillo preparing food for sale at a street stand.
(b) A teenage immigrant providing child-care facilities

Student reading: the Sanchez family

Teresa and Miguel Sanchez have seven children, all born in the Mexican village of San Felipe. Two of their three sons live in the village. Ricardo, at 18 the youngest son, lives at home. He left school at 15 and works with his father on the family's small piece of land. From time to time he also picks up jobs as a builder's labourer. Juan, 25, and the eldest, is recently married. He lives with his wife's family and drives a truck that brings soft drinks, canned foods, corn meal, beans and other supplies to the village. Ramon, the middle son, is now 22. He went to the nearest town when he was 18 and has a job as a night watchman. Ramon stayed at school till he was 16, and was able to get his job through the family of one of his teachers.

Three of the Sanchez's daughters live in Mexico City. Maria, now 23, left school at 11 to help her mother with housework and with the younger children, then at 14 went to the city for a live-in job as a maid with a family with which her cousin used to work. Now she is married and trying to find enough employment sewing at home so that she and her husband can afford to rent a room for themselves and their two children, sharing a house with his relatives. Rosalinda is 20. She wanted to be a teacher, but, like Maria, also left San Felipe after she finished primary school to work as a live-in servant. She still has ambition for a better job, perhaps working in a shop, but doesn't have enough education or the chance to get any more education because of the long hours she spends at her work. Luisa is 16. She left home when she was 13 to live with Maria. She helps Maria with the children and also babysits for several other families.

Carmen, the Sanchez's youngest child, is 13. Miguel and Teresa are not sure whether to send her to Mexico City. She is very attached to her parents, and likes the outdoor farm life. Her parents wonder what future the village holds for her. Ricardo would like to leave, but it is very hard for men with a village education to find even low-skilled jobs in the city. They need better education, good connections, and references. The Sanchezes expect Ricardo to take over more of his father's work on the land in the future. Miguel and Teresa have seen many changes in their lifetime in the village. When Teresa was young her mother used to spend hours every day grinding corn, and also had to haul water, weave and make their clothing, and make pottery for household use. Gradually life has changed. Now much of the food comes to the village already processed, ready-made clothes and material are available, and it is easier to carry water in plastic buckets from a nearby tap than it used to be in the old days when it had to be brought a long distance. But it is not easy to make money in San Felipe. Other than work on the land, there are only a few jobs: for teachers, with the government (for example, with the police or maintaining the roads and water supply), in construction, or bringing goods to the village and selling them.

8 Limits to geography: a feminist perspective

JANE WILLIAMSON-FIEN

Teaching geography for a better world involves a vision of a just society and an obligation to achieve that vision both in and through education. More specifically, it implies a belief that geography curricula are sufficiently flexible, or can be reformed adequately, to provide students with the necessary skills and knowledge to see where injustices lie and take action to eradicate them. In the light of such commitments, the position of women and the role of patriarchy in determining that position should be addressed in geography. What is less clear is whether the parameters of the discipline will allow this to occur. Two schools of thought exist here. The integrationist school takes the nature of geography as given and argues that justice for women can be achieved through the apparently simple mechanism of making existing curricula more inclusive of women's issues and concerns. A feminist perspective, on the other hand, is far less sanguine. It sees the necessity to question not only the content of geography courses but also the nature of existing geographical techniques and perspectives. Given the nature of patriarchy and its implications in geography, a feminist approach argues that justice for women can only be achieved through the development of feminised forms of knowledge which, though willing to use geographical insights, may bear little resemblance to the existing discipline of geography.

It may be more comfortable for many geographers, well-versed in male definitions of the world, to see the integrationist approach as providing justice for women since it fits reasonably into the existing disciplinary framework provided a little fine tuning is undertaken. However, this chapter suggests that the adoption of a feminist perspective has more potential to address the issue of injustices towards women and is more likely to engender a critical consideration of the processes of education generally.

Before a specific consideration of the integrationist and feminist perspectives, two points need to be emphasised. Arguably, these points will encourage the rejection of the old comfortable geographical position in favour of a new, if potentially unsettling, feminist approach. Firstly, geography has only ever provided a partial view of the world. It is neither god-given, value-free nor objective. Rather, it is historically and socially constructed (Harvey, 1984) and, as such, is both a manifestation and an instrument of the dominant ideologies of our society, namely patriarchy and capitalism. It is doubtful, therefore, whether geography is capable of posing questions on issues that lie beyond the purview of these ideologies. As Moira Gatens (1986) has observed with respect to the possibility of feminism in philosophy, what is important is not *what questions are not asked*, but, *what questions cannot be asked*. Similarly, in the context of Marxism and geography, Michael Eliot Hurst (1985) notes:

> In determining what is included geographers have also determined what is excluded! Excluded have been 'imperialism', 'class', 'capital', and all the Marxist conceptions that surround mode of production, ideology, and social formation. Included are 'space', 'environment', 'free market system', 'culture', and the cartographic display of such data.

He concludes that 'day-to-day geography' is both explicitly and implicitly ideological. It is also essentially a closed discourse confined:

> . . . to a limited domain of social reality and is unable to produce knowledge of anything outside this domain. Thus geographers can produce knowledge which is descriptive of 'spatial patterns', but they cannot give us knowledge of how these patterns are generated, and thus are severely constrained in advancing our understanding of the world (Eliot Hurst, 1985).

Secondly, it is important to emphasise that feminism is not merely for and about women. It is also about men and is genuinely visionary. As Hester Eisenstein (1984) has noted, feminism:

> . . . encompasses a concept of social transformation that, as a result of the eventual liberation of women, will change all human relationships for the better. Although centrally about women, their experience, condition or 'estate' . . . feminism is therefore also fundamentally about men and social change.

Feminists see social change as achievable via the identification and subversion of patriarchal structures. One such structure is the division of society into two distinct spheres: the *public* arena associated with institutionalised power, paid employment, religion, culture and men, and the *private* or *domestic* sphere – the emotional, particularistic world of women. These are not separate and equal spheres, however, as overwhelmingly it is the masculine world that is perceived to be important and to constitute the legitimate area of enquiry. Recognition of the public–private framework may provide a useful starting point for considering the condition of women, but its limitations as a phallocentric interpretation of reality are readily identifiable. For example, the public–private dichotomy not only discourages any focus on women, it also systematically places women's activities outside mainstream theory (Pateman, 1986; Thiele, 1986) and consequently denies the contributions that women make both to and in the so-called masculine public world (Davidoff, 1979; Game and Pringle, 1984). Small wonder that feminists see mainstream theory as constituting the *malestream* (O'Brien, 1981) – and how ironical that feminists are sometimes perceived to be introducing harmful separatist tendencies into theoretical investigations!

omissions, perceiving themselves redundant in the long term.

At its most superficial level, integration involves piecemeal tinkering with the curriculum. The implication is that sexism can be eradicated fairly quickly with goodwill and a few additional resources. This view of the problem is reflected in the comments of an American male feminist before his enlightenment:

> Sexism seemed infinitely less insidious than racism and far easier to overcome. All we needed was to be told what we were doing wrong and we would be happy to correct it. After all, what was involved? A more humane, sharing attitude wasn't exactly something one could argue against, and adopting one seemed easy enough to those of us who already felt we'd spent most of the '60s combating racism. At work, equal pay was eminently sensible and didn't affect our pocketbooks. At home, shared childcare seemed something we wanted in any case, and what was the big deal in doing the dishes once in a while? (Wetzsteon, 1979)

Much anti-sexist education and many well-meaning initiatives in geography classrooms have stemmed from the mistaken belief that a few marginal changes will dispose of sexism in education and, ultimately, in society. But what has really been achieved in terms of student awareness of patriarchal structures by the scramble to sit girls in front of computers, the inclusion of women in the keys of maps, or even the introduction of sex-neutral language? While some educationalists may argue that political pressures prevent a more thorough-going consideration of women's condition, these pressures need to be recognised for what they are: manifestations of the structures of patriarchy which will continue to

The integrationist approach

Louise Johnson (1985) describes the integrationist approach as 'putting women in'. Essentially, the proponents of integration have adopted the optimistic view that women will be conceptualised as the *equals* of men once existing discourses are inclusive of the activities, interests and concerns of women. This implies a pre-commitment to existing theoretical concerns, including current educational and epistemological frameworks, and integration is consequently ameliorative rather than transformative in character. Integrationists rarely dwell on why the omission of women existed in the first place (Allen, 1986). Instead, they concentrate their efforts on rectifying the

Figure 8.1 Women's condition: unrecorded

dominate and oppress while few people are willing to expose them (Figure 8.1). Pressure is needed for more significant and systematic changes to overcome the complacent notion that doing something is better than doing nothing. Indeed, doing little may be more dangerous than doing nothing for it implies that something positive is being achieved when, in reality, failure to address the enormity of the problem prevents the search for a real solution.

Integration and geography

To date, work undertaken on women by geographers has been overwhelmingly integrationist in character and, although it has been more systematic than piecemeal, and consequently more intellectually and educationally satisfying, it still lacks a critical focus. Patriarchal working assumptions remain intact as, for example, in the two reasons normally provided to explain the general absence, until recently, of a focus on women in geography. Wilbur Zelinsky, Janice Monk and Susan Hanson (1982) argue that this was because women were not 'prominent in the landscape' and, hence, 'the geographer's curiosity about the unchartered, but potentially no less important, worlds of half of humanity' has been stunted. The second explanation emphasises the fact that there have been few female geographers in the tertiary educational sector and, consequently, the geographical agenda has been dominated by male interests. It is expected that this situation will change when more women are absorbed into the discipline (Monk and Hanson, 1982; Women and Geography Study Group of the IBG, 1984). Both these assessments implicitly accept the legitimacy and paramount importance of the public sphere. Thus, in the first case, women were ignored because they were not visibly part of the public domain while, in the second instance, women can only expect to become important as more of them are incorporated into the public sphere. The presumption that female academics are bound, by virtue of their status in the public sphere, to promote the interests of women generally also needs to be queried. As Dorothy Smith (1978) notes, women in power

> . . . do not ordinarily represent women's perspectives. . . They are those whose work and style of work and conduct have met the approval of judges who are largely men.

The implicit messages of the integrationists contrast with their stated intention of promoting multiple perspectives to replace the 'single male as norm' approach (Maher, 1985). This pluralist vision implies the recognition of gender as a variable and the subsequent incorporation of the world of women into existing curricula with new areas of content opened up for exploration. For example, a consideration of 'domestic interiors and symbolic uses of space . . . indicates how the horizons of cultural geography might be extended' (Monk and Hanson, 1982). Similarly, geography

> . . . could profit from assessing the effects of the availability of such facilities as shopping areas, day care, medical services, recreation and transport on female labor-force participation and on labor in the home. (Monk and Hanson, 1982)

Although attractive, there are major problems associated with these new content areas. Firstly, some geographers imply that the extension of geography to incorporate new topics on women will not be easy. Thus, *Geography and Gender* (Women and Geography Study Group of the IBG, 1984) concludes with the challenge that geography nees to 'break out of established subdivisions and specialisms' otherwise 'certain sets of social and spatial relations are in danger of being overlooked'. *Geography and Gender* indicates some links between women and conventional geographical studies, but fails to demonstrate how the 'break out' is to be achieved. Secondly, while the public–private split remains unquestioned, it is not clear who is going to opt for consideration of private spaces over the apparently more important public arena. In these circumstances, even if domestic interiors, etc. are inserted into geography curricula, they are destined to be perceived as soft options, lacking the validity of hard core areas such as economic geography. Finally, although investigation of domestic spaces and access to facilities are undeniably geographical in orientation, none of these topics encourages a consideration of why women are associated with domestic environments, work in the home, shopping centres and day care! Commenting on the work of Jacqueline Tivers (1978), Jo Foord (1980) notes:

> Geographical studies centred on women (such as studies of journey to work/shop and comparisons of differential behaviour patterns) tend to reinforce 'expected' roles of male and female partners in the family unit. Women are seen, in such studies, only as 'household surrogates' and 'extensions of their families' engaged in the 'unpaid duty' of domestic labour.

Ultimately, integrationists may be doing little more than lending support to the status quo – and where is the justice for women in that?

Inevitably, integrationists are confined to the consideration of content. It could hardly be otherwise, for to question the fundamental concepts and approaches of geography would threaten the legitimacy of integrationists as spokespeople for the discipline. Some attempts have been made, nevertheless, to assess the broader curriculum implications of integration. Janice Monk (1983), for example, asserts the need for a 'transformation of the curriculum which involves the revision of theories, concepts and methodologies to reflect the experiences of women as well as men'. Precisely how this transformation will take place is never made clear, but the presumption appears to be that the new research on women, and the new geographical content so generated, will automatically inform and promote fundamental curriculum changes. If this interpretation of the argument is correct, the argument itself must be seen as illogical. New research on women in geography remains predicated on existing geographical theories and concerns and, as such, it is unlikely to provide information that will fundamentally alter geographical perspectives and approaches in academia or in classrooms. Thus, Louise Johnson (1985) has criticised the study undertaken by Anna Howe and Kevin O'Connor (1982), on the travel to work and labour force participation of men and women in Melbourne because, despite isolating women's experience for particular attention, they still defined the problem as a spatial one with a corresponding spatial solution. A similar problem emerges in *Geography and Gender* (Women and Geography Study Group of the IBG, 1984). Here, the authors are at great pains to explore the bases of both radical and socialist feminist analyses and, yet, the text slips back into a consideration of women in the context of conventional geographical subject areas; feminist perspectives remain peripheral to the discussion.

It would be unfair to deny integrationists any place in the debate on women and justice. After all, in some instances the adoption of the integrationist position may be seen as logically prior to the development of a feminist perspective (Gatens, 1986) and, indeed, many feminists recognise that their current approach has been reached via the integrationist position (Gatens, 1986; Gross, 1986, Williamson-Fien, 1986). Nevertheless, fundamental problems remain with the integrationist position because it confuses 'ends' with 'means' and thereby demonstrates either a naivety about where the power lies in our society or an unwillingness to confront it. Knowing about where women are, how they interact with their environments, what access they have to particular facilities, etc. must not be seen as ends in themselves, but as preludes to the posing of more critical questions relating to why women are confined to specific areas, why women might accept those areas as theirs and why those areas are associated with powerlessness. To refuse to come to grips with issues such as these is to confirm the legitimacy of existing power structures and to promote, albeit unwittingly, continued injustice towards women. Feminists would argue that solutions to the issue of justice for women do not lie in the structures currently constituting male power and that what is needed is a complete recasting of knowledge (Johnson, 1985).

The feminist approach

The central concerns of feminism are women as socially programmed, i.e. gendered, individuals and the patriarchal structures that create, reinforce and reproduce women's gendered identities. One manifestation of those structures is the current organisational framework of knowledge, including geography. Feminism reverses the priorities accepted by the integrationists in which women are objects of geographical investigation and argues, instead, that women's social experiences constitute the starting point with geography itself a potential object of investigation (see Gatens, 1986; Gross, 1986). Thus, a feminist approach to justice for women consists of an open-ended non-terminating critique of the epistemological status quo. Yet feminism seeks to be more than merely reactive, for the critique also emphasises where current and future research should begin. As Elizabeth Gross (1986) notes, feminism should be seen as a *strategy* rather than an immutable *theory*, a means 'of intervention into systems of power in order to subvert them and replace them with others more preferable'. More preferable structures would insure women's right to justice through autonomy (Gross, 1986), for women to be acceptable as women. Equality for women under existing structures only allows for women to be like men, and pale reflections at that (Thornton, 1986; Gatens, 1986).

A feminist approach has obvious implications for what counts as knowledge, what is taught in schools and how it is taught. Feminists recognise knowledge as socially created and that it is impossible, even undesirable, to create unadulterated feminist knowledge. While feminists have no commitment to the frameworks or assumptions of existing disciplines, they recognise that the disciplines, and their attendent methodologies, may have *tactical* value once women's social experiences have become central to the agenda (Gross, 1986). That is, geography and other disciplines have no primacy in terms of the questions asked, but some of their insights and techniques may have potential usefulness.

A feminist approach to education is also concerned with the general orientation of the curriculum and classroom practices. There is little point in attempting the difficult task of reconceptualising knowledge if the means by which it is to be presented to students are still suffused with patriarchal assumptions and attitudes. A feminist pedagogy is needed if justice for women is to be achieved. Some characteristics of such an approach are outlined below, together with an example of how a feminist perspective might structure the teaching of one sample topic, that of women's work and leisure.

Feminist pedagogy

Feminist pedagogy necessitates an awareness of classroom climate and, in particular, the way that girls and female experiences generally are devalued in that context. As Frances Maher (1985) expresses it:

> Women are silenced, objectified and made passive through both course content and the pedagogical style of . . . most classrooms.

A feminist pedagogy should enable both students and teachers to identify and resist the oppression of girls in the classroom and outside it. A three-fold strategy is suggested here as the means by which an immediate start may be undertaken. Firstly, teachers need to familiarise themselves with feminist literature and debate (see Oakley, 1982; Evans, 1982), concentrating specifically on the impact of patriarchal structures and attitudes in education (see Spender, 1982; Stanworth, 1983). To avoid feelings of isolation, frustration and the risks of constantly 'reinventing the wheel', teachers need to look for support and assistance from other feminist teachers and feminist activists outside education. Armed with information and backed by other like-minded people, feminist teachers can begin the long process of raising the consciousness of other educationalists and community members generally.

Secondly, teachers should start to take their female students seriously (Rich, 1979). Michelle Stanworth's (1983) evidence suggests that:

> . . . girls exist on the periphery of classroom life; their marginalisation in the classroom and the lesser attention they receive from teachers, results in girls appearing to others – and more importantly to themselves – as less capable than they really are.

Overcoming these problems involves teachers in not only monitoring their own attitudes towards their female students but also in engaging in positive action, even positive discrimination, in favour of those students. As Adrienne Rich (1979) puts it, teachers must ask themselves how women can be persuaded to move beyond the desire for male approval and learn to seek out and write about their own truths which culture has distorted or made taboo. She concludes:

> We can refuse to accept passive, obedient learning and insist on critical thinking. We can become harder on our women students, giving them the kinds of 'cultural prodding' that men receive, but on different terms and in a different style. Most young women need to have their intellectual lives, their work, legitimized against the claims of family, relationships, the old message that woman is always available for service to others. We need to keep our standards very high, not to accept a woman's preconceived sense of her limitations; we need to be hard to please, while supportive of risk-taking, because self-respect often comes only when exacting standards have been met. (Rich, 1979)

Significantly, Adrienne Rich's message should not be seen as merely encouraging girls to compete and thereby 'achieve' in the public domain like boys. Rather, the message is that girls, given appropriate teacher attitudes and actions, can move towards a position of positively valuing themselves, a position of autonomy. There will of course be those people who perceive problems when one group of students is treated differently from the other group. Committed teachers need to take a stand on this because adopting a particular perspective with girls does not necessarily mean that less effort will be put into the education of boys. Besides, the need to counter sexism, to expose patriarchy, has come about precisely because girls have been treated differently!

Thirdly, feminist pedagogy involves the adoption of appropriate teaching strategies. Frances Maher (1985) suggests that these must be collaborative, and interactive, facilitating the creation of co-operative learning environments. In order to make learning student-centred and on task, feminist teachers cannot rely on existing data sources, textbooks, teaching resources and packages, many of which emphasise, reinforce and perpetuate patriarchal values (Monk, 1978; ILEA, 1984; Wright, 1985). Rather, teaching must be geared to 'delegitimise' the information in such resources by the unveiling and evaluating of women's social experiences. Feminist teaching strategies, therefore, revolve around the collection, analysis and assessment of data on women, to expose and subvert patriarchal structures. This means utilising and incorporating the experiences of female students and other women into teaching programmes, emphasising student-based research and action, and locating the 'classroom' in the community, among women. In this context, many geographical and social science survey and field study techniques may prove useful.

Obviously, teaching that focuses on women's social experiences may alarm and antagonise male students, although girls have long been expected to accept male experiences as universal. It would be foolish to disregard this problem. Nevertheless, teaching programmes that emphasise the association of women's experiences with those of men, may help to allay male fears. For example, investigations focusing on women factory workers must ask why they are found overwhelmingly on the assembly line or in the typing pool, while men occupy the management positions (see Massey, 1984). Such investigations may not always be seen as complementary to men. However, a feminist approach would not, indeed could not, ignore the situation of men in the same way that existing discourses are structured to avoid consideration of women.

Feminist pedagogy, as Margo Culley and Catherine Portuges (1985) point out, challenges 'the economic, socio-political, cultural and psychological imperatives based on gender', and, in the process of applying feminist principles in the classroom, it has the potential 'for reconstructing and revitalizing the ways in which knowledge is acquired, sanctioned and perpetuated'. Further, it should not be viewed as the means to enforce feminist ideology but as the vehicle to empassion students with feminist knowledge (Raymond, 1979–80). Feminist teachers do not claim neutrality; they care passionately about their subject matter and, by caring, they assist their students to make the journey towards self-defined integrity (Raymond, 1979–80).

Feminising knowledge: women, work and leisure

Work is depicted in geography, as in other disciplines, to be synonymous with the male–public sphere, paid employment and so-called marketable skills. 'Real work' is seen to be closely linked with the production of material goods, for example in agriculture and industry, while the tertiary sector in which many women are employed is often omitted from consideration (see ILEA, 1984). Leisure constitutes the other side of the coin. It is identified as relaxation, as what occurs after work has finished or in spare time, and it is most frequently associated with the private sphere, particularly the home and its environs. Significantly, geography has rarely come to terms with the issue of leisure unless it becomes a component of the public arena via such enterprises as the tourist industry (see Prosser, 1982) or organised male sport (see Bale 1982).

Such definitions have implications for women. They suggest, for example, that women cannot be taken seriously as workers in the public sphere and, because the home is a place of leisure rather than work, the 'activities' that women undertake there cannot be construed as work. One result of such dicta is that girls learn to be 'non-workers'. They may drop subjects at school that might enhance their 'job prospects' and consequently find themselves, when circumstances demand it, in the lowest paid, least secure and most undesirable forms of paid employment (see Sharpe, 1976; Spender, 1982; Roberts, 1986). As 'non-workers', girls are persuaded that they need to attract men to work for them (Spender's (1982) interviews with girls are illuminating in this respect) and, if they are forced to find employment after marriage, they may still question whether they are entitled to it (Pollert, 1981).

Patriarchal definitions of work and leisure are also painfully confusing and contradictory for women. For example, girls probably accept, consciously or unconsciously, the notion that 'women don't work, and if they do they shouldn't'. Yet, girls must also be aware that their mothers and other female relatives work extremely hard at both paid and unpaid employment, that these women need an extraordinary range of skills, and frequently sustain longer working hours than their male relatives. At one level, therefore, girls know that women work, but at the same time they are being told, and appear to accept, that women do not work. Similar problems arise with the concept of leisure. If leisure is what occurs in the home, then are the activities that women do there a form of leisure? If the home is a place of work for women, then where are they to relax? What are appropriate leisure activities for them? As the one Women's Advisory Council has put it:

> . . . housewives cannot stop work, down tools and go home. . . For many housewives, whose work at home allows their families to have leisure at home, home may become a place where . . . (they) cannot relax, since the working day never seems to end. (New South Wales Women's Advisory Council, 1980)

The injustices and difficulties that women face in the context of work and leisure cannot be confronted and overcome while existing patriarchal definitions of work and leisure remain the unquestioned initial position. Instead, the starting point must be the work and leisure experiences of women themselves. (The practical activity on pages 112–16 indicates ways that the process of exploring women's work and leisure activities may be begun.) Once the spotlight has been turned onto women, once knowledge has been feminised, three areas of discussion emerge for consideration: the need for new definitions, the means by which existing definitions have been maintained, and the actions that need to be taken to change the current situation. A consideration of these issues should provide a basis for further activities after those on pages 112–16 have been completed.

The first issue concerns definitions of work and leisure. Any examination of women's work and leisure experiences quickly indicates that existing explanations of the nature of such activities only fit the male experience. It is necessary, therefore, to develop new ways of considering these concepts. For example, work is not merely income generating; it is also expenditure saving. The unpaid work that women do in the home is expenditure saving as anyone who has had to pay for home help or baby-sitting will testify. Hanna Papanek (1981) has noted the paradoxical nature of women's work: it is seen to be worth little, but substitutes for it are very expensive! Additionally, as consumers, women are not simply the passive end of the productive process. Shopping for food and other regular items, for example, is not a leisure activity despite the attempts of advertisers to paint it as such. It involves considerable planning, exertion and skilled management of time and money. Feminists are increasingly denoting such activities as consumption work (Weinbaum and Bridges, 1976; Game and Pringle, 1983). Reconceptualising what is meant by 'work' also requires recognition of the amount of paid work that women undertake in their homes in the forms of washing and ironing, child-minding, paying guests, outwork, etc. Paid work has never been confined to the public sphere. Sarah and Fugen (1982) have estimated, for example, that there were 400 000 paid homeworkers in Britain in 1982. Finally, any attempt to rewrite the definitions of work and leisure has to address the issue of skills. One of the enduring aspects of patriarchal ideology is that virtually any man, or even an adolescent, can undertake the sort of tasks a woman does in the home, so unskilled are the porcesses involved. While it may be the case that an element of deskilling is occurring in the domestic arena (Game and Pringle, 1983), it remains true that the effective operation of modern household technology requires many skills, perhaps more than in many of the jobs currently undertaken by men in paid employment.

The second issue is the question of why existing definitions of work and leisure have been maintained, even promoted, while they reflect only a partial male view of reality. Central to this discussion is the question of power, the conscious or unconscious power of men, and the means by which patriarchy can persuade both men and women that the dichotomy between public–male and private–female spheres is natural and desirable. At issue here are the processes of socialisation via received tradition, schooling, the media, advertising, etc. which continually institutionalise and reproduce the balance of power in favour of men and perpetuate injustices for women. The issue of patriarchal power means that questions relating to work and leisure need to be seen as specific aspects of a much broader problem.

The third issue focuses on the actions that need to be taken to undermine patriarchy and promote justice for women both in the context of work and leisure, and at a more general level. Arguably, the mere fact that

consciousness has now been raised will do much to reduce the potency and apparent naturalness of patriarchy and encourge girls to think more radically about their position. Paulo Freire (1970) has argued, for example, that for the oppressed to be liberated, their experiences have to be raised to the level of consciousness, then recognised and affirmed (see Maher, 1985). But, knowledge of oppression does not necessarily engender change, and critical consideration needs to be given to the efficacy of specific strategies currently promoted by feminists to achieve change. Such strategies include: payment for housework (Prescott, 1985); an independent income for all women regardless of household labour (see the Wageless Women's Charter in Parker, 1982); and suggestions that decreasing male working hours without reducing income may encourage men to undertake more domestic labour (Phillips, 1983).

These investigations and analyses certainly do not look too much like conventional geography, and yet it is possible to ask what geography might contribute to them. Feminist enquiries may alight on a particular aspect of women's social experiences that has a geographical component. For example, consider the following quotation:

> The undermining of self, of a woman's sense of her right to occupy space and walk freely in the world, is deeply relevant to education. The capacity to think independently, to take intellectual risks, to assert ourselves mentally, is inseparable from our physical way of being in the world, our feelings of personal integrity. If it is dangerous for me to walk home late of an evening from the library, because I am a woman and I can be raped, how self-possessed, how exuberant can I feel as I sit working in that library? How much of my working energy is drained by the subliminal knowledge that, as a woman, I test my physical right to exist each time I go out alone? (Rich, 1979)

Among the issues raised here are the existence of environments of fear and the impact they have on women's intellectual integrity and capacity to work. These questions are not to be answered by alternative approaches to architecture, town planning or the provision of more lighting in car parks. Instead, investigations must focus on the structures that create fear and persuade women not to frequent particular areas at certain times. In this context, it may be useful to undertake geographical studies into the character of environments of fear and where they are located, in order to ascertain how the structures that created such places might be undermined (see Women and Geography Group of the IBG, 1984; Matrix, 1984).

Conclusion

One of the difficulties of addressing the issue of justice for women is, as Kay Daniels (1985) has noted, that it is easy to see what is wrong but often hard to determine how to get to what is right. This chapter has suggested that part of the problem stems from the assumption that injustices against women can be confronted and the problems solved within existing disciplinary frameworks. The reality is otherwise. Geography, like all the other orthodox disciplines, is a creation of patriarchy and capitalism. Of itself, it *cannot* ask the questions that will expose the structures oppressing women and, consequently, attempts to provide justice by integrating women's concerns into existing geography curricula do little more than validate the status quo. What is needed is a feminist approach. Such a strategy focuses on women as patriarchally shaped individuals; it reorientates both classroom and teaching procedures, while retaining the right to use geographical techniques and insights when and where appropriate. A feminist approach exposes patriarchy and investigates the means by which it can be undermined.

It may not be easy to accept that geography has limitations. This is particularly true for people who care about their subject and who may be reluctant to accept that it cannot fully address issues of social equity. Nevertheless, it is precisely because so many geographers and geography teachers care about justice that it is possible to suggest that radical changes are necessary.

Activity 1: Women, work and leisure

Introduction

It is still widely assumed that 'women don't work and if they do they shouldn't'. This renders women's work invisible and confuses our female students as to their probable futures. It also grossly undervalues the direct contribution that women make to productive capacity, while providing no recognition of the double burden that many women face as labourers in both the *public* wage economy and the *private* domestic economy.

Similarly, notions that work occurs outside the home and that consequently home is associated with relaxation and leisure, causes further difficulties for women. For example, if leisure is what occurs in the home, then is the work women do there really a form of leisure? If home is a place of work for women then where are they to relax? What are appropriate leisure activities for women? Creating an environment of relaxation for others may mean that many women cannot relax at home, since the working day never seems to end.

This activity encourages students to revise their definition of work so that it includes both income-generating and expenditure-saving activities by exploring the appropriateness of the dichotomies of work/non-work and work/home through a study of the lives of women textile workers. The activity also uses information that students collect on the work and leisure activities of their mothers. By reflecting on the nature and scope of the work and leisure activities of these women, students are challenged to draw more general conclusions about female work and leisure.

Objectives

1. To examine the nature of female work and leisure.

2. To explore the range of duties undertaken by women in a typical working day, the conditions in which they work and the types of skills demanded of them.

3. To evaluate their own feelings about the nature of women's work and leisure.

Instructions

1. Divide the class into groups of two or three students. Ask each group to study Figure 8.2, which is an advertisement for a job, and answer the following questions:
   (a) Is the position being advertised a highly skilled one? Why/why not?
   (b) (i) What sort of people might apply for the position?
       (ii) Why do you think such people would apply for the position?
       (iii) What do you think they might expect to get out of this position?
   (c) Would you apply for this position if you were looking for a job? Why/why not?
   (d) Do you think at some stage in your future you might have a job like this? Why/why not?

2. After students have completed the questions, hear the responses from the groups. Debrief and make sure the students are aware that the position advertised was for a housewife. A thorough debriefing should allow discussion on problems that students may have with the idea of advertising for a housewife, for example: being a housewife is not a job, it is not done for pay. Additionally, it will enable you to explore differences in responses between boys and girls, whether girls are confused about their future expectations, the range of skills demanded of housewives, the work conditions, etc.

3. Ask students to study Figures 8.3 and 8.4. Figure 8.3 shows a day in the life of Helga, a textile worker in 1931. Figure 8.4 contains the story of Maria who is a modern-day

textile worker. Students should be assigned the following tasks.
(a) Examine Figure 8.3 and estimate the hours Helga spent.
   (i) doing housework
   (ii) travelling to and from work
   (iii) working in the factory
   (iv) sleeping and resting
   (v) engaging in leisure activities
   (vi) working in one way or another.
(b) Working in couples and using the clock graph in Figure 8.3 as your model, draw a similar graph of a day in the life of Maria. The story in Figure 8.4 gives you some information, but you will need to hypothesise about the rest.

Position Vacant

Applications are invited for the position of manager of a lively team of four demanding individuals of differing needs and personalities. The successful applicant will be required to perform and coordinate the following functions: companion, counsellor, financial manager, buying officer, teacher, nurse, chef, nutritionist, decorator, cleaner, driver, childcare supervisor, social secretary and recreation officer.

Qualifications: Applicants must have unlimited drive and the strongest sense of responsibility if they are to succeed in this job. They must be independent and self-motivated, and be able to work in isolation and without supervision. They must be skilled in the management of people of all ages. They must be able to work under stress, for long periods of time if necessary. They must have flexibility to perform a number of conflicting tasks at the one time without tiring. They must have the adaptability to handle all new developments in the life of the team, including emergencies and serious crises.

They must be able to communicate on a range of issues with people of all ages, including public servants, school teachers, doctors, dentists, tradespeople, business people, teenagers and children. They must be competent in the practical skills listed above. They must be healthy, creative, active and outgoing to encourage the physical and social development of the team members. They must have imagination, sensitivity, warmth, love and understanding since they are responsible for the mental and emotional well-being of the team.

Hours of work: All waking hours and a 24 hour shift when necessary.

Pay: No salary or wage. Allowances by arrangement, from time to time, with the income-earning member of the team. The successful applicant may be required to hold a second job, in addition to the one advertised here.

Benefits: No guaranteed holidays. No guaranteed sick leave, maternity leave or long service leave. No guaranteed life or accident insurance. No worker's compensation. No superannuation.

Figure 8.2 Position vacant (New South Wales Women's Advisory Council, 1980)

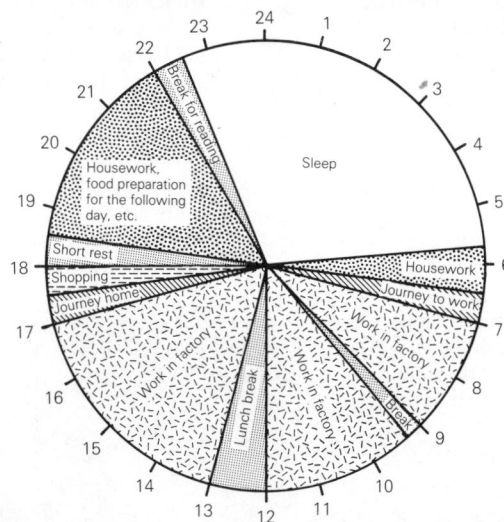

Figure 8.3 A clock graph of a day in the life of Helga, a 1931 textile worker (Herzog, 1980)

Maria's story

My husband, my children and I came to Australia from Greece ten years ago. My husband was working in a metal factory, but because his wages weren't enough for all our family's needs, I decided to look for a job too.

I began working nine years ago as a machinist in a factory making leather jackets. The factory was a long way from home and I had to get up very early to take my children to a child care centre before I went to work. The children did not like me to leave them – they cried every day, but what could I do?

One day, the boss asked me if I would like to work at home. I thought about it – I would need to buy my own sewing machine – but it would mean I could keep the children at home too. I decided to become an outworker.

I have been doing this work now for five years. My husband picks up the bundles of material at the factory each week and returns the finished articles. I work on piecework. I get $10 for every jacket I make and $1 extra for a coat. I usually earn $120–$140 per week. In the factory, I could earn $210. I know this is unfair, but at least at home the boss isn't always yelling at me.

Sometimes the boss is in a hurry to get the articles finished and he asks me to finish a large number by Monday. When this happens I work all the weekend sometimes from 8.00 in the morning till 11.00 at night. Otherwise, I try to work only on the weekdays – but somehow I always work more than 40 hours per week. Its good to be able to take a break when I want to, but I don't always have much time to spend with the children. Sometimes they help me by cutting the cottons or packing the jackets – then we talk a bit.

Recently my back has been troubling me and the doctor has told me it's due to the work I do. My husband wants me to stop working – but last month he was retrenched, so I must keep working. If I'm sick I don't get paid for time off and I don't get holiday pay. My husband contacted the Migrant Workers Centre about my bad back, but they said outworkers aren't entitled to worker's compensation.

Figure 8.4 Maria's story (Australia Asia Worker Links, 1982) (Photograph: Format/Jenny Matthews)

Ayshe's story

I am a Turkish–Cypriot woman living in Britain. I am an experienced machinist and ever since I left school 16 years ago, I have been sewing clothes in my home for factory owners. I'm an outworker.

The money I make is vital for my family. If I stop work even for one day my family will be affected. The amount I make depends on how many garments I make in a week but, generally, I don't earn much more than 40p per hour. It's not a lot of money, but I really don't have any choice; being an outworker is the only way I can earn money, look after the children and do the housework.

My boss says that I am self-employed but I cannot bargain with him. I have to accept my rate of pay and this can change at any time. Also, I don't get any benefits like sick pay, but I had to buy my own machine and I have to pay for my own heating and lighting. I can't complain to my boss because if I did he wouldn't give me any more work, and I don't want to talk to anyone in the government because I don't know whether I should have been paying tax or national insurance payments and so I might be in trouble.

Its very difficult working at home. You feel so cut-off from everything and everybody. I know there must be lots of other outworkers around, but I don't know where many of them are and I don't have the time or the money to try and find them. A lot of the time I feel really depressed and unhappy and this makes it hard for me to be nice and friendly towards my children and my husband. I cannot sleep at night because of my back. I cannot lie on my back... I've been to the hospital for an X-ray – its my muscles being bent all day they told me. They say I have to stop working for a while, but I can't afford to stop. I have to work.

Figure 8.5 Ayshe's story (adapted from information in Sarah and Fugen, 1982) (Photograph: Sally and Richard Greenhill)

4. Since the various groups of students are likely to have developed different clock graphs for Maria's day, you could initiate a class discussion to explore these differences and, in the process, uncover some of the assumptions about women's work that students have made in dividing up Maria's day.

5. Ask students to write three or four paragraphs that compare and contrast the working days of Helga and Maria. When outlining the similarities and differences in the lives and work experiences of the two women, students might consider:
   (a) the jobs they undertake and the range of skills that are needed
   (b) whether they have time to pursue their own activities
   (c) what the evidence suggests about their working conditions
   (d) any apparent changes/similarities over time of
       (i) the organisation of the textile industry
       (ii) women's work generally.

6. Get students to compare Maria's story and Ayshe's story (Figure 8.5). Both women are outworkers. Ask students to consider the following questions, and note that some of the questions will require further research.
   (a) What things are common to the lives and work of Maria and Ayshe?
   (b) What factors relating to women and women's work have encouraged both women to become outworkers?
   (c) Who benefits from the work of Maria and Ayshe? (Try to consider this question as broadly as possible.)
   (d) Are there any female outworkers in your community? If so, are they found in a particular part of town? Are they mainly migrant women? Has your local council appointed a Homeworker (Outworker) Officer to represent the interests of outworkers with employers and government officials?

7. Some students will be surprised to learn that 'sweated labour' is still a feature of life in developed nations such as Britain and Australia. It is worth while discussing with them why and how outwork remains hidden. They may also experience some frustration when trying to find out if outworking is a feature of their community. Nevertheless, this may crystallise their ideas about who gains from the system and help them to understand the problems that outworking women face in getting justice.

8. Get students to draw up a table of the activities undertaken by their mother – or some other female relative – on an average day. (Suggestions for the headings can be seen in instruction 9 below.) The table can be done partly by students' own observations and partly by what Mum indicates she has done during paid employment and/or their absence from home to attend school. Students must make sure they discriminate between the activities that Mum sees as leisure and those she sees as work. (For example, is knitting or sewing for the family work or leisure?)

9. Get students to draw a clock graph of their mother's activities during the day, including the hours spent:
   (a) doing housework
   (b) doing productive work other than housework (e.g. shopping, driving, children around)
   (c) doing paid employment
   (d) travelling to and from work
   (e) engaging in leisure activities
   (f) sleeping and resting.

10. You may wish to use the data collected by the students to explore the following with the class:
   (a) the range of leisure activities undertaken by the mothers and whether this range fits what the students expected
   (b) the amount of time taken up doing housework or other domestic duties
   (c) the percentage of mothers undertaking paid employment and the extent to which

this fits the national percentage of married women in the paid workforce

(d) the time that the mothers take to travel to and from paid work, what this might imply in terms of distance travelled and the type of transportation used.

11. Ask students to write three or four paragraphs that compare and contrast their mother's working day with either Helga, Maria or Ayshe. Some of the ideas listed in instruction 5 might be useful.

12. On the basis of what students have learnt in these activities, they should write four or five paragraphs on the issue of 'Women's work and leisure' considering whether conventional definitions of work and leisure are appropriate for women. They should express how they feel about the issues and indicate if their views have changed as a result of the activities.

Extension activities

1. Investigate the working days and leisure activities of other women, for example, Third World women textile workers such as the rural, outworking, lace makers of Narsapur (see Mies, 1982) and textile factory workers in Free Trade Zones (see Fuentes and Ehrenreich, 1984).

2. Consider the extent to which similarities and differences exist between the work and leisure experiences of the Third World women and the women whose lives have been considered in the activities above.

9 Third World studies: conscientisation in the geography classroom

TOH SWEE-HIN

Introduction

In teaching geography for a better world, Third World studies comprise a crucial arena for critical learning. How could our world be *better* if some 800 million human beings still remain afflicted by hunger, disease and acute lack of other basic needs; when over 40 000 children die daily from malnutrition and infection; and when the gap between rich and poor nations worsens? The 1985 Live Aid concerts revealed a considerable pool of compassion among citizens of affluent societies for suffering Africans. But much less clear is the degree of critical consciousness of the *root causes* of Third World poverty, as opposed to concern catalysed by exposure to the *symptoms* of under-development. Third World studies surely have a key role in educating young people about why the world seems unable to meet every person's basic needs. And hence, what societal changes, from local to national to global levels, might be necessary to facilitate *universal* development, the sine qua non of a *better world*. As Hicks and Townley (1982) stated, there is an urgent need for *global literacy*.

Paradigms of underdevelopment

While there is a general consensus about symptoms of Third World underdevelopment, there is considerable divergence in the realm of *causes* and *solutions*. After nearly four decades of theorising and practice, two major competing paradigms have emerged. The first, often called the *modernisation* worldview, has dominated mainstream academic analysis, and the policies of advanced industrialised governments, most

Third World governments, and large official aid agencies. The alternative paradigm, which I shall refer to by the acronym *PEACE*, emphasises *Participatory, Equitable, Appropriate, Conscientisation and Eco-developmental* principles in explaining the structural violence which keeps people hungry and poor, and in creating possible paths of liberation towards authentic mass development.

Have modernisation, will grow

Encompassing the gamut of social sciences, the dominant *modernisation* paradigm assumes that poor societies can and ought to progress along the path of industrialised states. Poverty resides in internal deficiencies, whether these be lack of capital, technology, expertise and modern infrastructure, or the stultifying effect of *traditional* values, or the problem of over-population (Hoselitz, 1960; Krause, 1961; Weiner, 1966; Hoogvelt, 1976; Little, 1982). Consequently, the channels of modern material and cultural inputs, such as trade, aid, foreign investment and transnational corporations, are upheld as essential and beneficial to development. Globally, the political-economic status quo is seen as capable of facilitating Third World economic growth while, within poor countries, a trickle-down approach to distributing the fruits of such growth is explicitly or implicitly adopted. And for modernisation to work, political stability is deemed imperative, even if repressive governments need to be bolstered by economic, political and military support (O'Brien, 1972).

These assumptions and themes of modernisation have generally held sway over development, aid, trade and global economic dispensation since the Second World War. During the 1970s the realities of continuing or worsening gaps between and within nations did force some reassessment among some modernisation theorists and policy-makers. Especially during Robert McNamara's term as World Bank president, the emphasis on *growth first* was admitted as inadequate. *Growth with equity* and *basic needs* became popular concepts (Chenery *et al.*, 1979; Grant, 1973; Brandt, 1980). Aid should be targeted at the hitherto neglected poorest, and even some international economic reforms were supported (McLaughlin *et al.*, 1979). In practice, though, growth with equity was only minimally institutionalised. Soon, with the deepening world economic crisis and the rise of the new right in core capitalist states, such 'global Keynesianism' ideas retreated before the reassertion of orthodox modernisation assumptions. The virtues of growth led by the private sector are sung loudly, as the World Bank, International Monetary Fund and other lending agencies stave off the Third World debt explosion. The path of export-oriented industrialisation, which has allowed a few countries to raise their populations' living standards, is urged as the model for the rest of the Third World.

Without PEACE no development

As modernisation policies took hold, radical social scientists and practitioners soon challenged trickle-down growth-biased development. Are mass-consuming free-enterprise societies necessarily the zenith of development? Is it just traditionalism and the lack of modern material and cultural factors which lead to poor nations? When modernity diffuses to Third World societies, who really benefits from that trade, investment, and aid (*New Internationalist*, 1978)?

In posing such questions, analysts of the dependency school undoubtedly pioneered the demystification of modernisation ideology. Drawing on Marxist or neo-Marxist theory, political economists such as Baran (1975) and Frank (1970) inspired the *development of underdevelopment* thesis. Contact between modern industrialised and traditional societies largely has not been and is not beneficent. Historically, colonialism and other processes of plunder and exploitation helped to lay the foundations of the modern capitalist world-system (Magdoff and Nowell, 1974; Rodney, 1972). As the west developed, the Third World experienced underdevelopment (Figure 9.1).

In the post-independence era, most Third World governments adapted to the requirements of this unequal world-system. Trade, investment and aid did benefit the ruling elites and the emerging middle classes, apart from serving the economic, political and/or strategic interests of the rich nations. The modernisation failed, however, to benefit the majority of Third World peoples. 'Trickle down' barely meant survival, providing an ideology for exploiting wealth, resources and the poor's toil for an *overdeveloped*

Figure 9.1 Faces of urban poverty in Mexico (Photograph: UNICEF/John Weisblat)

rich world and elite enclaves within unequal poor societies (Hayter, 1981; Alavi and Shanin, 1982; Harrison, 1981; Wilber and Weaver, 1979). Globally, trade remains unequal, skewed in favour of rich industrialised nations, while much talk of a New International Economic Order at various United Nations conferences and North-South dialogues to redress that inequality have seen few concrete actions (*New Internationalist*, 1981a; Brown, 1974; ACFOA, 1981; Duff, 1979).

Besides its expected rejection by modernisation proponents, dependency analysis has also been criticised by other radical thinkers (Blomstrom and Hettne, 1984). For instance, mechanistic application of the underdevelopment thesis meant ignoring the possibilities and actualities of development, depending on the mix of external political–economic factors and the complex nature of Third World societies. Such intra-paradigmatic debate is healthy, deepening critical understanding of underdevelopment and clarifying more realistic change strategies. For Third World studies in schools, however, it suffices to accentuate the counter-modernisation assumptions basically shared within the PEACE paradigm.

In particular, the concept of *structural violence* is crucial for understanding underdevelopment. No matter how hard they toil, the poor majorities are denied their rights and capacities to fulfil their basic needs. Children dying from lack of nutrition and health care, peasants and workers sweating with hungry stomachs, while their country has enough resources for all: such unnecessary phenomena are no less violent than the physical violence of wars and civil conflicts. And not surprisingly, these unjust social systems are maintained under threat and exercise of brutal repression dispensed by the military or para-military forces of the state and powerful elites (Falk, Kim and Mendlovitz, 1980; Herman, 1982; *New Internationalist*, 1980a). The activity at the end of this chapter is a simulation game based on the unequal interactions between two countries (Yellow and Green) and the structural violence that results. It is an excellent activity for helping even junior secondary school students to understand this abstract concept.

For much of the poor Third World, therefore, under-development emerges as internal social and political–economic structures interact with external advanced industrialised interests. Internally, power and wealth are concentrated among political/bureaucratic/technocratic elites, military leaders, entrepreneurs and/or landlords who form class alliances exploiting the poor. Often, political turmoil occurs as factions among these elites vie for power and privilege. But such changes in leadership do little to alleviate mass poverty, and usually make life worse for the poor entrapped in the accompanying factional violence and economic disruption. Externally, advanced capitalist states and transnational corporations seek accessibility to Third World raw materials, markets, super-cheap labour and profitable investment opportunities – vested interests which propel rich country governments to support those unjust political status quos. For the Soviet bloc, relations with the Third World, while similarly aimed at maintaining or expanding its sphere of influence, are much less impactful economically, concentrate on military aid, and occasionally assist liberation movements seeking to overcome structural violence (Pineys, 1983; Mack, 1981).

In counter-position to modernisation models, the PEACE paradigm upholds development policies which are *participatory* with the poor no longer powerless and passively accepting decisions dispensed from above by elites or experts (SID, 1981; Gran, 1983; Harrison, 1980). Participation allows the accu-mulated knowledge of the poor to be tapped, rather than ignored, to the detriment of many modernisation schemes. Social, political and economic structures

require radical transformation, so that societal resources and wealth are *equitably* distributed *within* and *between* nations (Nerfin, 1977; Falk, Kim and Mendlovitz, 1982). Methods and technology have to be *appropriate*, optimising use of local material, human and cultural resources and capable of maximising economic benefits to the poor majorities (Goulet, 1977; Reddy, 1975). But at the same time, such mass-oriented development should harmonise with, not destroy, the environment on which long-term human survival depends (*New Internationalist*, 1982c; Kothari, 1981). Above all, PEACEful development embodies the process of *conscientisation*, whereby the oppressed understand the political roots of their poverty and act to liberate themselves (Freire, 1972).

While the PEACE paradigm owes much analytically to the dependency and neo-Marxist traditions, it also includes non-Marxist radical perspectives such as liberation theology, which re-analyses Christian theory in the context of Third World oppression (Gheerbrant, 1974; Balasuriya, 1984); the ecological movement, whose concerns redress the environmental under-emphasis in radical political economy (Bookchin, 1980; Redclift, 1984); and the burgeoning analysis of women's double oppression with underdevelopment (Hill, 1983; ISIS, 1984). In the discussion below, three major groups of underdevelopment problems will illus-trate more concretely the differences between PEACE and modernisation thinking, and hopefully clarify how one paradigm is more consistent with a humanistic vision of a better world.

Food and population

Food and population issues must loom large in Third World studies, given that most poor people live agri-culturally, and global poverty's basic expression is hunger and malnutrition. To modernisation pro-ponents, two themes are prominent in the food–population equation: overpopulation and increased efficiency in food production. Too many children leading to more hunger is a popular view, at large and within aid/development circles, which therefore strongly urge birth control programmes upon the Third World (Ehrlich, 1968). In contrast, analysts such as Commoner (1975) have argued that poverty often underlies overpopulation. Under conditions of old age insecurity, high infant mortality and inadequate earn-ings, children are needed to help look after old parents and help them earn family income (Mamdani, 1972; *New Internationalist*, 1979a, 1980b; Hofsten, 1974). Within a PEACE paradigm, controlling population growth would only be one component of a development strategy meeting the poor's basic needs. The overpopulation ideology helps governments and ruling elites sidestep the difficult issues of global and naitonal structural violence.

More importantly, modernisation advocates believe hunger can and should be solved by making Third World agriculture more efficient to produce more food. This logic underpins the so-called Green Revolution, involving use of high-yielding varieties of wheat, corn, rice and other food crops. With aid from corporate foundations and bilateral/multilateral agencies, many Third World governments soon adopted the new technology (Borlaug et al., 1969; Swaminathan, 1983). But, although yields did increase, in many places this did not improve the livelihoods of poor rural majorities. Not surprisingly, the costly seeds, fertilisers, pesticides and irrigation required are more accessible to richer farmers and landlords. Increased landlessness has also occurred as tenant and poor farmers are squeezed out by over-mechanisation and indebtedness (Cleaver, 1972; George, 1976; Lappe and Collins, 1981). In sum, the Green Revolution is a technocratic fix to Third World hunger which avoids confronting the structures of inequalities and consequently continues to enrich the wealth of middle classes. Granted, some poor farmers also benefit, but the enormous national costs involved in importing such capital-intensive technology (including serious environmental negativities) cannot be justified when the vast majority of rural people remain unjustly marginalised.

Modernisation spokespersons do talk, of course, about the need for rural reforms too, such as reversing the urban bias in development expenditures and land inequalities (World Bank, 1975; ADB, 1978). But the preferred strategy is evolutionary piecemeal change, persuading governments and elites with incentives to give the poor a bigger piece of the national cake. The record, however, of such top–down reformism in much of the Third World is hardly encouraging, albeit not unexpected. Political and economic elites are powerful and resourceful enough to block, circumvent or co-opt paper reforms (Feder, 1971; Barraclough, 1979; ILO, 1979). This unwillingness of the modernisation paradigm to support radical structural transformations empowering the poor needs serious questioning. It is because vested interests of rich countries, transnational corporations or well-paid experts would be threatened by more participatory, equitable and technologically appropriate Third World societies? Here, case studies of revolutionary development models, such as China, Cuba and Nicaragua provide interesting insights (Aziz, 1978; Huberman and Sweezy, 1969; Collins, Lappe and Allen, 1982): albeit not as mechanistic formulas for emulation; rather as illustrations of how key PEACE paradigm principles can ensure at least the basic needs of all citizens.

Transnational corporations (TNCs)

In modernisation thinking TNCs are praised for providing the Third World with needed capital, technology, innovations, expertise, wider world markets and employment (Diebold, 1973; Galbraith, 1978; Vernon, 1973). As 'engines of growth' TNCs diffuse a logic of efficiency essential to development. While some costs (for example, excessive profit outflows; inappropriate technology transfers) and problems (for example, Third World nationalism) have now been acknowledged, modernisation experts and policymakers remain convinced that, overall, TNCs contribute positively to development. Codes of TNC conduct have been proposed, while TNCs are finding technology and management joint ventures as profitable as full ownership.

In contrast, the PEACE paradigm notes that TNCs are basically moved by their logic of profit maximisation and accumulation, a logic with counter-developmental consequences for poor Third World majorities (Barnet and Muller, 1974; Utrecht, 1978–1982; Widstrand, 1975). These include excess profits extracted from cheap natural and human resources; inappropriate technology; reinforcing industrial, mining or agribusiness enclaves serving rich country and local elite consumption at the expense of mass basic needs; and the shaping of consumer tastes to TNC products, wasting individual resources and even harming life. As an integral component of the world capitalist system, TNCs have been nurtured or protected by post-war economic and military aid. TNCs may efficiently meet their profit-seeking needs, and the wants of Third World elites for wealth and power. But they are not designed to promote equitable use of global resources efficiently for universal basic development.

Thus TNC-led agribusiness, including supply of farm inputs (for exmple, Green Revolution), food production (for example, ranching) and food processing (for example, canned vegetables), has capitalised on cheap Third World land and repressed labour. Cash crops for export provide more protein, other foods or even flowers for rich countries, and profits for TNCs and local elites, but less food for the poor (George, 1976; Burbach and Flynn, 1980). In popular discussions of the African food crisis, the focus has been on natural factors per se (for example, drought), rather than linking these factors to the web of unequal development structures, including the urban bias of most African governments and the role of agribusiness (Dinham and Hines, 1983).

Likewise, the profit-seeking logic of TNCs has led them to unethically and exploitatively market dangerous products in the Third World. Pesticides which poison oppressed farmers and labourers (Weir and Schapiro, 1981); harmful and over-expensive pharmaceuticals irrelevant to basic health care (Melrose, 1982); junk foods and drinks (Ledogar, 1975); infant formulas which, under poverty conditions, lead to unnecessary baby deaths (Chetley, 1979; *New Internationalist*, 1982a): all these negativities raise serious questions about the modernising beneficence of TNCs. This is not, of course, to apportion blame primarily on TNCs, since their ability to so practice arises out of the willingness of Third World governments and elites and the abetting role of mainstream aid agencies to promote such structurally violent modernisation.

Foreign aid

In a recent public survey, a majority of Australians supported foreign aid largely on humanitarian grounds. Rich countries should morally help the Third World poor (ACFOA, 1983). Modernisation advocates would maintain that official aid, whether bilateral or multilateral, do fulfil these humanitarian concerns by making available funds for modern infrastructure, technology, services, expertise and food (Pearson *et al.*, 1969; Clausen *et al.*, 1982; Jackson *et al.*, 1984). Aid provides a catalyst, demonstration models, trained personnel and physical resources for otherwise relatively stagnant, underproductive societies.

Viewed through PEACE paradigm lenses, however, official aid largely reflects vested political and economic interests. Humanitarian motives notwithstanding, rich countries and Third World elites manipulate aid to their mutual advantages. Hence tying of aid, common to bilateral programmes, serves to promote exports of goods and services of donor countries, and often accentuates the problems of inappropriate technology transfer (Figure 9.2). Fundamentally, economic aid embodies assumptions and strategies which modernise selected sectors of Third World societies so as to maintain poor countries within the donor's sphere of influence. Not surprisingly, advanced capitalist states prefer that aid help create suitable conditions for private investment and growth of free market forces (Lappe, Collins and Kinley, 1981; *New Internationalist*, 1979b, 1981b; Payer, 1983; Learmonth and Holt, 1982; Hayter and Watson, 1984).

The building of large-scale infrastructure (for example, roads, dams, irrigation); the commercialisation of agriculture via agribusiness; and the push for export-oriented industrialisation have yielded disproportionate benefits to donors, TNCs and Third World elites and middle classes. Hierarchically controlled by experts and officials, these projects or programmes not only treat the poor as passive receivers of 'good things from above,' but can often accentuate existing inequalities. Misappropriation of aid funds by corrupt officials and the usurping of resources meant for the poor by elites are prevalent in this modernisation aid system. Similar criticisms have been raised about official Australian aid (CAA, 1984b; Richards, 1981).

In the specific case of food aid, there are long-term counter-developmental consequences of creating a dependency complex (George, 1976; Choudhry, 1986). Relieving a recipient government from seriously tackling agricultural underdevelopment, it also depresses prices and hence earnings of poor farmers. Ruling elites often use food aid to keep urban classes content, instead of feeding the hungry, as well as to finance militarisation and luxury imports.

Military aid, overt or covert, has also been a crucial feature of official aid from both the superpower blocs, often buttressing unpopular repressive regimes (Chomsky and Herman, 1979; Randle, 1981; Agee, 1975; Pineye, 1983; Weissman, 1975). While some liberal modernisation analysts prefer to de-emphasise military assistance, others justify it as contributing to political stability and hence external confidence in recipient economies, as well as countering the alleged Soviet threat. Another not unimportant motivation is the highly lucrative arms sales spin-off from military aid programmes (Sampson, 1977; CAA, no date).

In PEACE paradigm terms, military aid cannot be left unquestioned, since it so often supports the structures of repression underlying socio-economic injustices and underdevelopment. The current case of Nicaragua is an instructive negative example. United States aid to the Contras is now inflicting unnecessary suffering upon a people who had sacrificed to overthrow the US-backed Somoza dictatorship and initiated basic needs reforms. In the case of Ethiopia, Soviet aid has bolstered a regime which devotes many times more expenditure to militarisation than food and rural development for starving Ethiopians.

Last, but not least, non-governmental organisation (NGO) aid deserves ample treatment in Third World studies, given the high mass-media profile of NGO programmes and the enthusiasm generated from recent aid rock concerts. For instance, the controversy over child sponsorship schemes should be clarified (*New Internationalist*, 1982b). Would handouts to individual children and families help them resolve the social roots of their poverty, or rather engender dependency and divide communities? Is is ethical or educational to advertise images of wretched starving children? Would not projects which emphasise participation, conscientisation and organisation of poor communities to challenge their unjust structures be more fruitful of authentic mass development? (*New Internationalist*, 1983, 1985; Lissner, 1977). Are Live Aid-type events, albeit useful in arousing compassion for the poor and starving, sufficient to weaken global/national/local structural violence? Or can rock stars and their youthful constituencies become aware and *committed* enough to protest against repressive or exploitative aid, and against the unequal world economic order?

Boomerang aid

'Tying' aid to exports from donor countries means that 7 out of every 10 aid dollars come straight back to the donors.

This diverts aid from its real purpose — the relief of poverty.

Illustration : Clive Offley

Figure 9.2 Boomerang aid (*New Internationalist*, no. 126, August 1983, p. 27)

Classroom ideas

Introducing underdevelopment

Patterns of global inequalities can initially be illustrated by various statistical indicators such as GNP per capita, life expectancy, infant mortality, literacy rates and the like. Useful sources are the World Bank's *Annual Development Report*, Sivard's (1983) compilation of social and military expenditures, the ODC's (1979) Physical Quality of Life Index, and the illustrated atlases of Kidron and Segal (1984) and the Open University (Crow and Thomas, 1983).

For most secondary school students, who usually have no direct experience of Third World poverty, films are essential to create interest and focus for analysis. It is important, however, to use (if possible) material which goes beyond symptoms (for example, *Five Minutes to Midnight*) to the roots of underdevelopment. Some good examples are *Children of the Miracle*, which exposes the structural violence of Brazil's growth-first development model; *Understanding Third World Poverty and Underdevelopment*, produced by the University of New South Wales Critical Social Issues Project (Trainer, 1984), which analyses world inequalities and emphasises the necessity of reduced consumption in rich countries; and *Tongpan*, a dramatic feature produced by Thai film-makers which movingly illustrates rural poverty in north-east Thailand and includes the counter-developmental impact of large dams.

In Australia, films and other audio-visual resources on development issues are now readily accessible from the National Film Library, and organisations such as Australian Freedom from Hunger Campaign, Community Aid Abroad (CAA), and Australian Catholic Relief. While the United Nations Association also has a large stock of material, care is needed in using these as many films tend to focus more on symptoms than causes of poverty. Likewise, in Britain, development-education films and other audio-visuals are obtainable from groups such as Oxfam, Christian Aid, Centre for World Development Education, Concord Films Council, International Broadcasting Trust, and various Development Education Centres found in many cities and regions (CEWC, 1984; Taylor and Richardson, 1979).

The key objective of watching films such as these is to 'unfreeze' the prevailing modernisation stereotypes that students tend to hold about Third World poverty (for example, overpopulation, technological backwardness and other blame-the-victim attitudes), and introduce some doubt about the meaning of development as well as some perception of relational analysis. Poor countries are no longer seen in monolithic terms: certain social, political and economic relationships determine access to and reproduction of wealth and poverty. Rich countries have vested political–economic interests in global inequalities. In this regard, simulation games such as 'Starpower' and 'The structural violence game' (pages 137–9) are useful in giving students a sense of how structurally unequal social systems and free-market forces tend to make the rich richer and poor poorer. Several scenes in the CSIP's (1984) role-play 'Market Forces' illustrate this logic in Third World contexts. It is also essential to check on the unfreezing process though periodic answering by the students of a questionnaire based on modernisation and PEACE views of underdevelopment.

While the references cited in my background discussion would be important for teacher understanding of the paradigm and the selected issues (and extracts from these references are often usable in class), there are several publications available which would complement that detailed literature either as student reference books or teacher guides. They include McGinnis (1979), Trainer (1984), Fyson (1984), Barke and O'Hare (1984), Bale (1983), Morrish (1983), AFHC (1978, 1982), Hicks and Townley (1982), DEC (1981), WSP (1976), Richardson (1977, 1978), Stuart (1977), Mountjoy (1978), Heatley (1979), Fallaw (1981), Jones and Wales (1982) and Fien (1985).

Food and population

An important objective in teaching about food and population is to make students aware of the class divisions within most rural Third World areas which underlie poverty and hunger. A useful stuctured role-play exercise is to prepare cards with statements reflecting the social status, wealth, income, political power, social relationships, division of labour, and access to services among different social classes in, for example, rural Bangladesh. The anthropological study by Hartmann and Boyce (1983) provides much rich meaningful data for such a role play.

On pages 132–4 are 25 of the over 40 role statements that I have been able to write on the Bangladesh case. *Sample teaching unit 1* on food and population issues (pages 128–31) explains how these roles may be used with a class. If time does not allow the full role play, four or five statements could be read out by individual class members, followed by discussion to link the symptoms of hunger with its structural causes.

Students will then be able to appreciate how the social, economic and political system is stacked against the poor. The usurious trap laid by money-lenders who are usually also rich farmers and landlords; the lack of basic health, education and other social services for the poor; the collaboration of government officials (for example, state warehouse managers) with rural elites to deny equitable prices for poor farmers' produce; the bias of banks, even government agencies, in dispensing credit to richer farmers; the hoarding of food even under famine conditions by merchants and landlords; the expansion of landlessness as the poor desperately sell their meagre holdings to stay alive; the patronage links between local and national politicians with rural elites; the waste of resources on militarisation and luxury consumption of the few; the diversion of food aid to urban middle classes and elite expenditures; and the complicity, wittingly or unwittingly, of large aid agencies and experts in programmes and projects whose benefits are usurped by elite groups because the agencies are unwilling to challenge the unequal power-structures: all these facets of the web of structural violence should be clarified and lead students to understand that physical factors (for exmple, weather, lack of resources) cannot be isolated from the political–economic fabric of underdevelopment. Hence that an alternative PEACE-oriented development path (for example, land reforms; breaking the economic elite–politician connections; substantial investment in mass-based agricultural development; organising and empowering the poor) could lead towards meeting the *universal* basic needs of even such a poor country as Bangladesh. For senior classes, this exercise can be elaborated into a full role play with scenes depicting various social and political–economic relations of production and distribution.

Simpler simulation exercises which combine values clarification with knowledge of food and hunger problems are also found in Otero and Smith (1977). Examples include brainstorming on causes of world hunger; a distribution model for deciding food allocation according to conservative, liberal and radical criteria; and experiencing poverty in the midst of affluence by unequally distributing food brought to class. However, apart from the need to adapt some of the exercises to your own local conditions, care is required to sharpen up the necessary political–economic analysis.

Some useful audio-visuals on food and population are *The Price of Hunger*, a UNESCO film; *An Interview with Susan George*, expressing some of George's cogent criticisms of the world food system; and several programmes in the International Broadcasting Trust series, *Utopia Limited*. The *Food First* comic issue of the *New Internationalist* (see Figure 9.3), the cartoon-based *Food for Beginners* book (George and Paine, 1982), and Third World First's (1985) special *Links* issue on the 'real causes of famine in Africa', are also very suitable for class use.

Teachers may use *Sample teaching unit 1* on food and population issues as a guide for teaching strategies on food and population (see pages 128–32).

Transnational corporations

A useful introductory exercise on TNCs consists of asking students to visit their local supermarket or department store to find out for themselves how pervasive TNCs are in their everyday lives as consumers. With the help of role plays and audio-visuals, class discussion should aim at illuminating the logic of TNC operations, how TNCs are part and parcel of advanced industrial overdevelopment, and the realities of TNC negativities not only in poor countries but also on the quality of life of affluent societies (for example, junk foods, circle of poison). The defence of TNCs can be illustrated by role playing actual statements of TNC executives on how they benefit the Third World, while contrasting expressions can be simulated via actors representing the victims of TNC exploitation. Such statements can be abstracted or derived from many of the detailed references cited in my background analysis above.

In agribusiness, for example, Burbach and Flynn (1980) provide detailed descriptions of how Latin American and Filipino labourers of TNCs such as Del Monte earn pittances, lack union rights and suffer indiscriminate pesticide spraying or excessive industrial accidents. The baby killer scandal can be objectively explored through a mock trial of Nestlé's formula marketing practices, having students act as defence lawyers articulating Nestlé's position and as prosecution lawyers as well as witnesses taking the stand. The teacher can act as judge, and other students as the jury (McGinnis, 1979). Huckle (1984) has designed an interesting simulation exercise based on TNCs in the global textile industry. Using jeans as a starting point, students are asked to discuss with the help of clue cards the connections between buying a pair of jeans and such issues as TNC control, technology transfer, free trade zones, sexism and trade agreements.

The films, *The Formula Factor*, which deals with the baby killer scandal, and *Controlling Interest*, a general overview of TNCs, provide good visual analysis of the profit-seeking logic of TNCs as well as the collaborative role played by Third World elites in sanctioning TNC operations. The *Utopia Limited* programmes on the Green Revolution and TNC involvement in Brazil also give stimulating discussions of the political economy of TNCs.

It is important, however, while acknowledging the realities of TNC power, not to leave students with a sense of hopelessness. At the least, they should feel that ordinary people, when aware and organised, can begin to challenge the logic and priorities of TNCs and even in a few cases check it. Many citizens have organised boycott campaigns of specific TNCs' products, petitions and stockholder resolutions to pressure TNCs to operate more ethically. Examples include the

Figure 9.3 Business of food (*Food First* comic, no. 543, 1982: Institute for Food and Development Policy, 145 Ninth Street, San Francisco, California 94103, USA)

INFACT and War on Want campaigns on infant formulas, which finally forced Nestlé, after a protracted struggle, to sign the International Code of Conduct; consumer groups protesting about pesticide and drug poisoning; and anti-apartheid organisations pressuring TNCs to disinvest from South Africa.

Foreign aid

A useful case study to illustrate how official aid can be counter-developmental is the Philippines (Figure 9.4). The structurally violent effects of export-oriented industrialisation on the urban poor, and agribusiness and Green Revolution policies on the rural masses are closely linked to established aid bodies like USAID, World Bank and the Australian Development Aid Bureau (ADAB) (Bello, Kinley and Elinson, 1982; CAA, 1984b; Leary, Ellis and Madlener, 1984). The films *To Sing Our Own Song, Collision Course* and *Celso and Cora* provide excellent analyses of under-

development and inequalities in the Philippines. The slide–tape kit, *Development Aid: Like It or Not*, illustrates and raises serious questions about Australian aid: who benefits, the poor or the political–economic elites, including one provincial governor who openly and happily thanks ADAB for his 'free ride' on ADAB's PADAP project.

In discussing NGO aid, an initial class activity is for students to look at mass-media advertisements of various agencies. What understanding of Third World poverty do the pictures, images and words of appeal of such child sponsorship agencies as World Vision or grass-roots project agencies such as Oxfam give? Class discussion can then compare aid that alleviates mainly *symptoms*, with aid that tries to overcome the *roots* of poverty (Figure 9.5). Students can also role play how they would react, and what would be expected of them, as sponsored children or sponsoring parents. In contrast, a more PEACE paradigm oriented NGO project is illustrated in the film Sangham about the group of landless Indian

Figure 9.4 Philippines: images

Filipino peasant toiling under inequalities and poverty

Rural-to-urban migration for a better life?

Urban poverty in the Manila slums

Repressive militarisation under Marco's dictatorship

Detention; human rights abuse; and political violence

Growth of armed liberation movements

Harijans who succeeded in organising themselves with NGO aid to challenge local landlords and other elites and to demand their constitutional rights to work and land.

I have noticed that young people, once aware of the relations between inequalities and structural violence, have little hesitation in supporting the basic rights of the poor oppressed to struggle against exploiting elites. At the same time, issues of aid in Third World studies provide the opportunity for citizens of rich countries to become self-critical of their indirect, if not direct, contribution to global and Third World under-development. Students should come to appreciate that much aid is really a rationale and vehicle for maintaining the rich world's share of the world economic pie. If aid is to lead to a better world, then it must be help which expresses solidarity with Third World peoples to liberate themselves from oppression and structural violence.

Teachers may use these ideas on foreign aid in a comprehensive teaching strategy on aid issues (see *Sample teaching unit 2* on pages 135–6).

Conclusion: geography as conscientisation

If the constant mass-media images of famine, deprivation and violence in the Third World are not to numb tomorrow's adults into hopeless despair or cynical apathy, geography lessons will need to play a *conscientisation* role. This means in the first place fostering an objective understanding of how global structural inequalities and external interventions in the name of profit or national interests are intimately linked to internal systems of class injustices and violence. Citizens of rich countries will need to realise that their willingness to consume less is one prerequisite for real Third World development. But such willingness cannot be left as *individual* choice and action. Rather, awareness and choice will have to be translated into *social* and *political* action to replace intra-societal and inter-societal values and relationships with alternative PEACE principles.

Secondly, it means to awaken the conscience and commitment of learners to exercise their democratic rights to express solidarity with the poor and oppressed. How consistent is western foreign policy, including aid programmes, with *participatory, equitable, appropriate, conscientising and ecologically* oriented development in the Third World? Why are so many experts and consultants promoting modernisation models of development? Whatever the degree of consistency, concerned citizens have the moral

Figure 9.5 A positive approach to aid: a community well-digging project in India based on participatory principles (Photograph: Community Aid Abroad)

responsibility to persuade decision-makers to effect policies transcending those contradictions. It is through encouraging this process of conscientisation that Third World studies can meaningfully contribute to teaching geography for a better world.

Acknowledgements

This chapter owes much to discussions and correspondence, recently and through the seventies, with mentors, colleagues as well as participants, including many teachers, in my Third World development-education courses. Particular thanks go to Kazim Bacchus, Robin Burns, Tessa Morris-Suzuki, Jen Burnley, Ted Trainer, Brian Gore, John Fien, Vanessa Letham, Geoff Arger, Chris Fox, and Sr. Margaret Chaplin, Jan Pitty and Jan Wilson, who kindly allowed me into their classrooms.

Sample teaching unit 1: food and population issues

Topic	Activity	Issues/questions	Values/attitudes
1. Patterns of world underdevelopment	Examine comparative indicators of development (e.g. GNP per capita; infant mortalities, etc.). Use maps, atlases. Compare military and social expenditures of a range of rich and poor countries. Show film, *Children of the Miracle* on rich–poor gaps in Brazil.	Rich world, poor world inequalities. Make clear 'average' nature of indicators. Many Third World states spend more on militarisation than basic needs. Ask for possible reasons. Gaps between elite minorities and poor majorities in life styles, work, basic needs, despite high growth rates. Role of external interests of TNCs, worker exploitation.	Ask (but leave open for future discussion): is it 'right' for global division into rich and poor? Initial awareness of inappropriate priorities, role of militarisation in maintaining poverty. Ask students to put themselves in 'shoes' of different roles depicted in film: homeless children, rich elites, worker, poor mother; how do they feel?
2. **Assess existing students worldview on causes/solutions of Third World poverty**	Answer questionnaire on causes of and possible solutions to Third World poverty. Use Bangladesh as context. Keep responses for comparison with end-of-programme responses.	Questions: 1. Describe in a few sentences your feelings about people of Bangladesh. 2. Write down four major reasons why you think Bangladesh is poor. 3. Say whether you agree or disagree with following statements on Bangladesh (use scale 'strongly agree' to 'strongly disagree', plus a 'not sure'): (a) Foreign aid is helping the poor people of Bangladesh. (b) Transnational corporations are helping Bangladesh to develop. (c) Poor Bangladeshis are poor because they have too many children. (d) Rich countries should pay only a low price for jute from Bangladesh as it is only a raw material. (e) Bangladesh should pay more for machinery from rich countries. (f) Rural poverty results from unequal distribution of land. (g) Bangladesh should buy modern medicines from rich countries for its people's health care. (h) Bangladesh needs more foreign aid experts to help development. (i) Foreign investment does not benefit the poor people of Bangladesh. 4. Would you be prepared to support the following aid projects? (yes/no/not sure): (a) sponsor a Bangladeshi child	An idea is obtained of students' existing values, attitudes and conceptions of causes and possible solutions to underdevelopment. Questions are a mixture of modernisation and PEACE paradigm perspectives. Detect whether any paradigm is favoured.

Sample teaching unit 1: food and population issues (cont.)

Topic	Activity	Issues/questions	Values/attitudes
		(b) help poor farmers form unions (c) support a well-digging project (d) give a scholarship to a Bangladeshi to study in your country (e) open a large modern hospital in the capital city (f) send food to feed children in Bangladesh	

3. Simulation exercises on power variables in all social, political and economic systems	(a) Warm-up simulation exercise. Bring two large cakes to class. Cut one cake into unequal pieces, total number enough for about two-thirds of the class.
	Cut second cake into equal-sized pieces, enough for at least one per student.
	Start with cake 1, give out slices on a first-come-first-served basis. Repeat with cake 2.
	(b) Follow up with the more elaborate simulation of 'The structural violence game' (see pages 137–9).
		If there is an unequal distribution of cake (equivalent to world's or national food supply) then some are fed well, others a little, and some actually starve.
		
		If there is an equal distribution, then all get at least something to eat and no-one starves.
		
		Give some statistics for share of rich and poor in Third World national income. For example, data for rural Asia:
		  income share of richest 5%
		  income share of poorest 20%
		
		Are there real life parallels to 'The structural violence game'?
		
		Power, privilege and wealth beget more, while poor gets poorer. Those who make unequal rules often win.
			Ask if it is fair or moral to have an unequal distribution system?
			
			Can the poor be blamed for being hungry?
			
			Clarify values of being powerful and rich, powerless and poor. Any feelings of 'guilt' or 'the losers deserve what they get'?

4. Bangladesh: example of a very poor country	Introduce Bangladesh: geographical characteristics – location, landscape, weather, history, economy, politics. Compare basic indicators with your country.	Difference in population density. Britain 65 times more GNP per capita than Bangladesh. Bangladesh infant mortality 13 times more than Britain's. Only half population in Bangladesh has access to safe water. Health personnel over 100 times more in First World. Bangladesh overspends on military compared with social expenditures. Note income inequalities: poorest 40% households receive under 20% national income; gaps increasing: 40% live below ILO poverty line (1960s), 80% (1970s); 20% peasants landless (3.4 million).	Development should at least mean fulfilment of basic human needs. Distorted government priorities.
5. Analysis of rural poverty in Bangladesh	Role play on Bangladesh rural underdevelopment (see Figure 9.3). Each student given a statement depicting a role (e.g. different social classes; officials, etc.). Divide class into	Goal: to give students a more realistic understanding of rural poverty as result of structural violence.	Aim to reverse view of Bangladesh as hopeless 'Basketcase'.

Sample teaching unit 1: food and population issues (cont.)

Topic	Activity	Issues/questions	Values/attitudes
	five groups (one for each group of statements). Have class discussion after each group has been read.		
	Group A statements	Existence of social class divisions in poor countryside (note land inequalities around Third World).	Is it fair to have unequal land tenure?
	Group B statements	Richer can store harvests until prices high. Poor forced even to sell meagre resources to survive. Labour exploitation by landed elites. Parental sacrifices to try to feed children.	Do poor deserve their 'fate'? Is system 'just'? How can rich behave in that manner?
	Group C statements	Usurious interest rates. Physical repression. Accompany economic exploitation. Illiteracy exploited by elites. Fatalism and religious values.	Are rates fair? (Compare to your country.) Are poor 'stupid'? Is poverty a matter of 'God's will'?
	Group D statements	Participation of government officials in structural violence. Corruption and inefficiency. Bureaucratic bias against poor.	Is corruption inevitable? How would students react if faced by poor dirty smelly people?
	Group E statements	Famine not because of absolute shortage of food in country, but lack of poor's purchasing power. No matter how hard poor toil, situation will not necessarily improve; often worsens. Women's double oppression (bring out general features of women in underdevelopment).	Understand that 'natural disasters' are not merely natural causes, but fused with political–economic causes. Dispel myth of women as 'unproductive'.
6. Green revolution simulation	Explain idea of Green Revolution (history, inputs, expected outcomes). Use Bangladesh case.	High-technology agriculture. Yields did increase in many Third World countries.	Is it appropriate technology for Third World conditions?
	Group F statements	Richer benefit more than poor. A few poor also benefit, but many poor unable to buy costly technology, lack land. Government resources monopolised by richer and powerful. Aid officials unwilling to question structural inequalities, so aid benefits rich more.	Recall lessons of 'The structural violence game'. What prerequisites are necessary to maximise potential benefits of Green Revolution (e.g. land reforms; participatory aid?) Is high-tech necessarily best?

Sample teaching unit 1: food and population issues (cont.)

Topic	Activity	Issues/questions	Values/attitudes
7. Overall discussion of food and population issues in unequal world order	Read extracts from *How the Other Half Dies, Food for Beginners* and *Food First* comic.	Overpopulation not primary cause of hunger. Population control desirable, but must be in conjunction with real agricultural development and other equitable social changes.	De-mystify popular conception of blaming poverty on 'too many babies'.
	See film, *Interview with Susan George*.	Enough food to feed everyone, if world political–economic order and national orders made more equitable.	Rich countries also part of Third World poverty; must take some responsibility.
	Utopia Limited film,	Underdevelopment, poverty and hunger caused unequal world-system interacting with Third World internal orders.	Whose interests served by rich world support of repressive regimes? Would students be prepared to 'de-develop' to facilitate Third World mass development?
	See slide–tape kit, *Nicaragua: Land for People*.	Explain pre-revolutionary structural violence in Nicaragua. Somoza supported by US.	Are poor justified in trying to obtain basic human rights and to struggle against oppression?
	Read extracts from Collins *et al.* (1982) *What Difference can a Revolution Make?*	Fundamental land and other social reforms after revolution enabled more food to be produced and to be shared more equitably.	Any student bias or fear about Third World revolutions?
	Read President Reagan's speeches on Nicaragua and Central America. See special issue of *New Internationalist* on Central America.	Counter-revolutionary intervention by US.	Is intervention to destabilise revolution in Nicaragua morally justified?
	(If time permits, see film *No Pasaran*)	(Dispel myth that Nicaragua is merely a Soviet or Cuban 'proxy'; liberation theology).	Be more critical of mainstream media discussions.
8. Post-programme assessment	Re-administer questionnaire on underdevelopment.	Compare pre-programme with post-programme responses. Explore with students what evidence and teaching activities helped changes, if any.	Have students changed paradigm emphasis? Have students more compassion (rather than pity) for poor?

Bangladesh rural poverty simulation: statements for role play

Group A statements

1. 'I am a landlord. I own 70 acres of land. I do not have to work on my own land. I hire labourers to grow rice on 20 acres. I rent the other 50 acres to poor farmers. Each farmer pays me half of his harvest as rent for using my land.'

2. 'I am a rich farmer. I own 10 acres of land. I work on my own land, but I also need to hire some labourers to help me grow my crops. I also rent out a few acres to poor farmers who pay me half their harvests as rent.'

3. 'I am a middle farmer. I own 2 acres of land, two cows, and some agricultural tools. I just have enough land to grow enough for my own family. Sometimes, for extra money, I also work for richer farmers or the landlords, but they don't pay much wages.'

4. 'I am a poor farmer. I own half an acre of land. I cannot grow enough food to feed my family. So I have to either work as a labourer or I have to rent out some land from a rich farmer or a landlord. At harvest time, I pay them half of my harvests as rent.'

5. 'I am a landless labourer. I own no land. I have no cows or agricultural tools, so I have to get work as a labourer. I earn about forty cents per day.'

Group B statements

1. 'I am a landlord. I live in a cement house. I own a motorcycle. It cost me as much as 20 years of the wages of one labourer. I have a large ware-house where I store my rice harvests. I only sell my rice when the price is high. I also own a small shop in town, where I can stay overnight in my second house. My shop is a pharmacy shop, but my most popular medicine is alcohol.'

2. 'I am a poor farmer. I live in a bamboo hut with my wife and my six children. My small piece of land does not grow enough food for all of us. Even though I also work for wages, still I cannot grow enough to feed my family properly. I have been sick for three weeks now. The doctor wants one hundred takas before he will cure me. I cannot afford to borrow any more money, so I will have to sell a part of my land to buy the medicine.'

3. 'I am a landless labourer. Once I had half an acre of land. Then two years of floods left me with no choice but to sell my land to repay the money-lender. It is difficult finding work, and the rich farmers or the landlords tell us: if you don't want to work for these wages, we can find lots of other workers who will.'

4. 'I am the wife of a poor farmer. My five children are always hungry. We eat rice once a day with wild vegetables. We have to share 250 g of rice among the eight of us, including my brother and sister-in-law. I often go without food to give more to my children. I chew on the betel nut to stop the pains of hunger in my stomach. I am afraid we shall have to chop down our only jackfruit tree to sell it as fire-wood, since my husband has been unable to find work this month. My children will have no chance to taste the jackfruit.'

Group C statements

1. 'I am a rich farmer. Because of the last three good harvests, I have been able to buy a shop in town selling cloth. Many poor farmers and landless workers also come to borrow from me. I lend it to them at high interest rates. Usually they pay me back by giving me half of their harvests.'

2. 'I am a poor farmer. I lost my land to the money-lender, so I moved my family to this small island near the coast to squat on one acre of land. Then the landlord and his men carrying big sticks came one day and threatened to beat me up if I did not work the land for him. So now I give him half my harvests. But last month, the cyclone came and washed away most of the island. I lost my wife and two of our children. How can I feed them now?'

3. 'I am a landless labourer. My family lives in this hut without walls. We use palm leaves to keep out the wind. In winter it is very cold for us. We have no money to buy more clothing. We sleep on straw on the mud floor and cover ourselves with sacks. My father used to own land, but he was careless and sold off 1 acre just for a wedding celebration. The rest of the land was cheated from him by money-lenders. I have been sick and weak from not enough food. Now the construction bosses will not hire me as they say I'm not strong enough to do the heavy work.'

4. 'I am the widow of a landless labourer. My husband fell ill and we had no money to see the doctor. So he died. Allah says the rich should help the poor, but sometimes I wonder if it's Allah's will or is it the work of men? Nobody can help me feed my children, and I must try to find some work or we will starve. The landlords pay us women workers so little, and I don't even have enough money to buy a new sari to replace this torn one, which is my only clothing.'

Figure 9.6 Transplanting rice seedlings, Bangladesh (Photograph: Panos Pictures/Tom Learmonth)

Group D statements

1. 'I am a government politician. The big landlords and the rich farmers are my strongest supporters. They make sure I get the votes, and I help them get government loans and aid equipment. The poor people are uneducated and have no manners. They are poor because they have too many children and do not work hard enough.'

2. 'I am a poor farmer. When I bring my harvest of jute to the government warehouse, the manager gives all kinds of reasons why he cannot buy my harvest from me. So we poor farmers have no choice but to sell our jute to the local merchants at 60 taka. The merchants then sell the jute to the government warehouse at the official price of 90 taka. The merchants then share their profits with the warehouse managers. That's why the managers will not buy from us poor farmers.'

3. 'I am a poor farmer's wife. I have six children. My husband and I need a large family so that we have sons to look after us when old. Our children also earn extra income, and work in the fields. But now that I have enough children I would like to stop having more children. But the government health workers do not like to visit my poor village. I hear that foreign countries have been giving free birth-control pills, but we hardly get any from the government. And nobody teaches us how to use them properly.'

4. 'I am a government bank manager. I approve low-interest loans from the government to help farmers buy fertilisers and seeds. I prefer to lend to the rich farmers. They know how to fill in the forms. They have enough land as security for the loan. They are always very friendly and take me out to lunch. The poor farmers cannot be trusted. They cannot even read the forms and waste my time. And if their harvests are bad, I cannot get them to repay their loans. So it's easier to lend to those richer farmers.'

5. 'I am a poor farmer's wife. My children often get sick from drinking the dirty water or not eating enough food. I cannot afford to take them to see the doctor and the government has very few health workers for us poor people. If I use what little money I have to buy medicine, how can I feed the other children?'

Group E statements

1. 'I am a poor farmer. In 1974, when the price of rice increased 5 times, more than 100 000 people starved to death. Some floods had destroyed crops in some districts. But the merchants had lots of rice which they bought and kept in their warehouses so that they can make higher profits when the price goes up again. The government was also inefficient and did not distribute available food to the starving people. I had to borrow money from the money-lender just to keep my family alive. Many of my neighbours even had to sell off their land at very low prices. After the famine, many of us still cannot afford to buy rice, so we live on cooked jute leaves.'

2. 'I am a landless labourer. There are more and more of us in the country as small farmers lose their land, but the number of jobs available has not increased. So our wages have gone down. Even the meal we get at work is less. Now we get only a pound of rice, with salt, a green chilli, and maybe a spoon of dal. I have six mouths to feed. I earn in one day 2 pounds of rice and 1 taka; 2 pounds of rice can feed only two people per day. Yesterday I did not work, so I did not eat. Finally, I had to tear out three bamboo poles from my house and sell them to buy some flour for us. How can we live like this?'

3. 'I am a poor Bangladeshi woman. When I was 13 years old, my parents arranged for me to marry a small farmer. My parents could only afford a small dowry, so my husband is a poor farmer. I try to be a good wife, but often he comes home and beats me up when he is unhappy or cannot get work. I have nowhere else to go; what else can I do but suffer quietly?'

Group F statements (For Green Revolution simulation, topic 6)

1. 'I am a Bangladesh official in the Ministry of Agriculture. Our country wants to increase food production, so we are encouraging our farmers to use the miracle seeds and lots of fertilisers, pesticides and irrigation. I am sure we shall be able to feed all our people soon.'

2. 'I am a rich farmer. I am the leader of the village co-operative. Our members are mostly rich and middle farmers since we can afford the membership fees. Our co-operative has obtained cheap loans from the government bank to buy the new seeds and fertilisers. The government has also given us a tube well and power pump for irrigation. We are very grateful to the government officials and thank them with gifts.'

3. 'I am a poor farmer. When the government told us to use the new seeds, we wanted to, but they were too expensive, and we could not afford the fertilisers either. We need water for the new seeds, but we have no wells or irrigation. One of my friends borrowed money to grow those new varieties; now he's in trouble, as the money-lender wants him to pay back quickly. He might now lose his land, too.'

4. 'I am an agricultural expert from the World Bank. I am responsible for bringing tube wells to improve irrigation for the farmers. Each tube well is supposed to serve 25 to 50 farmers, especially the poor farmers. But I now know who is getting the tube wells. All of them are going to the big farmers and to the politicians and civil servants who also own land. The rich farmers and landlords expect the poor to pay for getting water, but they can't afford that. My World Bank officials back in Washington know about this, but they are afraid to upset the Bangladesh government. I'm afraid to lose my job too if I complain too much.'

Based on and/or adapted from anthropological studies of Hartmann and Boyce (1983)

Figure 9.7 Bangladesh village life (Photograph: Panos Pictures/Mark Edwards)

Sample teaching unit 2: aid issues

Topic	Activity	Issues/questions	Values/attitudes
1. Introduction to aid	Introduce students to different kinds of aid and levels of aid.	Distinguish between bilateral/multilateral, NGO aid, relief aid.	
	Have class brainstorm in small groups on why they should give aid to Third World.	Differences between Western, Soviet bloc and OPEC aid. Open-ended exploration of possible reasons for giving aid. Concept of tied aid.	Ask each student to make a commitment on paper about giving aid; retain for post-programme comparison.
2. Existing views on causes of poverty	Optional: administer if Sample teaching unit 1 has not been taught. Retain responses for post-programme comparison.	See Sample teaching unit 1 (Activity 2)	
3. Case study of Philippines: introduction to inequalities	Basic knowledge of Philippines geography: social, political and economic conditions. Use CAA booklet on The Third World War: The Philippines. See film, To Sing our Own Song.	Rich–poor gaps; rural–urban gaps; urban poverty. Centralised power of Marcos regime. Militarised repression, human rights abuse. Role of church; liberation theology. Non-violent and revolutionary paths of opposition (aid involvement).	Is it moral for Filipino rich to spend $250 000 on a single watch while poor are hungry? Who do students identify with most in the film: Marcos family? Rich elites? Cardinal Sin? Workers? Urban poor? Rural poor? Tortured nun? Childred of murdered peasants? Senator Diokno? NPA guerillas? Clarify values of choices.
4. Father Brian Gore's case	Understanding of Father Brian Gore's work and circumstances leading up to arrest and voluntary exile from the Philippines.

Read extracts from McCoy (1984) Priests on Trial and Fr Gore's present criticisms of Australian aid and of Filipino system. | Functions of Basic Christian Communities: struggle for basic human needs and rights.

Why was Father Gore seen as threat?

Leave open detailed discussion of issues of Australian aid to next unit.

How has the overthrow of Marcos changed the situation of the poor? | Awareness that poor and oppressed can organise themselves to challenge elites and powerful: fatalism can be overcome through conscientisation.

Students' attitudes to common charge that Fr Gore mixing religion with politics. Clarify definition of politics. If they were priest in Fr Gore's position, what would they do? |
| 5. Australian–Philippines aid | Give class information on scale and type of Australian aid to Philippines.

See slide–tape, Development Aid: Like It or Not.

Read extracts of statements by Foreign Minister Hayden on justification of Australian aid, including military aid. | Economic aid programmes. Military aid programmes. (Also give some overview of US aid and influence in Philippines.)

Discuss the modernisation model of aid; then criticisms of that model by the PEACE paradigm. Who benefits from road building? Aid when given under conditions of inequalities tends to be usurped by rich and powerful. | Which model would students support? Clarify values for choice.

Is military aid morally justified?

Would students feel enough sense of injustice to engage in praxis to make Australian aid more peaceful? Explore |

Sample teaching unit 2: aid issues (cont.)

Topic	Activity	Issues/questions	Values/attitudes
		Would poor be 'hurt' if large-scale government-controlled aid projects stopped – could be diverted to partipatory small-scale NGO aid. Does military training in Australia necessarily produce more 'humane' soldiers?	options for alternative forms of aid and necessary prerequisites for basic needs aid.
6. Non-governmental aid	Describe types of NGO aid, various agencies. Distribute pamphlets from various NGOs. Analyse various mass-media advertisements used by agencies to raise funds.	Child sponsorship schemes, food aid, participatory grassroots projects. Explore differences in assumptions, explanations of poverty in different advertisements, e.g. compare 'Wealth: No. 1 World's Killer' to 'If you don't help, XXX will Die . . .' etc.	 Explore values when confronted by those different messages. Which ones are students most likely to respond to?
	Discuss child sponsorship schemes. Read extracts of children's letters to adopting parents (from New Internationalist special issues June 1985 and May 1982).	Social and psychological impact on adopted children, their families and community. Can it be long-term? Does it tackle roots of structural violence?	How would they feel to have to depend perpetually on hand-outs from rich foreigners? Can aid be more dignified?
	If possible, ask students to bring along samples of letters if their parents are child-sponsors (but ensure anonymity).		
	Live Aid concert and food aid.	While necessary for emergency relief, food aid has many disadvantages: diverted by government and corruption to non-needy groups; distorts indigenous agricultural development. Compassion raised by Live Aid shows rich-country people can care about Third World suffering, but such compassion needs to be informed by awareness of structural violence.	Did students support Live Aid? Is one rock concert enough? Do rock stars understand roots of structural violence? How would equalised world order affect rock stars' lifestyles?
	See film, Sangham	Landless organised through self-help NGO project to demand their rights to land and work and fair wages.	People can help themselves with support from outside. Aid without dependency. Long-term development better.
	Distribute literature of local groups supporting long-term participatory NGO aid, e.g. Oxfam. Invite their education officers to give talks.	Concept of aid as 'solidarity' rather than pity. Aid for justice for poor not serving rich-country interests or elites' interests.	Willingness to participate in fund-raising activities for such participatory projects, e.g. Walk Against Want. Encourage parents and family to participate also.
7. Post-programme assessment	Readminister questionnaire on causes and solutions to Third World poverty.	Compare pre-programme with post-programme responses. Explore reasons for change in terms of teaching/learning meterials.	Have students emerged from programme with greater compassion and respect for poor? Willing to de-develop?

The structural violence game

Vanessa Letham

Introduction →

I have found during the course of my work in the area of educating for peace and justice that young people are readily able to relate to the concepts of physical and verbal violence. They will often volunteer that there are physchological forms of violence too but, in my experience, no-one has yet mentioned structural violence unprompted.

Because structural violence is such a difficult concept to grasp, it could be treated in a way other than the traditional 'chalk and talk' method. *The structural violence game* is one such method.

However, it should be remembered that simulations oversimplify and mask the complex and deep-rooted nature of structural violence. Students will need to be guided towards an understanding of these complexities. Since the inception of the game during the last half of 1984, it has been changed and modified on a number of occasions. The original version appears in *Peacemeal* (Vol. 1. No. 3). In this version the 'oppressed' section of the class rolled newspapers to 'sell' to their 'oppressors' but the temptation to use them as weapons proved irresistable on a number of occasions. A potentially less violent version is printed here.

In a group that knows each other well and with a teacher who has good rapport with them, there may be a place for the original version. The evaluation session, particularly after 'violence' has broken out, is most revealing. Young people were very quickly able to see how oppression can lead to revolution.

Having used the game on numerous occasions, I have never ceased to be amazed at the range of strategies people use to procure a chocolate biscuit. In their simulated form I have seen the 'oppressed' try coercion, blackmail, selling-out their fellow sufferers, bartering, striking, sabotage and subterfuge. The 'oppressors' use stand-over tactics, threats, introduce 'agent provocateurs', withdraw the raw material, flaunt chocolate biscuits in front of the 'oppressed', make deals, bribe and cheat. In a number of cases the 'oppressed' have felt so disillusioned that they have stretched out on the floor and 'died'. A proportion of the 'oppressors' in every game feel dreadful about what they are doing and either withdraw from the playing of the game or try to make the conditions of the 'oppressed' a little better. The social change activists of the future perhaps? Leaders of the 'oppressed' usually emerge too, with well-orchestrated strikes and boycotts being organised.

On the occasions when teachers have joined in the game I have made sure that they join the ranks of the 'oppressed'. In this role they are far less likely to take over and try to direct proceedings. Many teachers have indicated that they felt powerless; squeezed in with others, unable to be in control and with their freedom of movement and speech curtailed.

It cannot be stressed too much that at the end of simulation games some people will have strong feelinngs evoked that will need to be dealt with. That is why it is very important to evaluate thoroughly the session straight away, allowing plenty of time for everyone to have their say. The de-role games suggested at the end of the game may at first seem silly and frivolous, but the intention is to release any tension that still remains, and restore group solidarity.

The structural violence game benefits from follow-up activities such as a media search, with the students finding as many examples of reported structurally violent situations as they can in any given week. A case study of one particular incident could be used for discussion of the ways in which the situation may be resolved non-violently.

Follow-up should include study of the less overt forms of structural violence. Elicit ideas on examples in a local context: at home, at school, in the governing of the country and the condition of the poor and oppressed here. Brainstorming is fast and efficient while allowing many people to contribute their ideas.

Small-group discussion is far less threatening to the individual in the group, giving them more freedom to discuss honestly an issue such as structural violence and how it relates to their life. This type of discussion may call into question the traditional forms of decision making. The group can find working alternatives to traditional hierarchical decision making, suggest ideas of their own and implement these in a classroom setting. For a whole day, all of the decisions could be made according to parliamentary procedures. On another day consensus could be used. An evaluation of the pros and cons of both systems could follow.

The game is a valuable teaching aid, but not the whole story in dealing with issues and concepts of structural violence. To be of any value at all, preparation, evaluation and follow-up are essential. Your own personal evaluation of the game would be most welcome to assist with the further development of this game and others to follow.

Objective

To explore the concept of structural violence through role play.

Materials

Ball of string or wool
Packet of chocolate-coated biscuits
Packet of plain dry crackers
Two ice-cream containers to store the biscuits
Computer paper for wall charts
Four (only) felt-tipped pens, various colours
Pile of scrap paper for folding and decorating
Wallcharts of 'rules'
Yellow and green sticky spots: ratio of 2:1
Blutak

Scenario

(Reproduce on a wall chart)
Yellow and Green are neighbouring countries.
Green supplies Yellow with paper to fold and decorate with pens (which are found only in the Yellow country).
Green buys the finished product and pays in biscuits.
Yellow depends on this industry to survive.
Green sells the finished product to the Green food distributor who pays her/his fellow Green in chocolate biscuits.
Green's lifestyle and status is measured by the quality and quantity of the folded paper.
Payment is calculated by quality and quantity.

General rules

(Reproduce on a wall chart)
Yellows may not leave their country.
Greens may come and go as they please.
Yellows may not talk to Greens or to more than one Yellow at a time.
Greens have no restriction on their freedom of speech.
Yellows may use paper and pens.
Green police enforce these rules.

Private rules:

(Reproduce on small sheet of paper for the Greens *only* to see)
Unless the paper is folded and decorated satisfactorily, Green will not supply Yellow with food.

Maximum payment is one biscuit per piece of paper.
Payment may be withheld if the workers are heard to complain.
Payment is actually in crackers, not in chocolate biscuits.

Instructions →

1. An open space is best. In a classroom it is best to clear desks and chairs.

2. Section off a corner of the room with the string and make it just large enough for two thirds of the group to fit in with standing room only.

3. Sit the participants in a circle to explain the rules of the game.

4. Distribute the spots (two yellow for every one green) separating friends where possible and making sure that the Greens are not all one sex.

5. Display wall charts and allow a few minutes for questions.

6. Send Yellows to the sectioned-off corner of the room.

7. Give the containers of biscuits to one of the Greens whose job it is now to distribute them.

8. Give one chocolate biscuit to one of the Yellows to share with the whole of the rest of the Yellow group and indicate that this is being done in the interests of fairness!

9. Make sure that the Greens do not declare that the other container holds crackers.

10. Appoint one or more Greens to be police.

11. Give the Yellows the felt-tipped pens, and give the paper to the Greens who will give it to the Yellows once the game starts.

12. Hand the 'Private rules' to one of the Greens.

13. Allow 3–5 minutes for the participants to get into their roles, then start the game. There is no set time for the running of this game. Much depends on the group. Fifteen minutes is a workable time. Some groups get very involved and time should be allowed for them to keep going. Other groups get disillusioned very quickly and the attention of some participants may wander. It is best to stop the game after the fifteen minutes if this is the case.

14. Stop the game. Call the participants to form a circle. Each participant in turn should now have the opportunity to state how they feel about their role. Individuals may 'pass' if they wish. This time is for sharing, not for discussing.

Evaluation →

Time should now be made available for discussion. Discussion starters such as the following may be used:
(a) What happened?
(b) How many forms of structural violence were observed?
(c) What did the Yellow group do? How did they react?
(d) What did the Green group do? How did they react?
(e) What positive steps could both parties have taken to improve the situation?
(f) Why did the Yellows allow themselves to be oppressed?
(g) What are parallel situations in the world that were reflected in this game?
(h) What do the two types of biscuits represent?

Conclusion →

Ask all the participants to remove their coloured spots. Share out the biscuits among the Yellows if there are any left.
Play an active de-role game such as 'Touch blue', 'Pruee' or 'Tangles'.

From: Letham, V. (1986) Educating for Peace, Justice and Hope, Peacemaking Project, P.O. Box, 452, Fremantle, Australia, 6160.

10 The geography of war and peace

DAVID HICKS

The geography of war

Understanding the world

Issues of war and peace are critical to the lives of everyone on this planet today. Helping young people to understand the nature of such issues is part of the geographer's broader task of exploring a wide range of contemporary issues. The breadth of these issues is admirably indicated in many maps in *The State of the World Atlas (SWA)* (Kidron and Segal, 1981), *The New State of the World Atlas (NSWA)* (Kidron and Segal, 1984) and *The War Atlas (TWA)* (Kidron and Smith, 1983). In various ways these maps graphically portray the problems of violence faced by many inhabitants of this planet today.

It is useful here to distinguish broadly between two sorts of violence: direct and indirect (see Chapter 1). Direct or personal violence occurs when someone is killed or physically hurt, whether as a result of warfare, terrorism, civil unrest or assault. The effects of indirect or structural violence may eventually be the same, but they relate to suffering caused by social, economic and political structures. Thus human beings suffer both subjectively and objectively from, for example, racism, sexism, apartheid, lack of food, lack of health care, lack of education. The atlases named above provide map resources for geography teaching on direct and structural violence:

Direct violence

- Military spending (*SWA* map 8; *NSWA* Map 7; *TWA* Maps 23, 24 and 25).
- Nuclear stockpiles (*SWA* Map 9; *NSWA* Map 8; *TWA* Map 9).
- Violent conflicts between 1913 and 1983 (*NSWA* Map 10; *TWA* Maps 1, 2, 3 and 4).
- Arms sales (*SWA* Map 11; *TWA* Maps 29, 30, 31, 32, 33 and 34).
- Refugee crises (*SWA* Map 32; *NSWA* Map 26).

Structural violence

- Proportion of GDP spent on education, health and armaments (*SWA* Map 29; *NSWA* Map 24; *TWA* Map 24).
- Languages and religions of rule (*SWA* Maps 33 and 34; *NSWA*, Maps 27 and 28).
- The treatment of ethnic minorities (*NSWA* Map 56).
- Inequalities in access to education (*SWA* Map 46; *NSWA* Map 41).
- The treatment of the earth and ecosystems (*SWA*, Maps 53 and 54; *NSWA*, Maps 45, 46, 47, 48 and 53; *TWA* Map 38).
- The control of economic wealth (*SWA*, Maps 36 and 37; *NSWA*, Maps 29, 30 and 31).
- Freedom of conscience (*SWA* Map 31; *NSWA* Maps 23 and 25).

With the help of these atlases, geographers can play a vital role in helping young people make sense of different conflicts in the world today. Apart from these atlases, a range of very practical materials exist which can be used even with younger pupils (Fisher and Hicks, 1985). The point to be stressed here is that the problems of violence and peace are various and numerous. They are the proper domain of human, political and economic geographers. War is but one of the issues that one might properly wish to teach about here.

Understanding war

'As a *professional* the grographer can and should be involved in issues of human survival' argue Pepper and Jenkins (1983). If we are concerned with spatial patterns and social processes then these need to be studied in relation to armaments, security and defence as well as in other contexts. The particular contribution of geographers, it can be argued, is to emphasise the spatial and environmental aspects of armed conflict and peace. Again, excellent maps and other data

(Sivard, 1986; Barnaby, 1988) are available for the use of teachers.

The topics that can be studied are many and varied and they can be developed in a wide variety of ways for the classroom. In terms of geopolitics one could study spheres of influence, heartlands, buffer zones, foreign bases and territorial expansion. One could also look at alliances such as NATO, ANZUS and the Warsaw Pact, the proliferation of nuclear weapons and the call for nuclear-free zones. Warfare has a very violent effect on both human welfare and on the natural and made landscapes. The outreach of both the military–industrial complex (Prins, 1983) and the arms trade have complex social and economic consequences.

In particular we should be studying that most vital and threatening of issues: the nuclear arms race. Openshaw and Steadman (1982) write:

> By solving a special type of geographical location-allocation problem it is possible to identify an optimal set of demographic targets which approximately maximise the number of civilian casualties in the event of a large-scale nuclear attack on Britain.

The threat of nuclear war to Britain is well described by Openshaw, Steadman and Greene (1983), as are important elements of the arms race and the peace movement by Sharp (1984) and the Australian legacy of British A-bomb tests in Australia during the 1950s by Tame and Robotham (1982) and Milliken (1986). It is worth noting that an Aboriginal geographer, William Jonas, was one of the three commissioners who investigated the social and environmental impacts of these tests for the Australian government. In all cases, both nuclear and non-nuclear, maps are of paramount importance: to show bomb targets, the effects of explosion, the location of weaponry, the distribution of military aid, theatres of war, power blocks, the climatic effects of a nuclear winter, and so on. But geographers should also be skilled at criticising maps and much of the propaganda of the cold war could benefit from dispassionate analysis here.

Important perspectives

It is vital when we teach about war that we raise a series of critical questions. The 'popular wisdom' about war does little to challenge its imperatives or its apparent natural momentum but, as with all the issues that geographers study, implicit ideologies need to be made clear.

One popular view of war argues that it is a natural outcome of human aggression. If people and countries are obviously aggressive by nature it is not surprising that we have wars. Now, while the causes of war are complex, the human aggression argument is a demonstrably false one. Conventional wisdom draws heavily on the writings of popular theorists such as Lorenz and Ardrey who have argued, often from the study of non-humans, that people are competitive, territorial and aggressive by nature. There is, however, considerable debate about the nature of human aggression and we and our pupils need to be aware of this. There is ample research evidence to suggest that aggressive behaviour may be something that is culturally learnt (Montagu, 1976), that it is the result of nurture rather than nature. If this is the case then we may need to rethink radically many of our assumptions about human behaviour.

It is also important to set war in the broader context of militarism generally. By militarism here is meant: taking as healthy and normal the use, or potential use, of armed force to resolve conflict. While actual war may be distant from many people's lives, militarism is not. The cost of militarism to any society can be considerable (Sharp and Trainer, 1984). Half of the world's scientists and engineers are occupied full-time in military research and development, while the budget of the US airforce is larger than the total educational budget for 1.2 billion children in Africa, Latin America, and Asia excluding Japan.

In political terms the insecurity generated in times of recession can easily be focused on enemies, both without and within. Accelerated arms races are also often associated with increased nationalism. The moral costs of militarism may be considerable as witnessed by our disinterested acceptance of indiscriminate killing and our learnt powerlessness in the face of the nuclear threat. Given the variety of war toys, war comics, war films and war games that are available in our society we should not be surprised. Perhaps we should reconsider our professional responsibilities here.

Feminist perspectives on militarism (Enloe, 1983) are particularly valuable and should be a staple part of any geographical consideration of war. If warfare is in fact a *male* construct through which some men as a group generally benefit and most women as a group suffer, we need to look carefully at the ways in which we socialise our children. After all, most boys learn that to be masculine is to be not feminine and that proving one's manhood against the 'enemy' is the ultimate test.

The geography of peace

Some definitions

One of the dangers of bracketing war and peace together is that they are taken to be opposites, the negation of each other. As indicated previously, war is best seen as but one form of male violence. Certainly the state of 'not war' is often called peace, but this is a totally inadequate definition of the word.

It is perhaps most helpful to return to the concepts of direct and indirect violence. If in a relationship, an institution, a country or the world, we have no direct violence between people, this may be defined as *negative peace*. Certainly such a state would be a dramatic step *en route* to a better world. It does, however, result in a definition of peace as 'absence of'.

However, if there is an absence of direct violence but injustice and inequality are present, this is hardly peaceful. Thus we need to develop the concept of *positive peace*, that is peace as both a state and a process, involving the presence of the goals referred to in Chapter 1: justice, equality, participation, non-violence and ecological balance.

Peace as well-being

To study the geography of peace is to analyse, reflect on, predict, map, and attempt to foster, human well-being on scales from the personal to the global. If we really do want to teach geography for a better world then our task can be nothing less than this.

Now, while such a task may at first seem impossible, each of us is responsible for the life-world that we find ourselves in. Although we can claim that it is not of our making, we do in fact have the choice of leaving it as it is, letting it get worse, or working to improve it. The first two courses of action have the same result: they support a status quo which is detrimental to the well-being of most people on the planet.

As educators we have a particular responsibility to young people. We need to ensure that we 'use the concerns and knowledge of [our] discipline to confront the central concerns of our times' (Pepper and Jenkins, 1985), however controversial these may be. If our pupils are to become informed citizens in

a democratic society then they need to explore and understand the debates, arguments, differing value-positions and perspectives on achieving human well-being at an early age. They can only do this effectively if our teaching styles are active, experiential, participatory and enquiry-based.

Strategies for geographical studies of war and peace

Some possibilities for making studies of war and peace are detailed in the curriculum project, *World Studies 8–13*, and the activities of groups such as the Peace Pledge Union. Three examples which geography teachers may choose to use are:

* Nuclear issues (a teacher activity)
* The nuclear chain (a student activity)
* The co-operative shapes/map game (a student activity).

Details of these activities are included in the following pages of this chapter. Each is based on discussion in small and large groups, using principles of the planning of structured discussion groups suggested by Richardson in Fisher and Hicks (1985). These principles for structured discussion are important not only for effective learning. They are also vital to help students learn about peace by learning peacefully in an environment free of structural pressures. Richardson's principles include the following.

1. *Things to handle.* Arrange for pupils to have things which are literally tangible: objects, pictures, slips of paper, which they can move around with their hands.

2. *Precise tasks.* Give precise instructions about what is to be done. For example: 'Here are pictures of six different people. Choose the two people you would most like to meet. For each of them, write down the one question you would most like to ask.'

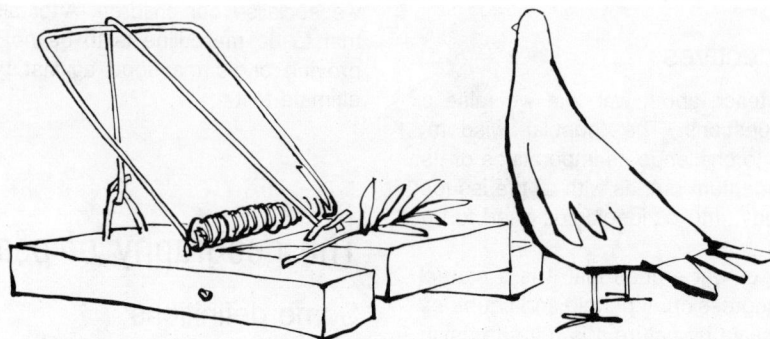

Figure 10.1 (Cartoon: Len Munnik)

3. *Co-operation.* Choose discussion tasks which require pupils to listen to each other and to help each other. For example, use 'jigsaw games', which can only be completed if everyone takes part.

4. *Small groups.* The smaller the group, the more pupils feel secure. Also, the more they're able to talk. Often arrange for them to work in pairs or in threes. The maximum for most group work is six.

5. *Controversy.* Choose subjects on which pupils are likely to have conflicting opinions. Or build controversy into a discussion by requiring some of the participants to play specific roles.

6. *Non-verbal materials.* Use material which communicates ideas symbolically and non-verbally rather than through words alone: photographs, cartoons, posters, statistical diagrams.

7. *Comparing, contrasting, selecting, justifying.* Provide a collection of things to be compared and contrasted with each other; require pupils to arrange them or to select from them; and to explain their arrangement or selection.

8. *Activity then reflection.* Give pupils an activity to perform, or require them to watch an activity: for example, a non-verbal game or exercise. Then invite discussion and clarification of what happened, and of how they felt, and of what can be learned.

9. *Not too easy, not too hard.* Definitely try to stretch pupils with discussion tasks you set. But do not depress them or annoy them by providing things which are too difficult. When you fail (as you sometimes will) to get the balance right, invite discussion of how people feel.

Activity 1: Nuclear issues
(A teacher activity)

Introduction ⟶

This activity is designed to encourage teachers to reflect on a range of nuclear issues and to select those they feel are relevant to geography.

Objectives ⟶

1. To reflect on the geographical nature of a range of nuclear issues.
2. To choose those that can be incorporated in a secondary school geography course.
3. To discuss appropriate resources and teaching strategies.

Instructions ⟶

Give all participants a copy of Figure 10.2, Nuclear issues. It describes nine nuclear issues and indicates how each one might be used with a class.

1. Participants read about the nine issues and consider their potential contribution to geographical education. These are ranked in the shape of a diamond with rank 1 being the most pertinent geographical issue. Teachers work in pairs to agree on their ranking.

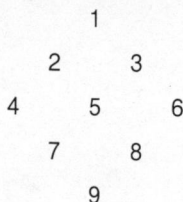

1

2   3

4   5   6

7   8

9

2. Briefly describe where in your courses you would include the three issues ranked 1–3, the resources you have, know about or would need, and the teaching strategies you would use.

Debriefing ⟶

The activity can be debriefed by considering the following.

1. What were your top three issues and why?
2. Which issues were not considered to be of great geographical importance?
3. What subjects should have responsibility for teaching about these other issues?
4. What educational benefits can be gained from teaching about the issues ranked 1–3 by most people?
5. What resources are available?
6. What are some appropriate teaching strategies?
7. Ask selected teachers to describe a successful lesson or unit on a nuclear topic.
8. Ask selected teachers to describe any lesson or unit on a nuclear topic that did not go very well.
9. Discuss the opportunities and difficulties geography teachers face in teaching about nuclear issues.

1. SUPERPOWERS

Students will examine the perceptions, mis-perceptions and stereotypes that the USA, USSR and their allies have of each other. They will evaluate the need for 'images of the enemy' to fuel the arms race.

2. ARMS RACE

Students will learn about the arms race, both conventional and nuclear. They will examine its history, its global dimensions, the arms trade and its effects on social and economic development, especially in the Third World.

3. FUEL CYCLE

Students will explore the links in the nuclear fuel cycle: from uranium mining, enrichment and nuclear reactors to re-processing, waste storage and the use of plutonium for weapons. British and overseas examples will be used.

4. NUCLEAR TESTING ·

Students will research the effects of nuclear tests on the environment and people in North America, the USSR, Australia and the Pacific Islands.

5. US BASES

Students will look at the location of American military bases in Europe, their global connections and their various functions. They will expand the scale of their study to compare USA and USSR military bases and operations world-wide. They will then weigh up the arguments both for and against their continued presence.

6. HIROSHIMA AND NAGASAKI

Students will examine the events that led up to the atomic bombing of Hiroshima and Nagasaki in 1945. They will study both the immediate and long-term effects on Japan and the world.

7. THE EFFECTS OF A POSSIBLE NUCLEAR WAR

Students will research the different sorts of damage that could be caused by nuclear weapons on people and the environment today. They will do this for towns in Britain and on a global scale.

8. LIVING IN A NUCLEAR AGE

Students will discuss the psychological effects on people, especially young people, of living in a society of mounting tension and the threat of 'the bomb'. They will see how other people feel, and contrast this with their own hopes and fears for the future.

9. THE PEACE PROCESS

Students will investigate the roles and aspirations of peace movements. The links between medical, scientific, educational, church and popularist groups in the peace movement will be explored, as well as international peace processes, such as disarmament conferences, and the work of various United Nations bodies.

Figure 10.2 Nuclear issues

Activity 2: The nuclear chain
(A pupil activity)

Introduction ⟹

This activity is designed to illustrate the key stages in what is sometimes known as the nuclear fuel cycle. In particular it attempts to draw out some of the dilemmas and hazards associated with this nuclear chain. It can form *one* part of a scheme of work on nuclear issues.

Objectives ⟹

1. To understand the main stages in the nuclear chain.
2. To illustrate the global nature of this nuclear chain.
3. To discuss the associated benefits and hazards.

Instructions ⟹

The class may work in pairs or in groups of five or six students. Give each pair or group a set of the seven title cards (Figure 10.3) and the seven nuclear chain cards (Figure 10.4). Their instructions are as follows:
1. Lay the seven title cards face up on the table.
2. Lay the seven nuclear chain cards face down on the table.
3. Take it in turns to pick up a nuclear chain card and to read out the description on it. Continue until all seven cards have been read out.
4. Match the descriptive nuclear chain cards to the appropriate title cards.
5. Arrange the paired cards in the sequence that seems most appropriate.
6. Write the title of each stage in the appropriate place on the world map (see Figure 10.5).
7. Pairs or groups discuss the possible benefits or hazards associated with each link in the nuclear chain.

Debriefing ⟹

The activity can be debriefed by considering the following questions.
1. Which title cards go with which nuclear chain cards?
2. Were they easy to match? Were any difficult to match? If so, why? It is not necessary to spend too long on this stage. Some terms on the nuclear chain cards may need explaining at this point.
3. What do you think is the appropriate sequence for the nuclear chain cards? How did you work this out? See how many variations pupils come up with. Discuss until a preferred sequence emerges.
4. Where have the stages in the nuclear chain been located on the world map?
5. How did you decide where each stage went?

It is possible at this point to discuss other routes of the nuclear chain. For example, uranium is mined in America, Canada, South Africa and the Soviet Union, as well as Australia.

6. What benefits are there for each stage in the nuclear chain?
7. What hazards might there be for each stage in the nuclear chain?

Answers to these questions will depend on pupils either (a) having done previous research on these issues, or (b) having access to information while they are involved in the activity.

Extension activities ⟹

1. How many other possible routes are there for the nuclear chain? Map as many of the global links as possible.
2. Many people talk about a *nuclear fuel cycle* in which the cycle is complete when the uranium becomes plutonium in a fast breeder reactor which can then be used again in a fast breeder. Which is the best description, cycle or chain? What are the implications of each term?
3. Develop detailed case studies of debates arising at different points of the nuclear chain: for example, uranium mining; the storage of nuclear waste; nuclear proliferation.

Uranium Mine

Uranium ore is mined and concentrated into yellowcake. Only 1% of this, however, is uranium that can be used to create energy. The mines create employment and revenue for the exporting country. Radioactive radon gas in mines and the waste, called tailings, can cause lung cancer.

Enrichment Plant

By various methods the uranium content is enriched from 2 to 4%. The plant is large, covering hundreds of acres. It requires high electricity consumption and provides many jobs. Later the uranium is packed into fuel rods.

Nuclear Reactor

The fuel rods are used in the reactor to generate heat for the production of electricity. The electricity is fed into the national grid to supply homes and industry. The waste from the reactor is radioactive.

Waste Reprocessing and Storage

Uranium and plutonium are recovered from the used fuel. They can be used again. The remaining waste has to be stored very carefully, however, as it will remain radioactive for many centuries. No totally safe way of storing it has yet been discovered.

Breeder Reactor

This sort of nuclear reactor runs on plutonium and it also converts uranium into more plutonium. This can be used to fuel more such reactors.

Nuclear Weapons Manufacture

Plutonium can be used in the manufacture of nuclear weapons. The two superpowers have thousands of such weapons and compete with each other in what is called the arms race. Some people think this helps to keep the peace, others feel it will sooner or later lead to nuclear war.

Nuclear Proliferation

Other countries also want their own nuclear weapons. Some have learnt to make their own using the plutonium from ordinary nuclear reactors. As nuclear weapons spread to more countries so their use becomes more likely.

Figure 10.3 Title cards

Figure 10.4 Nuclear chain cards

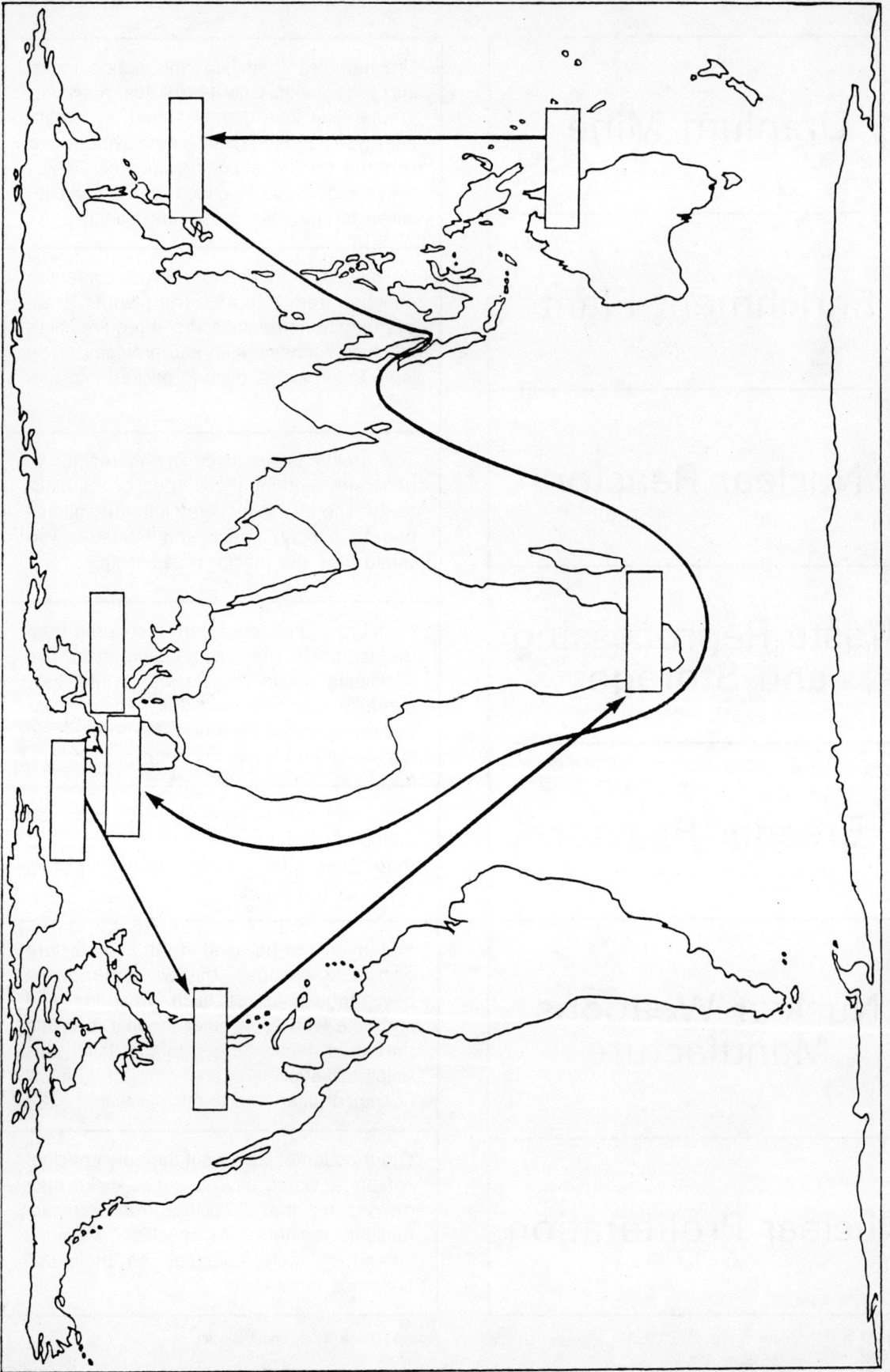

Figure 10.5 The global nuclear chain as it would appear with the starting point in Australia

Further reading ⟶

Bertell, R. (1985) *No Immediate Danger: Prognosis for a Radioactive Earth*, London, The Women's Press Ltd.

Croall, S. and Sempler, K. (1985) *Nuclear Power for Beginners* (revised edition), London, Writers and Readers.

Activity 3: The co-operative shapes map game

This activity is reproduced from *World Studies 8–13: A Teacher's Handbook* (Fisher and Hicks, 1985).

Objective ⟶

To encourage co-operation and empathy.

Preparation ⟶

This activity is for groups of five pupils. Enough copies of the maps in Figure 10.6 are needed for each group in the class to have a complete set. The maps should be cut up by the teacher along the lines indicated, and the pieces of the maps labelled A to E as shown. The appropriate pieces from each set of maps should then be sorted into five envelopes labelled A to E. Each group in the class will receive a complete set of envelopes, with five map pieces in each envelope.

Instructions ⟶

Each group of five sits round a table, and each member of the group is given an envelope with a different letter on it. The envelopes must not be opened yet. The following instructions are given:

- Each of you has an envelope with some pieces of a world map in it.
- Your group is going to make five maps which are exactly the same.
- You will not have finished until everyone has a map which looks the same as everyone else's.
- There are two simple rules. First, there is to be no talking during this game or any other kind of communication: no signs, winks or nods of the head. Second, you may not take a piece from someone else. You are only allowed to give pieces to other members of your group who you think need them.

Discussion ⟶

Pupils will probably want to talk initially about what happened. They can then go on to talk about their feeelings: frustration, irritation perhaps; anxiety at being unable to make a complete map; envy of those who can; dismay at having to dismantle their own map for the good of the group as a whole.

The class can further be asked how easy or difficult it was to put themselves in the position of other members of the group when at the same time they were probably anxious about their own map. And what of the difficulty of empathising with the group as a whole, of seeing the exercise as a task for all the members of the group to solve together rather than as a contest to be won or lost by individuals? How did pupils feel when others saw what pieces they needed and supplied them?

Variation ⟶

A more difficult version of the same activity uses squares instead of maps. Cut along the lines indicated in Figure 10.7.

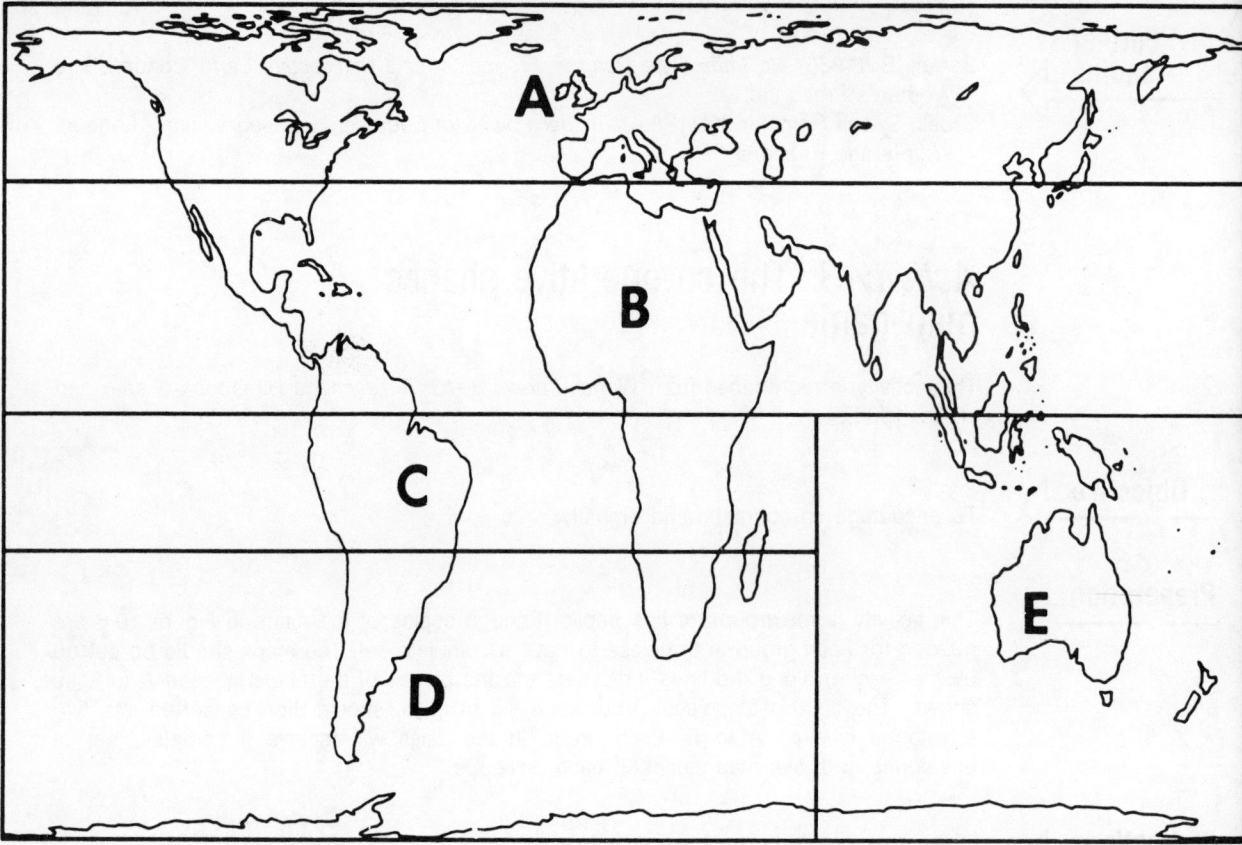

Figure 10.6 The co-operative map game

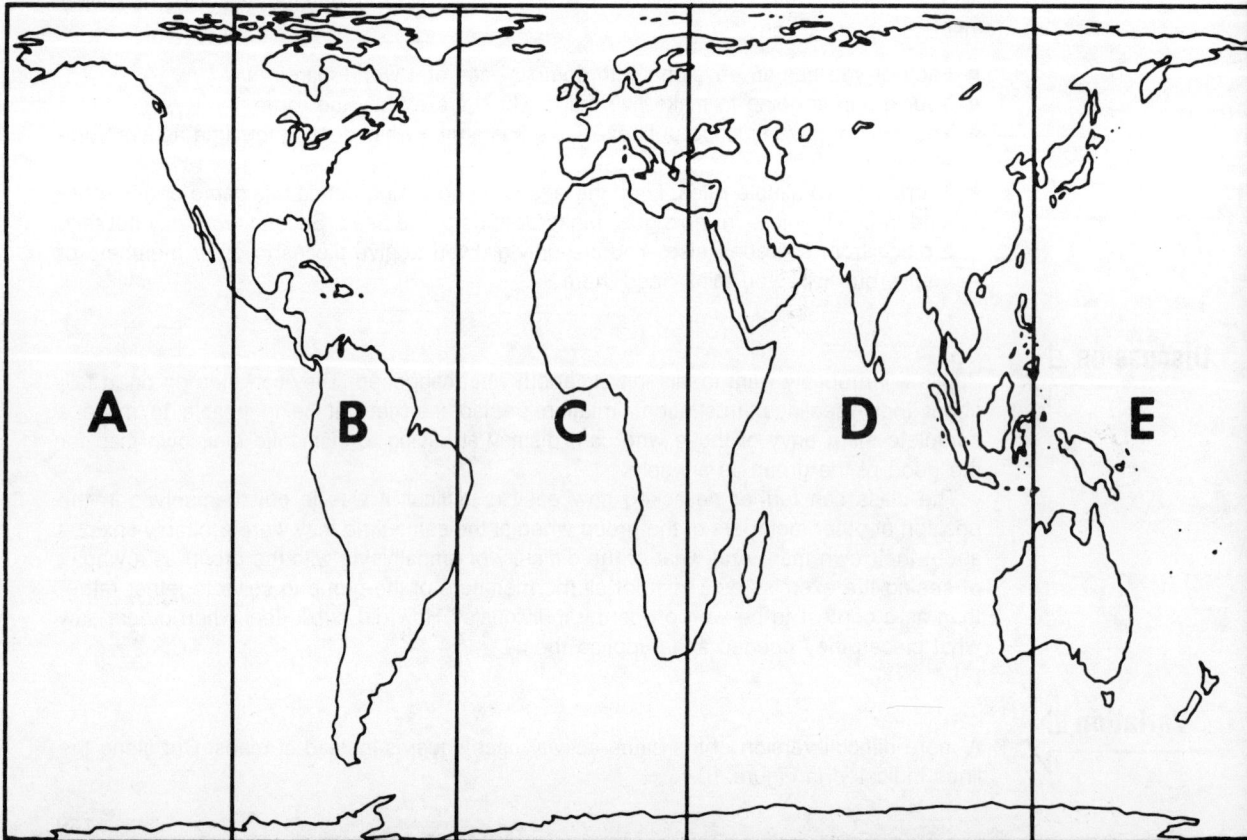

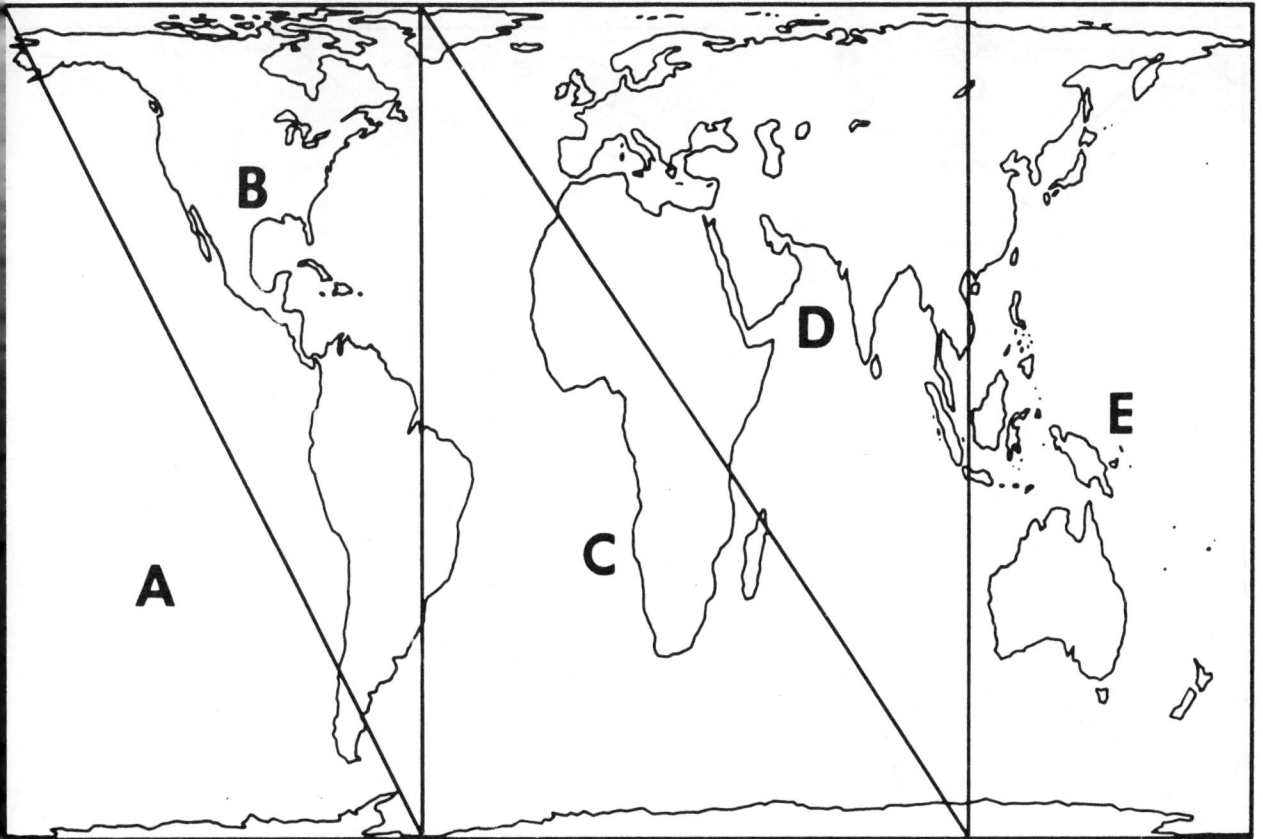

Figure 10.6 continued

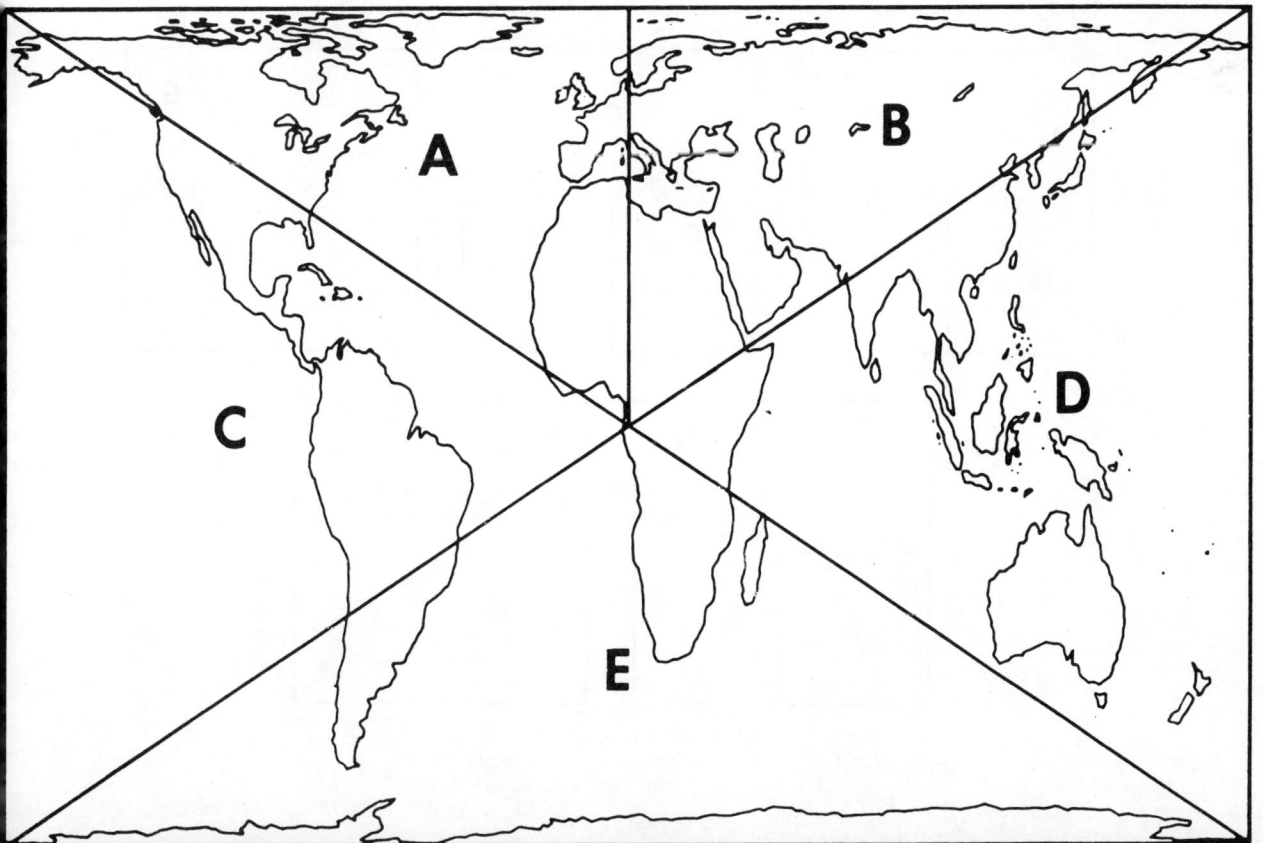

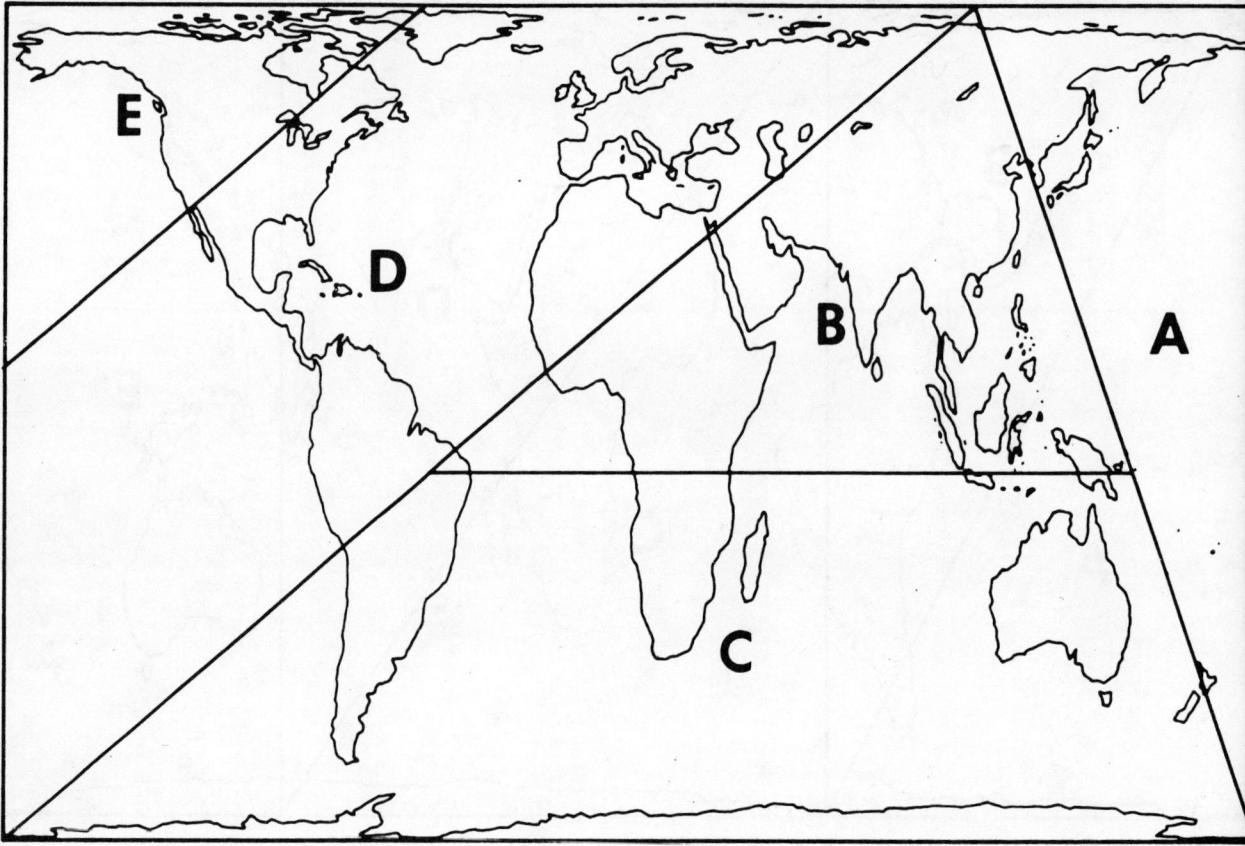

Figure 10.6 continued

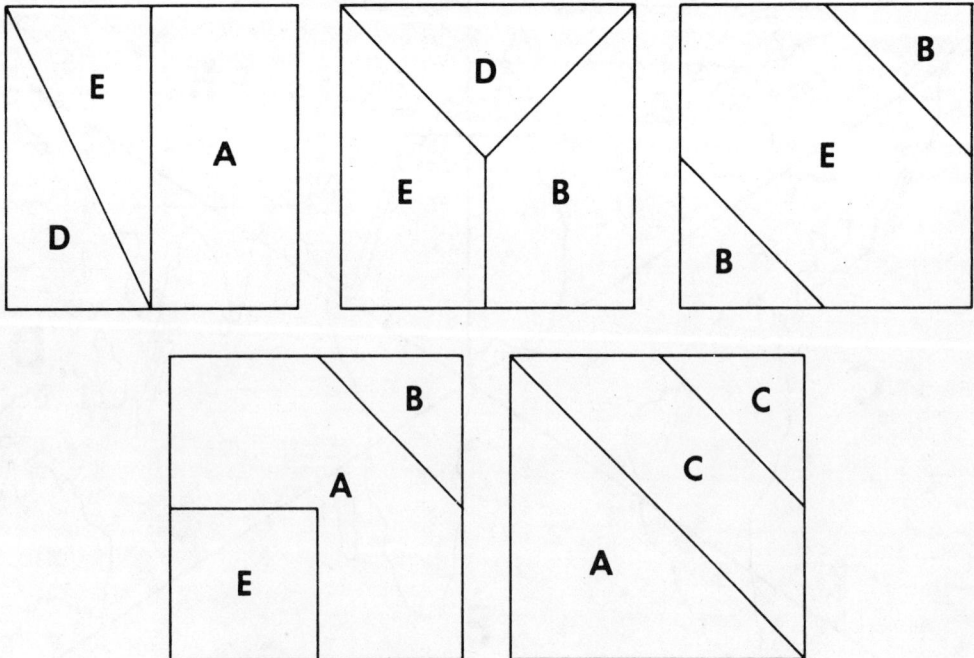

Figure 10.7 Co-operative squares (Source: Richardson, R., *Learning for Change in World Society*, World Studies Project of the One World Trust, 2nd edition, 1979)

11 Sport in geography

JOHN BALE

Introduction

It is too rarely recognised in geographical education that the knowledge which we seek to pass on to our students reflects the values, aspirations and interests of particular groups in society. In this sense most geograpical knowledge is *ideological* (Kirby, 1980). Many things which our students are deeply interested in and involved in outside school are ignored in the school curriculum, which suggests that the curriculum is biased in favour of dominant culture at the expense of cultural forms considered either 'low' or 'popular' in character. This chapter illustrates the biased nature of school geography by noting the absence of, and pleading the case for, sport studies in the geography curriculum.

Sport, one of the most lasting and widespread creations of the nineteenth century, was not only ignored by the political and social scientists of the day (Allison, 1980) but has also been conspicuous by its absence from the school and college curriculum (Thompson, 1980) ever since. Sport is the focus of more present-day media space than either industry, agriculture or politics; sport forms a major interest for many millions of young people; sport is an eminently geographical phenomenon. Yet we have tended to ignore the study (as opposed to the playing) of sport in schools in general, and in geography in particular. Indeed, geography seems more guilty than many other subjects in ignoring sport. A large number of academic journals exists for sports history, sport sociology, sport philosophy and sport psychology. Yet, oddly, geographers have been reluctant to embrace sport as a legitimate area of academic enquiry until very recently.

In this chapter I want to argue the case for sports geography and its greater visibility in the school geography syllabus. I want to suggest that a geographical approach to sport adds much to our knowledge of sport and that sport provides a fertile field for the exemplification of geographical ideas and the involvement of students in critical debate about such issues as environmental pollution and cultural imperialism. I want to add that a greater knowledge of sports geography will enhance the learning experiences of our students and hence their lives in general.

Arguments for sports geography

At least four arguments can be used to justify the study of sport in school in terms of both cognitive (knowledge) and affective (attitudinal) aims of education. Firstly, sport is a growth industry and a highly visible part of modern life. Secondly, sport is a particularly geographical phenomenon. Thirdly, sport forms a major part of the knowledge which children bring with them to school and upon which a student-centred and radical education might be partly based. Fourthly, sport provides a ready vehicle for the examination of some of the structures within which our deep-seated attitudes and behaviours are embedded.

Sport: a growth industry

Mass participatory sport and top-class achievement sport are both part of the recreation and leisure industries; mass sport because participants take part in it for recreational purposes, and elite sport because it attracts large numbers of spectators, either live or via television or radio, who watch sport as part of their leisure time. ('Playing' serious sport can be regarded more as work than play. See Rigauer (1981).) Few would deny that as we move into a post-industrial society the time spent on leisure and recreation is increasing. How leisure time is spent has obvious geographical implications in terms of land use, spatial interaction and regional variations in recreation opportunities.

Within the gamut of recreational activities a number of sport-oriented pursuits display dramatic growth. In Britain, activities such as swimming, golf, tennis, squash and running are growth sports, while team games tend to be in a relative decline (Blacksell, 1982). But even in football (soccer), which at the professional level has lost spectators steadily since the 1940s, the number of clubs at the recreational level continues to grow. New sports such as hang-gliding show spectacular growth rates; other sports such as orienteering, skiing, surfing and judo have been imported from overseas in attempts to satisfy our apparently insatiable appetites for new sports. Associated with sport are the sports goods industries which in many cases have transformed sports goods into fashion goods. Sports-centres, techno-sports and artificial sports surfaces are all part of the increasing commodification of sport and leisure (Kirby, 1985). All these activities have had considerable impacts on the urban, suburban and rural environments and, as a result, new landscapes devoted solely to sports have emerged.

In addition it can be argued that sport serves an ideological function in diverting our attention from more 'serious' matters. For this reason sport is some-times called the new opiate of the masses. Conversely, others prefer to regard it as the most enjoyable way of using one's body in public. Whatever one's view, it seems reasonable to argue that from a cognitive perspective it is worth while students knowing more about such an important phenomenon.

Sport is eminently geographical

Most geographical studies of sport (for example, Rooney, 1972; Bale, 1982) have tended to take sport as yet another thing to be mapped in order to show geographical variations. In other cases, sport has been used to illustrate notions of spatial diffusion (see, for example, Bale, 1978, 1984), geographic optimisation (Rooney, 1980), or a more welfare-geographic approach (for example, Humphreys, Mason and Pinch, 1983). Studies which look at the geographic origins of North American ice-hockey players (Ojala and Kureth, 1975) or stock-car drivers (Pillsbury, 1974), for example, prove interesting to geographers and physical educationalists alike. The former enjoy seeing sporting applications of well-known geographical ideas and the latter are often intrigued by the new insights a map provides on their stock-in-trade. Other studies utilise sport for teaching purposes. If we recognise that many students find sport interesting and school boring, sport can be used to motivate students in areas of the curriculum such as central place theory (Bale and Gowing, 1976), spatial interaction (Sas and Jones, 1976) and ecology (Baker, 1977).

What has rarely been recognised, however, is that the essentially geographical concepts of space and place are central to the very nature of (and actually help to define) sport *per se*. Wagner (1981) stresses the significance of space in defining sport. He argues that, unlike work and recreation, sport requires speci-fied sites: bounded fields, rinks, tracks, courses, etc. He points out that sport is a world of territoriality and hierarchy, that most sports are involved in the conquest of space where spatial violations are penal-ised. Once upon a time, sport took place in environ-ments designed with other things in mind but, over time, sport monoculture has emerged, and specialised sportscapes are now needed for top-class sport to take place. Record breaking becomes meaningless if one site is not exactly the same as another. This spatial specificity has been accompanied by artificial sports-spaces such as concrete stadiums, windowless halls, astroturf, indoor swimming pools and synthetic running tracks. In few areas of life is there such pressure to make one place the same — exactly the same — as another. Sport graphically illustrates what Edward Relph (1976, 1981) termed the 'Disney-fication' of place and the application of scientific humanism to the landscape.

Space in sport can also be interpreted as a symbol. In baseball it is used to recreate a lost pastoral world (Oriard, 1976) or in cricket the rustic myth of 'Merrie England'. At the same time it can be suggested that the symbolic attraction of sport may lie in its *similarity* to modern industrial society with its division of labour and limited independence (Gelber, 1983).

The geographic concept of *place* is important in sport in three main ways. First, sport provides the most obvious way (apart from war) in which ordinary people obtain status simply by belonging to a certain country or region, rather than by personal achieve-ment. The success achieved by individual countries in international competitions (such as the Olympic Games) affects the status of that country, and its citi-zens, worldwide. Sport provides a means of attach-ment to place, and pride in place, rarely found elsewhere in the modern world. Some years ago an unfashionable English soccer team, Sunderland, defeated the favourites, Leeds United, in the Football Association Cup Final. Following this victory, crime in Sunderland declined and industrial productivity increased (Derrick and McRory, 1973). However, when place pride becomes perverted it may contribute to more anti-social behaviour such as sport-induced violence (Bale, 1985).

Sport provides one of the few occasions when large, impersonal, functional units such as cities or nations can unite as wholes (Dunning, 1984). Sport can therefore be regarded as a force for conservatism and the reinforcement of status quo views of society at large since it stresses *place* rather than *class* differ-ences and, for a time at least, blurs class differences as communities and nations unite in support of 'their' team. Again, the analogy with war appears obvious.

A second way in which the concept of place is important in sport is in the phenomenon known as the 'home field advantage': in top-class sport more wins and higher scores tend to be achieved by the home team. To a degree, such widely observed sporting outcomes can be attributed to concepts related to territoriality (Edwards, 1979).

A third way in which place must be taken into account in sport is that different places, be they towns, regions or nations, put different emphases on different sports. Some regions clearly 'out-produce' others in terms of the number of athletes originating there (Figure 11.1). Some places have more sports clubs than others and some places are disadvantaged because of their lack of provision for sport or because they unwittingly consume sport-induced nuisances and hazards. Because sporting participation and 'production' is neither regular nor randomly distributed over the cultural landscape it is obviously a legitimate area for geographical enquiry.

Legitimising students' knowledge

The literature of the sociology of education reminds us of the ideological basis of what constitutes legitimate educational content, and draws attention, for example, to the paradox that the kind of knowledge about the world which students bring with them to school is often denied and devalued. The geography curriculum becomes 'things to learn' or 'steps on the way towards becoming a geographer' (to paraphrase Whitty and Young, 1976), rather than an opportunity 'for pupils and teachers to engage critically with the largely taken for granted knowledge of the social and natural world that they bring to school' (Whitty and Young, 1976). The study of geographical knowledge can be regarded as what Apple and King (1974) term:

> a study in ideology, the investigation of what is considered legitimate knowledge . . . by specific social groups and classes . . . The curriculum in schools responds to and represents ideological and cultural resources that come from somewhere. Not all groups' visions are represented and not all groups' meanings are responded to.

This is clearly exemplified in the area of recreational geography.

What is defined as recreational geography in the school curriculum constitutes a relatively minor element of what might conceivably be called recreational geography. Take, for example, the highly successful British curriculum development project, *Geography for the Young School Leaver*. Although one-third of the published curriculum materials is devoted to recreation and leisure (namely, the *Man, Land and Leisure* package), a whole area of recreational geography concerned with mass and spectator sport is defined out and much recreational experience is implicitly seen as 'not serious'. While the study of national parks and tourism appears to be legitimate, the kind of recreational experiences which are likely to be most meaningful to the majority of urban-based students are not. Among these is sport.

Thompson (1980) has argued that the omission of sport from the school curriculum is a form of cultural bias. While Bach and Beethoven are legitimate subjects for serious study, Bannister and Botham are not. It can be argued that it is not *what* is studied but *how* it is studied that is important. Given the significance of sport in society, its serious study can surely be defended. The serious study of sport might be illustrated by the kinds of syllabus units shown in Table 1, taken from a course on the geography of sport.

Depending on the length of each unit, others could be added: say, the 'Spatial organisation of sport' or 'Sport and the weather'. The arena of sport provides a milieu for fieldwork, decision-making exercises, values analysis, and much motivational 'traditional' geography. By studying sport, students come to value their own knowledge, rather than have it denied.

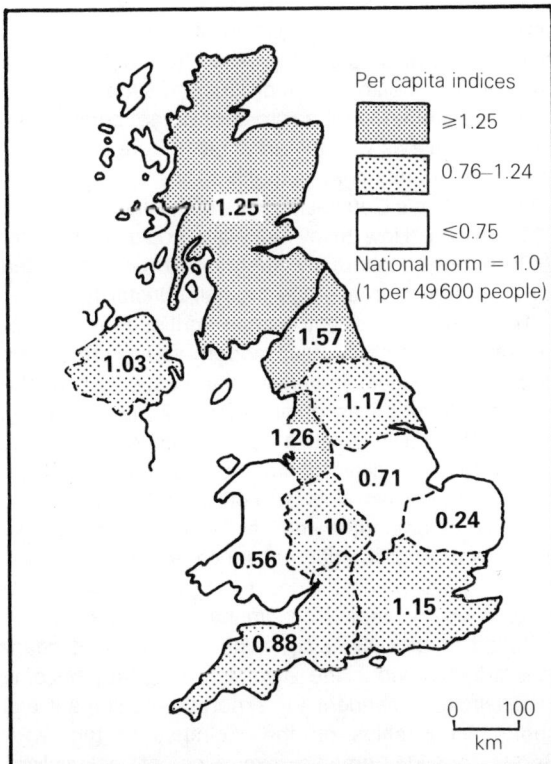

Figure 11.1 Regional variations in the per capita 'production' of British marathon runners, 1980

Per capita indices

≥1.25

0.76–1.24

≤0.75

National norm = 1.0
(1 per 49 600 people)

1.25
1.57
1.03
1.17
1.26
0.71
1.10
0.24
0.56
1.15
0.88

0   100
km

A critical engagement with sport

So far I have presented an essentially liberal view of sport studies in geography. However, a more radical dimension views sport (especially as reflected in top-class competitive sport) as a carrier of the deep structures of western culture and hence indicative of our lifestyles and priorities. For example, Galtung (1984) avers that, though playing a minor role, sport is essen-

Table 1 Three units for a course on sports geography

```
┌─────────────────────────────────────────────┐
│        Unit 1: Sport and the landscape        │
│                                               │
│ Ideas                                         │
│ • Sport affects the landscape directly by     │
│   producing distinctive types of sportscape.  │
│ • Sport affects the landscape indirectly by   │
│   generating many flows of traffic and pedes- │
│   trians.                                      │
│ • Land uses and property values are affected  │
│   by their adjacency to sportscapes of differ-│
│   ent kinds.                                   │
│ Skills                                        │
│ • Fieldwork, use of land-use maps, evaluation │
│   of sportscape quality.                      │
│                                               │
│          Unit 2: Diffusion of sport           │
│                                               │
│ Ideas                                         │
│ • Sports possess diverse geographical origins.│
│   The idea of serious competitive sport seems │
│   to have originated in Britain.              │
│ • Sports are innovations which can be studied │
│   through the framework of innovation         │
│   diffusion. Innovations in sports can be     │
│   studied in the same way.                    │
│ Skills                                        │
│ • Seeking generalisations, simple correlation │
│   analysis, use of secondary data (i.e. from  │
│   sports handbooks).                          │
│                                               │
│            Unit 3: Sports regions             │
│                                               │
│ Ideas                                         │
│ • Certain regions are associated with         │
│   particular sports.                          │
│ • Some regions significantly out-produce      │
│   others in terms of numbers of elite athletes│
│ • Some regions emphasise certain sports       │
│   rather than others in terms of the number of│
│   clubs or participants.                      │
│ • Facilities for sport are unevenly           │
│   distributed, at a variety of scales.        │
│ Skills                                        │
│ • Mapping, use of location quotients and other│
│   indices, identifying geographical attributes│
│   of sports data.                             │
└─────────────────────────────────────────────┘
```

tially anti-nature, since it decreasingly takes place in natural surroundings and increasingly in places possessing 'an overwhelming amount of concrete rather than just pure, uncontaminated, unmanipulated nature'. He elaborates on this point by noting that:

the sports palace and the stadium, Olympic or not, are anti-nature and have to be so because they are near laboratory settings in which the unidimensionality of competitive sports can unfold itself under controlled conditions. Pure nature has too much variation in it, too much 'noise'.

Concrete stadiums, windowless sports halls, synthetic tracks and surfaces are all examples of the 'improvement' of nature with the intent of providing either greater comfort or improved performance. Paradoxically, such environments often produce dissatisfaction from both spectators and participants alike (Oriard, 1976; Neilson, 1986). Astroturf may 'produce' more games but it can also produce horrendous injuries; 'players' seem universally to dislike the surface.

In addition, sport can create several forms of pollution. Perhaps the most well known is the social pollution resulting from crowd behaviour at sporting events (see the fieldwork project which follows). But, in a small way, visual and noise pollution can also result. Likewise, much sport can also be considered anti-people for a number of reasons. Firstly, contact sports thrive upon aggression and violence, both within and outside the rules. Apart from injury to and, sometimes, death of individuals, such violence demeans both the spectators and the combatants. Secondly, just as with the arms race, there is an enormous opportunity cost to much sports spending. The 1984 America's Cup yacht races in Australia cost over £100 million. How many hospitals could be built for £100 million? How many hungry children can be fed for the price of an average football transfer fee?

This anti-nature anti-human critique is complemented by the view that modern sports are classic examples of cultural imperialism and dependence. The invasion of American gridiron football into Europe is a current case in point: a not-too-subtle example of the further Americanisation of much of the world. Such cultural imperialism was, of course, writ large during the late nineteenth and early twentieth century diffusion of English sports to Africa and much of Asia. Such 'developments' occur at the expense of indigenous games. How many tribal games are included in the Olympics? When Third World countries are included in the Olympic arena, they become increasingly dependent for expertise, equipment and sports scholarships on the countries of the west. Sports provide graphic examples of colonialism, dependency, westernisation and the erosion of traditional cultures.

Practical activities

In this section I want to describe some practical exercises, noting the curriculum contexts in which they occur, which I have found encourage students to use the knowledge which they bring to school with them.

The first two exercises are simply brainstorming approaches which try to get students to recognise the strongly *spatial* and *confined* nature of sports. They may wish to trace the growing spatial confinement and artificiality in the environment or landscape of one particular sport. The third exercise gets students to draw similarities between sports and work in which they may be able to tease out the gradual imposition of worklike aspects in sports by identifying dates at which rules, regulations, bureaucracies, etc. were founded.

Activity 1: Geographical limits to sports

Instructions ⟹

1. Ask students to give example of sports with different degrees of exactness in their spatial limits. They should complete a table like the one below.

Precise limits		Variable limits		Very variable limits	
Sport	**Nature of limits**	**Sport**	**Nature of limits**	**Sport**	**Nature of limits**
100 m sprint	100 metres	Football	Max 130 yds long	Downhill skiing	Flags

2. Although all sports are physical activities, the amount of space used in sporting activity varies greatly. Some sports occupy micro-spaces, others meso-spaces and others macro-spaces. Ask students to complete the following table with appropriate sports.

Nature of spatial limits		
Micro	**Meso**	**Macro**
Squash	Cricket	Orienteering

3. Ask students if they think people with different personalities participate in environmentally different sports? Why?

Activity 2: Sport, space and society

Sport and modern industrial society share many characteristics. Some of these are included in the left-hand column of the table below. Ask students to complete the table by including examples from sports and the world of industry.

Features	Examples from sports	Examples from industry
Special times	20 mins in soccer	9-to-5 at work
Special places		
Profit focused		
Record keeping		
Record seeking		
Bureaucratic	International Olympic Committee	Confederation of British Industry
Rule bounded		
Needs an umpire		

Activity 3: Football comes to town

This activity is a role-playing simulation involving what many would regard as a noxious facility, namely a football stadium. It shows that sport can be a nuisance as well as a benefit. The activity has been used successfully with students aged 15–18 though it could be applied to virtually any age group in modified form.

A £10 million sports stadium is to be built in a small English town. It will have associated leisure facilities covering about 60 hectares, providing permanent employment for 750–1000 people and generating considerable traffic flows, with up to 60 000 people converging on the site on match days.

1. Have students discuss current nuisances generated by football stadiums (for example, crowds, hooligans, etc.). This forms an initial brainstorming session.

2. Now have students read the newspaper extract (Figure 11.2) describing how entrepreneur Robert Maxwell is planning a merger between two English football clubs: Oxford United and Reading Town.

3. An optional stage is to have students now suggest a suitable location for the newly merged club. In the version illustrated here, this is taken as given: i.e. the town of Didcot, located between Oxford and Reading (Figure 11.3).

4. Have students identify various interest groups who might react to the decision to put the club in Didcot. These would include the Maxwell empire, the Reading and Oxford teams' supporters clubs, the Oxfordshire County Council, the Didcot Traders' Association, Didcot residents, the local branch of the Council for the Preservation of Rural England, etc.

ALL LINES LEAD TO DIDCOT

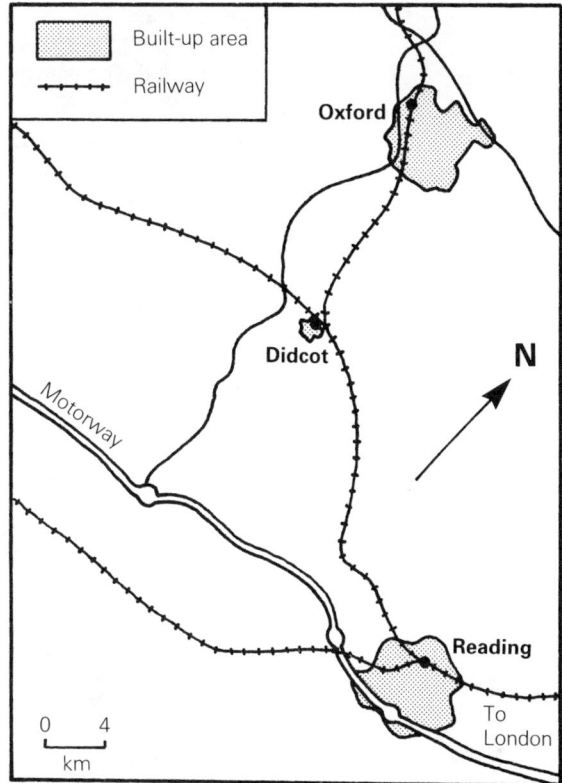

Figure 11.3 Oxford, Reading and Didcot: locations and major routes

Charles Burgess on the Maxwell vision

ROBERT MAXWELL's brave new world for football could be based in Didcot, Oxfordshire, the town where the millionaire chairman of Oxford United hopes the new Thames Valley club will build a £7 million to £10 million stadium and leisure complex and call on support from some of the 1.8 million people in the area.

But as yesterday's press conference at the FA headquarters in London illustrated there is still a long way to go before Oxford's takeover of Reading is completed.

Maxwell and the Reading chairman Frank Waller were photographed toasting the takeover with FA water while at the back of the hall, three of the six Reading directors made their opposition known. Maxwell described them as "gatecrashers" and had to remove one of them from the top table at the beginning.

At the end a solicitor acting for Toy Tranter, another of the objecting directors, bodyswerved through the throng to present Waller with a High Court writ preventing the Reading chairman from transferring 20,000 of his shares before May 3. Maxwell shrugged this off, saying it was a mere technicality and a publicity campaign and that there was "no way" the shares could be transferred before that date anyway.

The majority of fans from both Reading and Oxford are against the merger. But Maxwell, a past master at takeovers in printing and publishing who runs Britain's largest publishing group BPCC, is supremely confident.

He said, "You can take it from me that this will go through because it is what is best for football." None of the directors involved would make a penny from the deal, he said, and it could start a fashion. A complex, on a 150 acre site at Didcot would produce permanent work for 750 to 1,000 people in the shops, restaurants and other facilities it would attract. Tickets for a football match would include a train ticket from either Oxford to the north, or Reading to the south. It was the way ahead for football, said Maxwell, and the only way to survive.

(*The Guardian*, 2.4.83)

Figure 11.2 (*The Guardian*, 2 April 1983)

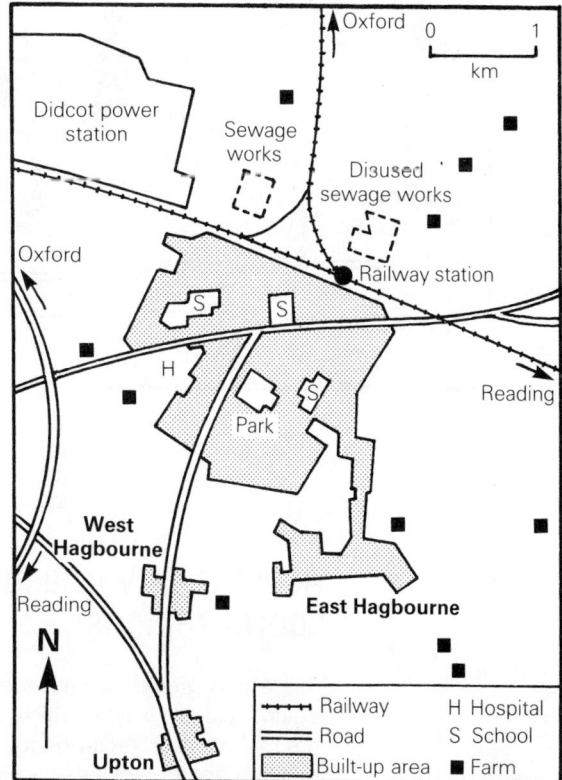

Figure 11.4 Didcot and its environs

159

5. Divide the class into groups, each of which identifies with one of the interest groups. Have each group prepare its case. Different values will emerge as group representatives present their case with regard to the proposal. This is an example of value analysis (Maye, 1984).

6. For the second half of the activity, divide the class into new groups, each group representing a consultancy firm who has been invited by Maxwell to select a site for the new football complex. Students use the map (Figure 11.4) to select an appropriate site, justifying their choice.

7. Have a spokesperson for each group report to the class, stating and justifying the group's locational choice.

8. Engage in a debriefing session, highlighting what other data and information might be needed in reality and the role of values in the growth of the sporting landscape. Have the class fill in the 'bubbles' in Figure 11.5.

Figure 11.5 Football comes to town . . . or should it?

Activity 4: Vernacular and geographical sports regions

This activity seeks to describe the ways particular sports are associated with particular regions and the way in which such sport–place associations may be at odds with reality, in so far as 'reality' can be identified and mapped. The activity, which would form part of a unit on sports regions, involves a mental mapping exercise and a geographical analysis of sports data.

Instructions ⟶

1. For a given sport (or sports) simply ask members of the class to indicate on a national base map (with county or state boundaries and major place names included as locational cues) the areas they associate with the particular sport(s). If more than one sport is being studied use a fresh map for each sport. Superimposed on each map is a grid co-ordinate system, the size of each grid square depending on the area of the map.

2. On an overhead projector transparency indicate the number – converted into percentages – of students who included *each* grid square in their perceived region.

3. When all grid squares have been covered ask the class in what ways they might represent the information cartographically. Choropleth mapping or isopleth interpolation are possible answers.

4. Have the class map the results and ask them to provide a title (for example, 'A regional map of British tennis'). Figure 11.6 shows an isoline map of British tennis.

5. Discuss with the class reasons for the pattern shown on the map.

6. Discuss whether the mental map corresponds to the reality. This will lead to consideration of the problem of how reality could be mapped.

7. Elicit from students the kinds of data which might be used to construct a map of the sport in question. They may suggest association handbooks, lists of clubs in the newspapers, birthplaces of famous players, etc.

8. Given appropriate data, per capita indices (Rooney, 1972; Bale, 1982) can be calculated for each state or county and the resulting map compared with the 'mental sports map' previously constructed (see Figures 11.6 and 11.7).

9. Have the class discuss the ways in which the vernacular regionalisation is different and the ways in which vernacular sports regions may be important in everyday life (in advertising, politics).

Figure 11.6 An isoline 'mental map' of British tennis

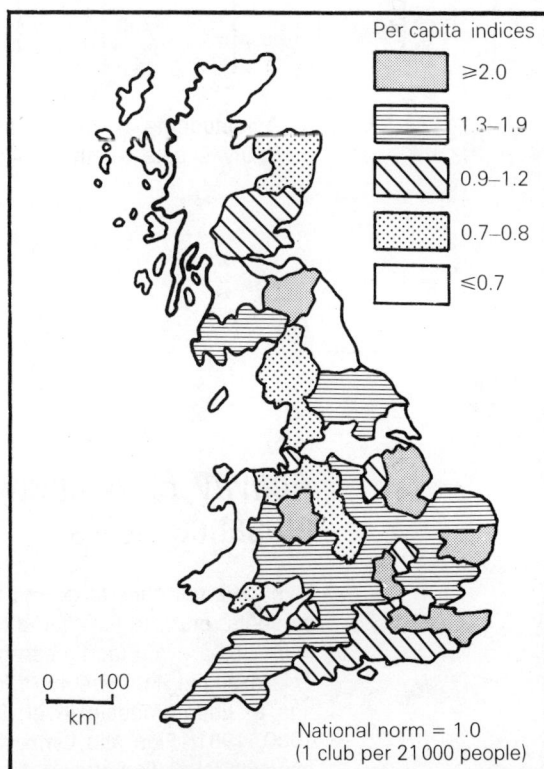

Figure 11.7 Per capita analysis of tennis in Britain, based on the number of clubs

Activity 5: Retailing and proximity to sports events

Instructions ⟶

1. Ask students to identify shops within about 2.5 km of a major sports stadium (for example, a cricket ground). Each shop should be marked (as a number) on a large-scale base map of the area.

2. In the field, students visit each shop and politely ask shopkeepers the following questions.
   (a) On match days are takings more or less than normal?
   (b) By approximately how much (e.g. $\times \frac{1}{2}$, $\times 2$, $\times 3$, $\times 4$ of the average takings) are they more/less than normal?
   (c) Why should takings change in this way?
   (d) On match days is there more or less shoplifting than normal?
   (e) On match days are trading hours longer, shorter, or the same?

3. Ask students to record their information in a table like the one below.

Survey point on map	Takings on match days			Shoplifting		Trading hours			Reason for change in takings	Type of shop
	More	Less	How much	More	Less	Longer	Shorter	Same		

Retail Survey

4. Ask students to write up and record their results using maps and diagrams. Get them to investigate whether distance from the ground seems to affect the results.

Activity 6: A fieldwork project on nuisance fields

This work unit tries to delimit the nuisance field of a professional sport club. In doing so, students return to the theme touched on earlier: that sport can be a bad thing. They also learn that a given facility can generate negative, as well as positive, spheres of influence. This example, in a variety of forms, has been undertaken with students from 14 years of age to undergraduate level. Examples have been described in detail elsewhere (Bale, 1980, 1981; Fien and Lynn, 1982; Humphreys, Mason and Pinch, 1983). Basically, the exercise takes five stages.

Instructions ⟶

1. An initial classroom session poses the problem, namely that of identifying the nature and spatial extent of sport-induced nuisances. Reference may be made to the popular press which, in Britain at least, regularly reports incidents of football hooliganism.
2. Have students suggest methods of delimiting the area of negative impact. Generally students are guided towards an approach which involves making up a simple questionnaire to give to 80 to 100 sample residences identified on a base map of the locality around the stadium. Residents are asked if on match days they consider the sports club to be: (i) a serious nuisance; (ii) a nuisance; or (iii) no nuisance. Students are also asked to enquire about the nature of the nuisances and whether the residents receive any compensation or not (for example, cheap tickets).
3. In the field, students (working in pairs) interview residents and allocate them value 2, 1 or 0, respectively, depending on the resident's replies about the nuisance level.
4. Back in the classroom get the students to collate their results by plotting and joining up on a map all the residences with the same nuisance value (2, 1 or 0). This will show the geographic extent of the nuisance (e.g. the limit of the value 1s). An example of a map constructed by using this approach is shown in Figure 11.8.
5. The nature of the perceived nuisance can also be tabulated or graphed by working out the total number of residences with each nuisance value. The locational implications of the project's findings can then be written up. It might be possible for the report to be sent to the local newspaper and the sports club involved.

Extension activities ⟶

It is possible to take this project one stage further by looking at the apparent effect that proximity to a stadium has on house prices. Local estate agents may be able to tell you whether there is a difference in price for a particular kind of house if it is located next to a sports stadium (or golf course, for that matter) rather than elsewhere in the town. How sensitive are house prices to proximity to different kinds of sports places?

Conclusion

In this chapter I have argued that sport, as opposed to recreation and leisure, is worthy of inclusion in the geography curriculum. The significance of sport, its geographic character and the fact that many students relate to it, together justify its presence in the geography syllabus. The practical ideas presented here suggest that sports geography has a good deal of motivational potential, plus the ability to enhance students' pride in their own knowledge and work. As sociologist John Loy (1975) put it, 'studying sport is often as much fun as playing sport and on occasion just as serious as well'.

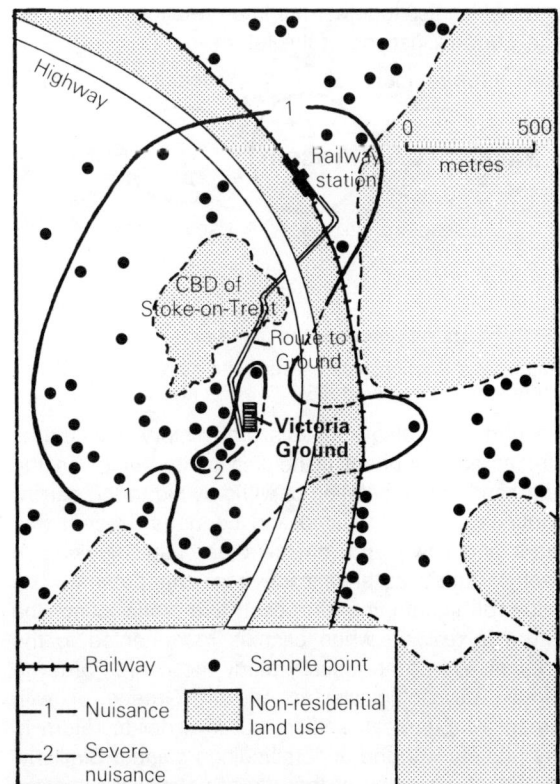

Figure 11.8 Nuisance fields around Stoke City Football Club

12 Alternative futures in geographical education

NOEL GOUGH

Introduction: the idea of futures studies

One useful way of thinking about futures studies is to see them as forward-looking equivalents of history. Studies of futures and pasts are certainly different, but they are interdependent and complementary. While history disciplines our **interpretations** of the past, futures studies attempt to discipline our **anticipations** of alternative futures. Richard Slaughter's (1985) elegant conceptualisation of relationships between past, present and future (Figure 12.1) suggests that the present can be thought of as a slipping 'knot in time' which ties together our interpretations of the past and our anticipations of the future.

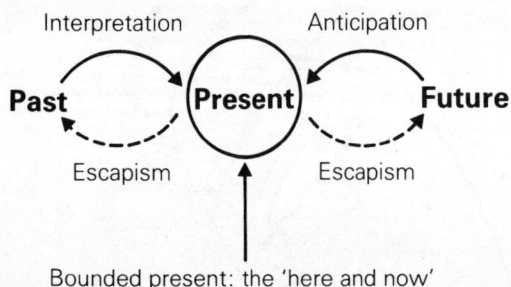

Figure 12.1 Relationships between the past, present and future (after Slaughter, 1985)

Figure 12.1 also suggests that history and futures studies are important in helping us to avoid, on the one hand, the temptation of withdrawing to the narrow confines of an attenuated and bounded present (the 'here and now') and, on the other hand, looking to past or future as an escape from the present. The value of interpreting the past and anticipating the future is realised when each is reconnected to the present. We do not usually study the past in order to remain psychologically in Ancient Greece or with America's European settlers but in order to return to the present with the understandings gained. Similarly, the finest examples of the arts of anticipation are not those which leave us in a future dreamworld, playing cosmic cops-and-robbers or cuddling cute extra-terrestrials, but those which invite us to think more clearly, critically and creatively about the changes and continuities that currently characterise our *real* journey through time.

This chapter presents a number of practical recommendations for exploring alternative futures in geographical education. For the most part, these recommendations are distilled from my own work as a teacher educator and curriculum designer. Some of this work, especially that related to the development of an 'Educating for the future' course for teachers, is described in more detail elsewhere (Gough, 1985).

Project IF (Inventing the Future): curriculum materials design principles

Project IF (Inventing the Future) involves the design of curriculum materials and teaching strategies for futures study in a variety of educational settings. Its products to date include a number of topic-centred worksheets which can be used as flexible resource materials in teaching a variety of subjects. The first Project IF worksheets (such as SIGNS, illustrated in Figure 12.2) originated from my long-held belief that teacher educators should pay teachers the respect of translating their abstract educational proposals into some sort of concrete form. Thus, Project IF worksheets began as an attempt to make the idea of educating for the future more meaningful by exemplifying it in tangible curriculum materials. Further worksheets (such as ANTARCTICA, illustrated in Figure 12.3) have been designed in workshops with classroom teachers and are being circulated through a network of interested teachers, student teachers and teacher educators.

PROJECT IF: INVENTING THE FUTURE WORKSHEET SERIES

TOPIC   SIGNS
INPUT

The first four signs shown above mean SCHOOL CROSSING, NO U-TURN, SLIPPERY WHEN WET and NO LEFT TURN. The sign at far right warns swimmers of crocodile inhabited waters in Australia's Northern Territory. Such wordless signs have been commonplace for many years and are especially useful in parts of the world where many languages are spoken.

OUTPUT   1 In the future we will probably require more wordless signs. Below are some signs that we might need in the near future. What do you think these signs mean?

2 Design wordless signs for the following messages (remember that a diagonal stripe is the usual way of indicating a forbidden activity):

DANGER: ULTRA-VIOLET ZONE   ELECTRIC AUTOMOBILES ONLY
CAUTION: POLLUTED AIR   ROBOT SERVICE STATION AHEAD
CAUTION: LASER CROSSING   NO-CLONE ZONE
REDUCED GRAVITY AREA   NO VERTICAL TURN
ANDROID SPOKEN HERE   GROKKING BAY AHEAD

3 What other wordless messages might be important in the future? Draw a sign that might be needed in 20 years' time and one that might be needed in 100 years' time.

Figure 12.2 Project IF SIGNS worksheet

PROJECT IF: INVENTING THE FUTURE WORKSHEET SERIES

TOPIC   ANTARCTICA
INPUT   Below is the latest travel poster from 21st Century Tours

It's just three hours away, and has more natural beauty than just about any country on earth.

You will find a range of hotels from top international standard to budget priced. And they are ideally located to suit your choice of outdoor activity, be it skiing, fishing, golfing, trekking or whatever.

For further details, see your travel agent.

Antarctica

the all-year paradise.

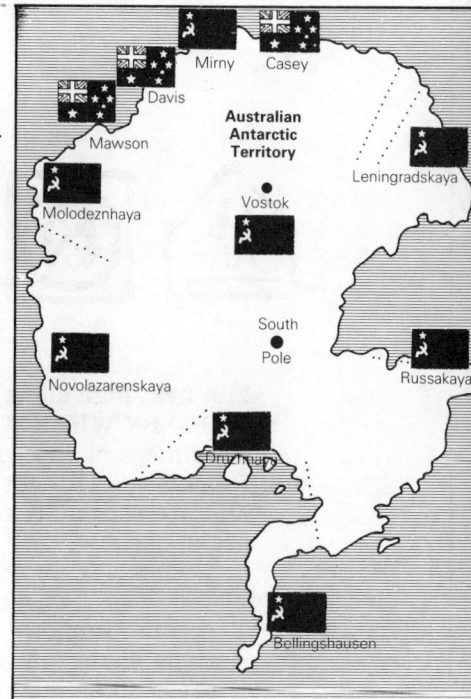

OUTPUT

1 What does this poster tell you about changes that have taken place since the present?

2 List possible reasons for the changes in Antarctica.
Try to find current evidence that suggests how these changes could be brought about.

3 In the 21st century, what other places in the world might be very different from the way they are today? Design a travel poster for one of these changed places and describe your holiday there.

4 Consider the place where you now live (suburb, town, city, etc). What changes would you like to have take place in fifty years' time? Describe how these changes might be brought about.

5 Many people are concerned that the world is losing its wilderness areas because humans want or need more places to be used for mining, hydro-electricity, timber, sport, tourism. etc.

What reasons can you suggest for conserving the "uselessness" of the world's wilderness areas?

Figure 12.3 Project IF ANTARCTICA worksheet

Project IF worksheets have so far followed a standard format which functions as a *creative limitation* in design workshops (in much the same way that choosing to write a sonnet, limerick or haiku can simultaneously constrain and liberate the poetic imagination). Each worksheet supplies some stimulus material (INPUT) related to the topic. This may be pictorial, graphic or written and may include press cuttings, cartoons, excerpts from science fiction stories, and so on. Pupil activities (OUTPUT) are also suggested; these are designed to encourage, through various forms of expression, critical and creative thinking about the topic.

Project IF materials embody a number of assumptions about the nature of futures studies which, in effect, function as design principles in the construction of Project IF worksheets. While the following list is not exhaustive, the assumptions detailed below are among those which are most significant in determining the content and character of the materials, and can therefore be thought of as principles which could guide the development of similar materials targeted more specifically to geographical education.

Assumption 1: Anticipation of a plurality of futures

At any given time many futures may be possible and we should be alert for the artificial narrowing of vision which characterises most attempts to predict or prescribe 'the' future (singular); futures (plural) thinking is mostly concerned with the elucidation and critique of *alternatives*, among which we may distinguish between those which are:

- probable – predicted in terms of present knowledge and trends;
- possible – virtually anything that can be imagined is possible, though some possibilities may seem to be more plausible than others;
- preferred – desirable alternatives among those which seem possible – they are not necessarily probable at present.

Therefore, Project IF materials encourage students to create images of *preferred* futures by imagining and exploring the implications of *possible* alternatives rather than by choosing among those alternatives which may now seem most probable. Question 4 in the OUTPUT section of the ANTARCTICA worksheet (Figure 12.3) is a geographical application of this principle.

Assumption 2: An eclectic approach to sources and methods

Images of alternative futures usually spring from four major sources and are elucidated by corresponding methods and procedures.

- Extrapolation: perceived consequences of present trends and events are elucidated by trend analysis and extrapolation.
- Consensus: opinions about what might or ought to happen are elucidated by monitoring cultural and sub-cultural consensus (for example, polls, commissions of 'experts', Delphi techniques).
- Imagination: the speculative imagination of people, especially artists in various media, produces images which are elucidated by connoisseurship, critique and, to some extent, by emulating their creative behaviour (for example, scenario-building frequently emulates science fiction).
- Combination: combining images from extrapolation, consensus and creative speculation produces further images of alternative futures; combinatory techniques (for example, cross-impact matrices, relevance trees, futures wheels) are among the most characteristic tools of futures research and study.

Project IF deliberately emphasises imaginative and combinatory methods. This is because extrapolative and consensus methods are used chiefly to generate *probable* futures and, as such, represent attempts to refine *predictions* about future events. But Project IF materials embody the assumption that the primary goal of futures study is not to predict the future but rather to help people create a better future.

Therefore, Project IF materials encourage students to invent the future rather than to predict it. Question 3 in the OUTPUT section of the ANTARCTICA worksheet (Figure 12.3) is a geographical application of this principle.

Assumption 3: Optimism and empowerment

Futures studies are motivated, in part, by a belief that humans are able to shape their own destinies 'if not entirely then at least to a degree which makes the effort worthwhile' (Gardner, 1975). Futures studies assume that this effort can be optimised and seek the knowledge and understanding which enables people to do so. In this sense, futures studies encourage optimism about the extent to which preferred futures are achievable and should thus empower people to take responsible action to achieve them.

Therefore, Project IF materials present visions of

alternative futures for critical examination, and encourage the investigation of further alternatives, as guides to responsible action in achieving preferred futures and avoiding undesirable alternatives. The INPUT section of the ANTARCTICA worksheet (Figure 12.3) is a geographical application of this principle.

Assumption 4: Variety and balance of problems, topics and issues

Much of the current impetus for futures studies is provided by a limited range of familiar concerns, including: technological change and its deleterious social consequences; the arms race and threats of nuclear war; environmental degradation; population pressures; difficulties in the supply and distribution of food and energy resources. A great deal of the publicity given to these matters is pessimistic or fatalistic about the human capacity to respond to them and may wrongly suggest that fear of the future is the major incentive to studying it. From an educational standpoint, the very familiarity of these concerns puts them in danger of becoming stereotyped and boring, or evoking other negative responses, when they are repeatedly put before students as topics for study. Problems relating to technology, global conflict, environment, population, food, energy, and the like, are too important to be trivialised by the superficial treatment which often characterises their relentless over-exposure in the media and in some classrooms.

Therefore, Project IF materials attempt to cover a wide variety of problems, topics and issues, balancing concerns which may be stereotypical of contemporary futures study with less conventional subject matter. The INPUT section of the Project IF SPORT worksheet (see the excerpt in Figure 12.4) can be thought of as

Figure 12.4 Excerpt from Project IF SPORT worksheet

New golf venue

- THE 1991 Australian Open Golf Championship will be held at the Sydney Showgrounds, following a 20-year, $62-thousand million deal between the Australian Golf Union and Lord Packer.

Lord Packer has just secured the Australian rights to the amazing American invention – the portable golf course. The new system allows holes to be placed in whichever venue an entrepreneur desires. Lord Packer has secured 36 separate holes from the US distributor.

"This is a great system," said Lord Packer. "We can roll the holes one after the other into the showgrounds. As one hole is completed, it will be removed, and replaced by the next. It's a revolutionary system, and allows spectators to watch 18 holes of golf from the one vantage point."

including geographical applications of this principle: the geography of sport provides a less stereotyped context for the consideration of future problems concerning location and space utilisation than the familiar topics referred to above.

Assumption 5: Rehearsal of surprise

Project IF materials embody the assumption than an effective way of preparing for the possible surprises of the future is to rehearse the experience of surprise. Surprise may be manifested in various ways and can entail, for example, being amused, amazed, bewildered or dismayed. The rehearsal of surprise may thus include seeking out, or inventing, images of alternative futures which are perceived to be humorous, fantastic, puzzling or disturbing.

Therefore, Project IF materials present images of possible futures which are intended to be surprising and deliberately encourage students to be 'playful' in their approach to futures studies, to view alternative futures as resources for 'mind games' which, by providing opportunities to surprise oneself and others, can be entertaining, enlightening and enriching. The INPUT section of the Project IF TREES worksheet (see excerpt in Figure 12.5) includes geographical applications of attempts to surprise students.

Assumption 6: Importance of speculation, science fiction and fantasy

Speculative literature and its equivalents in other media, including the popular genres of science fiction (SF) and fantasy, are among the most important resources for futures study and, indeed, to some extent chart its history. It can be argued that images of the future in any historic period have been generated by its creative artists or, as Jacques Ellul (1975) has said, 'its poets, mystics and visionaries'. These images are communicated to the larger society and transmitted from generation to generation through story telling (Green, 1975). These stories 'pull a culture forward in time' (Bundy, 1975). Thus, for example, the speculative storytelling of the eighteenth and nineteenth centuries, up to and including the utopian fiction of Jules Verne and the early writings of H. G. Wells, presented images of a future society in which the lot of humankind had been vastly improved through science and technology. Such images inspired confidence in the present and hope that the destiny foretold by those images would come true.

Much speculative literature of the early and mid-twentieth century is dystopian rather than utopian. Writers such as Karel Capek, Aldous Huxley, George Orwell and Yevgeny Zamyatin directed their readers' imaginations towards the grimmer possibilities of the

---

INPUT   Below is a newsplastic item from Age Videoprint dated 2083 06 30:

ARCHEOLOGISTS EXPLORING SYDNEY HARBOR SWAMP NEAR SPACEPORT 2 CONTINUE UNEARTH UNUSUAL OBJECTS   YESTERDAY LARGE DEPOSIT RARE ALUMINIUM CANS UNCOVERED   THESE BELIEVED BEEN THROWN FROM BRIDGE SPANNED HARBOR BEFORE SILTED   TODAY DISCOVERED LARGE CYLINDER LENGTH 10M DIAMETER 50CM HAD BROWN ROUGH TEXTURED SURFACE MOTTLED BLACK   EACH END MARKED PATTERN CONCENTRIC RINGS   INPERTS CLAIM OBJECT REMAINS   =TREE= =ANCIENT RELATIVE FRUIT PROPAGATERS HEIGHT 1M NOW AUSTRALIAN TALLEST LIVING VEGETATION= LOCAL HERSTORIANS IDENTIFIED BLACK MARKINGS =CHARCOAL=   =RARE SUBSTANCE BELIEVED ASSOCIATED ANCIENT CUSTOMS ?BUSHFIRES? ?BARBECUES?=

OUTPUT   1 Rewrite the newsplastic item in the INPUT in the style of a 1980s newspaper story

2 Why might bushfires and barbecues be regarded as 'ancient customs' in 2083? Try to think of as many different reasons as possible

3 How would your present way of life change if aluminium and timber became very rare in the near future (within ten years)?

4 Imagine that you are a 'herstory' teacher in 2083. Plan a lesson which helps your students to understand why there are no trees (and no vegetation taller than one metre), why Sydney Harbour has silted up and why there is no harbour bridge. Teach your lesson to someone.

Figure 12.5 Excerpt from Project IF TREES worksheet

future. But their stories were much more than mere warnings of potential dangers: each of these writers also provided the images, symbols or metaphors which have actually directed the decisions and shaped the expectations needed to *avoid* (to some extent and so far) the possible futures they depicted. Their vocabulary – *robot* (Capek), *brave new world* (Huxley), *big brother* (Orwell), *humanised machines* (Zamyatin) – is used in identifying and responding to the uncertainties and dangers that have accompanied technological progress.

Contemporary SF and fantasy reveal a wealth of imagined possibilities for the future and may also provide novel perspectives on the present. For example, 'parallel universe' stories, a major sub-genre of SF, challenge readers' assumptions about the present by depicting it as one among many possible alternatives. Stories in another SF sub-genre, the 'future history', commonly explore the consequences which might flow from present realities, such as new technologies, and in so doing often illuminate possibilities which might not otherwise have been considered. By metaphorically rearranging the world, such stories widen the possible boundaries of alternative futures and, perhaps more importantly, 'invite us to see our own lives in a longer time frame and in relation to future generations whose reality grows from, and is dependent upon, our own' (Slaughter, 1984).

Therefore, Project IF materials encourage critical appraisal of speculative fiction and fantasy and draw heavily on science fiction stories in depicting alternative futures and suggesting topics for study. The Project IF TREES worksheet (see the excerpt in Figure 12.5) is a geographical application of this principle.

Assumption 7: Critique and negotiation of meanings

Discussions about alternative futures often fail to penetrate the taken-for-grantedness of the inherited meanings embedded in language. A very simple example is the use of a phrase like 'future in balance' in reference to something about which there is some uncertainty (see Figure 12.6). Such a phrase encourages a polarisation of future possibilities, implying that the uncertainty will be resolved in one of only two ways which must be 'weighed' against each other.

The news item reproduced in Figure 12.6 implies that there are only two alternative futures for Antarctica, represented by two kinds of sub-cultural consensus (among 'conservationist' and 'exploitationist' scientists respectively) about what might or ought to happen.

An essential part of exploring alternative futures is critical analysis of the inherited meanings, traditions, values, paradigms, myths, metaphors, concepts and

THE TIMES THURSDAY JANUARY 10 1985

Science report
Antarctic's future in balance

By Bill Johnstone
Technology Correspondent

The Antarctic, often called the "world's science park", has been invaded this week by scientists and diplomats from about 30 countries in the latest attempt to agree on its future.

The debate will not centre on the scientific route of the ice-bound landmass, about one and a half times the size of the United States, but its political and economic significance. Antarctica is believed to be rich in minerals and oil.

There has been plenty of scientific research on minerals, plant and animal life in the region by about a dozen countries. The principal being France, Japan, Germany, Britain, the United States and Russia.

The obstacles to scientific research if minerals and oil were to be exploited in Antarctica have united many scientists against commercial explorations. The area has proved to be an unrivalled environment in which to study seals, whales, penguin, and krill, which would be immediately threatened, they say.

The 55 delegates to the five-day meeting on the Beardmore Glacier are there in a personal capacity, but if a new treaty were drawn up it would require official government signatures.

The scientists at Beardmore are likely to disagree about the continent's future. Their freedom of scientific work could cease if the seven countries who claim territorial rights attempt to formalize their claims.

The polar continent is governed by 14 countries, half of whom have territorial claims: Britain, Chile and Argentina (whose claims conflict), Australia, France, Norway and New Zealand. The United States, the Soviet Union, West Germany, Poland, South

Africa, Japan and Belgium are the other signatories to the Antarctic Treaty. They have no territorial claims but recognize none.

Scientists have uncovered evidence, since the Antarctic Treaty was drawn up in 1959, of the mineral wealth which lies below the polar cap. The ice, which is constantly shifting and is several hundred metres thick, would create great difficulties for those exploiting mineral deposits.

But mining is nevertheless an attractive prospect to many.

The polar researchers have already identified evidence of coal, iron ore, copper, titanium and gold among other minerals. The finds will raise the temperature of the debates at Beardmore during the next few days.

Source: International Institute for Environment and Development.

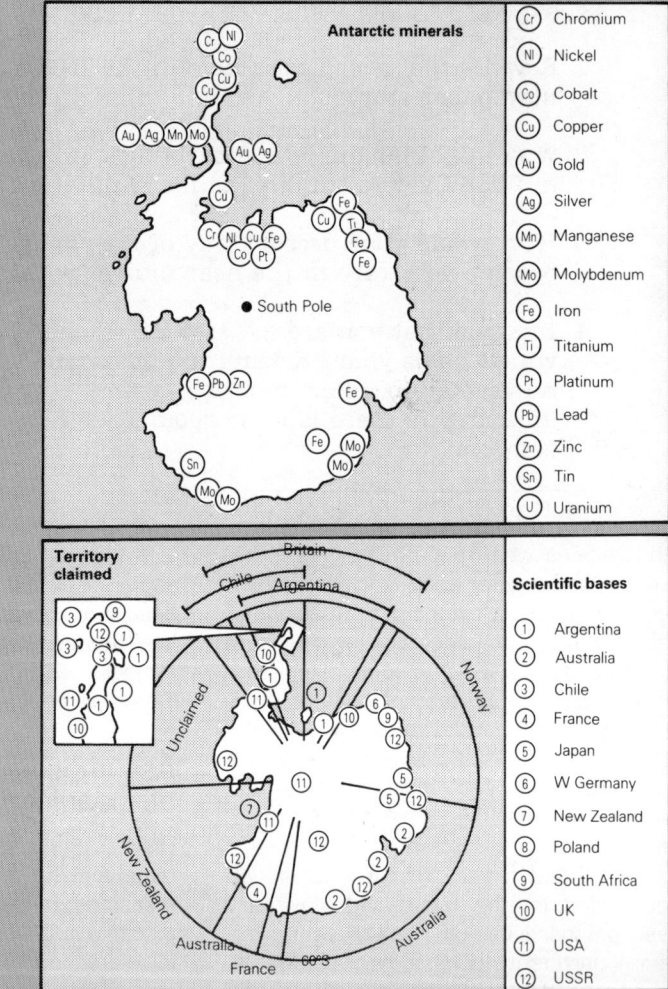

Antarctic minerals

Cr	Chromium
Ni	Nickel
Co	Cobalt
Cu	Copper
Au	Gold
Ag	Silver
Mn	Manganese
Mo	Molybdenum
Fe	Iron
Ti	Titanium
Pt	Platinum
Pb	Lead
Zn	Zinc
Sn	Tin
U	Uranium

Territory claimed

Scientific bases

1	Argentina
2	Australia
3	Chile
4	France
5	Japan
6	W Germany
7	New Zealand
8	Poland
9	South Africa
10	UK
11	USA
12	USSR

Figure 12.6 An example of the polarisation of alternative futures in everyday language

guiding images of various kinds that are embedded in everyday language, a language which mediates our interpretations of experience and our anticipations of future possibilities. Coupled with this critique must be a commitment to negotiating with wider publics the validity of emergent meanings and reconceptualisations and seeking practical strategies for the selective legitimation of new or renewed understandings.

Much discussion of alternative futures tends to focus on external change, such as new technologies, population pressures, environmental degradation, levels of resource consumption, threats of nuclear war, and so on. But underlying these visible changes, and the human response to (and responsibility for) them, are more subtle changes in values, interests and language. For example, the feminist critique of society and culture has shown that such global ills as the arms race, the shrinking of arable land, diminishing

food and fuel resources, and epidemics of diseases caused by industrial pollution, have less to do with the effects of new technologies than with the destructive power of patriarchy: with uncritical acceptance of an inherited myth of our own making.

The T-cycle (illustrated in Figure 12.7) is a tool which can help us to understand and anticipate the *changes in meaning* which occur through time. The language of geographical education includes many concepts, the meanings of which change from time to time (for example, *location, distance, distribution*). Slaughter (1986b) sees these changes in terms of a 'transformative cycle' which has four phases: breakdowns of meaning, reconceptualisations, negotiations and conflicts, and selective legitimation. Figure 12.7 illustrates a T-cycle for the concept of *work*. (NB, This form of the T-cycle is Gough's (1986) modification of Slaughter's version.)

Figure 12.7 A T-cycle: transformations in meaning through time for the concept of 'work' (Gough, 1986 and Slaughter, 1986b)

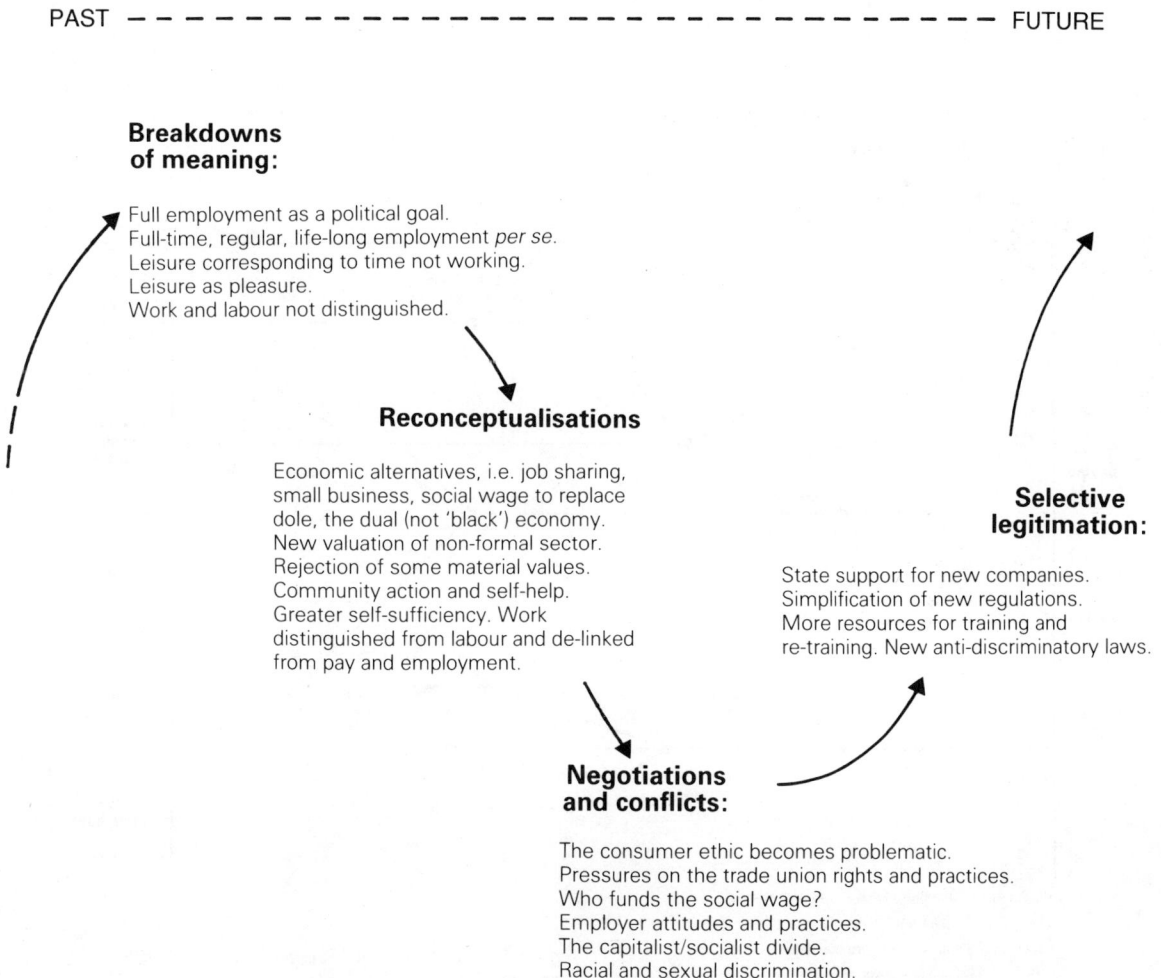

PAST — FUTURE

Breakdowns of meaning:

Full employment as a political goal.
Full-time, regular, life-long employment *per se*.
Leisure corresponding to time not working.
Leisure as pleasure.
Work and labour not distinguished.

Reconceptualisations

Economic alternatives, i.e. job sharing, small business, social wage to replace dole, the dual (not 'black') economy. New valuation of non-formal sector. Rejection of some material values. Community action and self-help. Greater self-sufficiency. Work distinguished from labour and de-linked from pay and employment.

Selective legitimation:

State support for new companies.
Simplification of new regulations.
More resources for training and re-training. New anti-discriminatory laws.

Negotiations and conflicts:

The consumer ethic becomes problematic.
Pressures on the trade union rights and practices.
Who funds the social wage?
Employer attitudes and practices.
The capitalist/socialist divide.
Racial and sexual discrimination.

171

Project IF teaching strategies

Curriculum materials, such as the Project IF work-sheets, can only be a part of classroom futures study. More important than the materials themselves are the kinds of classroom activities they stand for. Gwyneth Dow speaks of 'the preoccupation in western thought with both analysis and logicality as the prized intellectual pursuits which we set above imagination, insight, warmth and certainly (but why?) fantasy' (Dow, 1982). The 'prized intellectual pursuits' of western thought have shaped both the methods and the milieux of formal schooling – neither of which, it could be argued, lend themselves to imagination, insight, warmth and fantasy, let alone humour, which I would add to Dow's list. H. G. Wells once remarked that 'the crisis of today is the joke of tomorrow' (quoted in Teresi, 1982), and I can think of few more constructive ways of anticipating alternative futures than to look for, or to invent, humour in today's crises.

If teachers are to expect their students to be imaginative, to fantasise, or to learn from an incisive joke, they must themselves be prepared to seek out and to exhibit these forms of experience and expression. They must become connoisseurs, critics and, where possible, creators of alternative futures and of the ideas, media and settings which will encourage others to do likewise. Project IF work-

sheets illustrate several teaching strategies which can be used independently of the materials themselves. For example:

- SIGNS (see Figure 12.2) illustrates the strategy of focusing students' attention on an everyday phenomenon (in this case, non-verbal road signs) and inviting them to speculate, in a concrete way, about the projection of this phenomenon into the future.

  Evolution and change in place names is another example of a phenomenon which is taken for granted in everyday life and which could provide a useful focus for speculation in geography classrooms.

- ANTARCTICA (see Figure 12.3) illustrates the strategy of focusing students' attention on an imagined future possibility (in this case, the development of Antarctica for tourism) and inviting them to (i) appraise critically the possibility and/or invent further alternatives, and (ii) appraise critically the present concepts and circumstances on which the imagined future possibility is conditional.

- RELEVANCE TREES (see Figure 12.8) illustrates the strategy of focusing students' attention on key concepts and/or methods used in futures study and generating activities which encourage students to use the concept or method in addressing some real problem or issue (which could be drawn from the

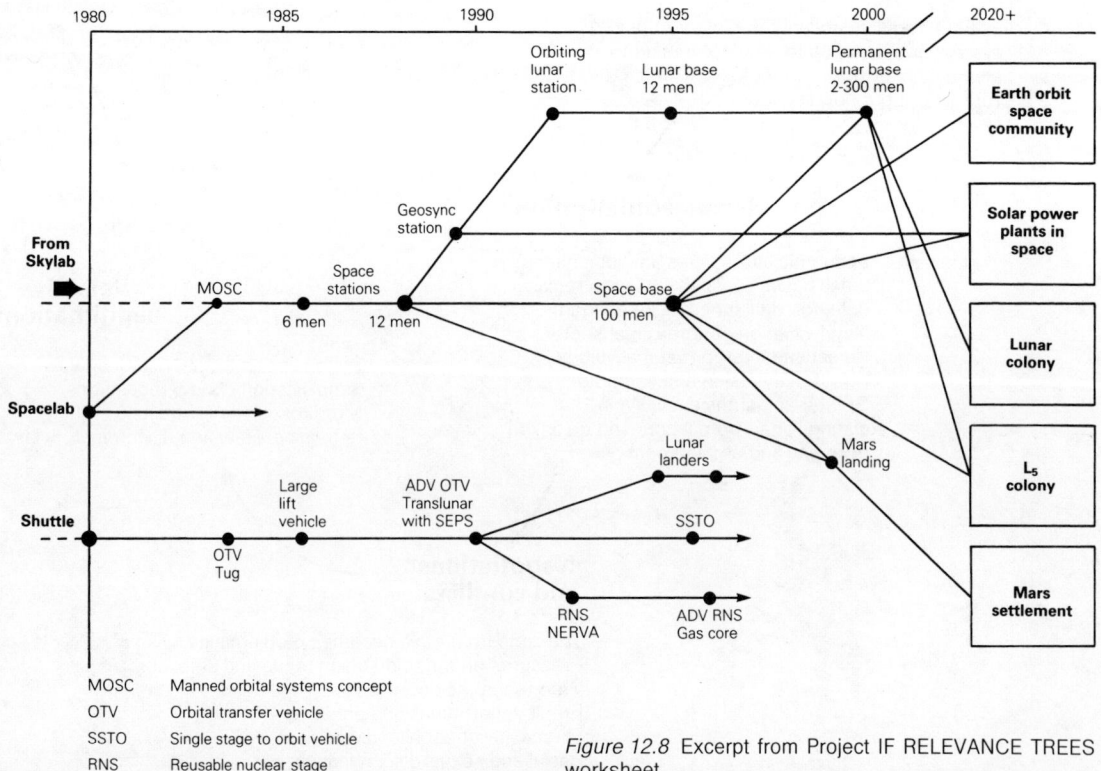

Figure 12.8 Excerpt from Project IF RELEVANCE TREES worksheet

MOSC — Manned orbital systems concept
OTV — Orbital transfer vehicle
SSTO — Single stage to orbit vehicle
RNS — Reusable nuclear stage

content of a school subject or from students' own interests and experiences). Techniques such as relevance trees, cross-impact matrices, and scenario-building and futures wheels have numerous applications in geography, particularly if the topic has a planning dimension: for example, considering a range of transport alternatives for a given locality. A common planning error is the failure to consider the implications, ramifications and consequences of predictions and intentions. Situations can arise where a plan of action, based on certain values, ends up working against those values, as the following example shows.

Intention : to relieve the congestion of a narrow road.
Plan : widen the road.
Result : more drivers are attracted to the improved road and it is even more crowded than the old one.

One way of anticipating consequences is to construct a *futures wheel*. A primary assumption, prediction or intention is placed at the centre of the wheel and first-order, second-order and third-order consequences (and beyond, if desired) are mapped onto successive rings. This method is particularly useful in analysing a proposed future. Although, on the surface, the proposal may appear to advance the values underlying its formulation, a closer examination may reveal that there are consequences which are not consistent with preferred futures.

The sample futures wheel illustrated in Figure 12.9 maps some consequences of doubling the human life span.

● REAL ESTATE (see excerpt in Figure 12.10) illustrates the strategy of transforming descriptive or explanatory material into a futures-oriented puzzle. This strategy incorporates very few preconceptions about students' responses.

Figure 12.9 A futures wheel: some consequences of doubling the human lifespan (Slaughter, 1986a)

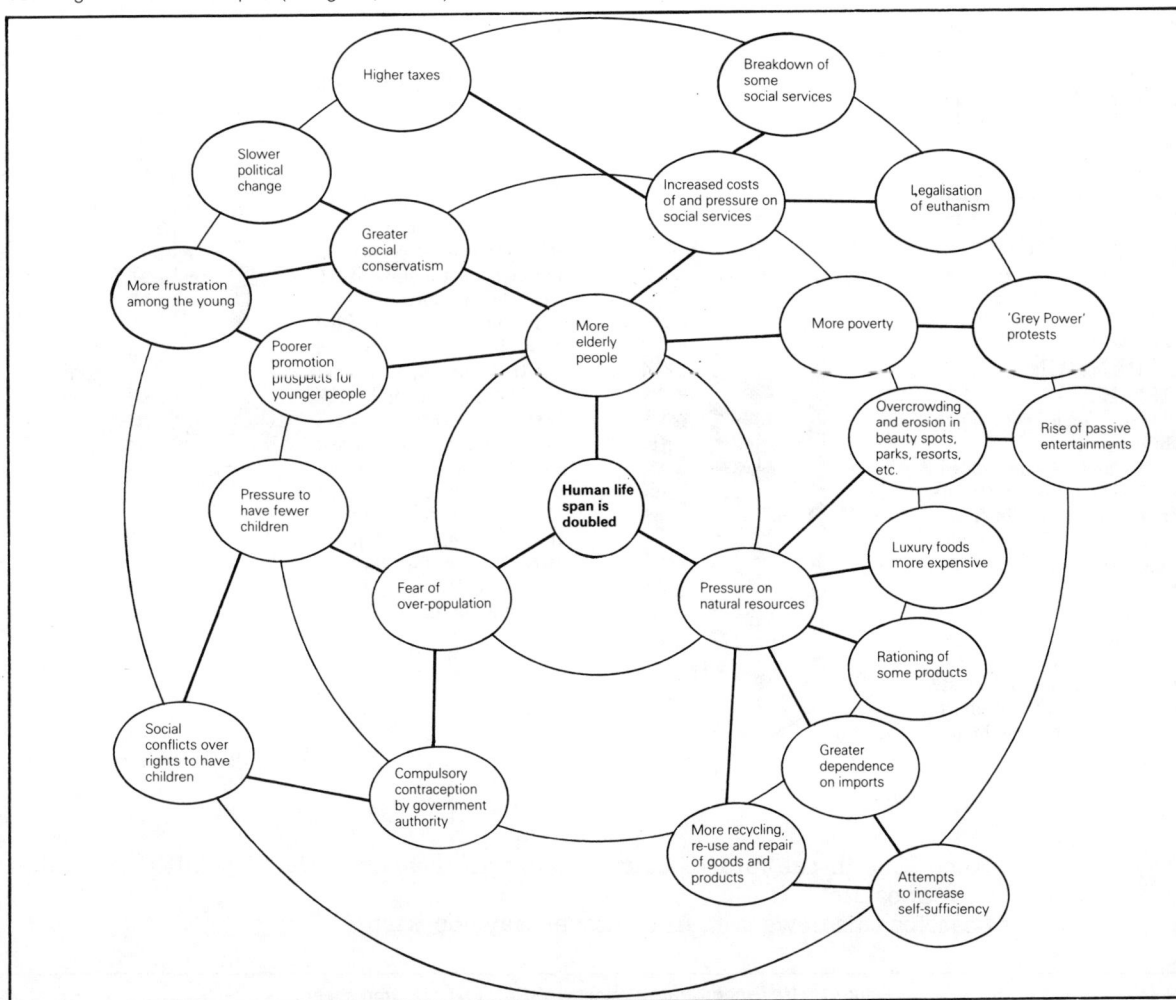

The fourth dimension in real estate

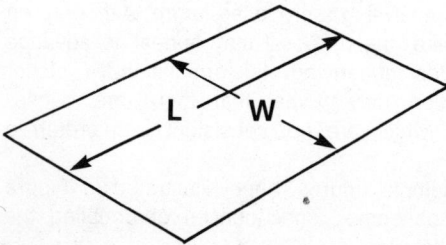

FIRST DIMENSION
LENGTH & WIDTH

One Deed for Each Piece of land.

Historically, private real estate ownership is a recent phenomenon. In Europe, it did not extend to the masses until after the Revolutionary War. In the early 1800's in Australia settlers used British recorded Deed system to show ownership – measuring length and width by feet with no pressing need to consider height.

SECOND DIMENSION
HEIGHT

One Deed for Each Building.

As land became filled, socio-economic impetus created the next dimension . . . height. Taller buildings became a prominent feature with the advent of improved engineering and materials. Still, only one Deed was needed to show ownership of the real estate – such as the 22 unit apartment building used in this illustration.

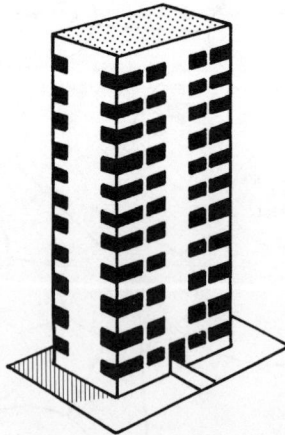

THIRD DIMENSION
STRATA TITLE

The ownership of apartment living created this 3rd dimension of real estate.

Dividing the height of a building horizontally or in Stratas allowed for as many Deeds (on one piece of property) as there were living units. Thus, ownership of this example apartment building (and facilities) is now jointly in the hands of 22 individuals.

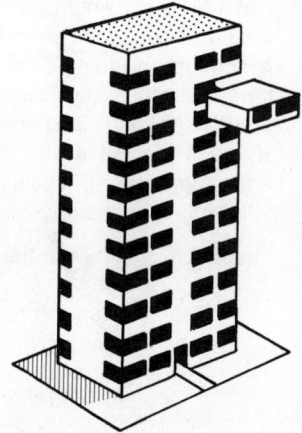

FOURTH DIMENSION
TIME

One Owner for Each Week of the Year.

TIME becomes the new dimension to its predecessors.

Now, ownership for the resort suite is on a weekly time interval – permitting the owner's use only to the time they require.

Ingenuity has propelled man into being able to control holiday resort ownership, bringing it back into affordable range. Ownership can be achieved by purchase of a Redeemable Preference Share in Chevron Queensland Ltd at the Chevron Hotel Surfers Paradise, entitling them to 20 years Holidays for a once only outlay.

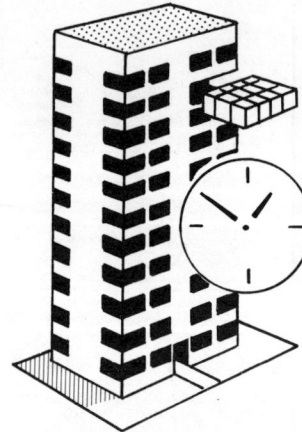

THE AGE, Monday 11 April 1983

Some time in the future, a news item will have the title, "The fifth dimension in real estate"
Describe this news item in whatever way you wish.

Figure 12.10 Excerpt from Project IF REAL ESTATE worksheet

Exploring future geographies: a practical activity

The technique illustrated here is of the kind I have dubbed 'time capsules'. When used in a group setting, I usually encourage individual written responses to time capsule A, followed by small group work on time capsule B. A rationale for the technique follows illustration of a sample time capsule exercise in Figures 12.11 and 12.12.

Time capsules: a rationale

The rationale for the time capsule technique springs directly from the Project IF assumption concerning the rehearsal of surprise. One of the surprises we can fairly readily rehearse is the debunking of our pet theories, such as our assumptions about the nature and effect of forces for social, technological and environmental change. But a realistic rehearsal of such surprises goes beyond attempting an academic answer to questions such as 'what if this theory, or that theorist, is wrong?'. Rather, we need to *simulate future hindsight*: to rehearse the *feeling of certainty* that, in an imagined future, such beliefs have been falsified.

Time capsule exercises begin, therefore, by confronting participants with dogmatic assertions from the past with which they are very likely to disagree. Ideally, time capsule A should provoke some sort of discernible 'gut reaction', such as laughter or anger. I usually encourage participants to write their responses individually, followed by a brief discussion during which their immediate reactions are shared.

Figure 12.11 Sample geographic time capsule A

GEOGRAPHIC TIME CAPSULE A: 1906 – OPENED 1986

Three Men in a Motor Car

From Winthrop E. Scarritt: "Three Men in a Motor Car" – E. P. Dutton & Co., New York, 1906

Let us now consider some of the modern problems which the motor-car will solve.

First. The congestion of traffic in our city streets. What would it mean to the city of New York if all the horse-drawn vehicles could be supplanted by motor-vehicles? . . . Indeed, I believe the automobile is the key, and the only key, to the problem of over-congested traffic in our city streets.

Second. It will solve the problem of overcrowding in the tenement-house district. Automobiles will become cheap, following the course of the bicycle. The laboring man, when the factory whistle blows and the work of the day is done, will step into his own car and in an hour's time be twenty miles away in the country beneath the blue sky, breathing God's pure air, listening to the music of the murmuring brook and the singing birds . . . * * *

Fifth. The motor-car is to emancipate the horse . . . The horse, man's best friend, is to be free. The day of his emancipation draweth nigh, when

Horse-drawn carts are seen no longer,
And the poor dumb beast is freed.
And the motor-car has conquered
Price and prejudice and greed.

Sixth. The automobile will do much to annihilate Time and Space.

Seventh. The automobile may revolutionize methods of farming.

The Automobile: Yesterday a Plaything of the Few; Today a Servant of the Many; Tomorrow the Necessity of Humanity.

1. Briefly describe your *immediate* reactions to the above statements – how did you *feel* as you read Scarritt's views?

2. In 1906, views such as those expressed by Winthrop Scarritt were widespread. It was generally believed that the motor car would solve many "modern problems".

   In 1986, it is clear that the social and environmental impact of the motor car has been rather different from that envisaged by Mr Scarritt. Briefly describe these differences and describe what has happened between 1906 and 1986 which accounts for these differences.

GEOGRAPHIC TIME CAPSULE B: 1984 – OPENED 2064

1. To some extent your responses to Time Capsule A are likely to have been a product of *hindsight*, of 80 years of change in our beliefs and understandings. The next piece you read was written recently. Try to imagine that you are now nearly 80 years in the future and that your immediate reactions are *exactly the same* as your reactions to Time Capsule A. That is, if you were amused by Mr Scarritt's views, imagine that you are equally amused by the following item.

THE AGE, Thursday 5 April 1984

Melbourne to keep on sprawling

by ROY ECCLESTON
urban affairs reporter

Melbourne's suburban sprawl would grow well into the next century, with the inner suburbs continuing to drop in population, a business analyst and forecaster predicted yesterday.

But Mr Phillip Ruthven, of Ibis Corporate Services, said it would be an oversimplification to say this would occur only because of the cheaper land and housing prices on the suburban fringe.

Mr Ruthven told suburban newspaper and marketing representatives that a big reason would be the increase in the free time that workers would have. With reduced working hours this was likely to be 50 per cent of a worker's time, with a consequent greater emphasis on living "where he wants to live rather than near work".

Mr Ruthven, who based most of his forecasts on examinations of figures from the Australian Bureau of Statistics, said the distance between wealthy and poor would also increase.

And many of the wealthy lived in the outer suburbs.

2. In 1984, views such as those expressed by Phillip Ruthven were widespread. It was generally believed that Melbourne's suburbs, like those of most major cities, would "keep on sprawling".

In 2064, it is clear that Melbourne's development (like that of many other cities) has been rather different from that envisaged by Mr Ruthven. Briefly describe these differences and describe what has happened between 1984 and 2064 which accounts for these differences.

Figure 12.12 Sample geographic time capsule B

These shared responses can then be drawn upon in providing the context for time capsule B. Thus, if participants have said that they found time capsule A to be 'pretty stupid' or 'a bit of a joke', they can be encouraged to sneer or laugh as they read time capsule B.

Time capsule B can be any current orthodoxy, and responses may best be elicited in small group settings. The purpose of the exercise is to imagine and invent alternative 'future histories' and my experience is that small groups are likely to be more creative than individuals, many of whom tend to be locked into one perspective of the future. The written responses to time capsule A may be used to suggest analogous explanations for change, for example, identification of assumptions in A now known to be false may lead to a search for assumptions in B which can be imagined to be falsified by future events.

The simulation of future hindsight is particularly useful in encouraging scepticism about the dogmatic assertions of so-called experts, who frequently pontificate about the future. With monotonous regularity, seemingly competent scientists and scholars have laid down the law about what is possible and impossible and, with the passage of time, have been proved utterly wrong. One among many failures of imagination by an eminent scientist was the following remark made by Ernest Rutherford in 1933:

> The energy produced by the breaking down of the atom is a very poor kind of thing. Anyone who expects a source of power from the transformation of these atoms is talking moonshine. (Quoted in Teresi, 1982, p. 141)

Any mild amusement or incredulity we might feel in response to Rutherford's assertion should be borne in mind when we read more recent pronouncements of a similar kind. For example, the following item appeared in *The Times* (22 November 1984):

PROFESSOR SCOFFS AT HOUSEHOLD ROBOT

by Pearce Wright, Science Editor

As if pitching balls at a coconut shy, Professor John Searle use the latest of his Reith Lectures, on BBC Radio 4 yesterday to shift his aim to a third area of "fashionable" scientific activity.

Loosening up for the throw, he said: "We are frequently assured that we are on the verge of having household robots that will do all the housework, babysit our children, amuse us with lively conversation, and take care of us in our old age. That is of course, so much nonsense."

The object of the attack by Professor Searle, Professor of Philosophy at the University of California, Berkeley, was the new discipline of cognitive science, which is at the centre of ideas for making possible computers with the same mental processes as the brain. . .

Of course, we may not need the analogy of Rutherford's assertion to help us imagine that Searle's statement could be falsified by future events; in some senses it is already false (most of us have had a machine which babysits children for many years, namely, television). However, the accuracy of Searle's prediction is not the point at issue. Rather, we should vigorously oppose any member of an opinionated elite who dismisses plausible speculations about possible alternatives as 'nonsense', as if they were not worth discussing or debating: such dismissals are an invitation to ignorance, whereas we should be encouraging anticipatory democracy through enlightened participation in the exploration of alternatives.

Section C

13 Reflections on teaching geography for a better world

BERNARD COX

Introduction

Teaching geography for a better world was the theme of the national conference of the Australian Geography Teacher's Association in 1986. This theme clearly permeates the chapters of this book. The theme certainly implies that the world is much in need of improvement and that geography teaching is one appropriate means for effecting improvement. Such a theme raises the following three matters for consideration.

- The idea of a better world: the criteria enabling us to identify what would make for a better world and the ideologies from which these criteria are derived.

- The character of geography as a discipline, and its capacity (as adapted to the school curriculum) to foster learning that might lead to a better world.

- Teaching/learning procedures enabling students of geography to conceptualise and work for a better world.

The authors of the various chapters have adopted several different approaches to identifying and working toward a better world. They include: studies of the nature of and need for political literacy (Huckle and McElroy) and human rights (Burnley), anti-racist approaches (Daws), women in geography (Monk and Williamson-Fien), Third World studies (Toh), applications of peace education (Hicks), and alternative futures (Gough). The chapters on these subjects convey the conceptions of a better world held by the editors and authors.

The idea of a better world

Assertions

Several chapters assert and exemplify that our planet and its people are plagued by problems which seriously limit the quality of life of the majority. This is established vividly by David Hicks who wrote:

. . . conditions for most of the 5000 million inhabitants on Planet Earth are far from good.

- *Tension and violence are on the increase in a world already dangerously overarmed and undernourished.*
- *30 children are dying each minute for want of food and inexpensive vaccines.*
- *At the same time $U.S. 1.5 million per minute are being spent on armaments.*
- *150 major wars have been fought in the last 40 years.*
- *Torture of people, animals and the environment have reached epidemic proportions.*
- *The male of the species, only half of the population, does barely one-third of the planet's work yet takes 90% of its income; direct and indirect violence against the female of the species is generally the norm.*
- *In 40 years the stockpile of nuclear weapons has grown from 3 to 50 000. (page 13)*

John Huckle reinforced this view of our world in a parlous condition and began to diagnose causes:

More and more of the earth's living and non-living resources become mere commodities to feed commodity chains and provide goods and services for the global market. Continual pressure to expand and cheapen production inevitably results in such social costs as pollution, resource depletion, habitat destruction, and species extinction. (page 22)

Toh Swee-Hin focused our attention specifically on the countries of the South:

Food and population issues must loom large in Third World studies, given that most poor people live agriculturally, and global poverty's basic expression is hunger and malnutrition. (page 119)

Geographical approaches to the study of life chances were extended by Janice Monk and Jane Williamson-Fien who examined gender challenges for the curriculum in geography. They have established their perspectives with the argument that our teaching materials commonly omit women's experiences, treat them in limited ways (for example, in discussions of population and fertility), or stereotype them. To rectify this situation, teachers must reach beyond the superficial addition of new material to transform the curriculum, revising the content and developing critical perspectives on existing materials and sources of data.

Criteria of a better world

The ideas presented in the earlier chapters of this book identified several criteria that might be used to judge how our world could be made better. These criteria all relate to anxiety over the state of the world and, perhaps more specifically, to a geography of welfare. The view of welfare is applied to humanity as a whole rather than to individuals or to specified groups. Obviously, individuals can and do benefit when welfare is considered in the context just noted but it is different from the traditional economics viewpoint of individuals making decisions favouring their own greatest material gain or of firms seeking to maximise profits.

Writing in this vein, Barrie McElroy argued:

While detachment may be an admirable procedural value for research it is not so appropriate for learning where participation in life is the constant goal. Effective participation grows from awareness, knowledge and the appropriate skills including one's understanding of and inclination to use political skills.

Implicit in the many general statements on the purposes of schooling is that education will result in changing the human, physical, social and economic environment for the better. At the same time some questions are not addressed. What kind of changes? Where should these changes occur? Better for whom? Who has the most say in decisions about change? The answers to such questions are generally implicit in the actual practice of schooling. (page 31)

David Hicks developed a concept of 'positive peace' which includes a list of goals which may readily be used as criteria for a better world.

We need to develop the concept of positive peace, that is peace both as a state and a process, involving the presence of the goals . . . .: justice, equality, participation, non-violence and ecological balance. (page 142)

Toh Swee-Hin also identified criteria derived from the PEACE paradigm elaborated in his chapter. He applied them to a better 'world' in countries of the South.

The PEACE paradigm upholds development policies which are participatory with the poor no longer powerless and passively accepting decisions dispensed from above by elites or experts. Participation allows the accumulated knowledge of the poor to be tapped. . . Social, political and economic structures require radical transformation so that societal resources and wealth are equitably distributed within and between nations. Methods and technology have to be appropriate, optimising use of local material, human and cultural resources and capable of maximising economic benefits to the poor majorities. But at the same time, such mass-oriented development should harmonise with, not destroy, the environment on which long-term human survival depends. Above all, PEACEful development embodies the process of conscientisation, whereby the oppressed understand the political roots of their poverty and act to liberate themselves. (page 119)

Traditional geographers who may be puzzling over the links between criteria for a better world and geography as they know it, may begin to identify these links in several phrases from the quotation from Toh, notably:

- 'resources and wealth are equitably distributed'
- 'use of local human and cultural resources'
- 'development should . . . not destroy the environment'

These are the traditional concerns of geography and are presented in several chapters from a range of distinct value positions. Zais (1976) writes that non-self-centred values relating to these include:

(1) the equality of selves; (2) an accepting, nonjudging attitude toward other individuals; (3) an absolute honesty in one's relations with others, so that the possibility of "using" another to achieve one's goals is precluded; (4) the rejection of competition among individuals; (5) high regard for town-meeting type participatory democracy; (6) the rejection of materialism; and (7) the notion that all people, whether they have met or not, are members of the same family — in short, brotherhood and community.

People act on these values in many different ways: some of us write, teach or lecture about them while others join conservation, peace and social justice groups. Some people engage in direct social action to protect these values while others are happy to live them in their own quiet way.

Distinguishing symptoms from root causes

Some causes of the plight of humanity were identified in several chapters. John Huckle offered a Marxist explanation.

The reason for this inequality and environmental destruction is that the world economy is a capitalist economy where the bulk of producers do not consume what they produce but exchange it in a competitive market for the best price. Such production is controlled by a rich minority who produce only what it is profitable for them to produce. Their motivation is the accumulation of capital; a process which can only take place through the exploitation of others. (page 20)

David Hicks argued that 'warfare has a very violent effect on both human welfare and on the natural and made landscapes' (page 141). Barrie McElroy decried the low levels of political literacy in many people, arguing that this dispossesses them of the knowledge and skills they need to take control over their own life-chances. Toh Swee-Hin stressed the crucial role of structural violence as a general cause of underdevelopment in the Third World and of the appalling living conditions of so many people. Leonie Daws identified racism as a strong source and form of structural violence while Janice Monk and Jane Williamson-Fien identified patriarchal structures and sexism as causes of inequality.

These are not the only causes cited in the chapters and they are not separate from each other, but they are diverse manifestations of violence resulting from the use and misuse of power in various ways. Geographers need to respond to the challenge of such contentions because they significantly affect the environments of our lives.

Frameworks for thinking about a better world

People see the roles of school in society in different ways. Indeed, when one considers carefully the impact that different approaches to schooling have on students, it may be realised that what different people want to make of society and what they want to do to or for students in schools are sharply contrasted. Ideologies provide background assumptions about ways people should lead their lives. These assumptions frame our everyday lives but not all of us put them to serious scrutiny. Different ideologies colour our beliefs about geography teaching for a better world. Many of the chapters in this book are orientated towards socially critical viewpoints. These approaches may be seen in perspective if brief descriptions are made of alternative ideologies.

Fundamentalists view education as the preparation of students for the workforce and, in doing so, tend to sustain present social structures. They press for conformity to a rigidly defined moral code which the school has some responsibility to maintain but not to question. The ways in which schools are run help select students for appropriate vocations. Fundamentalists argue that such an approach to schooling realistically prepares students for the conditions of life outside schools. Fundamentalism has been described as an 'ism' of defence in which standards, traditions, disciplined knowledge and the basics are conserved. Fundamentalists do not readily admit diverse points of view.

Socially critical educators often see the present society as characterised by inequities and injustices which result from the exercise of political power in the hands of a minority who control the world's capital. It is the task of schools to recognise this condition and to encourage students to be consciously and constructively critical of it. Rather than prepare students to meet the existing conditions of society, schools should encourage students to take action where appropriate to formulate and evaluate alternative solutions and remedy the problems.

The focus of liberal education is the multi-faceted growth of students as individuals. Liberals recognise the need to work towards the improvement of society. While many radicals assert that the power of the world's political and economic elites is so entrenched that reform cannot be brought about peacefully or without a struggle, liberals believe that reform is possible within the present system if people are guided by rational and moral principles. Liberalism is distinguished from other ideologies because it admits, and reflects on, diverse points of view. Such a liberal view of the world is not necessarily at odds with the perspectives of adherents to other ideologies. Liberalism is guided by such tenets as tolerance of diversity and respect for well-informed individual opinion which inhibit off-handed rejection of other ideas. Liberalism insists on plurality, often seeking answers to questions from other ideologies as to why they regard their system or solution as best. On the other hand, one problem with liberalism is that it ignores different levels of social power and, in trying to be neutral, may fail to take a stand for justice and equity in any conflict between the powerful and the powerless.

Noel Gough's paper on futures education in geography offered a different framework for thinking about a better world. He indicated that extrapolative and consensus methods are used to generate probable futures and refine our predictions about future events, but students can create images of preferred futures by imagining and exploring the implications of possible alternatives, rather than by choosing among those alternatives which may now seem most probable. This suggests a reconstructionist viewpoint.

Reconstructionists seek to build an ideal social order based on democratic principles. Their efforts in the past have often been expressed as utopian. The reconstructionist approach lies somewhere between the liberal and the socially critical approaches. Reconstructionists have a keen awareness of the changes needed to effect social justice but work constructively for social redirection. A school curriculum reflecting reconstructionism focuses on social problems, allows critical analyses of them and urges students to become involved in constructive action for the reform of society. Indeed the reconstructionists, along with liberals, place much reliance on the power of schools to redress major global problems, such as those which are the focus of this book: war, crime, oppression, environmental degradation, and others. On the other hand, socially critical teachers see schools as only one avenue of social change and argue for teachers to build links with the 'rainbow coalition' of social change groups increasingly present in the community (Huckle, 1986; Maher, 1986).

Comment: Teachers realise that their work is undertaken within one ideological framework or another. Ideologies usually contain assumptions that influence what and how we teach, but many of us are not aware enough of these assumptions to subject them to close scrutiny. It is important that all of us should know the intellectual and affective components of the ideology which contributes to the context of our work. We need to reflect on these components and to make curricular decisions informed by reflection.

Geography and teaching for a better world

Defining geography

It is not possible to provide a monolithic definition of geography. The diverse value-stances adopted by different geographers affect their interpretation and views of the world they are studying. For example, many physical geographers and the quantitative human geographers who flourished in the 1970s adopted largely empirical ways of knowing. This contrasts with David Hicks' reference to a 'geography of concern' which has emerged over the last decade or so. He described the main components of the geography of concern:

> *In particular we can look to developments in welfare geography, humanistic geography and radical geography to support us here. . . Welfare geography is concerned with describing, interpreting and predicting patterns of human welfare on a variety of scales. Humanistic geography focuses on our feelings, fears, perceptions and experiences, on our personal and private geographies. Radical geography asks critical questions about the unjust status quo and offers insights from Marxist and anarchist perspectives. (page 16).*

This geography of concern links humanistic geography and radical geography. Both tend to use methodologies of research based on the ways of knowing distinctive to such human studies as history, but their orientations to social criticism are different.

So what is geography? Writing in the *Dictionary of Human Geography* (Johnston *et al.*, 1983), Haggett says that geography:

> *occupies a puzzling position within the traditional organizations of knowledge. It is neither a purely natural science nor a purely social science.*

He identifies as the essential geographic characteristics:

- an emphasis on location;
- an ecological emphasis on people–land relations; and
- regional analysis in which the spatial and ecological approaches are fused.

He comments on the dynamism of the subject in the following way:

Geography today represents an amalgam in which the legacy of past ideas remains strongly embedded but current thinking is still being worked out. In some respects it resembles a city with districts of different ages and vitalities. There are some long established districts dating back to a century ago and sometimes in need of repair; areas which were once fashionable and are so no longer, while others are being rehabilitated. Other districts have expanded recently and rapidly; some are well built, others rather gimcrack. If we use the city metaphor, then geography has extended beyond its medieval walls to form a sprawling conurbation with other subjects.

Each of the chapters in this book suggested ways in which the concerns for a better world are related to the study of geography. John Bale, in writing that 'sport is eminently geographical', and David Hicks, in writing about the geography of war and peace, make it clear that content per se is not what makes a study distinctly geographical. The ways in which an idea is framed make it geographical. For example, it is possible to apply the concepts of 'spatial diffusion' and 'place' (in several ways) to sport. Both David Hicks and Barrie McElroy refer to 'social process and spatial pattern' as ways of developing geographical studies of their topics. McElroy offers a caution on the limits of the contribution that geography might make to a better world when he writes:

Neither the explanations and theories of geography nor our teaching give the average citizen or student much understanding of how power is exercised in decision making and how they might share that power. (page 31)

But John Huckle begins with a classic geographical contention that:

The location of production processes, in response to market forces, structures the world's spatial and environmental relations. The resulting spatial hierarchy of nation states, based on their dominant production processes, shows a threefold division, into core, periphery, and semi-periphery, which mirrors the global division of tabour. (page 21)

The consequences of this geographical pattern include marked regional variations in life chances. He asserts that these can only be explained by reference to cyclical and secular trends in the world economy and the ways in which political decisions affect the world economy. So explanation in geography must draw on a knowledge of how power is wielded and how political decisions are made.

The disparate social sciences are sharing ideas

Recent developments in the growth of various social sciences, such as history, geography, political science, sociology, psychology, economics, show that they are increasingly borrowing from each other with a view to making more elegant interpretations. For example, several premises of rational economic activity (such as, decisions are constantly taken for the purpose of maximising profits) are being reconsidered in the light of psychological knowledge. Historians are making more use of knowledge of past geographies and of sociological ideas in attempting to understand the human condition of ordinary people in past times. Humanistic geographers are enhancing explanations in geography by making use of what is known about the value systems adopted by people, their perception of place and their motivations. The study of people in social, economic and political contexts is increasingly a feature that the social sciences have in common. Thus, an overriding theme of this book is that a knowledge of ideologies is necessary if reflection and action in geography are to be purposeful. In recognising this, we have returned to John Huckle's contention that it is impossible to explain areal variations in welfare and life-chances without reference to the exercise of power evident in political decisions.

Teaching and learning geography for a better world

Moral growth in students

Teaching geography for a better world necessarily involves developing attributes of moral maturity in students. Knowledge and the exercise of reason are necessary but not sufficient for developing morality. Feelings and emotion are important in morality, both because they heighten sensitivity and also because the experience of concern for other people provides the motive for morality. So, important features of a moral person are readiness and skill in using content and reason, as well as admitting the experience of feeling as one comes to grips with issues.

Ethical decisions involving questions about right action cannot be avoided when we teach geography for a better world. Geography teachers contribute to moral growth in students when they encourage:

direct and indirect intervention of the school which affects both moral behaviour and the capacity to think about issues of right and wrong. (Purpel and Ryan, 1975)

The issues referred to here may relate to self, society and environments. Controversy emerges over issues on which there are different views that are both opposed and reasonable. Sometimes it is insufficient evidence that makes an issue difficult to resolve; sometimes people agree on criteria that might be used to resolve an issue but not on the relative importance of the criteria; often controversial issues derive from viewpoints supported by irreconcilable ideologies.

The kinds of issues which students of geography are often asked to ponder relate to:

- aspects of life in cities
- exploitation of natural resources
- food and poverty
- sources of energy
- development and environments.

These are general areas out of which issues may arise when they are brought to focus in a particular place. For example, 'using natural resources' is not generally an issue, but logging in the Daintree area of north Queensland is a controversial issue.

How we react to confronting issues

Past experiences colour our reactions to fresh stimuli. We are predisposed to react in various ways to people and ideas, and are often quite selective about the stimuli we respond to. So it is not surprising that perceptions of the world vary from one person to another and this contributes to the emergence of controversy among people. Teachers do well to be aware of diverse perspectives when they are fostering debate on controversial issues in class. Further, there are often inconsistencies among what an individual knows, values, says and does. Although personal values are more stable and enduring than attitudes, we need to recognise that values held by any individual are likely to be inconsistent. This is because they are often held relative to other values in life

Restraints on teaching about controversial issues in geography classes

We are not free to teach all issues in geography classes and the sources of restraints are quite varied. Restraints may come from the policy of employing authorities, from teachers' perceptions of their own lack of knowledge or skill in handling issues in class, and from the willingness of particular students to study certain issues. The views of the senior administrators of the school, other teachers, parents, and vocal members of the community may also inhibit discussion of controversial issues in class. Most of these restraints are issue-specific, work most keenly

in particular locations and tend to change with time. Recognising their existence does not imply condoning them.

Despite the operation of these restraints it is hard to exclude controversial issues from geography lessons. Further, it is arguable that it is educationally bad practice to do so. Denying students the opportunity of learning about controversial issues takes away their access to part of the subject they are studying, limits their opportunities for using the syntax of their subject to test the truth of ideas, and robs them of insights into ways in which human knowledge has developed. Many formerly controversial ideas have been resolved by advances in knowledge.

Teaching geography for a better world

Four major experiences may be combined in various ways to foster learning in geography for a better world. These are: inculcation, acquiring knowledge, reflection, and action. They are necessarily linked, combinations of them may occur simultaneously, and the order in which they may profitably be experienced can vary.

Inculcation involves instilling certain values in students and helping them internalise these values. It is widespread in classrooms and forms part of the general process of socialisation into the life of schools. Inculcation does presume widespread support for the values involved, but it should be distinguished from indoctrination which is characterised by persistent presentation of ideas from one viewpoint.

The acquisition of knowledge is essential to students learning geography for a better world. A wide range of possibe teaching/learning experiences may be used to good effect as students acquire knowledge. But it is arguable that it is important for students to learn how to learn, and their experiences might well focus on this. The overriding purpose of geography teaching for a better world is that students should take actions which are informed both by rational thinking and also by principled moral judgements. So learning experiences which promote the development of autonomy in students may well be extended to the acquisition of knowledge and the process of reflection.

Reflection can be undertaken individually or when working with a few other people. The term 'reflection' has been in the educational literature for a long time, at least since Dewey. He emphasised that the subject of reflection should be teased apart carefully. The logical supports and subsidiary ideas of the main contention should persistently be tested from diverse points of view in the process of reflection. Reflection helps us recognise inconsistencies and ambiguities in argument or viewpoint. It serves often to heighten awareness of the varied ways in which different people see the same object or event, person or idea. Self-evident or popularly accepted statements can be refined by the process of reflection.

Reflection involves both intellect and affect. It requires the use of what have commonly been called higher cognitive skills. Cognitive reflection can be enhanced by knowing the antecedents of the subject of study, by analysing the present situation in which it is placed, by undertaking case studies, by specific problem solving, by statistical analyses of numerical data, and other learning procedures.

The affective areas of reflection involve insight into the value premises of what is being studied, and also of the learner's own value-stance towards the same matter. Values analyses and values clarification are commonly-cited approaches to gaining these insights. Critical comment on them has pointed to uncertainty about their outcomes and to the claim that 'they can also be seen to convey a false view of politics which neglects issues of power' (Huckle, 1983).

Action is the fourth element in the complex of teaching/learning experiences that can be used in geography teaching for a better world. Action may lead to the acquisition of knowledge or may be an index of commitment which has been fostered during the process of reflection. Action or service learning has been popularised by some writers (Ball and Ball, 1973) as a way of developing a sense of commitment in learners and it is in this respect that it differs from 'learning by doing'. Action learning may well take place when someone does something for someone else who really wants the service provided.

Action has a different character when interpreted in the light of alternative views about education. Several chapters in this book present a case that it is the responsibility of schools to help students recognise social injustice and encourage them to use their skills in political literacy overcome the injustice. Many different actions have been suggested, including: writing letters to, or otherwise trying to influence, the people who make decisions in our society; publicising one's viewpoint; raising funds; taking collective action by joining organisations. These are all political actions because they involve the exercise of power in one form or another.

Where do we go from here?

An educational programme

The chapters in this book were prepared for an Australian geography teachers' conference which was held in Brisbane in January 1986. I was the conference moderator and had the opportunity to go to all the workshops to see how teachers were responding to the kind of messages explored in this book. These are some of the conclusions that I drew:

- Most of the teachers who attended developed

heightened awareness of the issues associated with geography teaching for a better world.
- There was debate about what really constitutes geographical study in secondary schools and why it should be a part of the curriculum.
- The significance of ideology in education was better known among teachers after the conference.
- Delegates accepted or rejected alternative perspectives on education but left the conference better informed about them.
- Delegates commented on 'practical realities' as limitations on the adoption of some of the ideas presented during the conference.

Which of these reactions do you share? Are you and your colleagues committed to teaching geography for a better world? If not, what are you teaching for? Are you aware of the issues involved and the role of ideology in education? What are the practical realities that you face in your adoption of some of the ideas in this book? What is the way forward from here?

One direction in which we might travel from here is to mount an educational programme involving inculcation, knowledge, reflection and action over the issues presented in this book. Decisions made by teachers about their own teaching during this process of re-education should thus be wise. Choices made by teachers about which of the suggestions, issues, content and methods they will adopt or reject are likely to be informed and studied.

It is hoped that our decisions will be made within a context of knowledge about such things as:
- the recent history of secondary education in the home region;
- the political climate in the home country;
- past and present syllabuses in geography; and
- 'images of preferred futures' gained through 'simulating future hindsight' (Gough).

It is hoped also that the decisions will be made within a context of feeling concern for people and environments (conscientisation), and a commitment to teaching geography for a better world.

14 Postscript

MICHAEL NAISH

What paragons of all the virtues we geographers are called upon to be! Within the span of my own experience as a teacher of children and adults over 25 years, geography teachers have been summoned to rally round an enormously diverse collection of banners, all held equally high. The strange messages on the banners have read:

- help them (the children) understand the great world stage
- enable them to read their newspapers with understanding
- play a key role in education for international understanding
- get them to learn through the soles of their boots
- help them develop skills of reading, writing, number and graphicacy (the fourth ace in the pack)
- develop scientific approaches through hypothesis testing – be objective
- theorise
- quantify
- develop problem-solving and decision-making modes of thinking
- focus on behaviourism and especially perception
- engage in systems analysis
- take the major responsibility for development education in the curriculum
- help develop language and mathematics across the curriculum
- enhance the role of geography in environmental education
- develop the place of geography in pre-vocational education and hence further the progress of the new vocationalism
- use geography to develop values education and political literacy

Yes, it is a long list, but it is only selective and most readers could probably add to it.

Now we are asked in this volume to teach geography for a better world. The book sets out, write Rod Gerber and John Fien, with a 'clear evangelical function': 'to increase the number of people who want to participate in teaching geography for a better world'. Learning geography is to be a means of putting the world to rights.

There are several problems facing those of us who would accept this invitation. These include the following.

- Our own inertia. Such inertia results from, for example, the nature of the education we have received; our own strongly reinforced personal attitudes, values and prejudices; and the limitations of our own understandings. This inertia must be broken down to achieve the emancipation necessary to take up the challenges posed in this book.
- Geography cannot do it alone. The issues and ideals addressed by authors in this volume are not of the kind of narrow focus accessible to a single discipline. Rather they demand concerted interdisciplinary analysis and planning for action.
- Geography teachers alone cannot achieve education for a better world. What is required is concerted curriculum planning at the level of the faculty, the school, the organising authority and beyond. At last in Britain, for example, we are beginning to realise the potential benefits for the curriculum of whole school planning.
- In most parts of the world curriculum control is a constraining factor. True curriculum reform – such as is needed if education is to address openly the kinds of issues raised in this book – is difficult to imagine in many administrations ranging from the authoritarian left to equally authoritarian right as they now exist. Generally speaking a genuinely enabling education which positively encourages critical thinking and autonomous initiative is

regarded with intense suspicion by authoritarian administrations. In some administrations, policies are devised to restrict access to knowledge, since knowledge is seen as a means to control.

- In some parts of the world public examination systems still strongly influence the nature of the curriculum, especially the quality of the experiences 'enjoyed' by the students. Generally speaking, and of course there are exceptions, the impact of public examinations is conservative and restrictive.

To expand on this list, as could easily be done, might be depressing for those who want to teach geography for a better world. The message to be derived from consideration of the entrenchment of curriculum constraints is that educationists, and that means teachers, clearly have a long way to go. It is sobering, in the midst of the effervescence which this book generates, to consider, for example, that new geography curricula are still being devised that place consideration of the demands of the discipline before the needs of the students.

What I want to say is that the kind of fundamental change of outlook proposed by reconstructionist educators will not be achieved overnight. How disappointing it will be if the teachers reading this book react in only a piecemeal way, revising certain lessons, perhaps introducing a limited amount of new material, but leaving the basic framework of their curriculum untouched. Tinkering with bits of individual school curricula may be where change has to begin, but it certainly should not stop there.

In my view the challenge is greater than this. It is a challenge concerned with matters as broad as the reconsideration of the aims and purposes of education at a global level, followed by fundamental curriculum reform.

Such reform must begin with consideration of what it takes to offer all children the opportunity to develop their understanding, their abilities and their sense of values in such a way as to provide them with the autonomy to be genuinely critical in their thinking and able to suggest and act upon initiatives to ensure the welfare of our small planet and the organisms which it supports. For humans, such welfare is concerned with social, ethical, economic, cultural and political matters as well as with survival.

A second step in fundamental curriculum reform must be to address the issues with which a child's education should be concerned. This book provides impressive lists of such issues. Critical planning would be needed then at institutional level in order to set out the contribution, in terms of knowledge, understanding, skills and values, of the various disciplines towards the analysis, explication and possible resolution of the issues.

A third step must be to devise the evaluation of curricula, pedagogy and student learning, with the main purpose of ensuring ongoing reappraisal and regeneration of the curriculum. Student assessment would be an incidental, but significant element of such evaluation, which could provide certification.

The purpose of such major reform would be to provide, for the first time, enabling frameworks within which we can realistically address the issues which make us wish to educate children for a better world. Is it an utterly utopian vision?

Reform of this nature may be asking for the world, but at least it might help to build a better one.

References

Introduction

Apple, M. (1979) *Ideology and Curriculum*, London, Routledge and Kegan Paul.

Apple, M. (1982) *Education and Power*, London, Routledge and Kegan Paul.

Association for Curriculum Development in Geography (1983) *Racist Society: Geography Curriculum*, London.

Bale, J., ed. (1983) *The Third World: Issues and Approaches*, Sheffield, Geographical Association.

Connell, R. W., Ashenden, D. J., Kessler, S. and Dowsett, G. W. (1982) *Making the Difference*, Sydney, George Allen and Unwin.

Donnelly, P. (1982) Geography for action: Criteria for choice of content in the 1980s, in *Geography: Action in Society*, Melbourne, Australian Geography Teachers' Association.

Geographical Association (1984) *Geographical Education for a Multicultural Society*, Sheffield, Geographical Association.

Gilbert, R. (1984) *The Impotent Image: Reflections of Ideology in the Secondary School Curriculum*, Brighton, Falmer Press.

Gilbert, R. (1986) 'That's where they have to go': The challenge of ideology in geography, *Geographical Education* 5(2), 43–6.

Gill, D. (1982) Geography 14–16 in London, *ILEA Geography Bulletin*, no. 14, 8–17.

Guilliatt, R. (1985) Youth: The generation that dances to an apocalyptic beat, *The Age*, Saturday Extra, pp. 1–3.

Hicks, D. (1981) Bias in Geography textbooks: images of the Third World and multi-ethnic Britain, Working paper no. 1, Centre for Multicultural Education, University of London Institute of Education.

Huckle, J. (1983) the politics of school knowledge, in J. Huckle, ed., *Geographical Education: Reflection and Action*, Oxford University Press, pp. 143–54.

Kemmis, S., Cole, P. and Suggett, D. (1983) *Orientations to Curriculum and Transitions: Towards the Socially Critical School*, Melbourne, Victorian Institute of Secondary Education.

Porritt, J. (1984) *Seeing Green: The Politics of Ecology Explained*, Oxford, Basil Blackwell.

Rawling, E. M. (1982) Geography for action, in *Geography: Action in Society*, Melbourne, Australian Geography Teachers' Association.

Reimer, E. (1971) *School is Dead*, Harmondsworth, Penguin Books.

Sibley, J. (1982) World views: A socio-economic paradigm – Energy policies and challenges for geography teaching, in *Geography: Action in Society*, Melbourne, Australian Geography Teachers' Association.

Whitty, G. (1980) *Ideology, Politics and the Curriculum*, Milton Keynes, Open University Press.

Wright, D. R. (1985) Are goegraphy textbooks sexist? *Teaching Geography*, Jan., pp. 81–5.

Chapter 1

Adams, D. (1979) *The Hitch-Hikers Guide to the Galaxy*, London, Pan.

Bailey, P. (1983) Editorial in *Teaching Geography*, 9(1).

Brandes, D. and Ginnis, P. (1986) *A Guide to Student Centred Learning*, Oxford, Basil Blackwell.

Capra, F. (1983) *The Turning Point: Science, Society and the Rising Culture*, London, Fontana.

Clarke, B. ed. (1979) *The Changing World and the Primary Classroom*, London, Centre for World Development Education.

Ferguson, M. (1982) *The Aquarian Conspiracy: Personal and Social Transformation in the 1980s*, London, Granada.

Fisher, S. and Hicks, D. (1985) *World Studies 8–13: A Teacher's Handbook*, Edinburgh, Oliver and Boyd.

Galtung, J. (1980) *The True Worlds: A Transnational Perspective*, New York, The Free Press.

Galtung, J. (1976) Peace education: problems and conflicts, in Haavelsrud, M. ed., *Education for Peace: Reflections and Action*, Guildford, IPC Science & Technology Press.

Guardian (1987) What are you worried about? *Young Guardian*, 7 January.

Hicks, D. and Townley, C. eds. (1982) *Teaching World Studies: An Introduction to Global Perspectives in the Curriculum*, London, Longman.

Hicks, D. (1984) Geography, in A. Craft and G. Bardell, eds., *Curriculum Opportunities in a Multicultural Society*, London, Harper & Row.

Huckle, J. (1982). Values education, in *Geography and Change: Teacher's Guide*, London, Nelson.

Huckle, J. ed. (1983) *Geographical Education: Reflection and Action*, Oxford University Press.

James, B. (1985) Lies that sully the empire, *Daily Mail*, 8 June.

Johnston, R. J. (1983) *Geography and Geographers*, second edition, London, Edward Arnold.

Johnston, R. J. and Taylor, P. J. eds. (1986) *A World in Crisis? Geographical Perspectives*, Oxford, Basil Blackwell.

Laing, R. D. (1978) *The Politics of Experience*, Harmondsworth, Penguin.

Observer (1987) Two-nation jobs shock revealed, Sunday 4 January.

Richardson, R. (1986) Understanding and misunderstanding: some thoughts towards a theory, in *Half the Lies Are True: Ireland/Britain: A Microcosm of International Misunderstanding*? Birmingham Development Education Centre/Trocaire, Dublin.

Smith, D. M. (1977) *Human Geography: A Welfare Approach*, London, Edward Arnold.

Chapter 2

Bahro, R. (1978) *The Alternative in Eastern Europe*, London, Verso.

Bahro, R. (1982) *Socialism and Survival*, London, Heretic Books.

Barratt Brown, M. (1984) *Models in Political Economy*, Harmondsworth, Penguin.

Blowers, A. (1984) *Something in the Air: Corporate Power and the Environment*, London, Harper and Row.

Boardman, R. (1981) *International Organization and the Conservation of Nature*, London, Macmillan.

Castles, S. and Wustenberg, W. (1979) *The Education of the Future: An Introduction to the Theory and Practice of Socialist Education*, London, Pluto Press.

Chaliand, G. and Rageau, J-P. (1985) *Strategic Atlas: World Geopolitics*, Harmondsworth, Penguin.

Cotgrove, S. (1982) *Catastrophe or Cornucopia: The Environment, Politics and the Future*, Chichester, John Wiley.

Connell, R. (1980) The transition to socialism, in B. Crough, E. L. Wheelwright and E. Wiltshire, eds., *Australia and World Capitalism*, Ringwood, Penguin.

Crick, B. and Porter, A., eds. (1978) *Political Education and Political Literacy*, London, Longman.

Croall, S. and Rankin, M. (1981) *Ecology for Beginners*, London, Writers and Readers.

Crough, B. L. and Wheelwright, E. L. (1981) *Australia – the Client State: A Study of the Effects of Trans-national Corporations*, Sydney, University of Sydney.

Crow, B. and Thomas, A. (1983) *Third World Atlas*, Milton Keynes, Open University Press.

Donelly, P. (1980) Ways of learning geography as social education for youth years 9–12, in *Focus on the Teaching of Goegraphy*, Adelaide, Australian Geography Teachers Association.

Donelly, P. (1984) Geography for action: Criteria for choice of content in the 1980s, in *Geography: Action in Society*, Melbourne, Australian Geography Teachers Association.

Earthscan (1982) *Stockholm Plus Ten*, London, Earthscan.

Falk, J. (1982) *Global Fission: The Battle Over Nuclear Power*, Melbourne, Oxford University Press.

Finer, S. E. (1974) *Comparative Government*, Harmondsworth, Penguin.

Freeland, J. (1985) Australia: The search for a new educational settlement, in R. Sharp and J. Freeland, eds., *Capitalist Crisis and Schooling*, London, Macmillan.

Galtung, J. (1975) Peace education problems and conflicts, in M. Haavelsrud, ed., *Education for Peace: Reflection and Action*, Guildford, IPC Science and Technology Press.

Gamble, A. (1982) *An Introduction to Modern Social and Political Thought*, London, Macmillan.

Gilbert, R. (1984) *The Impotent Image: Reflections on Ideology in the Secondary School Curriculum*, Lewes, Falmer Press.

Gorz, A. (1980) *Ecology as Politics*, Boston, South End Press.

Gorz, A. (1985) *Paths to Paradise: On the Liberation from Work*, London, Pluto Press.

Hague, R. and Harrop, M. (1982) *Comparative Government: an Introduction*, London, Macmillan.

Harris, K. (1982) *Teachers and Classes: A Marxist Analysis*, London, Routledge and Kegan Paul.

Harris, N. (1983) *Of Bread and Guns: The World Economy in Crisis*, Harmondsworth, Penguin.

Harrison, J. (1978) *Marxist Economics for Socialists: A Critique of Reformism*, London, Pluto Press.

Harvey, D. (1984) On the history and present condition of geography: An historical materialist manifesto, *Professional Geographer*.

Hornby, L. (1985) Conservation in the Third World, *Geofile*, 44.

Huckle, J., ed. (1983) *Geographical Education: Reflection and Action*, Oxford University Press.

Huckle, J. (1985a) Geography and schooling, in Johnston, R. J. (ed.), *Geography and the Future*, London, Methuen.

Huckle, J. (1985b) Ecological crisis: some implications for geographical education, *Contemporary Issues in Geography and Education*, 2(2).

IUCN, UNEP, WWF (1980) *World Conservation Strategy*, Geneva.

Johnston, R. J. (1982) *Geography and the State*, London, Macmillan.

Johnston, R. J. (1984) A materialist framework for political geography, *Progress in Human Geography*, 8(4), 473–92.

Kemmis, M., Cole, P. and Suggett, D. (1983) *Orientations to Curriculum and Transition: Towards the Socially Critical School*, Melbourne, Victorian Institute of Secondary Education.

Kidron, M. and Segal, R. (1984) *The New State of the World Atlas*, London, Pan Books.

Kliot N. and Waterman, S., eds. (1983) *Pluralism and Political Geography: People, Territory, and State*, London, Croom Helm.

Komarov, B. (1978) *Environmental Destruction in the Soviet Union*, London, Pluto Press.

Lowe, P. and Goyder, J. (1983) *Environmental Groups in Politics*, London, George Allen and Unwin.

Martin, B. (1979) *Changing the Cogs*, Canberra, Friends of the Earth.

Martin, B. (1984) Environmentalism and electoralism, *The Ecologist*, 14(3), 110–18.

McElroy, B. (1988) Geography's contribution to political literacy (Chapter 3 in this volume).

McCormick, J. (1985) *The User's Guide to the Environment*, London, Kogan Page.

McNally, D. (1980) *Socialism from Below: The History of an Idea*, Toronto, Workers' Action Books.

Myers, N., ed. (1985) *The Gaia Atlas of Planet Management*, London, Pan Books.

O'Riordan, T. (1976) *Environmentalism*, London, Pion.

Peet, R. (1985) An introduction to Marxist geography, *Journal of Geography*, 84(1), 5–10.

Pepper, D. (1984) *The Roots of Modern Environmentalism*, London, Croom Helm.

Porter, A. (1981) Political Literacy, in D. Heater and J. A. Gillespie, eds., *Political Education in Flux*, London, Sage.

Porter, A., ed. (1983) *Teaching Political Literacy: Implications for Teacher Training and Curriculum Planning*, London, University of London Institute of Education.

Porter, A. (1984) The principles of political literacy restated, in A. Porter, ed., *Principles of Political Literacy: The Working Papers of the Programme for Political Education*, London, University of London Institute of Education.

Redclift, M. (1984) *Development and the Environmental Crisis: Red or Green Alternatives*, London, Methuen.

Roberts, A. (1979) *The Self Managing Environment*, London, Allison and Busby.

Roddewig, R. J. (1978) *Green Bans: The Birth of Australian Environmental Politics* Sydney, Hale and Iremonger.

Sandbach, F. (1980) *Environment, Ideology and Policy*, Oxford, Basil Blackwell.

Sarup, M. (1982) *Education, State and Crisis*, London, Routledge and Kegan Paul.

Schnaiberg, A. (1980) *The Environment from Surplus to Scarcity*, Oxford University Press.

Sharp, R. (1980) *Knowledge, Ideology and the Politics of Schooling*, London, Routledge and Kegan Paul.

Sharp, R. (1984) Reclaiming the agenda: Socialist directions, in *Radical Education Dossier*, Autumn, pp. 25–9.

Short, J. R. (1982) *An Introduction to Political Geography*, London, Routledge and Kegan Paul.

Smil, V. (1984) *The Bad Earth: Environmental Degradation in China*, London, Zed Press.

Smith, M., McLoughlin, J., Large, P. and Chapman, R. (1985) *Asia's New Industrial World*, London, Methuen.

Stretton, H. (1976) *Capitalism, Socialism, and the Environment*, Cambridge University Press.

Sutcliffe, R. (1983) *Hard Times: The World Economy in Turmoil*, London, Pluto Press.

Taylor, P. (1985) *Political Geography: World-Economy, National State, and Locality*, London, Longman.

Timberlake, L. (1985) *Africa in Crisis: The Causes, the Cures of Environmental Bankruptcy*, London, Earthscan.

Wallerstein, I. (1979) *The Capitalist World-Economy*, Cambridge University Press.

Wallerstein, I. (1984) *The Politics of the World-Economy: The States, the Movements and the Civilizations*, Cambridge University Press.

Williams, R. (1982) *Socialism and Ecology*, London, Socialist Environment and Resources Association.

Wilson, D. (1983) *The Lead Scandal: The Fight to Save Children from Damage by Lead in Petrol*, London, Heinemann.

Chapter 3

Bradford, M. G. and Kent, W. A. (1977) *Human Geography*, Oxford University Press.

Carol, H. (1975) Geographic scenarios for an underdeveloped area: Alternative futures for Tropical Africa, in R. Abler, D. Janelle, A. Philbrick and J. Sommer, eds., *Human Geography in a Shrinking World*, Belmont, Duxbury Press.

Crick, B. (1978) Basic concepts for political education, in Crick, B. and Porter, A., eds., *Political Education and Political Literacy*, London, Longman, pp. 47–62.

Crick, B. and Porter, A., eds. (1978) *Political Education and Political Literacy*, London, Longman.

Freire, P. (1972) *Cultural Action for Freedom*, Harmondsworth, Penguin.

Gill, D. (1980) *Social Inequality: Spatial Form*, unpublished M. A. dissertation, University of London.

Kirby, A. (1981) A contemporary approach to urban areas, *Teaching Geography*, 6(3), 125–8.

Laver, M. (1979) *Playing Politics*, Harmondsworth, Penguin.

Porter, A. (1979) The programme of political education: A guide for beginners, *Social Science Teacher*, February, pp. 98–106.

Schools Council (1979) *Geography 16–19, Advanced Level Syllabus* (Trial Document),London, Schools Council.

Slater, F. and Spicer, B. (1980) Language and learning in a geographical context, *Geographical Education*, 3(4), 447–87.

Stradling, R. (1978) Notes for a spiral curriculum for developing political literacy, in B. Crick and A. Porter, eds., *Political Education and Political Literacy*, London, Longman.

Stradling, R. and Porter, A. (1978) Issues and political problems, in B. Crick and A. Porter, eds., *Political Education and Political Literacy*, London, Longman, pp. 74–81.

Teitelbaum, M. S. (1975) Relevance of demographic transition theory for developing countries, *Science*, 188, 4187, 420–5.

Vogeler, I. (1977) Dialectic teaching in geography, *Journal of Geography*, 76(7), 257–61.

Walford, R. (1973) *Caribbean Fishermen*, London, Longman.

Webb, C. (1979) Learning to change, *Bulletin of Environmental Education*, No. 103, pp. 27–30.

Willis, P. (1977) *Learning to Labour: How Working Class Kids Get Working Class Jobs*, Farnborough, Saxon House.

Chapter 4

Cohen, J. and Seed, J. (1980) In defence of Daintree, *The Ecologist*, 14(4).

Porter, A., ed. (1984) *Principles of Political Literacy: The Working Papers of the Programme for Political Education*, London, University of London Institute of Education.

A range of audiovisual resources on the Daintree rainforests is listed at the beginning of this chapter. The extracts on pages 54–60 provide useful textual resources, as do the following.

Australian Heritage Commission (1986) *Tropical Rainforest of North Queensland: Their Conservation Significance*, Canberra, Australian Government Publishing Service.

Borschmann, G. (1984) *Greater Daintree: World Heritage Tropical Rainforest at Risk*, Melbourne, Australian Conservation Foundation.

Gray, D., Thompson, D., Gray, C. and Mitchell, J. (1985) *The Trials of Tribulation*, Port Douglas, Douglas Shire Wilderness Action Group (P.O. Box 116, Port Douglas, 4871).

Liane, the newsletter of the Rainforest Conservation Society of Queensland (15 Colorado Avenue, Barton, Australia 4065).

Ord, W. (1984) Trouble at the Cape, *Wildlife Australia*, 21(1), 22–5.

Proceedings of the Rainforest Conference, Department of Geography, Sydney University, Geographical Society of NSW, 1981.

Stevens, N. C. and Bailey, A., eds. (1980) *Contemporary Cape York Peninsula*, Brisbane, Royal Society of Queensland.

Werren, G. and Allworth, D. (1982) *Australia's Rainforests: A Review*, Monograph No. 28, Geography Department, Monash University.

Chapter 5

Anderson, D. (1982) *Detecting Bad Schools: A Guide for Normal Parents*, London, SAU.

Hicks, D. (1981) The contribution of geography to multicultural understanding, *Teaching Geography*, November, 64–7.

Kidron, M. and Segal, R. (1981) *The State of the World Atlas*, London, Pan Books.

Kidron, M. and Segal, R. (1984) *The New State of the World Atlas*, London, Pan Books.

Chapter 6

Australian Ethnic Affairs Council Committee on Multicultural Education (1979) *Perspectives on Multicultural Education*, Canberra, Australian Government Publishing Service.

Brazier, C. (1985) The white problem, *New Internationalist*, 145, 7–9.

Bunge, W. (1984) Racism in geography. *Contemporary Issues in Geography and Education*, 1(2), 10–11.

Cook, I. (1984) Colonial past: post-colonial present: alternative perspectives in geography. *Contemporary Issues in Geography and Education*, 1(2), 2–9.

Craft, A. (1984) Curriculum for a multicultural society, in Skilbeck, M. ed., *Readings in School-Based Curriculum Development*, London, Harper and Row, pp. 53–61.

Curriculum Branch (1982) *Education for a Multicultural Society: Curriculum Guidelines for Primary Schools*, Brisbane, Queensland Department of Education.

Curriculum Branch (1983) *Multiculturalism in Geography (Draft Material)*, Brisbane Department of Education, Queensland.

Davey, C. (1978) Intercultural studies and the geography teacher, paper presented at the Australian Geography Teachers Association Sixth National Conference, Canberra, January, 1978.

Department of Education and Science (1986) *Geography from 5 to 16*, Curriculum Matters 7, An HMI Series. London, Her Majesty's Stationery Office.

Dunlop, S. (ed) (1976) *Place and People: A Guide to Modern Geography Teaching*, London, Heinemann.

Emery, J. S. (1980) Geographical education in a multicultural society, paper presented at the Seventh National Conference of the Australian Geography Teachers Association, Adelaide, 21–5 January, 1980.

Fien, J. (1984) Structural silence: Aborigines in Australian geography textbooks, *Contemporary Issues in Geography and Education*, 1(2), 22–5.

Fien, J. (1985) Taking a stand against racism in the classroom and in our textbooks, *Shared Experiences*, 3.

Fien, J., Gerber, R. and Wilson, P., eds, (1984) *The Geography Teacher's Guide to the Classroom*, South Melbourne, Macmillan.

Folds, R. (1984) Curriculum, culture and classroom social relations in South Australia's north west Aboriginal schools, *Curriculum Perspectives*, 4(2), 53–6.

Fraser, P. (1985a) Multicultural education is for geographers too, *Geography Bulletin*, January, 237–43.

Fraser, P. (1985b) You can't have worthwhile school based geography curriculum without thoroughly trained school based staff, *Geography Bulletin*, 17(1), 40–3.

Fyson, N. L. (1979) *The Development Puzzle*, London, Centre for World Development Education.

Geographical education for a multicultural society: an introduction (1983) *Contemporary Issues in Geography and Education*, 1(1), 5.

Gill, D. (1983a) Anti-racist education: of what relevance in the geography curriculum? *Contemporary Issues in Geography and Education*, 1(1), 6–10.

Gill, D. (1983b) Anti-racist teaching through geography, *Contemporary Issues in Geography and Education*, 1(1), 34–6.

Gill, D. (1984) GYSL education or indoctrination? *Contemporary Issues in Geography and Education*, 1(2), 34–5.

Gill, D. (1985) Geographical education for a multicultural society, in Straber-Welds, M. ed., *Education for a Multicultural Society: Case Study in ILEA Schools*, London, Bell and Hyman, pp. 58–69.

Hicks, D. (1984) The minority experience, *Geographical Activity Series*, Australian Geography Teachers Association.

Human Rights Commission (1984) The Teaching of Human Rights, Occasional Paper No. 6, Canberra, Australian Government Publishing Service.

Human Rights Commission (1985) Teaching, Enacting and Sticking Up for Human Rights, Occasional Paper No. 9, Canberra, Australian Government Publishing Service.

ILEA Centre for Anti-Racist Education (1984a) Is anti-racist education really necessary? *Contemporary Issues in Geography and Education*, 1(2), 26–9.

ILEA Centre for Anti-Racist Education (1984b) Annual Report, September 1983–August 1984, London.

ILEA (1987) Anti-racist resources for teaching geography, *Geography Bulletin*, 25, Spring Term.

Katz, J. (1978) *White Awareness: Handbook for Anti-Racism Training*, Norman, University of Oklahoma Press.

Lippmann, L. (1984) Multiculturalism and its implications for education, in Human Rights Commission, The Teaching of Human Rights, Occasional Paper No. 6, Canberra, Australian Government Publishing Service, pp. 113–23.

McKay, J. and Powell, J. (1985) Geography in Australian society, *Journal of Geography*, May–June, 98–104.

Murray, N. (1985) The multicultural mask, *New Internationalist*, 145, 26–7.

Office of the Race Relations Conciliator (Undated) *Let's Work Together: A Kit of Resources*, Auckland.

Pettman, J. (1983) Multicultural education or antiracist education, paper presented at the South Pacific Association of Teacher Educators Conference, 1983, Brisbane.

Pettman, J. (1984) Anti-racist teaching, in Human Rights Commission, The Teaching of Human Rights, Occasional Paper No. 6, Canberra, Australian Government Publishing Service, pp. 124–35.

Pettman, R. (1984) *Teaching for Human Rights*, Richmond, Hodja Educational Resources Cooperative.

Porter, E. (1973) *Appalachian Wilderness*, New York, Ballantine Books.

Queensland Multicultural Co-ordinating Committee (1982) *Education for a Multicultural Society: Policies and Practices*, Brisbane.

Richardson, R. (1985) Punch and the devil, *New Internationalist*, 145, 18–19.

Schools Council (1981) *Geography and Change: Teacher's Guide*, Walton-on-Thames, Thomas Nelson and Sons.

Simpson, A. (1984) The rich as a minority group, *Contemporary Issues in Geography and Education*, 1(2), 18–21.

Slater, F. (1983) Sexism and racism, *Contemporary Issues in Geography and Education*, 1(1), 26–9.

Working Party on Multicultural Education (1979) Education for a Multicultural Society: A Discussion Paper, Brisbane, Queensland Department of Education.

Wright, D. R. (1983a) They have no need of transport. . .' A study of attitudes to black people in three geography textbooks, *Contemporary Issues in Geography and Education*, 1(1), 11–15.

Wright, D. R. (1983b) A priority for the eighties, *Times Education Supplement*, 1 April 1983, p. 29.

Wundersitz, J. and Gale, F. (1985) Different offending patterns or differential treatment: a study of the over-representation of Aboriginal youths in the criminal justice system, paper presented at the Twentieth Conference of the Institute of Australian Geographers, 14–17 May 1985, Brisbane.

Chapter 7

Abadan-Unat, N. (1977) Implications of migration on emancipation and pseudo-emancipation of Turkish women, *International Migration Review*, 9, 31–57.

Ardener, S. ed. (1981) *Women and Space: Ground Rules and Mental Maps*, New York, St Martin's Press.

Bagchi, D. (1984) Rural renewable energy systems and the role of women, in J. H. Henshall and J. Townsend, eds., *Women's Role in Changing the Face of the Developing World*, Department of Geography, Durham University.

Beneria, L. (1982) Accounting for women's work, in L. Beneria, ed., *Women and Development: The Sexual Division of Labor in Rural Societies*, New York, Praeger.

Boserup, E. (1970) *Women's Role in Economic Development*, London, George Allen and Unwin.

Brouwer, L. and Priester, M. (1983) Living in between: Turkish women in their homeland and in the Netherlands, in A. Phizacklea, ed., *One Way Ticket: Migration and Female Labour*, London, Routledge and Kegan Paul.

Buvinic, M. and Youssef, N., with B. von Elm (1978) *Women Headed Households: The Ignored Factor in Development Planning*, Washington DC, US Agency for International Development.

Dixon, R. (1981) Jobs for women in rural industry and services, in B. C. Lewis, ed., *Invisible Farmers: Women and the Crisis in Agriculture*, Washington DC, US Agency for International Development.

Drake, C. (1983) Teaching about third world women, *Journal of Geography*, 82, 163–9.

Evans, M. D. R. (1984) Immigrant women in Australia: resources, family, and work, *International Migration Review*, 18, 1063–90.

Fagnani, J. (1983) Women's commuting patterns in the Paris region, *Tijdschrift voor Economische en Sociale Geografie* 74, 12–24.

Gale, F. (1985) Seeing women in the landscape: alternative views of the world around us, in J. Goodnow and C. Pateman, eds., *Women: Revising Social Science*, Sydney, George Allen and Unwin.

Guiliano, G. (1979) Public transportation and the travel means of women, *Traffic Quarterly*, 33, 606–16.

Hanson, S. and Hanson, P. (1980) Gender and urban activity patterns in Uppsala, Sweden, *Geographical Review*, 70, 291–9.

Hanson, S. and Johnston, I. (1985) Gender differences in work trip lengths: explanations and implications, *Urban Geography*, 6(3), 193–219.

Hayden, D. (1981) *The Grand Domestic Revolution: A History of Feminist Designs for American Homes, Neighborhoods, and Cities*, Cambridge, Mass., M.I.T. Press.

Hayden, D. (1984) *Redesigning the American Dream: The Future of Housing, Work, and Family Life*, New York, Norton.

Hayden, D. and Marris, P. (1981) The quiltmaker's landscape, *Landscape*, 25, 39–47.

Hess, J. (1981) Domestic interiors in northern New Mexico, *Heresies*, 11, 30–3.

Howe, A. and O'Connor, K. (1982) Travel to work and labor force participation of men and women in an Australian metropolitan area, *The Professional Geographer*, 32, 50–64.

ILEA (1984) Equal opportunities and sexism in geography, *Geography Bulletin*, 19, 20–5.

International Center for Research on Women (1979) *Women in Migration: A Third World Focus*, Washington DC, US Agency for International Development.

Jain, D. (1980) *Women's Quest for Power*, Ghaziabad, UP, Vikas Publishing House.

Journal of Geography (1978) 77(5), special issue on women in the geography curriculum.

Khatib-Chahidi, J. (1981) Sexual prohibitions, shared space and fictive marriages in Shi'ite Iran, in S. Ardener, ed., *Women and Space: Ground Rules and Mental Maps*, New York, St Martin's Press.

Kolodny, A. (1984) *The Land Before Her: Fantasy and Experience of the American Frontiers, 1630–1860*, Chapel Hill, University of North Carolina Press.

Larimore, A. (1978) Humanizing the writing in cultural geography textbooks, *Journal of Geography*, 77, 183–5.

Lloyd, B. (1975) Woman's place, man's place, *Landscape*, 20, 10–13.

Madden, J. (1981) Why women work closer to home, *Urban Studies*, 18, 181–94.

Mahajani, A. (1976) *Energy Policy for the Rural Third World*, London, International Institute for Environment and Development.

Matrix (1984) *Making Space: Women and the Man Made Environment*, London, Pluto Press.

May, N. (1981) *Of Conjuring and Caring*, London, Change.

Mazey, M. E. and Lee, D. R. (1983) *Her Place, Her Space*, Washington DC, Association of American Geographers.

McDowell, L. and Bowlby, S. (1983) Teaching feminist geography, *Journal of Geography in Higher Edcuation*, 7, 97–108.

McDowell, L. and Massey, D. (1984) A woman's place? in D. Massey and J. Allen, eds., *Geography Matters*, New York, Cambridge University Press in Association with the Open University.

McStay, J. R. and Dunlap, R. E. (1983) Male–female differences in concern for environment, *International Journal for Women's Studies*, 6, 291–301.

Monk, J. (1978) Women in geographic games, *Journal of Geography*, 77(5), 190–1.

Monk, J. (1983) Integrating women into the geography curriculum, *Journal of Geography*, 82, 271–3.

Monk, J. (1985) Feminist transformation: how can it be accomplished?, *Journal of Geography in Higher Education*, 9, 101–5.

Monk, J. and Alexander, C. S. (1986) Free Port Fallout: Gender, Employment, and Migration on Margarita Island, *Annals of Tourism Research*, 13, 393–413.

Monk, J. and Hanson, S. (1982) On not excluding half of the human in human geography, *The Professional Geographer*, 34, 11–23.

Monk, J. and Rengert, A. (1982) Locational decision-making: The case of the day care center, in A. Rengert and J. Monk, eds., *Women and Spatial Change*, Dubuque, Iowa, Kendall Hunt.

Nash, J. and Fernandez-Kelly, M. P. (1983) *Women, Men, and the International Division of Labor*, Albany, NY, State University of New York Press.

Nelson, K. (1986) Female labor supply characteristics and the suburbanization of low-wage office work, in M. Storper and A. Scott, eds., *Production, Work, Territory: The Geographical Anatomy of Industrial Capitalism*, London, George Allen and Unwin.

Norwood, V. and Monk, J. (1987) *The Desert is No Lady: Southwestern Landscapes in Women's Writing and Art*, New Haven, Yale University Press.

Pollock, N. (1981) Women on the inside: divisions of space in imperial China, *Heresies*, 11, 34–7.

Rengert, A. (1981) Some sociocultural aspects of rural outmigration in Latin America, in O. Horst, ed., *Papers in Latin American Geography in Honor of Lucia C. Harrison*,

Muncie, IN. Conference of Latin Americanist Geographers.

Rogers, B. (1980) *The Domestication of Women*, London, Tavistock.

Seager, J. and Olson, A. (1986) *Women in the World: An International Atlas*, London, Pluto Press (HB); Pan (PB).

Sharma, R. (1982) Greening the Indian countryside, *Mazingira*, **6**(1), 80–2.

Sivard, R. L. (1985) *Women. . .A World Survey*, Washington DC, World Priorities; London, Methuen.

Slater, F. (1983) Sexism and racism, *Contemporary Issues in Geography and Education*, **1**(1), 26–31.

Tivers, J. (1985) *Women Attached: The Daily Lives of Women with Young Children*, London, Croom Helm.

Ummayya, P. and Bandyopadhyay, J. (1983) The Trans-Himalayan Chipko footmarch, *The Ecologist*, **13**(5), 179–83.

United Nations Association of the United States of America (UNA/USA) (1980) Progress for half the world's people: The UN decade for women, in *Issues of the 80's*, New York, UNA/USA.

United Nations, Department of Economic and Social Affairs (1984) *Improving Concepts and Methods for Statistics and Indicators on the Situation of Women Studies in Methods* Series F, No. 33, New York, United Nations.

Watson, S. with Austerberry, H. (1986) *Housing and Homelessness: A Feminist Perspective*, London, Routledge and Kegan Paul.

Williamson-Fien, J. (1985) In pursuit of non-sexist geography–locating the invisible woman, *Queensland Geographer*, **20**(1), 17–37.

Women and Geography Study Group of the IBG (1984) *Geography and Gender*, London, Hutchinson Educational.

Wright, D. R. (1981) Are geography textbooks sexist?, *Teaching Geography*, Jan., 81–5.

Wright, G. (1983) *Building the Dream: A Social History of Housing in America*, Cambridge, Mass., M.I.T. Press.

Young, K. (1982) The creation of a relative surplus population: A case study from Mexico, in L. Beneria, ed., *Women and Development: The Sexual Division of Labor in Rural Societies*, New York, Praeger.

Chapter 8

Allen, A. (1986) Evidence and silence: Feminism and the limits of history, in C. Pateman and E. Gross, eds., *Feminist Challenges*, Sydney, Allen and Unwin.

Australia Asia Worker Links (1982) *Outwork*, Australia Asia Worker Links, December.

Bale, J. (1982) *Sport and Place*, London, Hurst.

Culley, M. and Portuges, C. (1985) Introduction, in M. Culley and C. Portuges, eds., *Gendered Subjects*, Boston, Routledge and Kegan Paul.

Daniels, K. (1985) Feminism and social history, *Australian Feminist Studies*, 1, 27–40.

Davidoff, L. (1979) The separation of home and work? Landladies and lodgers in nineteenth and twentieth century England, in S. Burman, ed., *Fit Work for Women*, London, Croom Helm.

Eisenstein, H. (1984) *Contemporary Feminist Thought*, London, Unwin Paperbacks.

Eliot Hurst, M. E. (1985) Geography has neither existence nor future, in R. J. Johnston, ed., *The Future of Geography*, London, Methuen.

Evans, M. ed., (1982) *The Woman Question*, London, Fontana Paperbacks.

Foord, J. (1980) Women's place – women's space, *Area*, **12**(1), 47–8.

Freire, P. (1970) *Pedagogy of the Oppressed*, New York, Continuum.

Fuentes, A. and Ehrenreich, B. (1984) *Women in the Global Factory*, Boston, South End Press.

Game, A. and Pringle, R. (1983) *Gender at Work*, Sydney, George Allen and Unwin.

Game, A. and Pringle, R. (1984) Production and consumption: Public versus private, in D. H. Broom, ed., *Unfinished Business*, Sydney, George Allen and Unwin.

Gatens, M. (1986) Feminism, philosophy and riddles without answers, in C. Pateman and E. Gross, eds., *Feminist Challenges*, Sydney, Allen and Unwin.

Gross, E. (1986) Conclusion: What is feminist theory, in C. Pateman and E. Gross, eds., *Feminist Challenges*, Sydney, Allen and Unwin.

Harvey, D. (1984) On the history and present condition of geography: An historical materialist manifesto, *Professional Geographer*, **36**(1), 1–11.

Herzog, M. (1980) *From Hand to Mouth: Women and Piecework*, Harmondsworth, Penguin.

Howe, A. and O'Connor, K. (1982) Travel to work and labour force participation of men and women in an Australian metropolitan area, *The Professional Geographer*, **32**, 50–64.

ILEA (1984) Equal opportunities and sexism in geography, *ILEA Geography Bulletin*, **19**, 20–5.

Johnson, L. (1985) Gender, genetics and the possibility of feminist geography, *Australian Geographical Studies*, **23**(1), 161–71.

Maher, F. (1985) Classroom pedagogy and the new scholarship on women, in M. Culley and C. Portuges, eds., *Gendered Subjects*, Boston, Routledge and Kegan Paul.

Massey, D. (1984) Foreword, in Women and Geography Study Group of the IBG, *Geography and Gender: An Introduction to Feminist Geography*, London, Hutchinson in association with the Explorations in Feminism Collective.

Matrix (1984) *Making Space: Women and the Man Made Environment*, London, Pluto Press.

Mies, M. (1982) *The Lace Makers of Narsapur*, London, Zed Press.

Monk, J. (1978) Women in geographic games, *Journal of Geography*, **77**(5), 190–1.

Monk, J. (1983) Integrating women into the geography curriculum, *Journal of Geography*, **82**(6), 271–3.

Monk, J. and Hanson, S. (1982) On not excluding half the human in human geography, *Professional Geographer*, **34**, 11–23.

New South Wales Women's Advisory Council (1980) *Occupation: Housewife*, Sydney, New South Wales Women's Advisory Council.

O'Brien, M. (1981) *The Politics of Reproduction*, London, Routledge and Kegan Paul.

Oakley, A. (1982) *Subject Women*, London, Fontana Paperbacks.

Papanek, H. (1981) The differential impact of programs and policies on women in development, in R. Dauber and M. L. Cain, eds., *Women and Technological Change in Developing Countries*, Boulder, Westview Press.

Parker, J. (1982) A right to an income, in H. Kanter, S. Lefanu, S. Shah and C. Spedding, eds., *Sweeping Statements*, London, Women's Press.

Pateman, C. (1986) Introduction: The theoretical subversiveness of feminism, in C. Pateman and E. Gross, eds., *Feminist Challenges*, Sydney, Allen and Unwin.

Phillips, A. (1983) *Hidden Hands*, London, Pluto Press.

Pollert, A. (1981) *Girls, Wives and Factory Lives*, London, Macmillan.

Prescott, M. (1985) Wages for housework, in J. Rigg and J. Copeland, eds., *Coming out!*, Melbourne, Nelson in association with the Australian Broadcasting Corporation.

Prosser, R. (1982) *Tourism*, London, Nelson.

Raymond, J. G. (1979–80) Women's studies: A knowledge of one's own, in M. Culley and C. Portuges, eds., *Gendered Subjects*, Boston, Routledge and Kegan Paul.

Rich, A. (1979) Taking women students seriously, in M. Culley and C. Portuges, eds., *Gendered Subjects* Boston, Routledge and Kegan Paul.

Roberts, N. (1986) *The Front Line: Women in the Sex Industry Speak*, London, Grafton Books.

Sarah and Fugen (1982) Homework: So what's changed?, in H. Kanter, S. Lefanu, S. Shah and C. Spedding, eds., *Sweeping Statements*, London, Women's Press.

Sharpe, S. (1976) *Just Like a Girl*, Harmondsworth, Pelican.

Smith, D. (1978) A peculiar eclipsing: Women's exclusion from man's culture, *Women's Studies International Quarterly*, 1(4), 281–96.

Spender, D. (1982) *Invisible Women*, London, Writers and Readers.

Stanworth, M. (1983) *Gender and Schooling*, London, Hutchinson in association with the Explorations in Feminism Collective.

Thiele, B. (1986) Vanishing acts in social and political thought: Tricks of the trade, in C. Pateman and E. Gross, eds., *Feminist Challenges*, Sydney, Allen and Unwin.

Thornton, M. (1986) Sex equality is not enough for feminism, in C. Pateman and E. Gross, eds., *Feminist Challenges*, Sydney, Allen and Unwin.

Tivers, J. (1978) How the other half lives: The geographical study of women, *Area*, .10, 302.

Weinbaum, B. and Bridges, A. (1976) The other side of the pay cheque, *Monthly Review*, July/August.

Wetzsteon, R. (1979) The feminist man? in E. Shapiro and B. Shapiro, eds., *The Women Say: The Men Say*, New York, Dell.

Williamson-Fien, J. (1986) Feminist geography – It's not just a mapping exercise, *Interaction*, 14(5), 31–47.

Women and Geography Study Group of the IBG (1984) *Geography and Gender: An Introduction to Feminist Geography*, London, Hutchinson in association with the Explorations in Feminism Collective.

Wright, D. R. (1985) Are geography textbooks sexist?, *Teaching Geography*, January, 81–5.

Zelinsky, W., Monk, J. and Hanson, S. (1982) Women and geography: A review and prospectus, *Progress in Human Geography*, 6, 317–66.

Chapter 9

ACFOA (1981) *North–South: Outlining the Issues*, Canberra, Australian Council for Overseas Aid.

ACFOA (1983) *Overseas Aid: What Australians Think*, Canberra, Australian Council for Overseas Aid.

AFHC (1978) *Development Dilemma*, Sydney, Australian Freedom from Hunger Campaign.

AFHC (1982) *Development Handbook: Speaker Notes and Reference Guide to Development Issues*, Sydney, Australian Freedom from Hunger Campaign.

ADB (Asian Development Bank) (1978) *Rural Asia: Challenge and Opportunity*, New York, Praeger.

Agee, P. (1975) *Inside the Company*, Ringwood, Penguin.

Alavi H. and Shanin, T., eds. (1982) *Introduction to the Sociology of Developing Societies*, London, MacMillan.

Aziz, S. (1978) *Rural Development: Learning from China*, London, MacMillan.

Balasuriya, T. (1984) *Planetary Theology*, New York, Orbis Books.

Bale, J. (1983) *The Third World: Issues and Approaches*, London, Geographical Association.

Baran, P. (1975) *The Political Economy of Growth*, New York, Monthly Review.

Barke, M. and O'Hare, G. (1984) *The Third World*, Conceptual Frameworks in Geography series, Edinburgh, Oliver and Boyd.

Barnet, R. J. and Muller, R .E. (1974) *Global Reach*, New York, Simon and Schuster.

Barraclough, S. (1979) Rural development strategy and agrarian reform, in B. Berchidewsky, ed., *Anthropology and Social Change in Rural Areas*, Paris, Mouton.

Bello, W., Kinley, D. and Elinson, E. (1982) *Development Debacle: The World Bank in the Philippines*, San Francisco, Institute for Food and Development Policy.

Blomstrom, M. and Hettne, B. (1984) *Development Theory in Transition*, London, Zed Press.

Bookchin, M. (1980) *Towards an Ecological Society*, Montreal, Black Rose.

Borlaug, N. E. *et al.* (1969) A Green Revolution yields a golden harvest, *Columbia Journal of World Business*, 4(5), 9–19.

Brandt, W. (1980) *North–South: A Programme for Survival*, London, Pan.

Brown, M. B. (1974) *The Anatomy of Underdevelopment*, Nottingham, Spokesmen.

Burbach, R. and Flynn, P. (1980) *Agribusiness in the Americas*, New York, Monthly Review.

CAA (no date) *The Arms Trade and the Third World*, CAA Discussion Sheet No. 4, Fitzroy, Community Aid Abroad.

CAA (1984a) *Overseas Aid: Review Fails to Tackle Basic Faults*, Fitzroy, Community Aid Abroad.

CAA (1984b) *The Third World War: The Philippines Front*, Fitzroy, Community Aid Abroad.

CEWC (1984) *World Studies Resource Guide*, London, Council for Education in World Citizenship.

Chenery, H. (1974) *Redistribution with Growth*, Oxford University Press.

Chetley, A. (1979) *The Baby Killer Scandal*, London, War on Want.

Chomsky, N. and Herman, E. S. (1979) *The Political Economy of Human Rights*, Vols. 1 and 2, Boston, South End.

Choudhry, S. A. (1986) Food policy, inequality and underdevelopment: The anatomy of an agrarian economy in bondage, *Journal of Contemporary Asia*, 16(2), 131–43.

Clausen, A. W. *et al.* (1982) We alleviate poverty and help the poor, *Far Eastern Economic Review*, September 3, Advertisement supplement.

Cleaver, H. M. (1972) The contradictions of the Green Revolution, *Monthly Review*, 24(2), 80–111.

Collins, J., Lappe, F. M. and Allen, N. (1982) *What Difference Could a Revolution Make?*, San Francisco, Institute for Food and Development Policy.

Commoner, B. (1975) How poverty breeds overpopulation, *Ramparts*, August–September, 22–5, 58–9.

Crow, B. and Thomas, A. (1983) *Third World Atlas*, Milton Keynes, Open University.

CSIP (Critical Social Issues Project) (1984) *Market Forces and Development: A Role Play*, Sydney, University of NSW Critical Social Issues Project.

DEC (Development Education Centre) (1981) *Priorities for Development*, Selley Oak, Development Education Centre.

Diebold, J. (1973) Multinational corporations: Why be scared of them? *Foreign Policy*, **12**, 79–95.

Dinham, B. and Hines, C. (1982) *Agribusiness in Africa*, London, Earth Resources Research.

Duff, P. (1979) What happened to the New International Economic Order 1974–1979, *Our Generation*, **12**(4), 30–40.

Ehrlich, P. R. (1986) *The Population Bomb*, New York, Ballantine Books.

Falk, R., Kim, S. S. and Mendlovitz, S., eds. (1982) *Toward a Just World Order*, Boulder, Westview.

Fallaw, S. (1981) *Geographic Perspectives on Development*, Melbourne, Heinemann Educational Australia.

Feder, E. (1971) *The Rape of the Peasantry*, New York, Anchor.

Fien, J. (1985) *Alternative Approaches to Development*, Harlow, Longman Resources Unit for Schools Council.

Frank, A. G. (1970) *Latin America: Underdevelopment or Revolution?*, New York, Monthly Review Press.

Freire, P. (1972) *Pedagogy of the Oppressed*, New York, Seabury.

Fyson, N. L. (1984) *The Development Puzzle*, London, Hodder and Stoughton.

Galbraith, J. K. (1978) In defense of multinationals, *Horizons USA*, **30**, 3–8.

George, S. (1976) *How the Other Half Dies*, Ringwood, Penguin.

George, S. and Paine, N. (1982) *Food for Beginners*, London, Writers and Readers.

Gheerbrant, A., ed. (1974) *The Rebel Church in Latin America*, Ringwood, Penguin.

Goulet, D. (1977) *The Uncertain Promise*, New York, IDOC/North America.

Gran, G. (1983) *Development By People*, New York, Praeger.

Grant, J. P. (1973) *Growth from Below: A People Oriented Development Strategy*, Washington, Overseas Development Council.

Harrison, P. (1980) *The Third World Tomorrow*, Ringwood, Penguin.

Harrison, P. (1981) *Inside the Third World*, Ringwood, Penguin.

Hartmann, B. and Boyce, J. (1983) *A Quiet Violence*, London, Zed Press.

Hayter, T. (1981) *The Creation of World Poverty*, London, Pluto.

Hayter, T. and Watson, C. (1984) *Aid: Rhetoric and Reality*, London, Pluto.

Heatley, R. (1979) *Poverty and Power*, London, Zed Press.

Herman, E. S. (1982) *The Real Terror Network*, Boston, South End Press.

Hicks, D. and Townley, C., eds. (1982) *Teaching World Studies*, London, Longman.

Hill, H. (1983) The impact of development policies on women, in J. Langmore and D. Peetz, eds., *Wealth, Poverty and Survival*, Sydney, George Allen and Unwin.

Hofsten, E. (1974) The family planning controversy, *Monthly Review*, **26**(6), 17–30.

Hoogvelt, A. (1976) *The Sociology of Developing Societies*, London, MacMillan.

Hoselitz, A. (1960) *Sociological Aspects of Economic Growth*, Glencoe, Free Press.

Huberman, L. and Sweezy, P. M. (1969) *Socialism in Cuba*, New York, Monthly Review Press.

Huckle, J. (1984) A multinational company at work, *Contemporary Issues in Geography and Education*, **1**(3), 36–9.

ILO (1979) *Profiles of Rural Poverty*, Geneva, International Labour Organisation.

ISIS (1984) *Women in Development*, Geneva, International Women's Information and Communication Services.

Jackson, G. (1984) Report of the Committee to Review the Australian Overseas Aid Program, Canberra, Australian Government Publishing Service.

Jones, B. and Wales, R. (1982) *Food, Farming and Famine*, Surrey, Thomas Nelson.

Kidron, M. and Segal, R. (1984) *The New State of the World Atlas*, London, Pan.

Kothari, R. (1981) *Environment and Alternative Development*, New York, Institute for World Order.

Krause, W. (1961) *Economic Development*, San Francisco, Wadsworth.

Lappe, F. M. and Collins, J. (1977) *Food First*, London, Abacus Books.

Lappe, F. M., Collins, J. and Kinley, D. (1981) *Aid as Obstacle*, San Francisco, Institute for Food and Development Policy.

Learmonth, T. and Holt, F. (1982) *Underdeveloping Bangladesh: 225 Years of British Involvement*, London, War on Want.

Leary, V., Ellis, A. A. and Madlener, K. (1984) *The Philippines: Human Rights After Martial Law*, Geneva, International Commission of Jurists.

Ledogar, R. J. (1975) *Hungry for Profits*, New York, IDOC/North America.

Lissner, J. (1977) *The Politics of Altruism*, Geneva, Lutheran World Federation.

Little, I. M. D. (1982) *Economic Development*, New York, Basic Books.

McCoy, A. M. (1984) *Priests on Trial*, Ringwood, Penguin.

McGinnis, J. B. (1979) *Bread and Justice* (Teachers Book and Student Text), New York, Paulist.

Mack, A. (1981) The Soviet threat: Reality or myth?, in D. Adlam *et al.*, eds., *Politics and Power*, London, Routledge Kegan Paul.

McLaughlin, M., ed. (1979) *The United States and World Development*, New York, Praeger.

Magdoff, H. and Nowell, C. E. (1974) Colonialism (c. 1450–1970), *New Encyclopaedia Brittanica Macropaedia*, Vol. 4, 879–906.

Mamdani, M. (1972) *The Myth of Population Control*, New York, Monthly Review.

Melrose, D. (1982) *Bitter Pills: Medicines and the Third World Poor*, London, OXFAM.

Morrish, M. (1983) *Development in the Third World*, Oxford University Press.

Mountjoy, A. (1978) *The Third World: Problems and Perspectives*, London, MacMillan.

Nerfin, M., ed. (1977) *Another Development: Approaches and Strategies*, Uppsalla, Dag Hammarskjold Foundation.

New Internationalist (1978) Answering Back: The Questions People Ask About World Poverty, **68** (October).

New Internationalist (1979a) Cracks and Chasms, **79** (September).

New Internationalist (1979b) The Foreign Aid Link, **82** (December).

New Internationalist (1980a) The Chosen Few, **93** (November).

New Internationalist (1980b) The Rich, the Poor and the Pregnant, **88** (June).

New Internationalist (1981a) Out of the Picture: The Brandt Report and After, **104** (October).

New Internationalist (1981b) Wisdom from Above, **96** (February).

New Internationalist (1982a) Stop the Baby Milk Pushers, 108 (February).

New Internationalist (1982b) Please Do Not Sponsor this Child, 111 (May).

New Internationalist (1982c) Assault on the Earth, 114 (August).

New Internationalist (1983) Reaching the Poorest: Six Rules for Real Aid, 126 (August).

New Internationalist (1985) Can You Help? Charity and Justice in the Third World, 148 (June).

O'Brien, D. C. (1972) Modernization, order and the erosion of a democratic ideal: American political science, 1960–70, *Journal of Development Studies*, 8(4), 351–78.

ODC (Overseas Development Council) (1979) *Measuring the Condition of the World's Poor*, Washington DC, Overseas Development Council.

Otero, G. G. and Smith, G. R. (1977) *Teaching About Food and Hunger: 33 Activities*, Denver, University of Denver Centre for Teaching International Relations.

PASG (Philippines Action Support Group) (1984) *Australia's Military Aid to the Philippines*, Canberra, Australian Council for Overseas Aid.

Payer, C. (1983) *The World Bank: A Critical Analysis*, New York, Monthly Review Press.

Pearson, L. *et al.* (1969) *Partners in Development*, New York, Praeger.

Pineye, D. (1983) The bases of Soviet power in the Third World, *World Development*, 11(12), 1083–95.

Randle, M. (1981) Militarism and repression, *Alternatives*, 7, 61–144.

Redclift, M. R. (1984) *Development and the Environmental Crisis*, London, Methuen.

Reddy, A. K. N. (1975) The Trojan horse, *CERES*, 9(2), 40–3.

Richards, R. (1981) *The Zamboanga Del Sur Development Project: The Impact on the Poor*, Sydney, Community Aid Abroad.

Richardson, R. (1977) *Progress and Poverty*, London, Nelson.

Richardson, R. (1978) *World in Conflict*, London, Nelson.

Rodney, W. (1972) *How Europe Underdeveloped Africa*, London Bogle-L'ouverture.

Sampson, A. (1977) *The Arms Bazaar*, New York, Viking.

SID (Society for International Understanding) (1981) Participation of the rural poor in development, *Development: Seeds of Change*, 1.

Sivard, R. L. (1983) *World Military and Social Expenditures*, Washington, World Priorities.

Stuart, J. (1977) *The Unequal Third*, London, Edward Arnold.

Swaminathan, M. S. (1983) Argicultural progress – Key to Third World prosperity, *Third World Quarterly*, 5(3), 553–66.

Taylor, N. and Richardson, R. (1979) *Seeing and Perceiving: Films in a World of Change*, London, Concord Films Council.

Third World First (1985) Dying for profit: the real causes of famine in Africa, *LINKS*, 22.

Trainer, T. (1984) The Limits to Growth (Issue Summaries, Documentary Evidence, Lesson Plans and Overhead Masters), Sydney, University of NSW Critical Social Issues Project.

Turner, J. (1978) *World Inequality*, London, Longman.

Utrecht, E., ed., (1978, 1978, 1981, 1982) *Transnational Corporations in Southeast Asia and the Pacific*, Vols 1–4, Sydney, University of Sydney Transnational Corporations Research Project.

Vernon, R. (1973) More on multinationals: Does society also benefit?, *Foreign Policy*, 1(3), 103–18.

Weiner, M., ed. (1966) *Modernization: The Dynamics of Growth*, New York, Basic Books.

Weir, D. and Schapiro, M. (1981) *Circle of Poison*, San Francisco, Institute for Food and Development Policy.

Weissman, S., ed. (1975) *The Trojan Horse*, Palo Alto, Ramparts.

White, M. B. and Quiqley, R. N., eds., (1977) *How the Other Third Lives*, Maryknoll, Orbis.

Widstrand, C. G., ed. (1975) *Multinational Firms in Africa*, Uppsalla, Scandinavian Institute for African Affairs.

Wilber, C. K. and Weaver, J. H. (1979) Patterns of dependency: Income distribution and the history of underdevelopment, in C. K. Wilber, ed., *The Political Economy of Development and Underdevelopment*, New York, Random House.

World Bank (1975) Land Reform: Sector Policy Paper, Washington DC, World Bank.

WSP (World Studies Project) (1976) *Learning for Change in World Society*, London, World Studies Project.

Chapter 10

Barnaby, F. ed. (1988) *The Gaia Peace Atlas*, London, Gaia Books Limited.

Enloe, C. (1983) *Does Khaki Become You? The Militarization of Women's Lives*, London, Pluto Press.

Fisher, S. and Hicks, D. (1985) *World Studies 8–13: A Teacher's Handbook*, Edinburgh, Oliver & Boyd.

Kidron, M. and Segal, R. (1981) *The State of the World Atlas*, London, Pluto Press.

Kidron, M. and Segal, R. (1984) *The New State of the World Atlas*, London, Pluto Press.

Kidron, M. and Smith, D. (1983) *The War Atlas*, London, Pluto Press.

Milliken, R. (1986) *No Conceivable Injury*, Ringwood, Penguin.

Montagu, A. (1976) *The Nature of Human Aggression*, New York, Oxford University Press.

Openshaw, S. and Steadman, P. (1982) On the geography of a worst case nuclear attack on the population of Britain, *Political Geography Quarterly*, 1(3).

Openshaw, S., Steadman, P. and Greene, O. (1983) *Doomsday: Britain After Nuclear Attack*, Oxford, Basil Blackwell.

Pepper, D. and Jenkins, A. (1983) A call to arms: Geography and peace studies, *Area*, 15(3).

Pepper, D. and Jenkins, A. (1985) *The Geography of Peace and War*, Oxford, Basil Blackwell.

Prins, G. ed. (1983) *Defended to Death*, Harmondsworth, Penguin.

Sharp, R. ed. (1984) *Apocalypse No: An Australian Guide to the Arms Race and the Peace Movement*, Sydney, Pluto Press.

Sharp, R. and Trainer, T. (1984) The real costs of military expenditure, in R. Sharp, ed., *Apocalypse No*, Sydney, Pluto Press, pp. 41–60.

Sivard, R. L. (1986) *World Military and Social Expenditures*, Washington, World Priorities.

Tame, A. and Robotham, F. P. J. (1982) *Maralinga*, Melbourne Fontana/Collins.

Chapter 11

Allison, L. (1980) Batsman and bowler: The key relations of Victorian England, *Journal of Sports History*, 7, 5–20.

Apple, M. and King, N. (1974) What do schools teach?, in J. Macdonald and W. Gephart, eds., *Humanism and Education*, Berkeley, Cal., McCutchan.

Baker, R. (1977) The ecology of association football, *Bulletin of Environmental Education*, 79, 19–22.

Bale, J. (1978) Geographical diffusion and the adoption of association football in England and Wales, *Geography*, 63, 188–97.

Bale, J. (1980) Football clubs as neighbours, *Town and Country Planning*, 44, 93–4.

Bale, J. (1981) Teaching welfare issues in urban geography, in R. Walford, ed., *Signposts for Geography Teaching*, London, Longman, pp. 51–63.

Bale, J. (1982) *Sport and Place*, London, Hurst.

Bale, J. (1984) International sports history as innovation diffusion, *Canadian Journal of History of Sport*, 15, 38–63.

Bale, J. (1985) This sick sporting world, *Geographical Magazine*, August, 404–5.

Bale, J. and Gowing, D. (1976) Geography and football, *Teaching Geography Occasional Papers*, No. 28.

Blacksell, M. (1982) Leisure, recreation and the environment, in R. Johnston and J. Doornkamp, eds., *The Changing Geography of the United Kingdom*, London, Longman.

Derrick, E. and McRory, J. (1973) Cup in Hand: Sunderland's self-image after the Cup, Working Paper, No. 8, University of Birmingham, Centre for Urban and Regional Studies.

Dunning, E. (1984) Scoial bonding and violence: A theoretical-empirical analysis, in J. Goldstein, ed., *Sports Violence*, New York, Springer-Verlag, pp. 127–46.

Edwards, J. (1979) The home field advantage, in J. Goldstein, eds., *Sport, Games and Play: Social and Psychological Viewpoints*, Hiddside, NJ, Erlbaum, pp. 409–38.

Fien, J. and Linn, G. (1982) The racecourse next door: yea or neigh?, *Geography Bulletin*, 14, 155–60.

Galtung, J. (1984) Sport and international understanding: Sport as a carrier of deep culture and structure, in Ilmarinen M, ed., *Sport and International Understanding*, Berlin, Springer-Verlag, pp. 14–19.

Gelber, S. (1983) Working at playing: The culture of the workplace and the rise of baseball, *Journal of Social History*, 16, 3–22.

Humphreys, D., Mason, C. and Pinch, S. (1983) The externality field of football clubs: A case study of The Dell, Southampton, *Geoforum*, 14, 401–11.

Kirby, A. (1980) An approach to ideology, *Journal of Geography in Higher Education*, 4, 16–26.

Kirby, A. (1985) Leisure as commodity: The role of the state in leisure provision, *Progress in Human Geography*, 9, 64–84.

Loy, J. (1975) Foreword, in D. Ball and J. Loy, eds., *Sport and Social Order*, Reading, Mass., Addison-Wesley.

Maye, B. (1984) Developing valuing and decision making skills in the geography classroom, in J. Fien, R. Gerber and P. Wilson, eds., *The Geography Teachers Guide to the Classroom*, Macmillan, Melbourne, 29–43.

Neilson, B. (1986) Dialogue with the city, *Landscape*, 29, 39–47.

Ojala, C. and Kureth, E. (1975) From Saskatoon and Parry Sound: A geography of skates and sticks in North America, *The Geographical Survey*, 4, 177–98.

Oriard, M. (1976) Sport and space, *Landscape*, 21, 32–40.

Pillsbury, R. (1974) Carolina thunder: A geography of southern stock car racing, *Journal of Geography*, 73, 39–47.

Relph, E. (1976) *Place and Placelessness*, London, Pion.

Relph, E. (1981) *Rational landscapes and humanistic Geography*, London, Croom Helm.

Rigauer, B. (1981) *Sport and Work*, New York, Columbia University Press.

Rooney, J. (1972) *A Geography of American Sport: From Cabin Creek to Anaheim*, Reading, Mass., Addison-Wesley.

Rooney, J. (1980) *The Recruiting Game*, Lincoln, Neb., University of Nebraska Press.

Sas, A. and Jones, A. (1976) Mapping the action!, *Journal of Geography*, 75, 231–8.

Thompson, K. (1980) Culture, sport and the curriculum, *British Journal of Educational Studies*, 28, 136–41.

Wagner, P. (1981) Sport, culture and geography, in A. Pred, ed., *Space and Time in Geography*, Lund, Gleerup.

Whitty, G. and Young, M. (1976) *Explorations in the Politics of School Knowledge*, Driffield, Nafferton.

Chapter 12

Bundy, R., ed. (1975) *Images of the Future*, New York, Prometheus Books.

Dow, G., ed. (1982) *Teacher Learning*, London, Routledge and Kegan Paul.

Ellul, J. (1975) Search for an image, in R. Bundy, ed., *Images of the Future*, New York, Prometheus Books.

Gardner, G. (1975) The case for social futurology in schools, in Tonkin, C. B., ed., *Innovation in Social Education*, Carlton, Pitman.

Gough, N. P. (1982) Futures study and science education: Some issues and suggestions, *Australian Science Teachers Journal*, 28(2).

Gough, N. P (1985) Teacher education for the future, *World Studies Journal*, 6(1).

Gough, N. (1986), Futures in curriculum: an invitation to action, *Curriculum Concerns*, 3(1).

Green, T. (1975) Stories and images of the future, in R. Bundy, ed., *Images of the Future*, New York, Prometheus Books.

Slaughter, R. A. (1984) An antidote to doublethink? Science fiction as a cultural resource, paper presented to the Sixth Annual J. Lloyd Eaton Conference, 1984: *Now or Never?* Science Fiction Foundation, North East London Polytechnic.

Slaughter, R. A. (1985) Rationale and content of an educational programme for schools, paper presented to 'The Place of Futures Studies in Education', an invitational workshop conducted by the UK Futures Network and the University of London Institute of Education.

Slaughter, R. (1986a), *Futures Across the Curriculum: A Handbook of Tools and Techniques* (Trial Version), Lancaster, University of Lancaster.

Slaughter, R. (1986b), Critical futures study – a dimension of curriculum work, *Curriculum Perspectives*, 6(2).

Teresi, D., ed. (1982) *Omni's Continuum*, London, Sidgwick and Jackson.

Chapter 13

Ball, C. and Ball, M. (1973) *Education for a Change: Community Action and the School*, Harmondsworth, Penguin Education.

Huckle, J. F. (1983) Values education through geography: A radical critique, *Journal of Geography*, 82(2), 59–63.

Huckle, J. F. (1986) Geographical education for environmental citzenship, *Geographical Education*, 5(2), 13–20.

Johnston, R. J. *et al.*, eds. (1983) *The Dictionary of Human Geography*, Southampton, Blackwell Reference.

Maher, M. (1986) Environmental education: What are we fighting for?, *Geographical Education* 5(2), 2–25.

Purpel, D. and Ryan, K. (1975) Moral education: Where sages fear to tread, *Phi Delta Kappan*, 56(10), June, 659–62.

Zais, R. (1976) *Curriculum Principles and Foundations*, New York, Harper and Row.